T0316634

Entrance to the Great Perfection

ENTRANCE TO THE
GREAT PERFECTION

━━━━━━━━━━ ❧❦❧ ━━━━━━━━━━

A Guide to the Dzogchen Preliminary Practices

Compiled, Translated, and Introduced by
Cortland Dahl

SNOW LION
BOULDER

SNOW LION
An imprint of Shambhala Publications, Inc.
4720 Walnut Street
Boulder, Colorado 80301
www.shambhala.com

Printed in the United States of America

⊗This edition is printed on acid-free paper that meets the
American National Standards Institute z39.48 Standard.
♻ Shambhala Publications makes every effort to print on recycled
paper. For more information please visit www.shambhala.com.
Distributed in the United States by Penguin Random House LLC
and in Canada by Random House of Canada Ltd

Designed and typeset by Gopa & Ted2, Inc.

The Library of Congress Cataloguing-in-Publication Data
Entrance to the Great perfection: a guide to the Dzogchen preliminary
practices/compiled, translated, and introduced by Cortland Dahl.
p.   cm.—(The heart essence series)
Includes bibliographical references and index.
ISBN 978-1-55939-339-3 (alk. paper)
1. Rdzogs-chen. 2. Rñiṅ-ma-pa (Sect)—Rituals—Texts. I. Dahl, Cortland,
1973–.
BQ7662.4.E58 2010
299.5'4—dc22
2009028293

Contents

—⟫⫶⟪—

This book is dedicated to the long life and flourishing activities of Chatral Sangyé Dorjé Rinpoche

Acknowledgments

This work would not have been possible without the blessings and guidance of Chatral Sangyé Dorjé Rinpoche. Rinpoche introduced me to the world of the Longchen Nyingtik and gave me permission to begin practicing its profound teachings. For his boundless blessings and compassion, I will be forever grateful. I am also indebted to Dzongsar Khyentse Rinpoche, who generously allowed me to include his penetrating teachings on the preliminary practices in this volume. In addition, I would like to thank the following teachers for contributing to this book in various ways: Dzogchen Ponlop Rinpoche, Khenpo Sherab Sangpo, Kyabjé Trulshik Rinpoche, Kyapchen Tulku Rinpoche, Matthieu Ricard, Semo Saraswati, Shechen Rabjam Rinpoche, Sogyal Rinpoche, Tulku Thondup Rinpoche, and especially Yongey Mingyur Rinpoche. If anything of the profundity of the Great Perfection teachings has made its way into this book, it is due solely to the blessings of these gifted teachers.

I would also like to express my gratitude to all those who helped improve the quality of the translation and introduction. First and foremost, I would like to thank Heidi Nevin for proofing my translation and providing excellent editorial feedback. I would also like to thank Kate Thomas and James Fox for their editorial work and Michael Wakoff at Snow Lion Publications for editing the final manuscript. Finally, I would like to express my gratitude to John Bohumil, Greg Johnson, Lama Tsomo, Mark Ackermoore, and Matthew Pistono for their insightful comments and suggestions concerning my introduction and to Adam Pearcey for helping clear up some difficult points concerning the translation.

There were also many individuals who contributed to the publication of Dzongsar Khyentse Rinpoche's commentary. First and foremost, I would like to thank Chanel Grubner for her careful editing work. Additional thanks goes to Doris Wolter for transcribing and editing the teachings, and to all the others who helped support the initial publication of Rinpoche's commentary.

This work would never have seen the light of day were it not for the generous support of many individuals. I would especially like to thank David Doth, Dan Pennie, Richard Perkins, and the Khyentse Foundation for sponsoring this project, and all those who have supported the Rimé Foundation in recent years, including John Bohumil, Molly Brooks, Kit Dahl, Beth Foss, Deborah Hopp, Evelyn Kaiser, David Lunsford and the Bodhi Foundation, Mary Marsden, Rob McIlhargie, Stephanie Chew Grossman, and the George Family Foundation. I am also grateful to my wife, Tenzin, and my young boy, Sangye, for their love and support, and for putting up with the nomadic lifestyle of a Buddhist translator.

Whatever goodness comes of this project I dedicate to the flourishing of the Great Perfection in all times and places, to the long lives of the masters who uphold its teachings, and to the enlightenment of all beings!

Tsultrim Shönu (Cortland Dahl)
Boudhanath, Nepal
November, 2008

INTRODUCTION

In the winter of 1757, a young man with little formal education but great spiritual potential began a long period of strict retreat in the highlands of central Tibet. In the months and years that followed, he experienced a number of visionary encounters with saints and buddhas, meetings that inspired him to compose some of the greatest masterpieces of Tibetan literature. His fame soon spread, and before long he was reputed to be a living buddha—one who has left behind every form of confusion and suffering and manifests the entire range of enlightened qualities. This spiritual adept came to be known as Jigmé Lingpa.

To this day, Jigmé Lingpa's legacy continues to shape the spiritual landscape of the Buddhist world. His philosophical works are studied in many of Tibet's prestigious educational institutions, while the ritual liturgies he revealed have become core practices in numerous monastic centers. The instruction manuals he wrote on profound and secret forms of meditation are widely taught to practitioners throughout Tibet and the Himalayas, and now in the West. Jigmé Lingpa was also instrumental in training some of the most influential Buddhist masters of his age. Many of the students he taught became great masters, embodying his example of deep meditative realization, profound insight, and vast compassionate activity. Yet despite his renown as a meditation master and philosopher of the highest order, he lived his entire life as a simple yogi, content to spend his days writing, meditating, and guiding the fortunate students with whom he shared a karmic bond.

Of all his achievements, Jigmé Lingpa's greatest contribution to Buddhism in Tibet lies in a revelatory collection of teachings and practices known as the Longchen Nyingtik, the Heart Essence of the Vast Expanse. The prayers, liturgies, and instruction manuals contained in this collection are at once practical and poetic. Jigmé Lingpa's elegant aspiration prayers inspire us to look beyond the ordinary deluded habits that propel the mind into suffering, and to refocus instead on the mind's true nature and pure expressions. Its liturgical arrangements, or *sadhanas*, provide a framework for meditation and are capable of transforming confusion into wisdom, eliciting a radical shift in consciousness. Finally, its numerous instruction manuals provide pragmatic advice on virtually every aspect of the spiritual journey, leading the beginning meditator step-by-step along the path of contemplation.

This series of prayers, practices, and meditation manuals lays out a clearly structured path to enlightenment. In the Heart Essence of the Vast Expanse, the spiritual journey begins with a set of preparatory practices, known in Tibet as *ngöndro*. These practices are designed to reorient the mind away from the mundane concerns of ordinary life toward the path to liberation, and then to build on that reorientation by creating an inner environment conducive to spiritual practice. Once the mind has been thoroughly trained and purified by these preliminary practices, the practitioner moves on to a series of advanced meditations that work to undo destructive habitual patterns and reveal the pure, luminous nature of mind that so often goes unnoticed.

As an introduction to the world of the Heart Essence of the Vast Expanse, and in particular to its teachings on the preliminary practices, this book explores the rich tradition that Jigmé Lingpa was a part of, examining the Nyingma school of Tibetan Buddhism and the unique approach of the Heart Essence of the Vast Expanse. The second part of the book focuses exclusively on this tradition's preliminary practices. This section contains translations of Jigmé Lingpa's writings on the preliminary practices, instructions that formed the basis for one of Tibet's most beloved literary compositions: Patrül Rinpoche's *The Words of My Perfect Teacher*. In his short instruction manuals, Jigmé Lingpa provides pithy instructions on these meditative exercises. Following these two texts are a short commentary on the preliminary practices by the great Rimé master Jamyang Khyentsé Wangpo and a contemporary commentary by Dzongsar Khyentse Rinpoche. While Jigmé Lingpa and Jamyang Khyentsé Wangpo present a traditional perspective on the preliminaries, Dzongsar Khyentse Rinpoche's lively instructions lend a modern sensibility to this ancient practice. Also included are two liturgies for the preliminary practices: the main Longchen Nyingtik ngöndro liturgy, compiled by Jigmé Trinlé Özer, and a short liturgy composed by Jamyang Khyentsé Wangpo. In short, this book is meant to serve as an entrance to the Great Perfection—to the innate purity and radiance of awareness, to the meditations and contemplative practices that reveal the mind's true nature, and to the lineage of enlightened masters that have passed these teachings down through the ages.

THE ORIGINS OF BUDDHISM IN TIBET

Tibetan spirituality is as rich and varied as the Tibetan landscape, which soars from the lofty peaks of the high Himalaya to the remote and hidden jungles of the Indian borderlands. Tibet is home to a multitude of Buddhist traditions and lineages, each with its own unique instructions, texts, and approaches to Buddhist practice. The influx of these lineages from India occurred in two phases.

The First Wave of Buddhism in Tibet

The first transmission of Buddhism to Tibet was initiated by a series of Tibetan monarchs that ruled the land at the height of its prestige and influence—in the seventh, eighth, and ninth centuries CE. King Songtsen Gampo was the first of these rulers. In addition to building numerous Buddhist temples, Songtsen Gampo formed links with the Buddhist cultures that bordered Tibet through his marriages to Chinese and Nepali princesses. Perhaps the most important development during his reign, however, was the creation of the Tibetan alphabet. In the middle of the seventh century, the king sent one of his ministers, Tönmi Sambhota, to India to study the Sanskrit language. The alphabet system created by Sambhota later allowed for the translation of the entire Buddhist canon into the Tibetan language and also served to bridge the geographic and cultural chasms that existed in Tibet at the time.

Though Songtsen Gampo is often credited with beginning the process of bringing Buddhism to Tibet, it was during the reign of his descendent, King Trisong Deutsen, that the Buddha's teachings truly took root in Tibetan soil. King Trisong Deutsen, who ruled the country in the eighth and ninth centuries and vastly expanded the Tibetan territory with fierce military campaigns, undertook the arduous tasks of building a major monastic center, translating the Buddhist canon, and inviting teachers from India to transmit the Buddha's teachings. The king also invited the abbot Shantarakshita and tantric adept Padmasambhava from India. Together, these two masters worked under the king's patronage to establish Samyé, Tibet's first monastery. Trisong Deutsen's work was later continued by his grandson, King Ralpachen, the third of Tibet's three "Dharma Kings." Along with many other scholars and translators, these monarchs inaugurated a tradition of Buddhist study and practice that continues to this day.

After this flourishing of Buddhist activity during the seventh to ninth centuries, the spread of Buddhism suffered a major setback at the hands of Langdarma, the brother of King Ralpachen. Langdarma was bitterly opposed to the spread of Buddhism, which he saw as a threat to the indigenous Bön tradition. During his short reign, Langdarma worked to undo the efforts of his predecessors. His violent persecution dismantled the community of ordained monks and nuns—nearly destroying Tibet's fledgling Buddhist community—and plunged the country into a period of political and cultural fragmentation.

Buddhism was not entirely wiped out during this dark period, however. While Langdarma and his cohorts decimated most of the monastic community, a few monks escaped to Amdo in northeastern Tibet, where they preserved the lineage of monastic ordination. The community of lay practitioners survived as well, and many tantric lineages that were transmitted by Padmasambhava and other Buddhist masters continued to be taught and practiced in secret. Thus, despite the great upheavals that took place in the ninth century, the work of Songtsen Gampo, Trisong Deutsen, and Ralpachen made a lasting impact in Tibet. The lineages that stem from this first spreading of Buddhism to Tibet came to be known as the *Nyingma*, or Ancient School.

The Nyingma tradition holds unique teachings that are not found in other lineages of Tibetan Buddhism. Among its distinct teachings are the *Tantra of the Secret Essence* and the Great Perfection. In the Nyingma school, the *Tantra of the Secret Essence* is regarded as the most significant work on Buddhist tantra, a form of spiritual practice that stresses using all facets of life as avenues to awakening. The teachings of this text lay out the theoretical foundations of tantric philosophy, in addition to offering a thorough treatment of the main principles of tantric practice. This text has given rise to a rich commentarial tradition, with works being composed by the greatest luminaries of the Nyingma lineage, including Rongzom Mahapandita (1012–1088),[1] Longchenpa (1308–1362),[2] and, in more recent times, Ju Mipam Namgyal (1846–1912).[3]

Despite the renown of the *Tantra of the Secret Essence*, it is the Great

Perfection, or *Dzogchen*, that is the hallmark of the Nyingma lineage. Though the term "Great Perfection" can be used to refer to the fundamental nature of reality as well as the state of buddhahood, it most commonly refers to a continually evolving set of spiritual instructions and the lineage of enlightened beings who have mastered these teachings and passed them down through the ages. This radically direct approach points out the mind's fundamental nature of luminous purity. According to its teachings, enlightenment is not a distant goal to strive toward, but an immanent reality that must be recognized in the present moment. Effort and agendas only serve to obscure the true nature of mind. Once this nature has been recognized, however, problems and negativity automatically dissolve, leaving the open space of pure awareness, in which the qualities of enlightenment spontaneously unfold.

We will return to the Nyingma school and its Great Perfection teachings later in this text. Now we turn our attention to the second spreading of the Buddha's teachings and the lineages that were brought to Tibet after the ninth century.

The Second Wave of Buddhism in Tibet

The Buddha's teachings regained their foothold on the Tibetan plateau one hundred years after the persecutions of Langdarma. In the middle of the tenth century, Yeshé Ö, king of a region in western Tibet called Ngari, abdicated the throne to devote his life to Buddhist practice. Aware of the setbacks Buddhism had faced in the previous century, Yeshé Ö worked to revive the spread of the Buddha's teachings by inviting Buddhist scholars from the Indian subcontinent to his kingdom and by sending a group of Tibetan scholars to learn Sanskrit and study the Buddha's teachings. One of them, Rinchen Sangpo (958–1051), became a skilled translator. The work initiated by Yeshé Ö and Rinchen Sangpo marks the beginning of the second phase of the transmission of Buddhism to Tibet. The lineages that were founded during and after this period are collectively referred to as the *Sarma*, or New Schools.

One of Yeshé Ö's initiatives was to invite the famed abbot of India's Vikramashila Monastery, Atisha (982–1054), to Tibet. Atisha initially refused Yeshé Ö's entreaties, but changed his mind once he learned that the former king had been imprisoned as a result of his efforts to spread the Buddha's teachings in Tibet.[4] Inspired by the former king's dedication, he left

India for Tibet and spent more than a decade in the land of snows, where he reinvigorated the monastic tradition and founded the Kadampa lineage.

The Kadampas stressed the importance of renunciation and monastic ordination. Above all, however, Atisha and his followers are remembered for their uncompromisingly simple lifestyle and the system of mind training, or *lojong*, that they espoused. The Kadampa mind-training teachings present the key ethical and philosophical principles of the Buddha's teachings in a pithy and accessible manner. Many of Tibet's most cherished literary works stem from this tradition, including Langri Tangpa's *Eight Verses on Training the Mind* and Geshé Chekawa's *Seven-Point Mind Training*. Atisha's *Lamp for the Path to Enlightenment* is a model for the various mind-training systems practiced throughout Tibetan Buddhism.[5]

Over time, the Kadampa tradition was absorbed into other lineages and ceased to exist as an independent entity. The Kadampa teachings were not lost, however, as they became the cornerstone of the Geluk school, a lineage founded in the early fifteenth century by Tsong Khapa (1357–1419). Like Atisha before him, Tsong Khapa stressed the importance of monastic ordination, celibacy, and academic study, especially as a prerequisite for the advanced meditations of Buddhist tantra. While the Geluk school has produced innumerable meditation masters, it is particularly well known for its rigorous philosophical training and skilled logicians.

The Kadam teachings were also incorporated into the Kagyü lineage, which was brought to Tibet by the translator Marpa (1002/1012–1097). Marpa had traveled to India to study with the enlightened scholar Naropa (1012–1100) and a number of other spiritual masters. In Tibet, he passed the Kagyü teachings on to Milarepa (1052–1135), his main student and Tibet's most famous saint, who in turn transmitted them to Rechungpa (1085–1161) and Gampopa (1079–1153). The Kagyü lineage then divided into a number of subgroups founded by Gampopa's primary students and those who followed in their wake.

It was Gampopa who integrated the Kagyü teachings of Marpa with Atisha's mind-training lineage. Prior to Gampopa, the instructions of the Kagyü lineage focused primarily on the Buddhist tantras and Mahamudra—a profound system of contemplation similar to the Great Perfection teachings of the Nyingma school. Gampopa had been steeped in the mind-training instructions of the Kadam school before meeting Milarepa. Once he attained enlightenment and began to pass on the teachings to his own students, he created a unique synthesis of the Kagyü and Kadampa teachings. To this day, the lojong instructions of Atisha are commonly taught alongside the Mahamudra transmissions of Marpa.

In the same century that Atisha reinvigorated the monastic traditions of Tibet and Marpa passed on the profound teachings of Buddhist tantra to Milarepa, the Sakya lineage was formed based on the instructions of the Indian siddha Virupa. Like Naropa of the Kagyü lineage, Virupa started as a monk and became a respected scholar at India's famed Nalanda University. After practicing Buddhist tantra for a number of years, he attained enlightenment and took on the role of a wandering yogi, adopting the "crazy wisdom" of living outside societal norms, with no fixed abode or established code of moral conduct to follow.

Virupa's teachings centered on the *Hevajra Tantra* and a related cycle of instructions known in Tibet as *Lam-dré*, or Path and Fruition. Eventually these instructions were passed down to the Tibetan translator Drogmi during the late ninth and tenth centuries. Drogmi followed the example of Virupa, beginning with the rigorous philosophical training of the sutra tradition and then moving on to the esoteric practices of Buddhist tantra, also known as *Vajrayana*. This became the established model for Buddhist practice in the Sakya lineage and was institutionalized at Sakya Gönpa in central Tibet, a monastery founded by Könchok Gyalpo (1034–1102) in the eleventh century. An unending stream of great scholars and saints has issued forth from this lineage, including unparalleled masters such as Sakya Pandita (1182–1251) and Gorampa Sonam Sengé (1429–1489).

The Nyingma, Sakya, Kagyü, and Geluk schools share many characteristics. Each, for example, synthesizes the relatively accessible teachings of the Sutra Vehicle with the more esoteric teachings of Buddhist tantra. In a Tibetan monastery today, you will find monks following both the Vinaya precepts (a set of guidelines for monks laid down by the Buddha roughly 2,500 years ago) and performing elaborate tantric rituals on a daily basis. Similarly, Tibet's monastic colleges traditionally focus on the teachings of the Sutra Vehicle, yet most include courses on the theoretical framework of tantra. Lamas give public tantric initiations as often as they explain fundamental Sutra Vehicle principles like impermanence and compassion.

All of these schools have thriving monastic traditions and long histories of philosophical and scholastic training. The Geluk monasteries of central Tibet are famed for their many learned scholars, yet the other three lineages have equally impressive monastic colleges, or shedras, such as the Shri Simha Shedra of Dzogchen Monastery, one of the six "mother monasteries" of the Nyingma lineage. The curricula of the four schools are also remarkably similar. When it comes to the Abhidharma teachings, for example, Vasubhandu's *Treasury of Abhidharma* is a mainstay in all four schools, just as the works of Nagarjuna, Chandrakirti, and Maitreya are widely viewed as the pinnacle of Great Vehicle thought.

The practice of meditation has always been the hallmark of the Buddhist tradition, and Tibet's many remote valleys and icy peaks are the perfect environment for those called to a life of contemplation. For these reasons, meditation and retreat play a vital role in all four schools. Each lineage nurtures communities of ascetic yogis dwelling in isolation and small bands of meditators living in strict retreat. In some schools, a regimented three-year, three-month retreat is a common form of intensive meditation practice, while in other lineages, meditators living together in small communities practice individually and at their own pace.

Despite these similarities, there are also differences between the four schools. One obvious example is lineage. As noted above, each of the four schools traces its ancestry back to ancient India and the teachings of the historical Buddha. Specific lines of transmission, however, vary greatly. The Great Perfection teachings of the Nyingma school, for example, are traced back through Padmasambhava, Vimalamitra, and Berotsana to Garap Dorjé, the first human Great Perfection master, and then to the buddhas Vajrasattva and Samantabhadra. The Kagyü lineage, meanwhile, is said to have originated with the primordial buddha Vajradhara, who transmitted the teachings to the Indian siddha Tilopa. The teachings then descended to Naropa, Marpa, Milarepa, and finally to Gampopa, before dividing into a number of sublineages. The Sakya and Geluk schools also possess their own lines of transmission.

Each school has a unique orientation. The Geluk and Sakya lineages stress the importance of philosophical training as a prerequisite for intensive meditation practice. For this reason, many lamas of these schools begin their training by studying in one of the lineage's major monastic colleges. This training can often take decades to complete.

The Nyingma school, in contrast, is the least monastic of the four lineages and tends to emphasize the practice of Buddhist tantra and Great Perfection meditation alongside scholarly study and philosophical inquiry. In the last century, Ju Mipam and Khenpo Shenga reinvigorated the model of the realized scholar-monk in the Nyingma school, but there have also been numerous lay masters. In fact, some of the greatest luminaries of this tradition were not monks, including great masters like Rongzom Mahapandita, Jigmé Lingpa, and, more recently, Dudjom Rinpoche Jigdral Yeshé Dorjé, the late head of the Nyingma school. The presence of a strong nonmonastic community of lamas and practitioners in the Nyingma school has also opened the door to a great number of female adepts.[6]

The Kagyü school emphasizes the practice of meditation. There is a rich scholastic tradition in this lineage as well, but the Kagyü school is known especially for its yogis and advanced meditators. In particular, this lineage is famous for its teachings on Mahamudra and the Six Dharmas of Naropa. Over the past thousand years, innumerable saints have based their practice on these teachings. Like the Geluk and Sakya lineages, this school places more emphasis on the importance of monastic ordination than the Nyingma lineage.

These four schools—the Nyingma, Sakya, Kagyü, and Geluk—are the most widely practiced lineages in Tibet. It is important to note, however, that there have been many other lineages and teachings on the Tibetan plateau. Some of these have died out, while others continue to flourish. The Chöd lineage of the great female master Machik Lapdrön (1031–1124), for example, continues to exert a powerful influence on the spirituality of Tibet, as do the Jonang and Shangpa Kagyü lineages, despite the fact that all three lack the institutional clout of Tibet's more prominent schools. Monks and nuns, householders and wandering ascetics, philosophers and simple yogis . . . there is enough variety in Tibetan Buddhism to accommodate them all.

THE NYINGMA SCHOOL

The teachings of the Nyingma school are one of the world's great spiritual treasures. They range from accounts of the mystical exploits of saints to sublime philosophical treatises, some spanning thousands of pages, on the nature of the mind and reality itself. Over the centuries, these teachings have inspired countless hermits and sages, monks and nuns, kings and laypeople. In the following pages, we will explore this lineage and its profound teachings, beginning with the kama and terma transmissions and a few short biographies of key Nyingma figures.

Kama and Terma

The instructions of the Nyingma school encompass the entirety of the Bu
dha's teachings. Like other Buddhist lineages in Tibet, Nyingma practitio
ers train in the three vehicles, or *yanas*, simultaneously. Pure monks and nu
practice tantra; eccentric yogis uphold the fundamental principle of nonvi
lence; and all practices are imbued with the altruistic attitude of bodl
chitta. What sets the Nyingma school apart, however, is the unique way th
these teachings have been passed down through the ages, and how the va
ous facets of the Buddhist path are formulated. These two issues relate to t
kama and terma transmissions, and to the nine vehicles, respectively.[7]

While all Buddhist teachings in Tibet can be traced back to ancient Ind
the Nyingma teachings came to the land of snows in the imperial peri
of Tibetan history, and especially with the transmissions that took pla
during the eighth- and ninth-century reign of King Trisong Deutsen. Sin
that time, the various lineages of the Nyingma school have been transm
ted in two distinct forms, known as *kama* and *terma*. The word *kama* lit
ally means "oral transmission," referring to teachings that have been hand
down from teacher to student for over a thousand years. Terma, on the oth
hand, are teachings or sacred objects that are hidden by a spiritual teach
for the benefit of future generations. These "treasures" are later revealed l
a reincarnation of the spiritual teacher or by a reincarnation of one of t
teacher's primary disciples.

The kama lineage has been transmitted as an uninterrupted continui
of study and practice since the time of Padmasambhava, Shantarakshi
and Vimalamitra. Over time, various masters have compiled collections
important texts from this lineage. In the twentieth century, for examp
Dudjom Rinpoche gathered together hundreds of texts from the kama li
eage, filling over fifty volumes.[8] This collection contains many of the ma
terpieces of the Nyingma tradition and addresses all aspects of Buddhi
thought and practice. The first twenty volumes or so contain the ritual ro
texts of the Nyingma school, including many tantric sadhanas, or practi
liturgies. The latter half of the collection is filled with commentaries on
vast range of Buddhist topics. As evidence of the Nyingma school's tantr
orientation, however, the vast majority of these texts relate to the theory a
practice of Buddhist tantra, and the Great Perfection in particular. Includ
in this compilation are works by the greatest masters of the Nyingma li
eage: Garap Dorjé, Padmasambhava, Vimalamitra, Rongzom, Longchenp

Jigmé Lingpa, and many others. These writings are unique to the Nyingma school.

The Nyingma tradition also accepts the canonical status of the writings found in the *Kangyur* and *Tengyur*. These compilations are held in common with the New Schools. Respectively, these two collections contain the sutras and tantras of the Buddha, and canonical commentaries by Indian masters. Many of the works from these compilations, such as the Middle Way writings of Nagarjuna and Chandrakirti, are studied in the monastic colleges of all four schools of Tibetan Buddhism.

Because the lineage for each of these teachings includes the countless individuals that have practiced, mastered, and transmitted these teachings over time, the kama lineage is often referred to as "the long lineage of oral transmissions." This continuity ensures that each teaching is grounded in the original teachings of the Buddha and the saints and scholars of times past.

This form of transmission is not without its disadvantages, however. With each successive generation, the chance of mistakes and corruptions slipping into the transmission increases, while broken samaya vows sap its vitality. Texts, for example, are especially prone to such degradations. Until recently, Tibetan texts were copied by hand or using woodblock prints. Each new version was susceptible to errors, omissions, and additions. For this reason, different versions of ancient texts often contain dramatic discrepancies in terms of both spelling and content. The oral commentary tradition that accompanies these texts is equally prone to corruption.

The terma lineage, by contrast, is less susceptible to such problems. Terma, or treasures, are typically revealed by reincarnations of those who initially received the teachings. When such a revelation takes place, there are very few intermediaries between the student that receives the teachings and the main gurus of the lineage, such as Padmasambhava and Vimalamitra. For this reason, terma transmissions are often called "the close lineage of revealed treasures."

Treasures may be teachings, statues and other blessed objects, or any other item that is destined to have a positive impact in a particular time and place. In Tibet, most treasures were hidden by Padmasambhava and his spiritual partner, Yeshé Tsogyal.⁹ Padmasambhava received a wealth of teachings. Though he was committed to passing them on to his Tibetan students, he saw that the time was not right for many of his transmissions and that they would have a much greater impact in the future. For this reason, he decided to transmit some teachings in private to a few close disciples and to have these teachings hidden until the time was ripe for them to be studied and practiced. He then charged a particular student with safeguarding the teaching he or she had received and propagating it in a future life.

Treasures are hidden in various ways. Some teachings, for example, are written down in coded language, called *dakini script*, and concealed in rocks, earth, or even in water. Of those that are concealed in the physical environment, one common form is *sa ter*, meaning "earth treasure." Other teachings, known as *gong ter*, or "mind treasure," are hidden in the mind of the student. In both cases, the individual meant to reveal the teachings—the *tertön*, or treasure revealer—typically meets with an auspicious circumstance that triggers a recollection of the teachings or an impulse to travel to the place where the treasures are located.

One well-known example concerns the transmission of the Heart Essence of the Dakinis, an influential treasure cycle propagated by Longchenpa. The custodian of this particular teaching was Princess Pemasel, the daughter of King Trisong Deutsen. Shortly before the princess passed away at the young age of eight, she received all the teachings and empowerments associated with the Heart Essence of the Dakinis directly from Padmasambhava. Yeshé Tsogyal, who was also present, transcribed the teachings and placed them in a small casket for safekeeping. Princess Pemasel then held the casket at the crown of her head and prayed, "May I meet with these teachings in the future and benefit beings!" To this, Padmasambhava added his own prayers and aspirations. Shortly thereafter, the princess passed away.

Yeshé Tsogyal kept a record of everything that transpired and asked the master whether the teachings should be propagated or concealed.

"The time has not yet come to spread these teachings," Padmasambhava responded. "They should be buried as treasure. Since the princess placed the casket of texts on the crown of her head and made aspirations for the future, these teachings are her heritage."

The texts of the Heart Essence of the Dakinis, along with princess's brocade cloak, were then hidden by Yeshé Tsogyal. At the end of the thirteenth century, Princess Pemasel was reborn as a man named Pema Ledrel Tsel. Once Pema Ledrel Tsel's karmic connection with the Heart Essence of the Dakinis was reactivated, he revealed the teachings that had been concealed centuries before and began to propagate them. He did, however, make one fatal mistake. The instructions he revealed stipulated that the teachings should not be transmitted immediately, but should first be practiced in seclusion. They warned that the treasure revealer would incur the wrath of the dakinis, the female protective spirits that safeguard the Great Perfection lineage, if this injunction were to go unheeded. Pema Ledrel Tsel ignored these warnings and soon began to transmit his revelations to a few close disciples. As the prophecy stated, this angered the dakinis, who soon created insurmountable obstacles to his life. He died shortly thereafter in his late twenties.

Because he died at such a young age, Pema Ledrel Tsel was unable to spread these precious teachings to more than a few close disciples. Princess Pemasel's next incarnation, however, was Longchenpa, who mastered the teachings through years of retreat practice before teaching them far and wide. Longchenpa's enduring reputation as an unparalleled master of the Great Perfection has ensured the place of the Heart Essence of the Dakinis as one of the most cherished treasure collections in the Nyingma lineage.

In addition to the Heart Essence of the Dakinis, innumerable treasure collections have been revealed over the centuries. Some fade into obscurity centuries after their revelation, while others continue to be taught and practiced for generations. One of the earliest treasure collections to be revealed, Rigdzin Gödem's (1337–1409) Unimpeded Wisdom Mind, or *Gongpa Sangtal*, has been held in high regard since its discovery in the fourteenth century. This collection is still widely practiced in certain regions, such as Sikkim, and at some Nyingma monasteries. Rigdzin Gödem is often mentioned alongside Guru Chöwang and Nyang Ral Nyima Özer as one of the three most important tertöns. Other collections, such as Namchö Mingyur Dorjé's (1645–1667) Space Dharma, or *Namchö*, and Longsel Nyingpo's (1625–1692) revelations, have also been integrated into the practice curriculum of some of the Nyingma tradition's main monastic centers and have made a lasting impact on the trajectory of Great Perfection thought and practice for this reason.[10] More recently, collections discovered by such masters of the Rimé movement[11] as Jamyang Khyentsé Wangpo and Chokgyur Dechen Lingpa (1829-1870) have profoundly shaped the Great Perfection tradition, as have the collections revealed by Dudjom Rinpoche Jikdrel Yeshé Dorjé (1904–1988) and Dilgo Khyentsé Rinpoche (1910–1991) in the twentieth century.[12]

Though the vast majority of treasures derive from the teachings of Padmasambhava, there are some that relate to other Buddhist masters. Two collections that relate to the teachings of Vimalamitra, for example, are the Heart Essence of Vimalamitra,[13] revealed by Dangma Lhungyal, and the Heart Essence of the Karmapa, revealed by the Third Karmapa, Rangjung Dorjé, a patriarch of the Kagyü lineage. More recently, an important treasure was rerevealed in the nineteenth century by Jamyang Khyentsé Wangpo, a master of both the Sakya and Nyingma teachings, entitled the Heart Essence of Chetsün.[14] Other collections, such as Terdak Lingpa's Essence of the Profound Nature of Ati, are considered distillations of the Great Perfection teachings of both Padmasambhava and Vimalamitra. Another such example is Jigmé Lingpa's Heart Essence of the Vast Expanse, which we will explore in the following pages.

PADMASAMBHAVA

The various lineages of the Nyingma school are united by their roots in the dynastic period outlined above and their shared reverence for Padmasambhava. While the life of Padmasambhava is shrouded in myth, it is clear that King Trisong Deutsen invited him to Tibet around the turn of the ninth century at the behest of the abbot Shantarakshita. At the king's request, Shantarakshita had come to the land of snows to transplant the monastic Buddhism of India on Tibetan soil and specifically to construct Samyé monastery. His initial efforts, however, met with failure. As legend has it, spirits and ghosts thwarted their every effort to build the monastery, mischievously undoing by night the work that was done each day. Frustrated by the lack of progress, Shantarakshita made a prediction that the building would only be finished if Padmasambhava were invited to Tibet to subdue the native spirits.

As predicted, Padmasambhava was found in India and invited to Tibet. Once there, he proceeded to subjugate the evil forces that were blocking the king's spiritual ambitions and to bind them under oath to serve the Dharma. With the spirits of Tibet working for the king and abbot rather than against them, the construction of Samyé continued without interruption. Eventually, it became hallowed ground where many teachings of the Nyingma lineage were transmitted, studied, and practiced.

Padmasambhava's reputation as a miracle worker did not begin in Tibet. The accounts of his birth, childhood, and upbringing are filled with inspiring tales of his unique and unconventional nature. One well-known story relates that Padmasambhava was born fully enlightened, appearing miraculously on a lotus flower in the middle of the ocean. He was found by Indrabhuti, the king of Oddiyana, who was searching for a wish-fulfilling jewel. In a rather humorous exchange, the king expressed his astonishment at finding a young boy in such strange circumstances. Responding to the king's inquiries, Padmasambhava exclaimed:

My father is Samantabhadra, self-awareness,
And my mother is Samantabhadri, the sphere of reality itself.
My caste is the indivisibility of this sphere and awareness,
And my name is Padmasambhava, the glorious Lotus-born.
My homeland is the unborn sphere of reality itself.
For sustenance, I consume dualistic appearances and thoughts
While engaging in the conduct of the buddhas of the three times![15]

This delighted the king, who promptly adopted the boy and proclaimed him heir to the throne of his kingdom.

After a number of years, the young Padmasambhava saw that a life of royal luxury would limit his ability to help others. To escape his responsibilities as prince, he began to act in an unconventional manner. One day, he let a trident slip from his hand as he played. The trident ended up hitting and killing a child of one of the king's ministers. Since the laws of the land stipulated that anyone guilty of such a heinous crime could not go unpunished, even a prince, the king and his ministers banished the young boy. When the king, with a heavy heart, told his adopted son the news, Padmasambhava responded:

In this world, one's mother and father are precious indeed.
You, my parents, have given me an entire kingdom!
Yet I have no attachment to this land, nor any fear of being banished,
And since birth and death are no different, I do not fear being killed.
Since the law of the land is strict, it is good that I am being banished!
Mother and father, may you live long and happily.
Our karmic connection is sure to bring us together once more.[16]

Padmasambhava traveled to a number of charnel grounds—wild, uninhabited locales where Indian villagers disposed of the dead and which were reputedly filled with demons and ghosts. There, he continued to engage in the eccentric behavior of a carefree yogi. Using his meditative powers, he brought these spirits under his control and charged them with serving the Buddha's teachings. Due to his spiritual accomplishment and deft skill in dealing with these malevolent forces, he came to be known by various names, including "Pema Tötreng Tsel" (Mighty One with a Garland of Skulls), "Dorjé Trakpo Tsel" (Mighty Vajra Wrath), and "Tsokyé Dorjé" (Lake-born Vajra).

Then Padmasambhava began a phase of study and practice. Despite being fully enlightened, he realized that he would be discredited if he did not have a lineage and spiritual mentors. For this reason, he sought out teachings from various masters. With Prabhahasti, for example, he took monastic ordination and received the name "Shakya Simha" (Lion of the Shakyas); from masters such as Ananda, Manjushrimitra, and Humkara he received vital tantric teachings.

In the course of his studies, Padmasambhava had visions of various deities and engaged in numerous miraculous feats. On one occasion, he defeated a group of Hindu philosophers in debate and proceeded to make a nearby jungle appear to burst into flames, thereby receiving the name "Sengé Dradrok" (the Roaring Lion). He was also given the names "Nyimé Ozer" (Light Rays of the Sun), as he was said to be able to ride the sun's rays, and "Loden Choksé" (Wise One with Passion for the Supreme) due to his encyclopedic knowledge of the Dharma.

Another story concerns Padmasambhava's relationship to a princess named Mandarava from the kingdom of Sahor. To further his meditation practice, he courted Mandarava and the two began to engage in various tantric practices secretly in a forest.[17] This scandalized the local population, who considered it a disgrace for a princess to be living in the jungle with an eccentric yogi. To avenge this affront, they set out to burn Padmasambhava and his spiritual consort at the stake. The villagers caught the two without fanfare. However, when they tried to burn them, they found that not only were Padmasambhava and Mandarava unharmed, but that the flames were actually spreading out and threatening to incinerate the immediate environs.[18] Seeing this, the people immediately stopped and begged the master's forgiveness. Showering him with praise, they called him "Padmasambhava," the Lotus-born. Mandarava became a teacher in her own right and is considered one of the first female masters of the Great Perfection.[19]

After leaving the kingdom of Sahor, Padmasambhava returned to Oddiyana and again faced persecution by the local population, which had not forgotten his expulsion from the country years before. True to form, he eventually impressed the king and his subjects with his miraculous powers and vast knowledge of the Dharma. He remained in the land for eight years, giving tantric initiations, teaching the Dharma, and eventually converting the entire land to Buddhism.

Padmasambhava traveled to the Wild Jungle Charnel Ground next, where he studied the Great Perfection with Shri Simha. According to the Heart

Essence of the Dakinis,[20] Shri Simha had been taught by Garap Dorjé, the first human master of the Great Perfection lineage. Padmasambhava stayed with Shri Simha for twenty-five years, studying and practicing the entire range of Great Perfection instructions. These teachings would become the basis for many influential collections in the Nyingma lineage, including the Longchen Nyingtik.

It was after this intense period of study and practice that King Trisong Deutsen invited Padmasambhava to Tibet. While there, Padmasambhava visited virtually every region in the land of snows and blessed thousands of places as sacred power spots. With his spiritual consort, the princess Yeshé Tsogyal, he traveled and worked tirelessly to help the Tibetan people establish the Buddha's teachings on the arid plains and isolated valleys of Tibet. Not only did he transmit the Buddhist teachings far and wide, he also gave secret teachings to his close disciples. Many of these teachings were written down and hidden for future generations. These terma teachings continue to be revealed to this day.

VIMALAMITRA

Along with Padmasambhava and the translator Berotsana, Vimalamitra was one of three key figures that transmitted the Great Perfection teachings to Tibet. Born in India, Vimalamitra eventually became a scholar and lived in the Buddhist center of Bodhgaya. One day, while on a walk with his friend, Jnanasutra, Vimalamitra had a vision of the buddha Vajrasattva, who told them that since their scholarly approach had not yet led them to enlightenment, they should travel to Siljin Charnel Ground in China to receive advanced teachings on the Great Perfection.

Vimalamitra set off immediately and soon met the great master Shri Simha. From Shri Simha, he received many teachings, including the Outer, Inner, and Secret Cycles of the Great Perfection's Key Instruction Section. He did not, however, receive all the instructions. After twenty years of study and practice, Vimalamitra returned to India. Some years later, his companion, Jnanasutra, decided to visit Shri Simha as well. In the end, it was Jnanasutra who received the full Great Perfection transmission from Shri Simha.

Once Vimalamitra heard that he had not received the teachings in their entirety, he became determined to find Jnanasutra and receive the Extremely Secret Unsurpassed Cycle of the Great Perfection. He eventually found Jnanasutra practicing in a charnel ground and was so impressed with his deep realization that he immediately became his old friend's devoted disciple.

Vimalamitra stayed with his teacher for over a decade and received all the teachings he had not previously received from Shri Simha.

When Jnanasutra passed away, Vimalamitra cried out and a jeweled casket fell from the sky into his hands. The box contained Jnanasutra's *Last Testament*, continuing a tradition that had started with Garap Dorjé, who had received similar teachings from Vajradhara himself. Jnanasutra's *Last Testament* presented a profound set of instructions called *The Four Ways to Rest*. In addition to the teachings he received from Shri Simha and Jnanasutra, Vimalamitra received visionary instructions from Garap Dorjé himself. After decades of practicing and transmitting the Great Perfection teachings in India, Vimalamitra was invited to Tibet by King Trisong Deutsen.

Vimalamitra's contribution to the spread of Buddhism in Tibet can hardly be overestimated. With many renowned translators, such as Yudra Nyingpo and Nyak Jnanakumara, he aided in the translation of tantric texts, such as the Mind Class teachings of the Great Perfection and the *Tantra of the Secret Essence*. Vimalamitra also transmitted the Heart Essence teachings, the most profound and secret instructions of the Great Perfection. He transmitted these teachings to only a few close students. These teachings, now known as the Vima Nyingtik, were eventually passed down to Longchenpa, the greatest exponent of the Great Perfection in Tibet.

It is said the Vimalamitra attained a rare level of spiritual accomplishment known as "the rainbow body of great transference," allowing him to remain in a body of light and reincarnate at will. He is said to have promised that he would return to Tibet every one hundred years to continue his work of spreading the Dharma. Some of the greatest luminaries of the Nyingma tradition are regarded as his incarnations, including Kumaradza, Jigmé Lingpa (1879–1941), Jamyang Khyentsé Wangpo (1820–1892), and the twentieth-century master Khenpo Ngakchung, also known as Khenpo Ngawang Pelzang.

BEROTSANA

The translator Berotsana is credited, along with Padmasambhava and Vimalamitra, with bringing the Great Perfection teachings to Tibet. His spiritual career began when he was still a young man. Following the advice of Padmasambhava, King Trisong Deutsen summoned Berotsana to Samyé Monastery, where he was ordained as a monk and trained as a translator. Shortly thereafter, he was sent to India to seek out Dharma teachings and bring them to Tibet.

Berotsana's journey was filled with hardship, but he eventually reached India and set off to find an enlightened teacher. The Great Perfection master Shri Simha was still alive and transmitting his precious teachings in a region known as Danakosha. The ruler of the area, however, had placed a strict injunction on transmitting the teachings, so the only way for Berotsana to receive them was to study in secret. By day, Berotsana received teachings on the Sutra Vehicle, which were taught openly throughout India. By night, Shri Simha gave him teachings on the Vajra Vehicle, especially the Mind and Space Classes of the Great Perfection. Berotsana also received instructions on the Heart Essence from Garap Dorjé in a vision.

The next difficulty he faced was getting the teachings to Tibet. Since any written teachings were likely to be confiscated by border guards, Berotsana recorded the teachings he had received on white silk using goat's milk, rendering them invisible to the naked eye. To read them, he had to hold the cloth over a smoking fire, thus revealing what he had written.

Once he was safe in Tibet, Berotsana transmitted the teachings he had received to the king. Just as he had studied, Berotsana taught the Sutra Vehicle teachings openly during the day, while teaching the king secretly about the Great Perfection at night. When the Indians found out that he had taken the teachings to Tibet and was teaching them, they began to spread malicious rumors about Berotsana. Members of the royal court hostile to the Dharma seized on these rumors and used them as a pretense to have him exiled.

Berotsana was later brought back from exile when his student, Yudra Nyingpo, encountered Vimalamitra. Yudra Nyingpo convinced Vimalamitra that his master was an authentic Buddhist teacher. Vimalamitra then used his influence with the king to have Berotsana summoned back to central Tibet. On his way, Berotsana ran into an old man named Pang Mipam Gonpo. Despite the fact that the man was eighty-five-years-old and had never studied the Dharma, Berotsana sensed that he had great spiritual potential and proceeded to teach him about the nature of mind. Mipam Gonpo was too old to sit in the traditional meditation posture, so he used a stick to keep his chin propped up. He progressed by leaps and bounds, however, and soon attained a very advanced level of realization.

Berotsana is widely regarded as one of the most gifted and realized of Tibet's many translators. He was responsible for bringing many teachings into the Tibetan language, especially those that concern the Great Perfection. Berotsana is also said to have reincarnated many times in Tibet. Terdak

Lingpa, founder of the Mindroling lineage, is considered to be such an emanation, as is Jamgön Kongtrül. Berotsana passed away in a secluded forest in Nepal, attaining the rainbow body like many of his students.

RONGZOM MAHAPANDITA

Rongzom Chökyi Zangpo, also known as Rongzom Mahapandita, is widely regarded as one of the two greatest exponents of the unique views and practices of the Nyingma school. Along with Longchenpa, he is known as an "Omniscient One." This rare title connotes both breadth of knowledge and depth of realization. His innate intelligence was so great, in fact, that Rongzom himself once remarked, "Since there is no teaching that I did not study, my learning is not insignificant. Yet, as I never needed to review the teachings I received more than once, neither is it great."

Rongzom was a contemporary of Atisha, Marpa Lotsawa, and many others who were instrumental in establishing new Buddhist lineages in the land of snows. He wrote extensively on a broad range of topics and demonstrated an unparalleled mastery of the Buddha's teachings.[21] The Indian scholars he interpreted often commented on his universal knowledge, encouraging him to write his own treatises. He was also praised by some of the greatest masters of the Sarma traditions, such as Atisha and Marpa. Echoing their sentiments, the great Gö Lotsawa wrote: "In the snowy land of Tibet, Rongzom remains unequalled as a scholar." The greatest testament to Rongzom's accomplishments, however, is the lasting influence he has had on the great thinkers of the Nyingma school. Mipam, perhaps the greatest Nyingma thinker of recent times, modeled his views on those of Rongzom and Longchenpa, a debt that he acknowledges repeatedly in his writings. Rongzom's thousand-year-old legacy continues to exert a powerful influence on spirituality in Tibet.

LONGCHEN RABJAM

Longchenpa is often singled out as the single greatest master in the history of the Nyingma lineage. Born in central Tibet at the beginning of the fourteenth century, his life was extraordinary from the very beginning. It is said that a fierce protective female spirit named Remati appeared as soon as he was born and pledged to protect him. Throughout his life, he had visions of buddhas and saints, including Manjushri, Tara, and Padmasambhava.

Longchenpa's spiritual training began when he was still a young child. His father offered him a series of tantric initiations when he was seven-years-old, and at nine, he was already memorizing lengthy sutras. He was ordained as a monk at age twelve and soon mastered the Vinaya. His mastery of the subject was so thorough, in fact, that he was able to give teachings on the Vinaya when he was only fourteen.

Though he is known primarily for his writings on the *Tantra of the Secret Essence* and the Great Perfection, Longchenpa studied and wrote about virtually every Buddhist teaching and lineage that was present in Tibet at the time he lived. In his mid-teens, he studied many collections from the New Schools, such as the Path and Fruition (*Lam-dré*) teachings of the Sakya school, the *Kalachakra Tantra*, and the Chöd instructions of Machik Lapdrön. At nineteen, he entered Sangpu Monastery, an influential Kadam institution of the time. There he studied the works of Maitreya, the valid cognition writings of Dignaga and Dharmakirti, the Perfection of Knowledge literature, and the Middle Way. With the Third Karmapa, Rangjung Dorjé, he studied teachings from the Kagyü school, including the Six Dharmas of Naropa. His learning was so vast that he came to be known as "Samyé Lung Mangwa," meaning "the One from Samyé with Many Transmissions."

In his late twenties, Longchenpa met his root guru, Rigdzin Kumaradza. The night before Longchenpa arrived at his teacher's camp, Kumaradza dreamt that a divine bird, accompanied by a thousand other birds, came and carried away his texts in all directions. He interpreted this to mean that someone would soon arrive that would be worthy of holding his precious lineage. Soon enough, Longchenpa arrived and was recognized as Kumaradza's prophesied heir.

Kumaradza was considered an incarnation of Vimalamitra and was the main lineage holder of the Vima Nyingtik, Vimalamitra's Heart Essence teachings. He transmitted all of these teachings to Longchenpa, who studied and practiced them in a state of such deprivation that he had only a single cloth sack to use as both blanket and bed. On five separate occasions, he offered his teacher all that he owned to rid himself of desire and attachment. Eventually, Longchenpa was appointed Kumaradza's main successor, and he set off to practice the teachings he had received for six years in strict retreat.

Longchenpa was considered the reincarnation of Pema Ledrel Tsel, who was himself the reincarnation of Princess Pemasel, the daughter of King Trisong Deutsen. As noted earlier, Princess Pemasel received a rare Heart Essence transmission from Padmasambhava shortly before she passed away at the age of eight. In her subsequent births, she evolved spiritually and was eventually reborn as Pema Ledrel Tsel. She then revealed the Great

Perfection teachings she had received from Padmasambhava as a treasure. These teachings came to be known as the *Khandro Nyingtik*, the Heart Essence of the Dakinis.

Though Longchenpa was the direct reincarnation of the very same *tertön*, or treasure revealer, who discovered the Heart Essence of the Dakinis, he made a point of seeking out his predecessor's Dharma heir and receiving the transmissions in person. He also had visions of Padmasambhava and Yeshé Tsogyal, who transmitted the Heart Essence of the Dakinis to him directly. When he first taught this collection, numerous miraculous omens appeared. Everyone present entered a state of deep meditation that lasted for an entire month and all experienced visions of dakinis and protective spirits.

As one of the most renowned scholars and meditation masters of his time, Longchenpa could have easily built large monasteries and institutions, yet he chose to live the life of a simple yogi. He lived out his days wandering from place to place, staying in solitary hermitages, and guiding the fortunate students that had gathered around him. Longchenpa passed away in his fifties while dwelling in the simplicity of the mountain retreats he loved. Surrounded by dedicated meditators, he manifested all the signs of a completely enlightened being and used his own death as a way to teach his closest students about the truth of impermanence.

Longchenpa composed numerous commentaries on both the Heart Essence of Vimalamitra and the Heart Essence of the Dakinis and then gathered all of these teachings, along with the root texts, into one collection. This collection, known as the *Nyingtik Yabshi*, or Fourfold Heart Essence, spans thousands of pages and contains hundreds of individual titles. It is the single most comprehensive collection of writings on the practice of the Great Perfection. He also penned a series of treatises on the theoretical underpinnings of the Great Perfection, entitled the Seven Treasuries. This collection is widely regarded as one of the great masterpieces of Tibetan literature.[22] The same can be said of Longchenpa's Three Cycles of Rest.[23] While the Fourfold Heart Essence focuses on the secret and advanced meditations of the Great Perfection, and the Seven Treasuries stress its theoretical foundation, this series presents the entirety of the Buddhist teachings, and the Great Perfection in particular, in an accessible, easy-to-practice manner. Longchenpa also composed a commentary on the *Tantra of the Secret Essence*, entitled *Dispelling the Darkness of the Ten Directions*, that is widely studied to this day.

No Tibetan figure in the Nyingma lineage is as esteemed as Longchenpa. His writings on the Great Perfection are so extensive, profound, and clear that it is hard to see how they will ever be matched. As a student, his diligence, renunciation, devotion, and thirst for the Dharma were unparalleled, while as a teacher, his lack of concern for wealth and power and his ability to guide others made him the ideal guru. As we will see, it was Longchenpa who inspired the revelation of the Longchen Nyingtik and prompted Jigmé Lingpa to compose many influential works.

THE HEART ESSENCE OF THE VAST EXPANSE

The Heart Essence of the Vast Expanse is one of the most profound spiritual teachings ever revealed. Since the time it was discovered in the eighteenth century, it has given rise to innumerable enlightened lineage holders and masterpieces of spiritual literature. Many well-known masters of all lineages were practitioners of these teachings, including Jamyang Khyentsé Wangpo, Patrül Rinpoche (1808–1887), and the successive incarnations of the Dodrupchen Rinpoches. In more recent times, Dilgo Khyentsé (1910–1991), one of the Dalai Lama's main teachers, and Chatral Sangyé Dorjé (b. 1913), a living buddha of the Dzogchen lineage, have been outstanding exemplars of this tradition. In the following pages, we will explore the origins and contents of these teachings, beginning with the man who revealed these profound treasures, Jigmé Lingpa.

Jigmé Lingpa and the Revelation of the Longchen Nyingtik

Jigmé Lingpa was born in Southern Tibet in 1730, on the anniversary of Longchenpa's death. He was a spiritual prodigy from a young age, with an unusual degree of compassion and intelligence. He also experienced visions of his past lives, which are said to include King Trisong Deutsen and Longchenpa.

At the age of six, Jigmé Lingpa entered Palri Monastery as a novice monk. Though his parents were from a noble family, they were of simple means and unable to provide their son with anything more than the basic necessities of life. Because of this, his life at the monastery was extremely spartan. What he lacked in material comforts, however, he made up for with the richness of his inner life. Throughout this time, he possessed an insatiable thirst for the Dharma and was blessed with visions of saints and buddhas. Though Jigmé Lingpa took every opportunity to study and practice, he was never able to enter a formal education program. The amazing spiritual masterpieces that he penned later in life were the flowering of deep realization, rather than the product of study.

A pivotal period in Jigmé Lingpa's spiritual development came in his late twenties, when he began a series of solitary meditation retreats that would last seven years. He followed an extremely strict code of conduct over the course of these retreats and vowed to limit his contacts with the outside world until he had perfected his own practice of the development and completion stage yogas. He had many visions throughout this period, including visions of Padmasambhava, Yeshé Tsogyal, and the Great Perfection master Manjushrimitra. He also experienced the opening of his throat chakra, the energetic center associated with enlightened speech, and from that point on was able to spontaneously compose beautiful songs of realization and learned treatises on a variety of Buddhist topics.

Jigmé Lingpa revealed the Heart Essence of the Vast Expanse in the year 1757. One evening in the midst of his retreat, he was overcome with devotion for Padmasambhava. With tears streaming down his face, and unable to bear being separated from this great master, his consciousness soon shifted, and he became immersed in a state of luminous clarity.

After some time, he found himself in a visionary dream, bounding through the sky on the back of a white snow lion. He eventually arrived at Boudhanath Stupa in Kathmandu valley.[24] Soon enough, he arrived in the eastern courtyard of the monument, at which point he met a wisdom dakini face-to-face. Handing him a large wooden locket, she told him that within it he would find the symbolic script of Padmasambhava—the mind treasure of Samantabhadra and the secret treasure of the dakinis. The dakini then vanished.

Thrilled, Jigmé Lingpa opened the box and found five yellow scrolls and seven crystal beads. As he unrolled one of the scrolls, he noticed the smell of camphor and his entire body began to vibrate, which he took to mean that the guardian of the teachings was Rahula, an extremely wrathful Dharma protector—an enlightened manifestation that protects the Buddha's teachings. Unrolling the scroll further, he saw the symbolic script of the dakinis. The script was unintelligible to him, unfortunately, so he began to roll the scroll back up. Immediately the writing transformed into ordinary Tibetan script, revealing the sadhana of Mahakaruna, a form of Avalokiteshvara, one of the main yidam deities of the Longchen Nyingtik cycle.

The script aroused his curiosity about the teachings, prompting him to look for clues that would indicate who was meant to reveal the teachings.

When he found the line, "These instructions are a gift for the Dharma king and his son," he saw that the teachings were meant for him, and a spontaneous understanding of all the words of the cycle and their underlying meaning arose in his mind. Shortly thereafter, he once again experienced a state of deep meditation.

Jigmé Lingpa then placed one of the crystals in his mouth and picked up the scrolls. Just as he set off to return home, the protector Rahula appeared in the form of a smiling monk and gave him words of encouragement. Next he ventured to the northern quadrant of the stupa and paused once again to look at the scrolls. The text he saw this time was the guide to the collection, with an inventory of its contents and information concerning its origins and destiny. Seeing this text, he felt a sudden inspiration to show it to his mother, believing that merely seeing the revelation would bring liberation.

In that instant, a woman appeared in the sky before him, and he presented her with the scroll. In response, she warned him of the danger of revealing the teachings to others prematurely. At her prompting, Jigmé Lingpa then swallowed the remaining crystals, and finally even the scrolls, triggering a surge of excitement. Feeling that the teachings of the treasure were etched in his mind, he woke from his vision and found himself immersed in a nonconceptual, blissful state.

As mentioned, Jigmé Lingpa was the reincarnation of King Trisong Deutsen. In that life, Jigmé Lingpa had received the teachings of the Heart Essence of the Vast Expanse directly from Padmasambhava. The teachings then lay dormant in his mind stream until the time was ripe for them to be revealed and propagated. He eventually transcribed all the teachings and practiced them in secret for seven years.

When he was thirty-one-years-old, Jigmé Lingpa began a second three-year retreat at Chimpu, near Samyé Monastery in central Tibet. During the course of this retreat, he experienced a series of three visions of Longchenpa, who empowered him as a master of the true lineage of realization and authorized him to compose texts. Despite these visionary experiences, however, he also took the time to seek out Great Perfection teachings from living masters. Among these transmissions were the key works of Longchenpa: the Fourfold Heart Essence, the Seven Treasuries, and the Three Cycles of Rest.

Eventually, a series of auspicious events indicated that it was time to propagate the Heart Essence of the Vast Expanse. He began by codifying the outer guru yoga teachings, and then proceeded to the sadhanas of the Three

Roots, further guru yoga practices, and the sadhana of Mahakaruna mentioned earlier. In addition, he also composed some of his most well-known works, including *Treasury of Precious Qualities* and *Supreme Wisdom*. Then, in 1765, he gave the empowerments and teachings of the Heart Essence of the Vast Expanse to a group of fifteen disciples.

From that point on, Jigmé Lingpa continued to teach and write about the teachings he had revealed. He had students from the six "mother monasteries" of the Nyingma lineage, such as Rigdzin Chenpo, the main lama of Dorjé Trak Monastery, Shechen Rabjam of Shechen Monastery, Getsé Mahapandita of Katok Monastery, and the Third Dzogchen Rinpoche of Dzogchen Monastery. His students also included masters from the Sarma schools, including the heads of the Sakya and Drikung Kagyü schools, leaders from two of Ganden Monastery's monastic colleges, and also political figures like the king and queen of Dergé, a powerful region of eastern Tibet.

Though he soon became one of the foremost spiritual teachers in all Tibet, Jigmé Lingpa steadfastly refused to surround himself with the pomp and splendor enjoyed by others. Instead, he lived in a simple hermitage, where he spent his days writing and teaching. The offerings he received were used solely for spiritual projects. He was particularly devoted to the traditional Buddhist practice of ransoming life, in which an animal scheduled for slaughter is purchased and either set free or kept as a pet.

The writings he composed in these years continue to exert a powerful influence on the Nyingma lineage. In all, his collected works fill fourteen volumes, each of which would equal numerous volumes in English. In addition to the three volumes of the Heart Essence of the Vast Expanse, Jigmé Lingpa also composed two lengthy autocommentaries on his *Treasury of Precious Qualities*. These profound texts cover the entire Buddhist path, from the foundational teachings all the way up to the Great Perfection. He compiled an entire volume of teachings on the yidam deity Vajrakilaya and also a collection of Nyingma tantras, entitled The Hundred Thousand Tantras of the Nyingma School, for which he wrote an extensive history.

Jigmé Lingpa's highly regarded works on meditation practice are widely studied to this day. In all, he penned three works on the preliminary practices. The first two, included in this book, later became the basis for Patrül Rinpoche's *The Words of My Perfect Teacher*. His third work, *Staircase to Liberation*, presents a unique mind-training system from the Heart Essence of Vimalamitra.[25] On the development stage, he wrote a commentary entitled *Ladder to Akanishta*, which provides an overview of the main principles and many key instructions on this style of tantric practice. Jigmé Lingpa also wrote what is perhaps the most widely taught Great Perfection instruction manual, *Supreme Wisdom*, which is more commonly known by its Tibetan title, *Yeshé Lama*.

Leaving behind a magnificent legacy, Jigmé Lingpa passed away in 1798. His students built upon the foundation he erected in the centuries that followed, emulating his lifestyle of simplicity and devotion, and spreading his teachings throughout Tibet.

The Expansion of the Heart Essence of the Vast Expanse

Following the passing of Jigmé Lingpa, the Longchen Nyingtik lineage was carried forward by a number of outstanding Tibetan masters. Though listing all the sublineages that eventually arose is beyond the scope of this introduction, a few major lines of transmission warrant special attention. Jigmé Lingpa's two "heart sons" were Jigmé Trinlé Özer, the first Dodrupchen Rinpoche (1745–1821) and Jigmé Gyalway Nyugu (1765–1843). Both of these individuals were true masters in their own right, as well as completely devoted to Jigmé Lingpa and his Heart Essence teachings. These disciples initiated two enduring Longchen Nyingtik lineages.

Like Jigmé Lingpa before him, Jigmé Trinlé Özer counted some of the most renowned lamas of the Nyingma lineage as his students. His reincarnation, the second Dodrupchen, Jigmé Puntsok Jungney (1824–1863), established the famed Dodrupchen Monastery, which became central to the transmission of the Heart Essence of the Vast Expanse. The subsequent incarnations of the Dodrupchen lineage have all been outstanding masters as well, especially the third, Jigmé Tenpey Nyima, a renowned author and teacher. When the Chinese invaded Tibet in 1959, the fourth Dodrupchen, Jigmé Trinley Pelzang (b. 1927) escaped and built a monastery in Gangtok, Sikkim. This is now one of the primary Longchen Nyingtik centers outside of Tibet.

Jigmé Gyelway Nyugu, Jigmé Lingpa's second heart son, transmitted the teachings to Patrül Rinpoche, one of Jigmé Lingpa's three reincarnations.[26] The lineage then descended to Lungtok Tenpey Nyima (1829–1901/2), who passed on the teachings to Khenpo Ngawang Pelzang.[27] As noted above, Khenpo Ngawang Pelzang—also known as Khenpo Ngaga and Khenpo Ngakchung—was reputed to be an emanation of Vimalamitra. He taught many outstanding masters of the twentieth century. Though the majority have passed away, his heart son, Chatral Sangyé Dorjé, now in his mid-nineties, currently lives on the outskirts of Kathmandu valley in Nepal, where he maintains a hermit lifestyle and teaches only a few close disciples. Though not a direct student of Khenpo Ngawang Pelzang, another notable figure in this lineage was Nyoshul Khenpo Jamyang Dorjé (1931–1999).[28] Nyoshul Khenpo passed on his lineage to a number of lamas who actively teach in the West, including Sogyal Rinpoche, Tsoknyi Rinpoche, and Yongey Mingyur Rinpoche.[29]

In addition to Patrül Rinpoche, Jigmé Lingpa's two other reincarnations were Do Khyentsé Yeshé Dorjé (1800–1866) and Jamyang Khyentsé Wangpo. These masters are widely regarded as two of the greatest masters of the past few centuries. In particular, Jamyang Khyentsé Wangpo helped initiate the Rimé movement, along with Jamgön Kongtrül (1813–1899) and Chokgyur Dechen Lingpa (1829–1870).[30] In the twentieth century, two notable incarnations from this lineage were Jamyang Khyentsé Chökyi Lodro (1893–1959) and Dilgo Khyentsé Rinpoche. Jamyang Khyentsé Chökyi Lodro's reincarnation, Dzongsar Khyentse Rinpoche (b. 1961) teaches widely throughout the world, while the reincarnation of Dilgo Khyentsé Rinpoche, Urgyen Tenzin Jigmé Lhundrup (b. 1993), lives primarily in Bhutan and is still studying. In addition to these influential teachers, the Longchen Nyingtik is taught by scores of other teachers in Tibet, South Asia, and the West.

The Texts of the Heart Essence of the Vast Expanse

Despite its great profundity, the Heart Essence of the Vast Expanse is surprisingly accessible. Unlike many treasure cycles, which often contain hundreds of liturgies and other related materials, the *Longchen Nyingtik* spans only three volumes.[31] Contained in these three volumes are some of the Nyingma lineage's most well-known prayers, sadhanas, and instruction manuals.

The first volume opens with two autobiographies by Jigmé Lingpa, followed by a guide to the collection that lists its contents, as well as information concerning its revelation and propagation. The remainder of the volume consists primarily of sadhana texts, their associated instruction manuals, and prayers. This includes the *Outer Guru Yoga* (which was later incorporated into the preliminary practices), *The Gathering of the Masters of Awareness* (*Rigdzin Düpa*), and sadhanas related to Yumkha Dechen Gyalmo, Tara, Lion-faced Dakini, and various practices related to the Palchen Düpa collection. Each of these sadhanas is accompanied by numerous subsidiary texts, some of which are supplementary liturgies, and others that are practical instructions on sadhana practice.

The second volume contains additional texts from the Palchen Düpa collection, followed by Jigmé Lingpa's explanation of development stage meditation, *Ladder to Akanishta*. Also included are sadhanas related to Mahakaruna and Hayagriva, an extremely secret guru yoga practice entitled *Tiklé Gyachen*, the wrathful guru yoga practice Takyung Barwa, and a series of prayers and aspirations. The volume concludes with a number of texts associated with the one hundred peaceful and wrathful deities and the protectors of the lineage.

The third and final volume contains texts related to completion stage practice, including texts on transference, yogic heat, and trülkhor (yogic exercises), followed by a text on chöd. The remainder of the volume consists of Great Perfection tantras and commentaries, instruction manuals, and additional texts on practice, such as Jigmé Lingpa's three texts on the preliminary practices and the Great Perfection manual *Yeshé Lama*.

Practicing the Heart Essence of the Vast Expanse

The Heart Essence of the Vast Expanse presents a comprehensive path to enlightenment, beginning with essential contemplations that provide inspiration for spiritual practice, and continuing up to the most profound and secret practices of the Great Perfection. Each stage of the path builds upon earlier teachings, preparing the student for the steps that follow. Renouncing worldly concerns and recognizing the absence of self, for example, lay the foundation for cultivating compassion and understanding the principle of emptiness. These factors, in turn, eventually help the practitioner to recognize the pure, luminous nature of mind.

THE PRELIMINARY PRACTICES

The preliminary practices erect a solid foundation for dedicated spiritual practice. Indeed, they are often said to be even more profound than the various development and completion stage yogas, precisely because success in meditation depends largely on how effectively one has practiced the preliminaries. For this reason, the preliminaries are perhaps the most commonly practiced teachings in the Nyingma lineage.

The preliminary practices are divided into two groups: the common outer preliminaries and the unique inner preliminaries. The terms "common" and "unique" indicate that the outer preliminaries are held in common with the Sutra Vehicle, whereas the inner preliminaries are unique to the Vajra Vehicle. The outer preliminaries consist of a series of contemplations that elicit a feeling of disenchantment toward mundane activities, along with a sense of enthusiasm toward the state of liberation and the practices that lead to this state. This attitude of joyful renunciation ensures that one's spiritual practice will not end up reinforcing ordinary states of desire and attachment. The inner preliminaries build on this foundation by clearing away obstacles and obscurations, while simultaneously creating circumstances that set the stage for awakening to take place.

The outer preliminaries consist of six contemplative exercises. In order, the six topics that are addressed in these contemplations are:

- ▸ The precious human existence
- ▸ Death and impermanence
- ▸ The shortcomings of samsara
- ▸ The principle of karma
- ▸ The benefits of liberation
- ▸ The guru principle

Each of these contemplations plays a different role on the spiritual path. The first two contemplations undermine the tendency to become obsessed with trivial matters and shortsighted goals, and instead help the practitioner to focus on what is more meaningful and of lasting benefit. Contemplating the shortcomings of samsara and karma, on the other hand, dislodges the notion that we can attain lasting happiness in future existences. All together, these four thoughts show us that no matter where we are born in samsara, there is no end to suffering. Building upon this recognition, the fifth contemplation offers an alternative—liberation—helping us to see the virtues of attaining freedom from confusion and suffering. The sixth and final contemplation takes this one step further by exploring the role of the spiritual teacher on the path to liberation.

The inner preliminaries are also broken down into six parts:

- ▸ Going for refuge
- ▸ Cultivating bodhichitta
- ▸ The meditation and recitation of Vajrasattva

- Mandala offering
- The offering of the simple beggar
- Guru yoga

All six practices contain a component that, according to tradition, should be repeated one hundred thousand times. As before, each practice serves a specific function. The act of taking refuge is the foundation for all Buddhist practice, insofar as it involves committing oneself to viewing the Buddha as one's source of guidance and inspiration, his teachings as the path to be followed, and the spiritual community as one's companions on the spiritual journey. In this practice, the meditator imagines him- or herself to be in the presence of the Three Jewels and Three Roots and recites a four-line refuge prayer, eventually accumulating one hundred thousand repetitions. Whereas the refuge prayer is often accompanied by full-body prostrations in the other lineages, in the Longchen Nyingtik prostrations are typically performed in the context of guru yoga.

Bodhichitta is the wish to attain enlightenment for the benefit of others. In the context of the preliminary practices, the cultivation of bodhichitta is formalized by visualizing the Three Jewels and Three Roots, as before, and reciting a four-line stanza in their presence. This stanza is usually recited one hundred thousand times as well, though there are certain traditions where this is not the case.[32] In addition, there are also a number of contemplations that are practiced, including the cultivation of empathy and the willingness to consider the needs of others before one's own. This practice serves to dissolve self-centeredness and replace it with a more altruistic attitude, and eventually with the mind-set of bodhichitta.

The third inner preliminary practice is the meditation and recitation of Vajrasattva. Here, one visualizes Vajrasattva, the embodiment of purity, above the crown of one's head and imagines a stream of purifying nectar flowing out from his divine form. This nectar fills the entire body and purifies all forms of ignorance, negativity, and suffering. Along with this imaginative process, one also acknowledges the negative actions one has committed in the past, vows to refrain from doing them in the future, and recites the one-hundred-syllable mantra of Vajrasattva to purify the latent habitual tendencies that lead to such negativity. Here, it is this mantra that is accumulated one hundred thousand times. This practice effectively eliminates the various factors that block realization from taking place.

Following Vajrasattva practice is the mandala offering, in which one makes real and imagined offerings to a visualized assembly of enlightened beings. For this practice, the meditator holds a small mandala plate and repeatedly places offerings on top of it, while simultaneously reciting a short offering prayer and visualizing a host of enlightened beings. The physical act of offering and recitation of the prayer are repeated one hundred thousand times. This is taught to be a particularly effective way to gather the two accumulations of merit and wisdom. To this, the Longchen Nyingtik adds the offering of the simple beggar, which involves the imagined offering of one's own body. In addition to being a powerful way to gather merit and cultivate wisdom, this practice also functions to eliminate fixation related to the physical body.

The fifth and final practice of the inner preliminaries is guru yoga. In this practice, the animate and inanimate universe is viewed as a pure realm populated with buddhas. Within this divine atmosphere, the meditator supplicates the guru, makes offerings, and then merges his or her mind with the wisdom mind of the guru. When the devotion of the student is sincere and heartfelt, this merging of minds can bring about an immediate and profound shift in consciousness. Guru yoga serves to infuse the meditator's mind with the blessings of the lineage.

These outer and inner preliminaries prepare the mind of the student for advanced meditations like the Great Perfection. Once complete, the student receives guidance from his or her teacher concerning the appropriate course of meditation to follow. This may include development stage meditation (visualization and mantra recitation), completion stage with symbolic attributes practice (working with the body's subtle energies), and/or formless completion stage practices (recognizing and familiarizing oneself with the nature of mind).

As noted above, these practices are typically followed under the guidance of an experienced spiritual teacher. Once a student has requested permission to begin the preliminary practices and the teacher has consented, the first steps are to receive the appropriate empowerments, reading transmissions, and instructions. These three are known in Tibet as *wang, lung,* and *tri.* There are numerous empowerments that may be given to prepare the student for the preliminaries. Ideally, an empowerment for the one hundred peaceful and wrathful deities would be received, or empowerments associated with Vajrasattva and Padmasambhava.[33] Along with these empowerments, the reading transmission for the preliminary practices liturgy would be given. In certain situations, empowerments may be dispensed with and the reading transmission is given alone. Finally, the student must also receive practical instructions on the practices. This may involve receiving an explanation of the liturgy itself, or a commentary on the preliminary practices, such as those contained in this book or Patrül Rinpoche's *The Words of My Perfect Teacher*.

In some sublineages, there are specific requirements for both the outer and inner preliminaries. In the lineage of Khenpo Ngakchung, for instance, the first stage of practice involves a one-hundred-day retreat, during which one spends approximately eight hours each day contemplating the outer preliminaries and the various bodhichitta meditations, and only four hours accumulating the required numbers to complete the inner preliminaries.[34] By the end of this retreat, the student will have completed one hundred thousand refuge prayer recitations and thirty thousand bodhichitta prayer recitations, in addition to having spent eight hundred hours contemplating the various topics outlined above. The student then proceeds to accumulate one hundred thousand recitations of the one-hundred-syllable mantra, one hundred thousand mandala offerings, one hundred thousand prostrations in conjunction with the seven-branch offering, and 12 million repetitions of the vajra guru mantra—*om ah hum vajra guru padma siddhi hum*. In other traditions, the requirements are much less demanding. There may be no specific requirement for the outer preliminaries, other than a strong recommendation that the student spend ample time contemplating them, and the guru yoga requirement may be 1.2 million recitations, rather than 12 million.

In terms of study, the Longchen Nyingtik lineage has one of the richest bodies of practice literature in Tibet, especially concerning the preliminary practices. The main preliminary practice liturgy itself, *The Sublime Path to Omniscience*, was compiled from the writings of Jigmé Lingpa and other authors by the first Dodrupchen Rinpoche. This lengthy liturgy, included at the end of this volume, is regarded as one of the most inspiring and lyrical compositions of the Tibetan tradition. A concise liturgy composed by Jamyang Khyentsé Wangpo, entitled *The Sublime Path to Enlightenment*, is also included in this volume.

The two works by Jigmé Lingpa contained in this book are considered the primary instruction manuals on the preliminary practices and the basis for all others. In addition to Jigmé Lingpa's writings, there are two other works of primary importance concerning the preliminary practices: a short text by Jamyang Khyentsé Wangpo entitled *Illuminating the Sublime Path to Omniscience* and Patrül Rinpoche's *The Words of My Perfect Teacher*. There are numerous other commentaries in addition to these four texts. Of particular interest are Khenpo Ngakchung's *A Guide to "The Words of My Perfect Teacher"* (which contains the author's notes on Patrül Rinpoche's work) and Chökyi Drakpa's *A Torch for the Path to Omniscience* (a word-for-word commentary on the liturgy).

Traditionally, the preliminary practices are completed when the student has completed the required number of accumulations for each practice. Once again, however, there is no standard rule that applies in all cases. Some teachers may instruct their students to practice until certain signs manifest that indicate their success in practice. Such signs may be the occurrence of auspicious dreams, or a marked decrease in negative emotions and increase in virtues like wisdom and compassion. Another alternative, though less common, is to practice the preliminaries for a set length of time. Once complete, students typically proceed to a particular development stage sadhana.

DEVELOPMENT STAGE

Following the outer and inner preliminary practices, the student will ideally be ready to start the main practices of the Vajra Vehicle: the development stage and completion stage. In development stage practice, the meditator uses the visualization of pure realms and deities, mantra recitation, and meditative absorption to disrupt the ordinary processes of distorted perception and replace them with the pure appearances of a mandala—a divine palace and the deities that inhabit it. Such practices may have one deity or a pair of deities as their focal point and typically involve the recitation of lengthy liturgies and numerous repetitions of sacred mantras. By absorbing one's mind in these visualized appearances and mantric sounds, the habitual tendency to view the mundane world as impure and problematic is progressively refined away. Eventually, one's mind, and then even the body, merges with this divine identity.

Each development stage practice is centered on a particular yidam deity or group of yidam deities. Yidams are not gods, but rather archetypal projections that enable the practitioner to connect with certain aspects of his or her own buddha nature. Manjushri, for example, is the embodiment of wisdom. Thus, imagining oneself to be Manjushri is a skillful way to actualize one's indwelling wisdom. Likewise, one may focus on Avalokiteshvara to develop compassion, Vajrakilaya to overcome obstacles, or Vajrasattva to purify negativity. By repeatedly envisioning oneself as an enlightened being, any lack of confidence in one's own enlightened potential is gradually worn away.

As with the preliminary practices, the development stage begins with an empowerment, reading transmission, and practical instructions. The empowerment one receives depends on the yidam deity one is going to practice. If one has been advised to practice *Gathering of the Masters of Awareness*, for instance, one would receive a specific empowerment for that practice. Likewise, one would also receive a reading transmission for the liturgy, or sadhana, that is used in daily meditation and then instructions on how to do the practice.

Each development stage practice has an associated sadhana—a structured liturgy that guides the meditator step-by-step through the practice.[35] Typically, sadhana practice begins with a series of preliminary steps that serve to remind the meditator of the basic principles of the Buddhist path. These preliminary steps consist of cultivating renunciation, taking refuge, and generating bodhichitta. There are also preliminary steps that are unique to the development stage, in which one expels malicious forces, establishes a protective boundary, and then consecrates oneself and the environment by invoking the compassion of the Three Roots—the guru, yidam deity, and Dharma protectors and dakinis.

The main practice opens with the three absorptions. In these three contemplations, the meditator becomes absorbed in emptiness, compassion, and the expression of these two, visualized as a seed syllable. Following this, one will visualize a mandala, with the practitioner imagined to be the deity that resides at its center. Depending on the style of practice, the visualization may be developed in an instant, or constructed in a step-by-step manner.[36] Once the visualization is complete, the meditator proceeds to invoke the blessings of all the buddhas and bodhisattvas and to imbue the visualized images with this enlightened energy. One then visualizes the surrounding deities making offerings and praising the central deity (or deities, should there be a pair of deities in union).

When visualizing, there are three main elements that one should not lose sight of: clear appearance, stable pride, and the purity of the visualized imagery. Clear appearance refers to the visualized image of the deity, which should be clear and precise. It is also worth noting that the visualized forms are not solid, corporeal entities, but rather ethereal and made of light. Stable pride indicates that the practitioner should have the confidence that he or she truly *is* the deity. In recollecting the purity of the deity, one recalls that the imagined deity is actually an expression of the mind's enlightened nature.

Once the visualization is clear and stable, one may add the practice of mantra recitation. Each yidam deity has its own mantra, which is recited a certain number of times to complete the practice. Typically, the number of mantras that need to be recited is determined by the number of syllables in the mantra, with one hundred thousand repetitions for each. Thus, since the mantra of Padmasambhava—OM AH HUM VAJRA GURU PADMA SIDDHI HUM—has twelve syllables, it would be recited 1.2 million times. Depending on the number of deities in the mandala, the practitioner may have to recite numerous additional mantras, though for the surrounding deities the number of mantras that must be accumulated is substantially less.

The final step of development stage practice is the dissolution phase. Here, the visualized mandala is gradually dissolved from without: the external world melts into light and dissolves into the surrounding deities, the surrounding deities dissolve into the central deity, and finally the central deity dissolves into emptiness. The meditator then rests in an open, nonconceptual state. During the post-meditation period, the goal is to experience all forms, sounds, and thoughts as the display of deity, mantra, and wisdom.

When studying the development stage, one typically receives teachings on the sadhana one is going to practice. While most sadhanas have their own instruction manuals, it is also helpful to study works that discuss the general principles of development stage practice. In the Longchen Nyingtik lineage, Jigmé Lingpa's *Ladder to Akanishta* and two texts by Patrül Rinpoche—*Clarifying the Difficult Points in the Development Stage and Deity Yoga* and *Four Stakes That Bind the Life-Force*—are considered authoritative works on this subject.[37]

As with the preliminary practices, there are various ways to gauge whether or not one is ready to move on to more advanced forms of practice. Common requirements relate to duration, number of recitations, and experiential signs of success. For the first, one may be instructed to practice for a certain number of months. With the second, one commits to accumulate a set number of mantra recitations. The ideal, however, is to practice until one has experienced the signs of success that are spelled out in the relevant instruction manual. Such signs may manifest in dreams or waking life.

COMPLETION STAGE AND THE GREAT PERFECTION

Though development stage practice is an effective method for undoing the habitual patterns associated with impure perception, it can also lead to a fixation on the newly developed pure vision of reality. The completion stage functions to counteract this tendency and also to help the practitioner identify and directly experience the subtle energetic body and the empty radiance of pure awareness. There are two main divisions of completion stage practice: completion stage with symbolic attributes and completion stage without symbolic attributes. In the former, emphasis is placed on working with the subtle energies, channels, and essences of the body and, in particular, on bringing the energies of the right and left channels into the central channel. In the completion stage without symbolic attributes, the nature of mind is emphasized. This includes effortless practices such as Mahamudra and the Great Perfection.

In the Heart Essence of the Vast Expanse, there are texts and practices associated with both forms of completion stage meditation. The first completion stage practice contained in the root texts of the collection concerns the practice of transference, or *powa*, in which the practitioner projects his or her consciousness into a different plane of existence.[38] Following this are a number of practices that allow one to work directly with the body's subtle energies to elicit an experience of bliss-emptiness.

When it comes to the completion stage without symbolic attributes, the Longchen Nyingtik focuses on the Heart Essence teachings of the Great Perfection. These profound instructions are contained in a meditation manual by Jigmé Lingpa, entitled *Supreme Wisdom*. This manual, often referred to by its Tibetan title, *Yeshé Lama*, fuses the Heart Essence teachings of Vimalamitra and Padmasambhava.

According to this system, once the student has completed the outer and inner preliminaries, the next step is to practice the unique preliminaries of the Heart Essence teachings: the outer and inner separations of samsara and nirvana, or *kordé rushen*; the physical, verbal, and mental preliminaries; and the practices of resting in the natural state and revitalization. These practices prepare the student for the advanced practices of breakthrough and direct leap—*trekchö* and *tögal*. Breakthrough is intended for those inclined to an effortless approach, where the focus is on emptiness and original purity. In this phase of practice, the meditator is introduced to awareness, or *rigpa*. Once awareness has been pointed out and recognized, one repeatedly familiarizes oneself with this pure awareness until it becomes a stable, living experience. The direct leap focuses on the radiance of pure awareness, rather than emptiness. This style of practice is geared toward those who are more industrious by nature.

The general progression of practice in the Heart Essence tradition contains these four steps: the preliminary practices, development stage, completion stage with symbolic attributes, and Great Perfection. There is, however, no standard approach that each student must follow. The Buddha's teachings are noteworthy for their willingness to accommodate differences in aptitude, personality, and character. Not surprisingly, the approach of the Longchen Nyingtik reflects this outlook. While most students do follow the progression outlined above to some degree, there is a great deal of flexibility when it comes to the specific practices one does, for how long, and how these practices are integrated with different life circumstances. Some practitioners, for instance, may be advised to do an abbreviated version of the preliminaries, while others may practice an intensive retreat-based version, which can involve nearly ten thousand hours of cumulative practice. Similarly, practitioners may practice sadhanas associated with one or more yidam deity, depending on their personal connection with a particular buddha family and the advice of their spiritual guide, or they may practice none at all and proceed directly to the Great Perfection.

THE ORIGINS OF THIS WORK

The following translations of Jigmé Lingpa's writings on the preliminary practices were completed in two stages. I initially became interested in these texts shortly after meeting Chatral Rinpoche, a living master of the Great Perfection. At the time, I was beginning to learn Tibetan but was not yet able to read or speak fluently. Chatral Rinpoche kindly gave me the appropriate transmissions to begin the preliminary practices and then instructed me to visit one of his close students, Kyapchen Tulku Rinpoche, to receive detailed instructions on ngöndro practice. As I would soon find out, however, Kyapchen Tulku spoke no English, and since I was still unable to communicate in Tibetan, I had no way to receive the instructions I needed to begin practicing.

This turned out to be a great motivation to learn Tibetan. For the next year, I studied colloquial and literary Tibetan diligently, visiting Chatral Rinpoche when I could at his monastery on the outskirts of Kathmandu, Nepal. During the course of my studies, I had the good fortune to meet an extremely learned lama named Khenpo Sherab Sangpo, who was teaching at the Centre for Buddhist Studies in Boudhanath at that time. Khenpo had already been teaching Western students for a number of years and was eager to learn English, so we made a deal: I agreed to teach him English every day for an hour, and in exchange, he agreed to help me read Jigmé Lingpa's writings on the preliminary practices, which I had recently begun to translate with the permission of Chatral Rinpoche. For the next six months, we met a few times each week to work on his English and revise my translation. Eventually, my Tibetan improved to the degree that I was able to approach Kyapchen Tulku Rinpoche, who generously explained the entire ngöndro liturgy to me word-by-word. I then moved to a small retreat center near Chatral Rinpoche's monastery in Pharping to practice.

A few years later, I came across the draft translations I had prepared under the guidance of Khenpo Sherab Sangpo. I was struck by the beauty and profundity of Jigmé Lingpa's instructions and also the utter inadequacy of my initial efforts to render his words into English. I was, however, inspired to revisit the text and correct the many mistakes I had made. It also occurred to me that the translation might be of interest to other practitioners, so I visited Chatral Rinpoche to ask his advice. Rinpoche is known, not only for his mastery of the Great Perfection, but also for his strict approach to transmitting teachings. For this reason, I was not sure what he would say. I asked him whether or not it would be a good idea to revise the translations and have them published and was pleasantly surprised when he responded enthusiastically.

With Chatral Rinpoche's blessings, I then set to work correcting the translation. My first step was to check the entire text against the original Tibetan, which I did during a two-month retreat in Namo Buddha, Nepal. As luck would have it, shortly thereafter I found myself in close proximity to Khenpo Sherab Sangpo once again, who was teaching in Minneapolis. I consulted Khenpo about the many questions I had and clarified difficult sections in the text. Finally, I sent the translation to Heidi Nevin, a gifted translator and close student of Chatral Rinpoche's. Heidi generously checked the entire translation against the Tibetan and also offered insightful editorial advice, greatly improving both the quality of the translation and the readability of my prose.

When I was working on the translation, a friend told me about a wonderful commentary on the preliminary practices by Dzongsar Khyentse Rinpoche. I eventually found a copy and read it eagerly, finding it incredibly beneficial for my practice. It occurred to me that an excerpt from his teachings would make a superb introduction to Jigmé Lingpa's translations. I asked Dzongsar Khyentse Rinpoche for permission to use an excerpt, and he generously agreed. Once I began to read through the text to find the right passage, however, it was clear that I had a big problem: there was simply too much good material ... I couldn't choose. I then made another request to Khyentse Rinpoche, this time asking if I could include the manuscript alongside my translations, and once again he agreed.

This, of course, left me without an introduction. After mulling it over, I decided to write this explanatory introduction and numerous appendices that would help the reader contextualize the teachings of Jigmé Lingpa and Dzongsar Khyentse Rinpoche. I wrote about the topics that I myself would have been interested in when I first set out to study and practice the preliminaries. I also thought it would be helpful to include Jamyang Khyentsé Wangpo's commentary along with the long and concise ngöndro liturgies, as well as an extended reading list and glossary. Eventually, Snow Lion Publications agreed to publish the book. Under the auspices of the Rimé Foundation, I completed this project as a member of the Nitartha Translation Network.

HOW TO PRACTICE

*Instructions on the Common Great Perfection Preliminaries of
the Heart Essence of the Vast Expanse*

JIGMÉ LINGPA

Homage to the buddhas and bodhisattvas!

This text presents the common preliminaries of the Great Perfection: Heart
Essence of the Vast Expanse, condensing these teachings into a practical set
of instructions containing six topics:

1) The rarity of the freedoms and riches
2) The impermanence of life
3) The shortcomings of samsara
4) The principle of karmic causality
5) The benefits of liberation
6) How to follow a spiritual teacher

THE RARITY OF THE FREEDOMS AND RICHES

This topic entails four steps:

- ▸ A contemplation of the essential freedoms
- ▸ A contemplation of the specific riches
- ▸ A contemplation of the metaphors that illustrate their rarity
- ▸ A contemplation of their relative improbability

The Eight Freedoms

When you are born into one of the eight restricted states, you will lack the power to practice the Dharma, and in this sense you will not be free. This occurs in the following way: If you are born in the hell realm, you will suffer relentlessly from agonizing heat and cold, and therefore have no opportunity to practice the Dharma. As a spirit, you will be unable to practice due to painful experiences of hunger and thirst. As an animal, you will be kept from Dharma practice by the suffering of enslavement or by being preyed upon. Likewise, if you are born as a long-life god, your time will be passed in a blank state of mental dullness, and you will have no opportunity to practice. If you are born in a borderland, you will be unable to practice the Dharma due to the absence of the Buddha's teachings. If you happen to be born in the unfortunate position of one who practices non-Buddhist faiths or one who has a similar outlook on life, your own mind will be tainted with distorted beliefs that will keep you from practicing the Dharma. If you are born in a dark age, you will not even hear the words "Three Jewels," nor will you be able to tell virtue from vice. Thus, if you are born at such a time, you will be unable to practice the Dharma. If you are mentally retarded, your consciousness will be unfit to practice the Dharma. Not being born into any of these eight states is what we mean by the term "opportunity," and since one will then have the chance to practice the Dharma, the word "freedom" is used.

Therefore, begin by taking refuge and cultivating bodhichitta, and then rejoice in the fact that right now your mind hasn't taken birth in one of these eight restricted states. Think to yourself, "In essence, these eight freedoms will be extremely difficult to come by in the future, so if I don't apply myself diligently to the Dharma now, my human existence will be rendered useless!" Reflect on this again and again. To conclude, dedicate the virtue you've accumulated to all sentient beings, and do the same for the topics that follow.

To supplement this contemplation, carefully examine your mind to see if it has fallen prey to any of the eight incidental circumstances or eight factors that cut one off from the Dharma. All of these will restrict you from practicing. Exposing your own faults in this manner is extremely beneficial.

Concerning the two sets of eight incidental circumstances that restrict Dharma practice, the *Precious Wish-Fulfilling Treasury* states:

> Disturbed by the five poisons, ignorant and stupid, caught in
> Mara's grasp,

Lazy, bursting with an ocean of negative karma, being dominated by
others,
Practicing out of fear, and being a spiritual person only in appearance—
These are the eight incidental circumstances that restrict Dharma
practice.

And:

Bound tight, with extremely degenerate behavior,
No disenchantment with samsara, without even a shred of faith,
Engaging in nonvirtue and negativity, with no interest in the Dharma,
Lax when it comes to keeping the vows and samayas—
These eight will cut your mind off from the Dharma.

These two sets of eight circumstances can befall one very easily. Therefore,
if you fail to approach them with some sense of discernment, merely attaining the essential freedoms will not necessarily prevent you from eventually
falling into a situation where you will not have the opportunity to practice
the Dharma. Keep in mind that this kind of freedom is simply the ordinary
leisure one might experience in old age.

The Ten Riches

The five personal riches are as follows: You will not encounter the Dharma
without being born as a human. That you have such a human form at present
is the *richness of support*. Neither will you encounter the Dharma if you're
born in a borderland or some other location where the Dharma doesn't exist.
Since you have been born into a central location where the Dharma is present, you have the *richness of place*. Not having a full set of correctly functioning sense faculties is an obstacle to practice. Now that you are free of such
problems, you possess the *richness of the quality of sense faculties*. If you lead
an immoral life and continually engage in nonvirtue, you will effectively be
turning your back on the Dharma. That you are now inclined toward virtue
is referred to as the *richness of a special attitude*. However, if you don't place
your faith in the right place, meaning the teachings of the Buddha, your
mind won't be directed toward the Dharma. That you are now able to direct
your mind to the Dharma is the *richness of faith*. Since the presence of all
five of these factors depends on you, they are referred to as "the five personal
riches."

The five circumstantial riches are as follows: If you haven't been born in an enlightened age, in a world where a buddha has appeared, you won't even hear the word "Dharma." That you now find yourself in an age where a buddha has appeared is the *richness of a special teacher*. However, even if a buddha does appear, if he or she doesn't teach the Dharma, it won't be of any benefit. That the Buddha has turned the wheel of Dharma three times is the *richness of Dharma*. Nevertheless, if these teachings have been given but then enter a state of decline, they won't be able to help us. Since the period in which the doctrine will remain has not yet ended, we have the *richness of time*. If you don't practice the teachings, they won't do you any good, even if they are still present. Having entered the door of the teachings is the *richness of your own good fortune*. Once you've entered the teachings, if you haven't met with conducive circumstances for practice, meaning that you have not been accepted by a spiritual teacher, you won't gain a true understanding of the Dharma. If you have been accepted by a teacher, this is the *richness of superior compassion*. As the presence of all five of these factors depends on other conditions, they are referred to as "the five circumstantial riches."

When complete, these eighteen factors form the support for practicing the sacred Dharma, hence the term "precious human body." On the other hand, if just one of these is missing, you will be unable to genuinely traverse the path to liberation. If this is the case, what you have is called an "ordinary human body." Therefore, from today onward, you should rejoice in the fact that you now have what can truly be called "a precious human body." Still, since immoral activity, the waning of faith, and other such conditions can lead to the loss of these eighteen factors, you must be on guard. This is an important point! A situation like this will not be found again.

If you don't do something meaningful with your freedoms and riches now, you will end up in the unfortunate position of having fallen into the lower realms, where you won't be able to tell right from wrong. Even if you do manage to be reborn in the higher realms, it will be difficult to meet a spiritual teacher. Whatever you do will end up creating negativity, and it will become impossible to be freed from the sufferings of samsara. In a heartfelt manner, think to yourself, "What a fool I've been not to see this problem!" Even when you're in the city or the middle of a large market, you should carefully examine your situation to see if you have this precious human body with all of these eighteen factors. Then, using your own existence as the basis for your considerations, ponder again and again how difficult it is to find such a fortunate situation.

A Metaphor

The Buddha likened the rarity of finding such a precious human existence to the following situation: Imagine a wooden yoke with one hole floating on the surface of an ocean churning with huge waves. In the depths of this ocean, there is a blind turtle. This wooden yoke doesn't stay still for even a moment, and the turtle comes to the surface only one time every hundred years. The support of a human body, the Buddha said, is even more rarely met with than the turtle putting its neck through the hole of the yoke.

The Probability of Obtaining the Freedoms and Riches

Likewise, if you observe the various numbers and types of sentient beings, you'll see that obtaining a human body is virtually impossible. If you equate the number of hell beings to the stars seen in the night sky, for example, spirits are as rare as a star seen in daylight. Likewise, when the number of spirits is compared to the stars in the night sky, animals are no more numerous than the number of stars seen during the day. And again, the same can be said of the number of animals compared to a rebirth in the higher realms. This latter point is a fact that we can directly perceive: Just examine how many parasites live on or inside a single human body.

Furthermore, if you consider the number of people who have no interest in the Dharma or who have fallen away from it, you'll see that those who lead a spiritual life are extremely few in number. Therefore, obtaining a mere human existence, and especially a Dharmic human existence, is extremely difficult. Contemplating this over and over again, cultivate a sense of certainty regarding the difficulty of obtaining the freedoms and riches.

THE IMPERMANENCE OF LIFE

The External Universe

To begin, meditate on impermanence by contemplating the external universe. The four continents, Mount Meru, and the heavenly realms, with their firm and stable enclosure, last for an entire eon. Nevertheless, one day these too will perish, at which point they will be completely destroyed by seven fires and one flood, with not even a bit of ash left behind. Contemplate this process and cultivate a sense of sadness.

Living Beings

Second, meditate on the impermanence of the beings that inhabit the universe. Even the sages and gods, with their eon-long life spans and majestic brilliance, cannot escape their own mortality. What, then, of those of us on earth, born as we are at the end of an age in a place where the life span is indefinite? We too will soon be dead.

What were once thriving villages and monasteries are now empty and deserted. Once inhabited by great individuals, they are now home to nothing more than birds and mice. Just look at your own parents, friends and relatives, fellow villagers, neighbors, pets, and so on. Of those that you can recall, most of them are now gone. Some of them were alive just last year, but this year they are no more.

More specifically, in your present circumstances you feed your body good food, dress it in the finest clothes and jewelry, and maintain a healthy lifestyle. Despite all this, your life is getting shorter with each passing day. Death will arrive before long, and when it does, your breathing will become labored and your face will grow pale. Your limbs will twitch and your mind will grow delusional. In the end, you will end up a corpse, your body tied and covered with cloth. Cast naked into a charnel ground, your limbs will be hacked apart and eaten by vultures and wild beasts, with even your hair and bones torn apart and scattered here and there. When all this happens, your loved ones and possessions will not go with you, yet leaving them behind will seem unbearable. Your karma alone will dictate what happens.

Such a time could even arrive today or this evening. You can't be sure! With a sense of urgency, think about how unbearable this actually is. As you continually familiarize your mind with this idea, when you move, sit, or lie down, you can even say to yourself, "This is my very last act in this world!"

THE SHORTCOMINGS OF SAMSARA

General Presentation

The term "samsara" refers to our continuous journey through the six classes of existence, the realms that beings inhabit in all their various forms. Within these six realms, there isn't a single form you haven't had, nor is there a single being that hasn't been your parent, child, enemy, friend, or simply an indifferent stranger. As such, every single being has helped us as our own parent or loved one at some time, just as they have harmed us as an enemy. Furthermore, the number of heads, limbs, and body parts that you've severed to sate your desires is beyond reckoning. If you were to gather together the small insect bodies that you've had, the pile would be even higher than Mount Meru. What's more, the tears you've cried would surely fill an ocean.

If even beings like Brahma and Indra, with their long lives and marvelous bodies and riches, still die and end up having to endure the most miserable sufferings of the lower realms, the prosperity, good health, and other trifling pleasures that you are experiencing in your present form may keep you fooled for a few years, months, or days. But once the pleasant results of the higher realms have run out, your condition will be extremely poor and wretched, or you'll have to experience the unwanted and unbearable sufferings of the lower realms. What is the point, then, of your present happiness and contentment? It's just like being woken in the middle of a nice dream. Think to yourself, "In this present life I must do whatever it takes to liberate myself from samsara, this ocean of suffering!" Then, with this thought, put the teachings into practice, making sure to include the preparation, main practice, and conclusion.[39]

The Specific Sufferings of the Six Realms

THE EIGHT HOT HELLS

In the Eight Hot Hells, you won't even have the pleasure of being able to put your foot down in peace, as the ground and the entire surrounding enclosure are like a burning-hot piece of iron and the whole environment is a blazing expanse of hot flames. These characteristics are common to all eight of the hell realms.

The inhabitants of the Reviving Hell are gathered together in an expanse of glowing embers. There, with minds overcome by hatred, they see one another as mortal enemies and attack each other with weapons. The moment they die, a voice from the sky bellows, "Revive!" and they are immediately brought back to life. They must then continue to undergo this same suffering until all of their negative karma is exhausted. For this reason, the name "reviving" is given to this karmic experience.

Imagine that you are undergoing these experiences and focus on how this affects your mind. If merely meditating on these planes of existence creates such suffering, how would you be able to cope if you actually experienced the ripening of such karma yourself? The main cause of rebirth in hell is a mind filled with anger. Hence, you have the cause of such karma in abundance since you've been conditioning yourself in this manner from the past up to the present moment. You should be terrified! Think to yourself, "There's no doubt that I too will have to experience the result of this karma, whether I want to or not!" Give rise to a fierce sense of remorse for all that you've done up until the present. Confess it all and vow to restrain yourself in the future. Apply the antidote to your mind by thinking to yourself, "I'd rather die than commit such acts from here on out!" Then cultivate an intense feeling of compassion for all the hell beings who are actually undergoing this resultant suffering right now, as well as for those who are engaging in the causes that will condition them for this in the future. This is a genuine method for reducing the negativity in your own mind stream. Hence, be mindful of this for all that follows.

The bodies of those in the Black Line Hell are laid out like chunks of charred wood by the terrifying henchmen of the Lord of Death. Eight, sixteen and even more black lines are then drawn on their bodies, marking them from the crown of their heads to the soles of the feet. These lines are then used as guides to dismember their bodies. The moment they finish, their body parts rejoin and the process starts all over again, bringing immeasurable suffering.

The Crushing Hell is a land of burning-hot iron. Its inhabitants find themselves between mountains that they perceive as the heads of horses, camels, bulls, and other animals. They are then caught in the middle when fights break out between these creatures, and they are crushed like blisters. At other times, they are beaten with a blazing hammer and ground like sesame seeds in an iron mortar. The instant this befalls them, they are revived, only to suffer just as before.

Those in the Wailing Hell cry out intensely as they're boiled in molten iron. The inhabitants of the Howling Hell are forced into a two-level building made of blazing-hot iron. There they are beaten with red-hot hammers and suffer when they see that the entrances are sealed shut. In the Inferno, beings are boiled in an iron vessel filled with molten metal. Whenever they make it to the surface, they are hit with hammers and lose consciousness, only to suffer once they become accustomed to this pleasant respite. As for the Great Inferno, the beings there are put into a blazing-iron building, where they are impaled on three-pronged stakes straight through to their shoulders and the crown of their heads. They are then wrapped with red-hot blankets of iron. Their suffering is immense.

The Hell of Incessant Torment is surrounded by the Sixteen Neighboring Hells. There, in a blazing-iron building, the inhabitants are burned alive until their bodies become indistinguishable from the flames. Their suffering is incredibly harsh. Since their bodies can't even be seen, the only indication of their presence is the sound of their agonized wailing. Their desire to be freed is incessant. Although they occasionally see what appears to be a door, it gradually recedes into the distance and then disappears altogether, making them suffer anew. Thus, the very building where they live harms them, as do the spears that stab them, the clubs they are beaten with, the molten iron that is poured into their mouths, as well as other forms of external torment. In short, the beings in this hell must continually endure the sufferings found in the previous seven hells. These beings live for an entire intermediate eon without even a moment's respite. For this reason, it is called the "Hell of Incessant Torment without Respite."

Since the sensations experienced in each of these Eight Hot Hells grows gradually more intense by a factor of seven, the suffering in each of them increases by a factor of seven as well. Imagine yourself undergoing these experiences. In the same way that you wouldn't want to go back to a place where you once experienced great suffering, meditate and think to yourself, "I must really put some effort into these methods that will keep me from being born in these places!"

THE NEIGHBORING HELLS

The Neighboring Hells are the sixteen areas that surround the Hell of Incessant Torment. In each of the four directions there is a Pit of Burning Embers, a Swamp of Decomposing Corpses, a Plain of Weapons, and a Forest of Sword Blades. When the karma of the denizens of the Hell of Incessant Torment eventually diminishes, they manage to escape, whereupon they find a shady trench and approach it with delight. Once they arrive, however, they sink into a pit of burning coals and hot ashes. Next they see a river, only to find a foul-smelling swamp of decomposing corpses once they approach. Again they fall in and metal-beaked parasites bore into their flesh. On the plain of weapons, they first catch sight of a pleasant-looking meadow, but it turns out to be filled with razor-sharp iron blades. They suffer with each step they take, as blades slice straight through their feet each time they step down and then heal when lifted back up. Similarly, they may see a lush, green forest and again approach it optimistically. Once there, however, the leaves turn to swords, and their bodies are cut to pieces by a pelting rain.

There is also the Hill of the Iron Shalmali. At first, they see a loved one calling out to them from a hilltop. As they get closer, sharp iron blades on the path slice into their legs, and when they finally arrive on top, ravens and vultures bore into their brains and dig out their eyeballs. Then again they see their loved one calling out, but this time from below. As before, their legs get cut open when they descend to meet them, and when they get to the bottom, their loved one will turn into an iron man or woman, blazing with fire, who will then proceed to scorch them in their embrace and devour them.

THE EIGHT COLD HELLS

The Eight Cold Hells are all situated among glaciers and snow-capped mountains, where the ground is such that one's own footsteps cannot be seen and the body is frozen by the blizzards that continuously rage. In the Blistering Hell, blisters break out all over the body, which is naked and exposed to the freezing cold. In the Hell of Burst Blisters, these blisters burst open and leave wounds. In the Hell of Clenched Teeth, the pain becomes unbearable, causing the teeth to clench shut. Beings in the Hell of Lamentation wail incessantly. In the Hell of Groans, the sound of the voice breaks, and all that comes out is a pitiful moan. In the Hell of Utpala-Like Cracks, the skin splits open into four pieces, just like the utpala flower. In the Hell of Lotus-Like Cracks, it splits into eight pieces and then further into sixteen, thirty-two, and then even into countless pieces in the Great Hell of Lotus-Like Cracks. As the skin splits open in these hells, small, sharp-beaked insects crawl into the cracks and eat the flesh. As before, imagine what it would be like to be in these eight hells, each of which is named for the intolerable suffering of cold found therein.

THE EPHEMERAL HELLS

There are many different forms of suffering in the Ephemeral Hells. Some beings are crushed between rocks or encased in boulders. Others are frozen in glaciers, boiled in hot springs, or burned in fires. Some may suffer as their own limbs and digits are hacked apart, the visceral result of having cut down and split up trees. Still more experience the unbearable suffering of thinking themselves to be something that is continually in use, such as a pestle, broom, pot, door, mat, post, hearthstone, or rope. Some spend their days suffering in an iron house and are freed at night. Others kill one another, and so on. Once again, cultivate a sense of sadness as you imagine yourself undergoing all these different experiences and forms of suffering.

THE SUFFERING OF SPIRITS

Subterranean Spirits This class of spirits is subdivided into three categories. All three possess the common characteristics of having emaciated, skeletal bodies, and not even hearing the words "food" and "drink" for months and years on end, not to mention that they never actually find any. Spirits with external obscurations experience the four misperceptions, such as experiencing heat as though it were cold. They also have the experience of seeing rivers, fruit, and so forth, only to have them vanish as soon as they chase after them, leaving behind inhospitable ravines and desert. Alternatively, they may find these things to be guarded by weapon-wielding beings, and then suffer by being beaten, struck, and stabbed.

Spirits with internal obscurations have mouths the size of needle tips and throats no bigger than the hair of a horse's tail. Even if one were to drink the water of an entire ocean, the heat of its mouth would evaporate it in an instant, before it even reaches the throat. Their stomachs are the size of a whole country and can't be supported by their limbs, which are only as big as a blade of grass. Even if one were to get a bit of water, it would turn into burning sand by the time it entered its mouth. Throughout the night, their hearts and lungs burst into flames, smoke bellowing from their noses. These spirits are referred to as "those with obscurations related to food and drink."

The third class of spirits are those with specific obscurations. These spirits' bodies are filled with parasites that devour them from within. Whenever they happen to meet one another, they are overcome with rage and end up attacking and beating each other. Goiters erupt from their throats, and when they turn into pus, they are forced to eat it as food. Experiencing these sufferings and more, their plight is extremely wretched.

Celestial Spirits The spirits that move in space are ghosts, demons, harmbringers, flesh-eaters, powerful ghosts, the king spirit, and others. Celestial spirits are a class of malevolent beings called harm-bringers. This class includes spirits that cause insanity, amnesia, and so forth, and also the powerful ghosts, king spirits, and others. Although these beings may have some magical powers or wealth, what they possess is unstable due to the many dangers they face. In addition, they experience the seasons in a distorted manner and are continually tormented by all the sensations explained above. Malicious in thought and deed, they try to transfer their suffering to others. Just as in the Ephemeral Hells, in their suffering, these beings may take different forms, at times manifesting as dogs, birds, and so on. All members of this class experience the four misapprehensions as well; they are quite a miserable lot.

The fact that their thoughts and actions continually revolve around harming others also means that they are conditioning themselves to experience their own future suffering. In these and other ways, their lives are filled with evil. Hence, such forms of existence are said to be "on their way to the land of the Lord of Death." Relate this to your own situation and think, "I must really put some effort into the methods that will keep me from being born in these places!"

THE SUFFERING OF THE ANIMAL REALM

Animals that Live Scattered in Different Places This group includes birds, wild herbivores, and other nondomesticated animals. These beings prey on one another and are killed by hunters, butchers, and others, who use a variety of means to separate them from their life force. Horses, cows, water buffalo, goats, sheep, and other domesticated animals are kept in fenced enclosures and tortured by their karma. Their noses are pierced, they are castrated, killed, and their blood is extracted. Moreover, those indigenous to primitive border regions suffer just as if they were in hell. There they are sacrificed and endure other cruelties, and although they see all this directly, they just sit passively and wait until their own time comes.

Oceanic Animals It is said that this form of life is experienced as a result of having abandoned virtue that is conducive to liberation. These animals live in the pitch-black ocean and the four seas that lie between the continents, where they prey upon one another. It is so dark in these places that they cannot perceive anything. They are afflicted by all manner of suffering: heat and cold, hunger and thirst, and stupidity and ignorance. Once again, cultivate a feeling of sadness as you take the nature of these states of existence as your focal point and imagine yourself to be directly undergoing these experiences.

THE SUFFERING OF HUMANS

At the moment, you have managed to find a physical body in a fortunate existence. Although what you are experiencing may seem like happiness, it won't last forever. Sooner or later, whether tomorrow, the next day, or some other time, a fresh experience of suffering will come along and plague your body and mind, bringing great torment in its wake. This is the suffering of change, which we can all clearly perceive.

When another experience of suffering is suddenly added to this initial experience, you have suffering upon suffering. For example, if you've taken rebirth as a cannibalistic demon as a result of the suffering of change, to then be punished by a king constitutes the suffering of suffering.

Right now you may have many experiences that are superficially pleasurable, but such worldly grandeur is only achieved by committing nonvirtuous acts like killing. For example, when you go out to a pleasant park to enjoy yourself, you may experience some pleasure as you play dice, gamble, and do other such things, all the while eating meat and getting drunk. Yet even in this simple situation, the cause of all these experiences is nothing but negativity, and as a result you are conditioning yourself for nothing but suffering in the future. In just the same way, when you harm someone else, what you are effectively doing is conditioning yourself to be harmed. This is the law of nature. It pervades all forms of worldly enjoyment, even though initially it may not be very obvious that these activities involve suffering. Hence, this is termed "the pervasive suffering of conditioning."

As human beings, we are born from the womb. Our conception takes place when, as a disembodied spirit, we unite with our father's sperm and mother's ovum. From that point onward, the body goes through various phases of development, first taking an oval shape and then developing further until it becomes a fully formed body.

As our senses begin to awaken to their objects, we experience nausea and foul smells while inside our mother's womb; we feel constricted and suffocated as well. When our mothers eat certain foods, wear certain clothing, or do anything wrong, it feels as though we are being burned alive, plunged into freezing water, squished beneath a mountain, or hurled off a cliff. When we fall onto the mattress or are touched, it feels like someone is cutting into an open wound. When we are bathed, it feels so hot that it is as though we are being flayed alive. The birth process entails an incalculable number of sufferings.

Once born and in the full bloom of youth, things may seem to be improving. Nevertheless, our lives are headed toward their own dissolution. Before long we will have to suffer through the aging process, at which point our bodies' strength will diminish, and we will no longer have enough energy to carry on. In addition, we won't be able to digest our food, our eyesight will dim, and we will go deaf. Our speech will become unintelligible and our thought patterns confused. Our teeth will fall out and, although we will still be attracted to sense pleasures, we will no longer have the strength to enjoy them. Both heat and cold will become intolerable, and others will belittle and annoy our overly sensitive minds. All in all, just about everything will manifest as suffering. We can see all this for ourselves, so think it over.

By their very nature, our bodies are conglomerations of the four elements. When these four are in a state of imbalance, we are continually plagued by various illnesses, such as those of wind, bile, phlegm, and those that are a combination of these three. This, in turn, brings the five perpetuating aggregates nothing but suffering. Even things that we love and enjoy can backfire and become a cause of illness. Ponder this carefully, and let it evoke a feeling of fear. Think to yourself, "Such illnesses will be the death of me . . . and they could be here any moment!"

After this the moment of death will arrive. You will collapse onto your bed, not knowing if you'll ever rise again. You will have no appetite for the food and drink that you see. Instead, you will be joyless, afflicted by the pangs of death. With your vanity and pride slipping away, hallucinatory premonitions will manifest. Once the moment of death has arrived, your friends and family will surround you, but they won't be able to delay your departure. You must face the pains of death alone. Though you may have incalculable riches, you'll be powerless to take them with you. Your mind won't let them go, but go they must. Your body will begin to twitch, and, with your eyes barely open, the elements will dissolve and you will grow delusional.

Finally, leaving a tear-stained, lifeless corpse, you'll move on to a new existence and the visions of the intermediate state will arise. When all this comes to pass, you will have no one to call on for protection and nowhere to go for refuge. All that you see will terrify you, and everything you feel will be an experience of suffering. Once this befalls you, this body to which you cling so dearly will be tied up, trampled on, and cast into a horrid charnel ground. Once wealthy, the time to wander as a disembodied spirit will be upon you. You'll have no choice but to go wherever your karma leads.

As you ponder all this, you may think to yourself, "I haven't given any thought to my own mortality up until now. Instead, I've just been trying to get the better of my enemies and protect those I love. I've been making plans to get a big house and strike it rich, concerning myself with my close relations and those that I hold dear. All the while, I've passed my time in attachment, aggression, and ignorance. What a huge mistake!"

There are other forms of suffering that you may experience in addition to these four. You may suffer and experience mental unease when you encounter your enemies and other objective circumstances that you dislike, despite your desire to avoid them. Likewise, being separated from the people and things you love and then reminiscing about their qualities pains your mind. Here in this world, we are slaves to thoughts of hope and fear, and consequently we suffer when things don't turn out as we planned.

It is the five defiled aggregates that perpetuate the truth of suffering. Once these five are present, form serves as the support, while sensation perceives its nature. Perception forms the continuity, and seeds are then sown by karmic formations. Finally, consciousness views all this as "mine." Thus, because they are the place where suffering occurs, its support, and because they are in possession of its source and are interrelated, they are referred to as "the aggregates of samsaric suffering."

Human beings are especially susceptible to these eight forms of suffering, which bring them perpetual torment. Think about the way this occurs and, with this recognition, cultivate a sense of sadness regarding the nature of birth.

THE SUFFERING OF DEMIGODS

When the force of your previously accumulated nonvirtue results in your taking on the form of a demigod, you will be immediately overcome by coarse feelings of envy. These feelings cause disputes over territory, internal quarrels, and fights over the necessities of life. Demigods are plagued continually by such things and this upsets them physically and mentally.

In addition, their envy is directed toward the glory and prosperity of the gods, whom they find intolerable. They perpetually wage war on the gods, and this only adds to their affliction and suffering. Due to differences in their previously accumulated merit, the gods are roughly seven times taller than humans. Unless they are hit in a major organ with a weapon, they will not die. The demigods, in contrast, are shorter. If they take a hit in a vital organ, they immediately experience the agony of death.

Although it may be possible for intelligent individuals to appear in this realm, karmic obscurations prevent them from perceiving the truths of the listeners and solitary buddhas, and such unfortunate beings constantly endure the sufferings of battle and strife. Thinking this over, diligently cultivate the methods that will allow you to rid yourself of these causes and results.

THE SUFFERING OF THE GODS

The heavens of the desire realm stretch from the Heaven of the Four Great Kings up to the Heaven of Mastery over Others' Creations. Although there is a short-lived experience of superficial happiness in these realms, previously accumulated virtuous karma is exhausted here. This temporary happiness causes the gods to be free of any sense of disenchantment or renunciation. Consequently, they idly neglect to do anything that will benefit them in the future.

When the virtuous karma they gathered in the past runs out, they experience death and transmigration from their respective realm and class. There are five omens [that indicate the coming of this impending disaster]: The luster of their bodies fades; their thrones become uncomfortable; their flower garlands rot; their clothes begin to smell; and sweat appears on their bodies. Upon seeing these five omens, dying gods panic and fall unconscious. They endure this unbearable suffering for seven of the gods' days, which is a long time.

As for the form and formless realms, these gods are sustained for a short while by the bliss of their meditative concentrations. Nevertheless, since these are worldly absorptions precipitated by [virtue] that accords with merit, they are states that lack the karmic background needed to see the truth. When their karma runs out, they are conditioned to fall into a lower state of existence.

Because the aggregates will be reborn, the suffering of change will be experienced. Therefore, no matter where you are born within the three realms and six classes, you will never transcend suffering. Contemplate this carefully and think to yourself, "What a fool I would be not to exert myself in the methods to free myself from samsara!" With this thought, make a firm pledge to do so, and then dedicate the virtue.

THE LAW OF KARMA

Samsara arises from karma and is produced as a result of karma. There is no other force that makes you go to the higher and lower realms. It does not happen just by chance either. Therefore, you should examine the causes and effects of both virtue and nonvirtue, in all their various permutations, and then work tirelessly to abandon nonvirtue and practice virtue.

The ten nonvirtues are the physical, verbal, and mental actions that need to be abandoned. First are the three physical nonvirtues. The first physical nonvirtue is the taking of life. The fully ripened result of taking life depends upon your motivation. Killing motivated by anger, desire, and ignorance leads to rebirths in hell, the spirit realm, and the animal realm, respectively. The same applies to the remaining nine nonvirtues as well. As the experiential result that resembles its cause, even if you manage to attain an existence in one of the higher realms, you will have a short, illness-ridden life. The dominant result ripens as the environment in which you live, causing rebirth in unpleasant, dangerous places with ravines, gorges, cliffs, and other such features.

With stealing, the result that resembles its cause is a state of poverty. Even if you manage to find some wealth, it will end up being shared with others. As the dominant result, your crops will be destroyed by frost and hail, trees will not bear fruit, and you will be born in lands plagued by famine. These days, to take something furtively is regarded as stealing, and, as far as this form of theft goes, taking the property of the Three Jewels is the most serious. Stealing also includes taking something by overpowering another or to do so by deception, such as purposely miscalculating to trick your customers in business. Although there are many who think nothing of such activities, this is exactly what is meant by the term. Thus, you should be aware that these are specific instances of the act of stealing.

With sexual misconduct, the most serious act is to be the condition for another individual to break their vows. This also includes masturbation, adultery, and prostitution. Similarly, even if your partner is not committed to another, it is not permissible to engage in sexual conduct during the day; while holding temporary vows; while sick, pregnant, or grieving; during menstruation or while recovering from childbirth; or in front of representations of the Three Jewels. Nor is it permissible to engage in sexual activity with a parent or family member, with a child, or to have oral/anal intercourse. In these and other ways, sexual misconduct can take place with reference to the particular place, time, or circumstances in which the act is committed. For such acts, the experiential result that resembles its cause is to have an unattractive, promiscuous spouse and to encounter rivals. The dominant result is that you will end up in unpleasant, foul-smelling places filled with excrement, cesspools, and the like.

Next are the four verbal nonvirtues, the first of which is lying. Lying includes all false statements that are motivated by the desire to deceive someone else. This especially applies to assertions that one has achieved certain levels of spiritual realization when one has not, that one has clairvoyance when one does not, and to other such claims. In particular, this includes the act of slandering a buddha. As the result that resembles its cause, if you tell lies you yourself will be frequently slandered and deceived by others. As the dominant result, your finances will be unstable and your mind will be perpetually in a state of panic, encountering frightening places and conditions.

Divisive speech refers to all acts of consciously sowing discord among others. Creating a schism in the Sangha is particularly serious. The result that resembles its cause for this type of activity is that your family, friends, and acquaintances will not get along, and you will encounter those who oppose you. As the dominant result, you will be forced to live in environments that are difficult to traverse, places with ravines, cliffs, and the like.

Harsh speech is anything that pricks another's heart like a thorn. Openly stating the faults of another, such as pointing out that a particular individual is unattractive, typifies this type of nonvirtue. In particular, this includes saying something unpleasant to a noble being. The result that resembles its cause for harsh speech is that you will always hear unpleasant things and what you say will create discord. As the dominant result, you will end up in unpleasant places that have thorns, gravel, and other such features.

Pointless speech includes uttering Brahmanic mantras and other topics that are mistakenly thought to be Dharma; tales of prostitutes, lewd songs, and other discussions that stir up lustful feelings and cause one to be distracted from the Dharma; and words of anger that are uttered when discussing such topics as war and banditry. The result that resembles its cause for this category is that your manner of speaking will be ignoble and lacking confidence. The dominant result is that your labors will not bear fruit, and the seasons will be unpredictable and untimely.

Since these seven types of physical and verbal karma are observable, obstructive physical forms, their potential is fully expressed when the four aspects of a karmic act are complete, these four being the basis, intention, execution, and completion.[40]

Third are the three mental nonvirtues: covetousness, malice, and wrong view. Covetousness is a frame of mind in which one becomes attached to, then obsessed with, another's belongings, and then asserts ownership over them with a malicious mind-set. In terms of the result that resembles its cause, your wishes will go unfulfilled, and you will encounter what you do not want. As the dominant result, you will have problems with your crops and will experience many forms of suffering due to bad times and environments.

Malice is a hate-filled, angry mind-set in which one wishes terrible suffering upon another. As the result that resembles its cause, you will live in a state of constant paranoia and experience many torments. Its dominant result is an experience of fear concerning evil dictators, bandits and thieves, snakes, wild animals, and so on.

A wrong view is the thought that causality is not true, and the belief that the superior position to take is either a nihilistic or eternalistic view. As the result that resembles its cause, you will continue to hold such beliefs and have a mind disturbed by craft and deceit. As the dominant result, you will have few belongings and be born with neither protector nor comrades.

Since these three mental states are grouped into the category of obstructive, yet unobservable forms, only two of the four previously mentioned factors need be present to create a full karmic act.

All of these ten nonvirtuous acts will also give rise to behavioral results that resemble their respective causes, which is to say that you will take on a form similar to the one in which the initial karmic act was committed, and then continue to engage in the same negative behavior you committed before. This, in turn, will cause the karma to proliferate endlessly, and consequently you will experience a tremendous amount of suffering. Thus, you should understand both the ten nonvirtues and the various forms of suffering they produce. With this understanding, you should then go on to cultivate a stable mind-set committed to avoiding these ten nonvirtuous acts, and an appreciation for the results of the ten virtues.

The way to put these into practice is as follows: Give up taking life and you will have a long life and good health. Give up stealing and you will be wealthy. Give up sexual misconduct and you will have a beautiful spouse and few rivals. Give up lying and you will be universally praised and adored. Give up divisive speech and you will have respectful companions. Give up harsh speech and you will hear pleasant things. Give up pointless speech and your speech will be given due respect. Give up covetousness and your wishes will be fulfilled. Give up malice and you will be free from harm. Give up wrong views and the sublime view will take birth in your mind. Give rise to a courageous attitude and think to yourself: "I shall strive to accomplish the positive causes of goodness and virtue!"

THE BENEFITS OF LIBERATION

Whether one attains the level of a listener, solitary buddha, or complete buddha, all are endowed with the coolness of peace and free from the precipitous defile of samsaric suffering. How wonderful! Moreover, from among these three divisions, at present you have met with the teachings of the Great Vehicle, the Mahayana. Thus, think to yourself: "The ten virtues, the four immeasurables, the six perfections, the four absorptions, the four formless absorptions, tranquility, insight, and so on—all these are said to be none other than perfect enlightenment. I must achieve them!" Having prepared yourself by cultivating bodhichitta in this way, carry out the main practice by remaining free of any reference point and conclude by sealing what you have done with dedication and aspirations. Thus, you should embrace your practice with the three sacred principles.

SERVING A SPIRITUAL TEACHER

In no sutra, tantra, or shastra will you ever hear of someone who attained buddhahood without serving a spiritual teacher. We can also see for ourselves that there isn't a single person who attained the excellent qualities of the paths and levels by sheer willpower and self-confidence alone. As sentient beings, we are exceedingly clever when it comes to leading ourselves astray. On the path to liberation and omniscience, we are like a blind man left alone and confused on a deserted plain. Just as there is no example of someone who ventured to a treasure-filled isle without the guidance of a captain, it should be obvious that spiritual teachers and virtuous companions are the ones who will guide us on the path to liberation and omniscience. Thus, you should serve them with the utmost respect. Do their bidding without displeasing them for even a moment.

The excellent qualities that arise from serving a teacher in this way are beyond reckoning, so generate a sense of enthusiasm. Without falling under the sway of bad influences or the ignorant, work tirelessly to serve your teachers. Pray fervently that you may meet superior teachers and be accepted by their great compassion in future lifetimes as well.

By Dzogchenpa Rangjung Dorje [Jigmé Lingpa].

THE APPLICATION OF MINDFULNESS

⊰∥⊱

*Instructions on the Unique Great Perfection Preliminaries
of the Heart Essence of the Vast Expanse*

JIGMÉ LINGPA

Homage to the self-occurring primordial sphere!

Once your mind has been made open and receptive through the seven-point mind training of the common preliminaries, the unique and specific preliminaries will enable you to establish yourself at the exalted level of the Luminous Heart Essence of the Natural Great Perfection, the supreme king of vehicles.[41]

The multitude of approaches to teaching the stages of these practices that have emerged over time has made the Heart Essence teachings seem like a mere painting of a butter lamp. Saddened by this state of affairs, I hereby pledge to establish a foundation for the teachings by setting forth the enlightened intent of the lord of victorious ones, Longchen Rabjam, the master of the teachings of this exalted vehicle.

TAKING REFUGE

The topic of taking refuge addresses 1) a delineation of the different motivations for taking refuge, 2) how to take refuge, and 3) a contemplation of its benefits and advantages.

Differences in Motivation

Those who fear the sufferings of the three lower realms and take refuge in the Three Jewels to pursue the pleasures of higher, pleasurable states of existence are known as *lesser individuals*. They do not pursue any goal aside from a mere temporary pleasure. Those who fear the sufferings of samsara and take refuge in the Three Jewels to pursue a state of peace and bliss for themselves alone are known as *middling individuals*. Their goal is a mere individual liberation from samsara. Those who see the suffering of other sentient beings throughout limitless samsara and take refuge to free them from their plight are known as *superior individuals*. They focus on the desire to attain buddhahood for the sake of all sentient beings. Of these three, reject the motivations of the lesser and middling individuals and form the correct motivation by thinking to yourself, "For the sake of all sentient beings, I will now train following the example of the superior individual!"

How to Take Refuge

The approach of the common vehicle is to take refuge by regarding the Buddha as one's teacher, the Dharma as one's protection, and the Sangha as one's companions while practicing the path. Generally speaking, the unique approach of the Secret Mantra Vehicle is to take refuge by offering one's body, speech, and mind to the guru, relying upon the yidam deity, and taking the dakinis as one's companions. In the tradition of the Vajra Essence, with its extraordinary and exalted methods, one takes refuge in the swift path in which one utilizes the channels (*nadi*) as the nirmanakaya, refines the energies (*prana*) into the sambhogakaya, and purifies the essences (*bindu*) into the dharmakaya. Finally, the ultimate and undeceiving refuge is the true vajra nature, the wisdom that dwells in the enlightened minds of these objects of refuge. This wisdom is empty in essence, clear in nature, and all pervasive in its compassion. Here one aims to bring the great indivisibility of these three qualities into one's own being and resolve them once and for all.

To acquaint yourself with the principles outlined here, visualize as follows for the main practice of taking refuge: Imagine your surroundings to be a beautiful and enchanting pure land made of various jewels. In the center of this land is a wish-fulfilling tree, its five branches filling the entire sky. Its perfect leaves, flowers, and fruit are ornamented with webs of jewels, tiny bells, and the like, and in its center is a jeweled throne supported by snow lions and stacked with a multicolored lotus, sun, and moon. Upon it sits your root guru, the essence of all buddhas, in the form of the Vajradhara of Oddiyana and his spiritual partner. Seated in tiers above him are the gurus of the Great Perfection lineage, with the yidam deities, warriors, and dakinis surrounding them. On the front branch of the tree are Buddha Shakyamuni and the buddhas of the ten directions and three times. On the right branch are the Eight Close Sons, the Sangha of bodhisattvas. On the left branch are the assembly of realized beings, the supreme pair, and the rest of the Sangha of listeners. On the branch behind the throne is the Jewel of the Dharma, represented by a stack of texts humming with the natural sounds of the vowels and consonants of the Sanskrit alphabet. Every gap between all these beings is filled with a virtual ocean of oath-bound Dharma protectors, both those arisen from wisdom and those produced by karma. All these beings possess qualities of knowledge, love, and power that defy the imagination. Looking upon you with love, they now dwell before you as your great guides.

You and all sentient beings, including your parents and those who have caused you harm, are gathered together on the ground before the jewel tree with joined palms, thinking, "From now until we attain the very essence of enlightenment, we rely completely on you! We offer ourselves to you! We have no one in whom we can place our hopes, no one to whom we can turn for refuge, aside from you!" As this thought occupies your mind, stirring up intense feeling, recite the following lines:

> In the true Three Jewels, the sugata, and Three Roots; 8
> In nadi, prana, and bindu, the nature of bodhichitta; 8
> In the essence, nature, and compassion mandala, 8
> I take refuge until the heart of enlightenment is attained! 8

Once you have recited this prayer as many times as possible, imagine that you and all sentient beings dissolve into the Three Jewels and the other objects of refuge, all of which then dissolve into the central figure of the guru, who embodies all three sources of refuge. Finally, the guru as well dissolves into the dharmakaya, the primordial state free from elaborations. To conclude, simply rest evenly in the true nature as long as you are able; this is the ultimate act of taking refuge.

The Benefits of Taking Refuge

Taking refuge is the foundational support for all of the Buddha's teachings. The mere act of taking refuge plants the seed of liberation, distances one from the accumulation of nonvirtue, and causes virtue to develop. It is both the basis and support for all vows and the source of every excellent quality. Even on a temporary level, taking refuge will prompt beneficial divine forces to offer their protection, bringing success to whatever one aims to achieve. It ensures that one will never be apart from the presence of the Three Jewels and that one will recollect one's past lives. Hence, as it leads to happiness here and hereafter, and ultimately to the attainment of buddhahood, the virtues of taking refuge are simply too numerous to count.

As a related topic, I will also summarize the defining characteristics of the precepts associated with taking refuge, as these ensure that the refuge vows remain present in one's mind stream. Once you have taken refuge in the Buddha, you should no longer look to worldly gods, fickle and malicious tyrants, and other such individuals for protection and refuge, as they themselves are still caught up in samsara. In addition, always maintain an attitude of reverence for any representation of enlightened form, even a broken piece of a statue. Once you've taken refuge in the Dharma, avoid thinking of harming another sentient being, even in a dream. You should also cultivate respect for any representation of the Dharma, even for a tiny part of sacred script. Having taken refuge in the Sangha, you should no longer associate with those who adhere to non-Buddhist philosophies and others whose beliefs and conduct are misguided. You should also show reverence for any representation of the Sangha; avoid stepping on even a piece of yellow fabric.

To sum up, in this Vehicle of the Supreme Secret, the guru is the main object of refuge: The guru's enlightened mind is the Buddha, the guru's enlightened speech is the Dharma, and the guru's enlightened form is the Sangha. Therefore, if you displease the guru, you will have abandoned all objects of refuge. Apply yourself diligently to the vital points of taking refuge, as this is the foundation and support of all the Buddha's teachings.

CULTIVATING BODHICHITTA

Cultivating bodhichitta lies at the root of the Great Vehicle. In this section there are three subtopics: 1) training the mind with the four immeasurables,

2) cultivating bodhichitta, and 3) maintaining the precepts of aspiration and application bodhichitta.

The Four Immeasurables

For equanimity, the first of the four immeasurables, meditate as follows: In our present circumstances, we are extremely attached to our parents, relatives, friends, and other loved ones, while we feel intense aversion toward our enemies and those associated with them. The problem here is that we have not examined the situation clearly. In previous lives, our enemies have undoubtedly been our friends, and vice versa. Though we may now think of some people as our enemies, there is no definitive proof that they will be able to harm us. It is even possible that if we know how to get along with them, they may end up helping us as a friend would. Moreover, we can also see with our very own eyes that sometimes loved ones ally themselves with those who oppose us, rob us of our wealth, create disputes, and so on, like a child who deceives his parents. Even if someone may appear to be a close friend, when that person doesn't get his way, he may end up creating suffering for us as well.

This will not only destroy whatever temporary happiness you may have, it will ultimately create a great flood of obstacles to your virtuous endeavors and cast you into the lower realms. What could be a worse enemy than that? In the future, your enemies could become friends and your friends, enemies . . . there's no way to tell. To think otherwise is simply insane! Therefore, practice remaining in a state of equanimity, free from attachment and aversion to those near and far. Start with one being, then two, and then gradually expand your equanimity toward all beings in the entire universe.

Next, meditate on love. Take all sentient beings as your focal point. Cultivate an intense desire for them all to be happy and prosperous. Your desire should be as intense as the love that parents feel for their small children and their willingness to tolerate ingratitude. With this wish, meditate on compassion and advance your practice by thinking to yourself, "By any means necessary, I will help all sentient beings!"

To meditate on compassion, take as your mind's object someone who is afflicted with intense suffering, such as a criminal who has been thrown into a dungeon and is soon to be executed, or an animal that is about to meet its death at the hands of a butcher. Make this being the object of your love as though you are a mother and this being is your own child. Meditate with such unbearable compassion that tears well up in your eyes, as you think, "I would do anything! If only this being could be freed from this suffering soon. Now. This very instant!" Then meditate on the lower realms and all those who are creating the causes to be born there. Finally, rest in a state free of any reference point.

Next, meditate on joy. As the object of your meditation, focus on a being in the higher realms, someone who is happy and content, with a long life, a large retinue, and great wealth. Without feeling competitive or envious, think to yourself: "May this person continue to dwell in the higher realms and acquire prosperity even greater than this! May he or she be secure, wise, and acquire other magnificent things! How wonderful it would be if other sentient beings were to live in such a state!" In particular, completely uproot any negative attitudes you may have toward those who have wronged you or those whom you envy; do away with your inability to tolerate the wealth and prosperity of others. Cultivate extraordinary joy for all who are happy. To conclude, rest in a state free of any reference point.

The Cultivation of Bodhichitta

One's mind-set determines the type of bodhichitta that should be cultivated. The wish to establish other beings in the state of liberation having first attained such a state for oneself is the *guidelike cultivation of bodhichitta*. The wish for oneself and other beings to be liberated simultaneously is the *ferryman-like cultivation of bodhichitta*. Not wishing to attain liberation for oneself until all other sentient beings have done so first is the *shepherdlike cultivation of bodhichitta*.

The cultivation of bodhichitta can also be described in terms of the levels of the spiritual path. On the paths of accumulation and connection, bodhichitta is cultivated through devoted conduct. From the first through seventh levels, one cultivates the bodhichitta of superior, completely pure intention. On the three pure levels, fully matured bodhichitta is cultivated. Finally, at the level of buddhahood, one cultivates the bodhichitta in which all obscurations have been abandoned.

These conventional designations notwithstanding, relative bodhichitta is attained through ritual practice, while ultimate bodhichitta arises through the power of meditation on its characteristics. The beginner, however, must rely on the first of these two; you may consult other sources for the ritual conferment of the cultivation of bodhichitta.

To begin, visualize the assembly of buddhas and bodhisattvas in the sky before you as witnesses. Then cultivate the bodhichitta of vast intelligence as follows: There is not a single sentient being who has not been your mother or father at some time in the past. When they were your parents, they nurtured you with the greatest care, just as your present parents have. Giving you the best food and dressing you in the finest clothing, you can be sure that they reared you with great love in both thought and deed. As this is the case, think: "How could I be liberated when my parents are still here in samsara? I must cultivate supreme bodhichitta and act on a vast scale for the benefit of all sentient beings! So long as there is even a single being left in samsara I will work with great diligence!" With this thought in mind, recite the following stanza as many times as possible:

> Oh!
> Dazed by myriad appearances, like the reflection of the moon, 𐤀
> Beings wander endlessly through the cycles of samsara. 𐤀
> So that they may rest in the space of luminous self-awareness, 𐤀
> I arouse bodhichitta within the four immeasurables. 𐤀

To conclude, imagine that the field of merit dissolves into you and the absolute bodhichitta present in the minds of the buddhas and bodhisattvas arises vividly in your own mind. Then, rest in the nature of emptiness.

The Bodhichitta Precepts

Training in bodhichitta relates to both aspiration bodhichitta and application bodhichitta. Training in aspiration bodhichitta is likened to wanting to go somewhere. This involves three meditations: equalizing self and other, exchanging self and other, and cherishing others more than oneself. Until you have mastered these practices, meditate by thinking repeatedly: "Though I and all sentient beings want to be happy and do not want to suffer, most sentient beings do not know what causes suffering. Unable to tell right from wrong and how to act accordingly, they suffer continually. How sad! Now that I have immersed myself in the Dharma, I have some understanding of the benefits and dangers involved. Hence, I should tolerate ingratitude and prejudice and see myself and others as equals!"

To cultivate bodhichitta by exchanging self and other, focus either on a being plagued by suffering that you see in front of you, or imagine such a being before you. As you breathe out, send them your happiness, goodness, body, belongings, and even your basic virtues, just as though you are dressing them in your finest clothes. Then, as you breathe in, envision yourself taking upon yourself whatever suffering they may have. Practice sending and taking in this manner, such that the being you are focusing on becomes happy and free of suffering. Then, gradually extend your meditation until you are doing this for all sentient beings.

Once you are adept at this practice, meditate on cherishing others more than yourself. To do so, from the depths of your heart, think: "I can stay in samsara or be born in hell; whatever sickness, pain, and hardship I encounter, I will bear it! May the suffering of other sentient beings ripen in me! May my own happiness and the fruits of my virtue be completely transferred to them!" Then, rest in a state free of any reference point.

The second set of precepts concerns application bodhichitta, which is likened to actually going to the place you initially aspired to go to. The perfection of generosity is to be unattached to wealth and possessions and to give, give completely, and give utterly to the virtuous for the benefit of all sentient beings.[42] The perfection of discipline is to restrain whatever negative activities you happen to be engaged in and instead to work for the benefit of others. Specific instances of the latter include the completely pure sphere of activity outlined in the *Buddha Avatamsaka Sutra* and the meditation on the eight thoughts of great beings.[43] To undergo hardships for the sake of the Dharma and to tolerate the ingratitude of others is the perfection of patience. To overpower laziness, which wastes the freedoms and advantages, and apply oneself to the ten Dharma activities[44] and the ten perfections is perfection of diligence.

Concerning the perfection of concentration, that which comes together is also subject to separation, and desire is the source of all faults. Greed develops by not being satisfied with what one has. Since these qualities are common in thieves and others who create discord, they are in conflict with the doctrine of complete liberation. For this reason, such factors are reviled by realized beings. Immature companions are base by their very nature; they are difficult to please and will not return your favors. Merely associating with those who are jealous and other such people will cause your virtue to wane. Distractions will just make you busy and have no real importance; whatever energy you put into them will be pointless. Moreover, defeating enemies and caring for loved ones is an endless process, so you should abandon them both once and for all!

Having left all this behind, settle in a solitary forest retreat. These are places where the buddhas and bodhisattvas of times past have found peace—places free from busyness and distractions and without any commerce or agricultural activity. If you part ways with immature companions and make birds and animals your only friends, you will find contentment. Find a place that has the requisite water and plants—the food needed for an ascetic lifestyle. In such places, awareness naturally becomes clear and concentration develops on its own; such places are free from enemies and loved ones alike, the companions of aversion and attachment. In a place with such excellent qualities, seat yourself in the seven-point posture of Vairochana[45] and rest your mind in a state completely free from thought activity and fixation—this is the perfection of concentration.

External appearances of the five objects do not exist, yet at the same time they do appear from the perspective of delusion, like the experiences in dreams. Like an illusion, they manifest incidentally when the right arrangement of causes and conditions comes together. Like an optical illusion, they appear to exist, while in fact they do not. Like a mirage, they appear yet are not truly there. Like an echo, they can manifest outside, inside, or anywhere else. Like a city of spirits, there is neither support nor supported. Like the appearance in a reflection, what appears has no nature of its own. Like a magically emanated city, nonexistent appearances can manifest as anything whatsoever. By observing these insubstantial reflections of emptiness, as exemplified by these eight examples of illusoriness, you will come to understand the deceptive nature of external objective appearances. In a similar manner, by analyzing the basic nature of the mind—the subjective mind that creates all these appearances—objective appearances will not cease, but the conceptualization and fixation related to them will be put to rest. You may then rest in the state of realization—reality itself—empty and clear like space. This is the perfection of wisdom.

The understanding of this explanation encompasses all the profound points of the Perfection Vehicle. Since these are the fundamental teachings of the Great Vehicle, thoroughly understanding them will protect one from the sufferings of samsara; elevate one from the Vehicles of the Listeners and Solitary Buddhas; ensure that the roots of virtue do not exhaust themselves, but develop; bring the attainment of a vast amount of merit; make one a successor to the buddhas; ensure that one benefits others on a vast scale; and so on. There are innumerable reasons to do these practices, so you should do so with the complete preparation, main practice, and conclusion.[46]

THE MEDITATION AND RECITATION
OF VAJRASATTVA

Negativity and obscurations interfere with the arising of the extraordinary experiences and realizations of this profound path. The supreme way to purify these factors is to practice the yoga of Vajrasattva. In this practice, the vital points of the four powers are as follows: The *power of support* is to take Vajrasattva as your refuge and maintain both aspiration and application bodhichitta. The *power of remorse* for one's misdeeds is to generate an intense feeling of regret for all the negativity and nonvirtuous karma that you have committed. The *power of refraining from negative behavior* is to think: "From now on, I will not commit such deeds even at the cost of my life!" The *power of applying the antidote* is to remedy all that you have done in the past by reciting the one-hundred-syllable mantra and meditating on Vajrasattva.

While recollecting the purity of these four powers, recite the one-hundred-syllable mantra and meditate on Vajrasattva as a unity:

> AH ༔
> On the crown of my head, in my ordinary form, ༔
> Upon a white lotus and moon disc seat, ༔
> Appears guru Vajrasattva from the syllable HUM. ༔
> Brilliant and white, with sambhogakaya ornaments, ༔
> He embraces Vajratöpa, holding vajra and bell. ༔
>
> Please grant me refuge and purify my negativity. ༔
> With intense remorse, I confess all I've done! ༔
> I will restrain myself from now on, even at the cost of my life! ༔
>
> Resting on the full moon in his heart center ༔
> Is the syllable HUM, surrounded by the mantra. ༔
> Reciting the mantra invokes his wisdom mind, ༔
> Causing clouds of bodhichitta nectar to flow ༔
> From the union of the consorts' blissful play, ༔
> Raining down like a shower of camphor. ༔
>
> May this purify the karma and afflictions that create suffering, ༔
> Both my own and those of all beings throughout the three realms. ༔
> May it refine away all illness, along with harmful forces, ༔
> Our negativity, obscurations, misdeeds, and broken vows! ༔

With one-pointed concentration and devotion, recite the hundred-syllable mantra without distraction. As you do, visualize the wisdom nectar of great bliss emerging from the HUM syllable and mantra garland in the heart center of Vajrasattva. As though the moon itself were melting, the nectar travels through Vajrasattva's body and drips down from the point where the two deities' bodies unite, falling into the aperture of Brahma at the crown of your head. From the pores of your body and your two orifices, all sickness pours out in the form of blood and pus, all negative forces in the form of insects, and all negativity and obscurations in the form of smoke and black liquid. All this flows out, falling nine stories below you into the open mouth of Yamaraja, the karmic lord of death. Entering into his stomach, untimely death is averted. As you imagine this, recite the mantra as many times as you can. Then, conclude by visualizing that your four chakras are completely permeated by nectar, intoxicating the body and mind with undefiled bliss.

Vajrasattva is delighted by all this. Smiling, he says, "Noble child, all of your negativity, obscurations, misdeeds, and broken vows are purified!" Granting you his approval, he melts into light and dissolves into you. This causes you to become Vajrasattva, with a form apparent yet empty like the reflection in a mirror. Visualize the four seed syllables around the life force syllable in your heart. Light radiates out from the four seed syllables, transforming the world and its inhabitants—the entire three realms—into the enlightened nature of the support and supported of the five classes of Vajrasattva.[47] Then recite the mantra OM VAJRASATTVA HUM. This is a particularly special key instruction.

To conclude the session, with free-flowing, mindful awareness, seal the session without conceptualizing the three spheres; let go of all thoughts concerning the basis of purification and that which does the purifying. This is the ultimate purification of obscurations. Continue with this practice until you see signs that indicate your obscurations have been purified, reciting at least one hundred thousand mantras.

MANDALA

Gathering the Accumulations and Conducive Conditions

The mandala offering is used to create conducive conditions and gather the accumulations. The result of the strength of merit and wisdom is the twofold purity of buddhahood. Therefore, in the context of the path, gathering these two accumulations is also the perfection of skillful means.

To begin, acquire a mandala according to your means. The best is a mandala made with precious jewels. Next best is a mandala made from bronze or another pure substance. At the very least, you can use a piece of stone, wood, and so forth, as long as it has a smooth, even surface. Clean the base of the mandala well and anoint it with saffron water and the five substances that come from cows. As a support for the visualization, arrange piles on the mandala plate. Ideally, jewels should be used, though medicinal fruits or, at the very least, grains and other such substances will suffice.

Next, visualize the victors and their offspring, the field of merit, in the space before you as the essence of the three kayas. As you do so, think that in an ordinary sense, you are offering the nirmanakaya mandala. This is the billionfold pure realm, the third-order thousandfold universe with the four continents, Mount Meru, and the heavens.[48] In particular, you are offering your own wonderful body, wealth, entourage, and subjects. In short, completely offer all that you cherish and cling to without being bound by greed and avarice. This is also an antidote for the belief in the self.

In the space above this mandala is the extraordinary, sambhogakaya mandala—the self-appearing, Richly Arrayed Supreme Realm. This includes the wisdom jewel palace, various primordially and spontaneously present enlightened forms, and pure realms that are beautifully arrayed with Lashya and the other goddesses of sense pleasure. In the space above this mandala is the special dharmakaya mandala. On this birthless, original ground, arrange piles of the apparent quality of unceasing luminosity, the full expression of awareness.

Meditating in this manner makes it easier to bring to mind the individual focal points of the three kayas. In reality, however, self-appearing pure realms are unconfined and unrestricted; they cannot be measured in terms of breadth and height. These self-arisen and spontaneously present places have no fixed dimensions; within one minute particle there may be innumerable other pure realms. With this understanding, recite the following lines with intense devotion:

OM AH HUM ᢀ
The third-order thousandfold universe with its billion realms, ᢀ
Filled with the seven jewels and the wealth of gods and men, ᢀ

In offering all this, along with my very own body, ৪
May I attain the ability to turn the wheel of Dharma! ৪

The Richly Arrayed Supreme Realm of great bliss, ৪
With its five certainties and piles of the five families, ৪
Filled with immeasurable clouds of pleasurable offerings— ৪
With this offering, may I enjoy the sambhogakaya realm! ৪

The youthful vase body, the purity of all that appears and exists; ৪
Adorned with unceasing compassion, the play of reality itself— ৪
Completely purified of any fixation on the kayas and bindus— ৪
With this offering, may I enjoy the dharmakaya realm! ৪

With these words, offer this with the knowledge completely purified of the three spheres.

THE ACCUMULATIONS OF THE SIMPLE BEGGAR

Conquering the Four Demons in a Single Blow

In the sky before you, visualize your kind root guru sitting on a jewel-encrusted throne, piled with silk brocades and cushions. All around him are the lineage gurus, yidam deities, oceans of mandalas, dakinis, and Dharma protectors. Below you are the six classes of beings, including your enemies. Visualize all this in a single instant. Then, coordinate the visualization with this recitation:

P'ET ৪
Casting aside my treasured body, I conquer the demon of the divine child. ৪
My mind shoots out from the aperture of Brahma, projected up into space, ৪
Then transforms into Tröma, conquering the demon of the Lord of Death. ৪
With a hooked knife in my left hand conquering the demon of affliction, ৪

I slice off the skull of my corpse, conquering the demon of the
   aggregates. 8
With my right hand I take this skull cup, enacting enlightened
   activity, 8
Placing it on a trikaya hearth, fashioned from three human heads. 8
Inside it I place the corpse, now big enough to fill one billion
   worlds. 8
Melted into amrita by the AH stroke, it flows down from the syllable
   HAM, 8
Purified, multiplied, and transformed by the power of the three
   syllables. 8

Recite the syllables OM AH HUM innumerable times and then chant:

P'ET 8
Fulfilling my sacred bond with the offerings to the guests above 8
Completes the accumulations, bringing siddhis, common and
   supreme. 8
Pleasing the samsaric guests below, all karmic debts are now paid, 8
While malicious and obstructive forces in particular are appeased. 8
Illness, negative energies, and obstacles recede into space. 8
Adverse circumstances and ego clinging are reduced to dust. 8
In the end, all the offerings, recipients, and the one making
   offerings, 8
Dissolve into the Great Perfection, the basic nature of simplicity, AH. 8 8

With these words, rest in equanimity.

The benefits of this practice are innumerable. Among others, it allows one
to amass the accumulations on a vast scale, it fools death and cuts through
and pacifies illness, and it enables one to grasp the luminosity of the intermediate state.

GURU YOGA

Guru yoga is the ultimate method for actualizing the wisdom of realization in one's own mind stream. This practice has three parts: 1) visualizing
the objects of refuge, 2) offering the seven branches, and 3) supplicating
the guru.

Visualizing the Objects of Refuge

Cultivating a pure realm is a special activity for those with great strength of mind. Therefore, begin by visualizing the infinite range of appearances to be the Palace of Lotus Light, complete with all its structures and qualities. In the midst of this palace, visualize yourself in the form of Vajrayogini, while in essence you are Yeshé Tsogyal. Visualizing yourself in this manner makes you a suitable vessel for empowerment, arouses the wisdom of bliss-emptiness, and creates the auspicious link of being accepted as a student. Gaze devotedly at the heart center of your guru, who sits on the crown of your head on a lotus, sun, and moon. Inseparable from the Vajradhara of Oddiyana, your guru takes on the complete appearance of this master, who manifests as an eight-year-old youth. With his right hand, he holds a vajra at his heart. His left hand is in the mudra of meditative composure, upon it a skull cup and vase. He sits in the posture of a reveling king within a sphere of rainbow light and a latticelike net of five shining lights. With him are the eight masters of awareness from India, as well as the twenty-five disciples of Tibet, the Three Roots, and an ocean of oath-bound protectors, without a single one missing. Their presence is so overwhelming that your ordinary perceptions are automatically arrested. As you visualize this, link the words with their meaning and recite the lines that begin, "Ah! I appear in the midst of a buddha realm. . ."

The Seven-Branch Offering

As the path of the Vajra Vehicle is rich in methods, free from hardship, and intended for those with sharp faculties, here one gathers the accumulations of those with great strength of mind. By training continuously in this practice, one can amass with each passing moment the accumulations gathered over an entire great eon in the Vehicle of the Perfections, for a lifetime of this practice will bring liberation. For this reason, since we can be sure that the most sublime, supreme, secret, and unsurpassed field of merit is the vajra master alone, here the seven-branch offering is linked with guru yoga. All the innumerable approaches one can take to gather the accumulations are condensed in this seven-branch offering.

The individual visualizations for this practice are as follows: For the branch of prostrations, visualize hundreds, thousands, or even infinite manifestations of your own body. These manifestations then join all sentient beings of the three realms in prostration. Together, you join your hands and bring them to your crown, throat, and heart, then drop down to your knees in prostration, lowering the five parts of your body to the ground.

For the branch of offerings, set out whatever physical offerings you have and mentally offer all of space and the entire earth; offer flowers, incense, butter lamps, and other offering substances used by gods and men, as well as celestial palaces, countries, fortresses, delightful parks, the seven royal emblems, the eight auspicious symbols, the sixteen offering goddesses, and so on. Following the example set by the bodhisattva Samantabhadra, offer up clouds of offerings, filled with song, dance, and music.[49]

For the branch of confession, with intense shame and regret, confess all the negativity, downfalls, and nonvirtue that you have committed from time immemorial up to the present. Confess everything, whether you remember doing it or not. This includes the ten nonvirtues that you have engaged in physically, verbally, and mentally; the five acts of immediate retribution and the five that are almost as severe; the five heavy acts, the eight perversions, the misuse of offerings made to the Three Jewels, and so forth. Imagine that all this gathers on your tongue in the form of a black mass. Light then radiates out from the enlightened body, speech, and mind of those in the field of merit and hits this mass, purifying you as though your impurities were being washed away. You then apply the antidote, pledging to refrain from committing such acts in the future.

For the branch of rejoicing, from the very depths of your heart, rejoice in the great wheel of Dharma that is turned for the benefit of beings by the victorious ones; in the vast activity carried out by the bodhisattvas; in the virtue of sentient beings, both that which is meritorious and that which leads to liberation; and in all the virtuous things that you have done in the past, are doing in the present, and are certain to do in the future.

For the branch of turning the wheel of Dharma, imagine that you are in the presence of those buddhas, bodhisattvas, and spiritual teachers who shoulder the burden of benefiting all beings, yet who are worn out and fatigued by ingratitude and are now absorbed in a state of peace and bliss, no longer teaching the Dharma. Just as Brahma and Vishnu made offerings and requested the Buddha Shakyamuni to teach, emanate millions upon millions of bodies and use them to offer sacred wheels, jewels, and the like, supplicating these enlightened beings to turn the wheel of Dharma.

For the branch of requesting enlightened beings to remain, envision yourself in front of the gurus, buddhas, and bodhisattvas that dwell in this and other worlds, who have completed their activity for the welfare of sentient beings and wish to pass into nirvana. Just as the layman Tsunda did, multiply your body many times over and supplicate them to remain in samsara. Then imagine that, as the result of your supplication, these beings remain to carry out the welfare of sentient beings until samsara is emptied.

For the branch of dedication, dedicate all the merit you and others have accumulated throughout the three times, as exemplified by the virtue that is being gathered right now, to the welfare of all sentient beings. Like the complete dedication of the youthful Manjushri, seal your dedication with the knowledge free of any reference point.

Along with these seven branches, recite the lines that begin, "HRIH I bow down in prostration . . ." and include one hundred thousand prostrations with your practice.

Supplication and the Four Vajras

As the essence of the heruka in each mandala, the sacred guru, the glorious protector, has complete power. Merely seeing, hearing, remembering, or touching the guru plants the seed of liberation. Since his or her activities are the same as the enlightened activities of all the buddhas, the guru is the fourth jewel. It is our guru that will swiftly establish us in the state of Vajradhara in this very life and body. This will come about only through the guru's compassionate blessings and the profound path of ripening and liberation we are shown. For these reasons, from our own perspective, our guru's kindness is supreme and superior even to that of the buddhas. When appraised in terms of his or her excellent qualities, the guru possesses enlightened intent as vast as space and wisdom and love as boundless as the ocean. With compassion fierce and powerful like a waterfall, the guru's nature is steadfast like the king of mountains, and like a parent, the guru regards all sentient beings with equanimity. Indeed, you could never quantify each and every sublime quality the guru has. Merely supplicating the guru will effortlessly bring you whatever spiritual attainments you desire.

With devotion so intense that tears well up in your eyes, think to yourself, "Oh precious, wish-fulfilling jewel, I put myself completely in your care! I place all my hopes in you! You alone will be the focal point of my practice!" As you think this, recite the lines of the liturgy that begin, "Noble Lord Guru Rinpoche, you are the embodiment . . ." down to, "O Padmakara, my precious master, keep me in your heart!" With these lines, supplicate as much as you can, and then recite the lines, "Apart from you, there is no one in whom I can place my hopes!" to "Please purify the two obscurations, O Guru with your might and power!" a suitable number of times. Following this, combine supplication, the yoga that invokes the wisdom mind of the guru, with the vajra guru mantra.

To receive the four empowerments, imagine that your intense longing causes the guru to regard you with love. In between his eyebrows there is an OM syllable, dazzling like crystal. From it, a ray of light is emitted that penetrates the crown of your head, purifying all of your physical karma and the obscurations of your energetic channels. The blessings of vajra form infuse your being, you obtain the vase empowerment and become a vessel for the development stage. The seed of the matured master of awareness is implanted in your being, as is the fortune to attain the level of nirmanakaya buddha.

In the guru's throat is the syllable AH, blazing like a ruby. From it a second light streams out and enters your throat center, purifying your verbal karma and energetic obscurations. The blessings of vajra speech infuse your being, you obtain the secret empowerment and become a vessel for the practice of mantra recitation. The seed of the master of awareness with power over longevity is implanted in your being, as is the fortune to attain the level of a sambhogakaya buddha.

In the guru's heart center is a sky-blue HUM syllable, from which light streams out and penetrates your heart, purifying your mental karma and the obscurations of the energetic essences. The blessings of vajra mind infuse your being, you obtain the knowledge-wisdom empowerment and become a vessel for bliss-emptiness, the practice of yogic heat. The seed of the master of awareness of the great seal is implanted in your being, as is the fortune to attain the level of a dharmakaya buddha.

Like a shooting star, a second HUM syllable shoots out from the HUM in your guru's heart center and merges inseparably with your mind. This purifies the karma of the universal ground and cognitive obscurations. The blessings of vajra wisdom infuse your being, you obtain the empowerment in which the absolute is indicated through words, and you become a vessel for the Great Perfection of original purity. The seed of the spontaneously present master of awareness is implanted in your being, as is the fortune to attain the ultimate result, the level of a svabhavikakaya buddha.

Once you've received the four empowerments, mingle your own three gates and the body, speech, and mind of the guru, becoming of one taste.

Then, simply rest in this state as you maintain the natural radiance of the view and exert yourself in the supplication approach. This is referred to as "observing the face of the dharmakaya guru."

Your mind stream has been linked to the seeds of the four vajras from the very beginning. To awaken their potential, the vajra master ripens these seeds by allowing you to enter the mandala. In this context, we refer to this as the "ground empowerment." When practicing guru yoga, this is to be practiced at all times; there is no need to rely on other conditions. This is termed the "path empowerment." There is a great need to plant an ocean of seeds related to purification, perfection, and maturation, so those who have been ripened by the supreme vajra path should always practice the path empowerment. In addition, one must also recite ten million approach supplications.

The fruitional empowerment occurs once all that obscures has been exhausted, as illustrated by the sutra tradition's convention in which the buddhas confer the empowerment of great light. In this unsurpassed vehicle, it is said:

> The dharmakaya Samantabhadra has no active guru.
> There is no preceptor who gives empowerments
> Or who explains the Dharma.
> When you know your own mind to be the dharmakaya,
> You have received the empowerments
> And transmissions of the buddhas of the three times.
> To hold the lineage is realization.

In the context of this guru sadhana, there are various details concerning the stages of visualization and the projection and absorption of light, that are discussed in the footnotes of the root text of the sadhana.

At the end of each session, the completion stage practice of dissolving the visualization is a profound, vital point. Be sure to give it a place of importance. As you recite the verses that begin, "When my life has come to an end . . . ," simultaneously imagine that your intense longing for the great vajra master arouses his compassion, prompting him to direct all his attention to you. Smiling with an active gaze at once joyful and engaging, a dazzling warm red light emanates from his heart center. The moment it reaches your heart, your body, still visualized as Vajrayogini, transforms into a small sphere of light the size of a pea. This sphere shoots up like a spark and merges with

Guru Rinpoche's heart. Once this happens you can simply rest in equanimity. In the post-meditation state, dedicate the virtue and recite *The Prayer of the Copper-Colored Mountain*. These are very sacred points.

For those whose devotion and samaya vows are completely pure, merely completing the path up to this point will ensure their rebirth on the Glorious Mountain of Chamara, even without performing the main practices. In that pure realm, they will proceed along the path of the four awareness holders, reaching the abode of Samantabhadra even more swiftly than the movements of the sun and moon.

Mangalam!

The Quintessential Nectar
of the Profound Meaning

⸻ ❧❦❧ ⸻

*A Concise Explanation of the Great Perfection Preliminary Practices
of the Heart Essence of the Vast Expanse*

JAMYANG KHYENTSÉ WANGPO

Homage to the guru!

What follows is a guide to the various stages of the Great Perfection preliminary practices of the Heart Essence of the Vast Expanse.

PREPARATION

To begin, when it is time to get up at dawn, imagine your guru in the space
before you in the form of Padmasambhava, surrounded by a group of dakas
and dakinis. With their damarus resounding with the sound of mantra, they
rouse you from your slumber. As you get up, imagine your body [to be the
deity] and your environment to be a pure realm. Next, visualize the guru in
your heart center. He then ascends through the central channel to the space
above the crown of your head, where he dwells with obvious delight. Following this, sit in the correct posture, exhale the stale breath nine times, and
then rest for a few moments, simply letting your consciousness settle into its
natural state. These steps will prepare you for deep meditation.

To practice the blessing of speech, recite the lines that begin, "OM AH HUM.
Burning fire emerges from the syllable RAM, incinerating my tongue . . ." If
you like, you may insert the supplication that begins, "You, whose immense
kindness brings great joy . . ."[50] prior to *Calling the Guru from Afar.*[51]

THE MAIN PRACTICE

The Common Preliminaries

The main practice contains two sections: the common preliminaries and the unique preliminaries. The first section is broken down further into six topics:

- ► The precious human birth
- ► Death and impermanence
- ► The principle of karma
- ► The suffering of samsara
- ► The virtues of liberation
- ► The guru principle

To practice all six topics one after another, recite the lines from the liturgy that begin, "From the blossoming flower of faith in the center of my heart . . ." as you contemplate the following.

There are eighteen factors that constitute a precious human existence: the eight freedoms, which are the opposites of the eight restrictions, and the ten riches. Of these two groups, the freedoms are the essential qualities of the precious human existence, while the ten riches are its specific attributes. An existence with these eighteen qualities is exceedingly rare and inconceivably advantageous. Indeed, you can see this for yourself by considering this situation from the point of view of its causes, the analogies that demonstrate its rarity, and the probability of its attainment.

Nevertheless, while you may have such an existence right now, you are sure to die one day. Even the world around us, solid and stable though it seems, will eventually be destroyed by seven firestorms and one flood, until not even ash remains. Similarly, all the beings that are born into this world will one day pass away; no one can escape this fate. In fact, not only will you die, there is no way to be certain that death will not strike this very evening!

When you pass away, nothing will do you any good except for the pure Dharma. You will not simply disappear when you die. Rather, what happens next will be dictated by your previous actions. Negative actions will bring you a rebirth in one of the three lower realms, where the suffering of suffering is intolerable. Tainted virtuous actions, on the other hand, will cause you to be reborn in one of the three higher realms, where you will still be subject to the suffering of change and the universal suffering of conditioned existence.

For these reasons, you should exert yourself by whatever means necessary to free yourself from samsara, which is nothing but a vast ocean of suffering! To do so, you need to rely upon a qualified spiritual teacher of the Great Vehicle, pleasing him or her in the three ways. Practice your teacher's guidance concerning what to do and what to give up to the letter, without falling under the influence of immature friends or bad influences. To the best of your ability, incorporate this genuine teaching on the certainty of death into each and every day.

Keeping all this in mind, arouse faith in the Three Jewels so that you will be able to practice in this manner, thinking to yourself, "Think of me, Three Jewels!" At the same time, be sure to generate an intense sense of renunciation and subdue your mind stream.

The Unique Preliminaries

The unique preliminaries also contain six sections:

- ▸ Refuge
- ▸ Bodhichitta
- ▸ The meditation and recitation of Vajrasattva
- ▸ Mandala offering
- ▸ The offering of the simple beggar
- ▸ Guru yoga

REFUGE

To take refuge, adopt the attitude of a great being, thinking to yourself, "I now take refuge in the guru and Three Jewels to free all sentient beings, both myself and others, from the terrible sufferings of samsara." With this mindset, envision your surroundings as a beautiful pure realm with a ground made of jewels. In the midst of this enchanting environment is a wish-fulfilling tree that fills the entire expanse of space, its five branches filled with leaves, flowers, fruit, garlands of precious jewels, and small bells. In the center of the tree is your root guru, the embodiment of all the buddhas, in the form of the Vajra Master of Oddiyana.[52] He sits upon a jeweled throne held aloft by snow lions, resting upon a multicolored lotus and sun and moon discs. Blue in color, he holds a vajra and bell and embraces his spiritual partner, Yeshé Tsogyal, who holds a curved knife and skull cup. They are both clad in silk and wear bone ornaments. He sits in the vajra posture, while above his crown, the gurus of the Great Perfection lineage are seated one above the other. These gurus are surrounded by the realized root and lineage masters, the yidam deities associated with the six major classes of tantra, and an inconceivable number of the dakas and dakinis of the three abodes. On the branch in front of the guru are Shakyamuni and the rest of the buddhas of the three times in their nirmanakaya form. To his left and right are the assemblies of realized beings: On the right branch is the sangha of the Great Vehicle, including the Eight Close Sons, and on the left, Shariputra, Modgalyayana, and the sangha of listeners. On the branch behind the guru sits the Jewel of the Dharma in the form of stacked books, red in color and emitting the sounds of the vowels and consonants of the Sanskrit alphabet. All the space between these figures is completely filled with a veritable ocean of oath-bound Dharma protectors, both wisdom protectors and karmic guardians. Since all of these possess the infinite qualities of wisdom, love, and power, they accept you lovingly and are now actually present before you as your great guides.

You stand before them, with your father to your right, your mother to your left, and those who have done you harm in front. Surrounding you are the sentient beings of the six realms. Joining your palms as a physical gesture of respect, you all chant the refuge liturgy and think, "From now until we attain the essence of enlightenment, we take the guru as our guide, the yidam deities and buddhas as our teachers, the Dharma as our path, and the daki-nis, Dharma protectors, and sangha as our companions along the way. We rely on you; we offer everything to you. We have no other refuge or hope but you. Whatever we do, please care for us!" With intense yearning, take refuge as many times as you can.

At the end, light rays stream out from the heart centers of the sources of refuge, entering the bodies and minds of you and all other sentient beings. Imagine that this completely purifies the two obscurations and their habitual patterns, extends your lifespan, increases your merit, and causes the qualities of learning and realization to evolve. Finally, rest for a short time in a state free from mental fixation.

BODHICHITTA
Start by cultivating the four immeasurables. Begin with equanimity, arous-ing an attitude free from attachment to loved ones or aversion to those you do not like. Consider the fact that there is no telling whether someone will be a friend or enemy, whether in this life or a future life. Indeed, our rela-tionships with others are never set. In all our lifetimes, which stretch back

infinitely into the distant past, the limitless number of sentient beings have played different roles in our lives. Our friends have harmed us, our enemies have shown us kindness, and so on. You can then take this one step further by considering how all of these beings are none other than our kind parents. On this basis, cultivate the wish to repay their kindness: Arouse love, the wish for them to be happy; compassion, the wish to free them from suffering; and joy, the delight you would feel were they never to be parted from such a state.

With the objects of refuge dwelling before you as witnesses, cultivate aspiration bodhichitta with the following thought, "By all means, I must attain the precious state of perfect buddhahood to bring all sentient beings the perfect happiness of complete liberation." Next, cultivate application bodhichitta, thinking, "To this end, I will train in bodhisattva activity on a vast scale, as represented by this profound path, working diligently until not a single sentient being remains in samsara!" Without losing sight of these motivations, recite the bodhichitta liturgy three or another suitable number of times.

If you are unable to do this as a regular practice, simply cultivating aspiration and application bodhichitta will suffice. On the other hand, if you prefer, you may train your mind in equalizing and exchanging self and other. In particular, you can imagine sending out happiness with the out breath and taking in the suffering of others as you breathe in. You may also cultivate ultimate bodhichitta, the union of tranquility and insight, prompted by a definitive understanding of the twofold absence of self.

To conclude, imagine that both you and sentient beings dissolve into the objects of refuge. The objects of refuge, in turn, dissolve into the guru at the center. Finally, dissolve the guru into the primordial space of the dharmakaya, beyond elaborations, and then rest in meditation.

THE MEDITATION AND RECITATION OF VAJRASATTVA

During the meditation and recitation of Vajrasattva, chant the lines that begin, "AH. On the crown of my head, in my ordinary form . . ." At the same time, imagine yourself in your ordinary form, with an eight-petaled white lotus on the crown of your head. The stem of the lotus, four finger-widths in length, is inserted into your crown aperture. At its center is a white moon disc, equal in size to the lotus's orange anthers. Resting upon the disc is a white HUM syllable. In an instant, the HUM syllable transforms into guru Vajrasattva, brilliant white in color and radiating light. Peaceful, smiling, and replete with all the marks and signs of buddhahood, Vajrasattva wears five garments: a white silk upper garment, a multicolored lower garment, a crown with silk ribbons, and sleeves like those depicted in ancient paintings. He is also wearing eight jewel ornaments: a jeweled crown, earrings, a necklace, bracelets, anklets, a waistband, a long jeweled necklace that hangs below the navel, and a shorter necklace that hangs to the breast. With his right hand, he holds a vajra at his heart. With his left, he holds a bell at his hip. He sits in vajra posture in union with his spiritual partner Vajratöpa, who is white, holds a curved knife and a skull cup, and sits in the lotus posture.

As you imagine all this, practice the meditation and recitation of Vajrasattva with the vital points of the four powers. For the power of support, think the following with intense devotion, "Please purify all the negativity and obscurations in my mind stream! Think of me!" As the power of remorse, generate an overwhelming feeling of regret for all the negativity that you have carried out in the past. For the power of restraining negative behavior, think to yourself, "I will not engage in such activities in the future, even if it costs me my life!" Finally, as the power of applying the antidote, do the following to remedy what you have done in the past: Imagine a HUM syllable sitting on a moon disc in the heart center of Vajrasattva. A strand of letters that form the hundred syllable mantra circle clockwise around the HUM syllable. The letters are white and so fine that they appear to be written with a single strand of hair.

As you visualize this, recite the letters of the mantra for a short while as if you are reading them. This will cause the nectar of great bliss to flow forth, white and radiating light. The nectar flows through the bodies of the male and female deities, emerging from their point of union before it winds down the stem of the lotus and enters your body through the crown aperture. Like trash carried away by a great flood, all illness flows out of your pores and two lower orifices in the form of pus and blood, negative forces emerge as insects, and negativity and obscurations pour out as black liquid. Flowing out, all of this falls into the gaping mouth and down into the stomach of the Lord of Death, who awaits nine stories below in the form of a red bull. This averts untimely death.

Imagining this, recite the hundred-syllable mantra. Ideally, you should recite the mantra as many times as possible. Second best is to recite it one hundred times. At the very least, recite it twenty-one times.

Next, imagine that the nectar completely fills the abodes of the four chakras, thereby purifying the negativity and obscurations of the three gates in equal proportion. The wisdom of bliss-emptiness, the four joys, arises in your mind stream, causing undefiled bliss to permeate your body and mind.

Following this, offer confession and pledge to restrain yourself in the future. With intense devotion, request Vajrasattva to grant you refuge by reciting the lines that begin, "Protector, under the sway of unknowing and ignorance . . ." Guru Vajrasattva, delighted that you have purified the negativity and transgressions present in your mind stream, laughs with a broad smile. "Fortunate child," he says, "All of your negativity, obscurations, breaches, and transgressions of samaya are now purified!" With these words, he absolves you, whereupon he melts into light, as the essence of great bliss-emptiness, and dissolves into you.

This sets the stage for you to manifest instantaneously as Vajrasattva in union with his spiritual partner, with all their color, implements, and ornamentation distinct and complete. In the heart center of your body, which should be imagined to be apparent, yet empty like the reflection in a mirror, is the syllable HUM. Surrounding it in the four directions are the seed syllables of the mantra: OM, VAJRA, SA, TVA. An infinite number of white light rays stream out from these syllables, making offerings to the realized beings. Gathering in all their blessings and spiritual attainments, the light then reconverges and dissolves into you. Next, the light radiates out once again and purifies all of the negativity and obscurations of sentient beings. This transforms the entire external universe into the Unsurpassed Realm of Complete Joy and brings all sentient beings of the three realms to the state of Vajrasattva and the five buddha families. Imagine that you and all these beings then recite the quintessence mantra in unison as much as you are able. This purifies the obscurations by specifically utilizing the development stage.

To conclude, gather the elaborations of deity and mantra back into the basic state of luminosity and look at the original face of the true Vajrasattva—the empty awareness that is primordially and naturally unestablished, where the discursive thoughts of something to purify and something that purifies do not exist. Settling into this state is the supreme way to purify the obscurations. Here, one utilizes the ultimate completion stage.

MANDALA

Fourth is the mandala offering. Begin by imagining the field of merit in the space before you, as you did when taking refuge. Clean a mandala plate made from a precious metal or another material and then anoint it with scented water and the five substances that come from cows. Arrange either thirty-seven or seven piles of flowers on the plate. If you are not doing this as your daily practice, however, you may simply visualize this. Whatever the case, you may then offer the common mandala of the nirmanakaya realm: the billion world systems of the third-order thousandfold universe, each of which has its own four continents, Mount Meru, and heavens and is filled with all the abundance of mankind and the natural world. In particular, offer your own body, belongings, and all the virtue you've amassed with a sense of detachment. In the space above the nirmanakaya realm is the extraordinary sambhogakaya mandala, the pure land of the Richly Arrayed Supreme Realm, in which the play of the kayas and wisdoms manifest as infinite clouds of offerings. In the space of that realm is the special dharmakaya mandala, where the apparent aspect of unceasing luminosity is arranged as piles of the full expression of awareness on the primordial unarisen ground. Offer all of this with the understanding that there are an infinite number of pure realms within each subatomic particle that you offer and that reality itself surpasses the imagination and can manifest in any way whatsoever.

As you offer this, make the following supplication with overwhelming devotion a suitable number of times:

> Through these offerings, may the two accumulations, both my own
>   and those of all sentient beings, be perfected!
> May the two obscurations be purified!
> May the sublime qualities of experience and realization take birth
>   in my mind stream!
> Ultimately, may I enjoy the ocean of pure realms of the three kayas!

THE ACCUMULATIONS OF THE SIMPLE BEGGAR

As before, begin by imagining the field of merit, beneath which you can instantaneously visualize all the sentient beings of the six realms, headed by those who have done you harm. At the same time, recite the lines that begin:

> P'ET
> Casting aside my treasured body, I conquer the demon of the
>   divine child . . .

Relinquishing self-centeredness and fixation toward the body, imagine the essence of your mind, in the form of a sphere of white light the size of a pea, shooting out into space from your crown. The sphere then transforms into the wisdom dakini, the Black Wrathful One, who is adorned with silks and the five bone mudras. The head of a sow protrudes from her crown. With her right hand, she swings a curved knife through the air and slices off the top of the skull, at the level of the eyebrows, of the corpse you left behind. The skull then grows to the size of a third-order thousandfold universe, and you place it on a hearth fashioned from skulls, each the size of Mount Meru. You then dismember your corpse and place it inside the skull. From below, the fire of wisdom blazes forth from the stroke of the syllable AH. From above, a stream of nectar drips down from an upside down HUM syllable into the skull. The contents of the skull then melt and boil.

Reciting OM *purifies* all impure entities, which are then expelled in the form of purple steam. Reciting AH *multiplies* the pure contents—the nectar of wisdom—to expand beyond the scope of the imagination. Reciting HUM *transforms* the essence of this wisdom nectar into a great cloud of wheels of the treasury of space, which manifest as all manner of sense pleasures. Recite these three syllables—OM AH HUM—many times.

Next, emanate an infinite number of offering goddesses from your heart center and offer the select portion to the field of merit, thereby sating their enlightened mind streams with undefiled bliss. This, in turn, perfects the two accumulations, both your own and those of all sentient beings. It also purifies the two obscurations and accomplishes the two spiritual attainments.

Following this, give the remainder of your offering to the beings of the six realms, especially to those who have done you harm. For each recipient, your gift transforms into whatever it is that they desire. For malevolent entities, your gift turns into heaps of flesh, blood, and bones. This purifies any karmic debts you may have with them and purifies their malicious and vindictive mind-sets. Your body then becomes an immaculate rainbow body, and your mind undergoes a fundamental transformation into the nonconceptual dharmakaya.

To conclude, all dualistic thought patterns, as represented by the notions of offering and recipient, are purified into the space of the luminous Great Perfection, the mind's fundamental nature, free from inherent existence. Rest in this natural and uncontrived state, free from the concepts of the three spheres.

GURU YOGA

The first stage of guru yoga addresses the visualization of the objects of refuge. As you recite the lines that begin, "How wondrous! I appear in the midst of a buddha realm . . ." imagine that your perception pervades all of space and that the entirety of your perception is a pure realm, in which all forms of ordinary fixation have dissolved into space. In its place, a realm of infinite purity manifests spontaneously and naturally: the Sublime and Supreme Great Palace of Lotus Light, with its limitless shape, ornamentation, and structure.

You yourself dwell in the center of the palace. You are Yeshé Tsogyal in essence, yet your form is that of Vajrayogini. Red in color, you hold a curved knife and a skull cup filled with blood in your right and left hands, respectively. A khatvanga rests in the crook of your left arm. Standing upon a lotus, sun disc, and corpse, your right leg is extended while your left is bent slightly inward. Your body is adorned with silks and bone ornaments and your eyes, filled with devotion, gaze longingly at your master's heart center.

A multicolored lotus with a hundred thousand petals is present in the space before you, level with the top of your head. There sits your own root guru, the embodiment of all sources of refuge, resting upon sun and moon discs as wide as the anthers of the lotus. With the appearance of an eight-year-old boy, he manifests in the form of the Lake-born Vajra of Oddiyana, his skin white with a tinge of red. His two eyes stare straight ahead intensely. For clothing, he wears a white vajra undergarment, on top of which he wears a red robe, a dark blue tunic from the mantra tradition, a red shawl with a gold floral pattern, and a maroon cloak made from silk brocade. He has one face and two arms. In his right hand, he holds a five-pronged vajra at his heart. The left hand, resting in the mudra of meditation, holds a kapala, within which is a longevity vase filled with the nectar of the wisdom of immortality. In the crook of his left arm, he cradles a three-pronged khatvanga, symbolizing his spiritual partner Mandarava. Radiant with the signs and marks of buddhahood, he smiles wrathfully and wears a five-petaled lotus hat on his head. He is seated in the posture of a reveling king, completely surrounded by a tent of rainbows and a lattice of multicolored rays of light, within which swirl orbs of rainbow-colored light.

Within this expanse, the learned and accomplished masters that dwell on the ground of the masters of awareness are present as the play of the great wisdom of your root guru's enlightened mind. This includes the eight masters of awareness from India, the eighty-four powerful yogis, and the twenty-five disciples, the mahasiddhas of Tibet. Also present are the limitless peaceful and wrathful yidam deities associated with the six major classes of tantra, the dakas and dakinis of the three abodes, Dharma protectors, wealth deities, and the guardians of treasures. All of these figures are gathered together like billowing clouds, yet they are also the union of clarity and emptiness, like a rainbow or the moon's reflection in a pond. Bringing them to mind naturally causes your ordinary state of consciousness to cease.

Next, invoke Pema Tötreng Tsel of Oddiyana[53] by reciting the *Seven-Line Supplication* with fervent devotion. He then arrives swiftly from the emanated realm of the Glorious Mountain in Chamara to the southwest, accompanied by the three roots and a veritable ocean of victorious ones. They emerge like sesame seeds bursting forth from a pod and then merge inseparably with the samaya beings.

Seven-Branch Offering For the seven-branch offering, emanate a hundred, thousand, or an infinite number of replicas of your own body, then prostrate together with the sentient beings of the three realms, showing respect physically, verbally, and mentally. Next, present offerings. These offerings can include things that you have actually prepared, as well as the offering clouds of Samantabhadra that you imagine, which you can multiply until they fill the entirety of space. Following this, acknowledge all the negativity and transgressions you have engaged in via the three gates throughout your infinite lives, confessing them all with an overwhelming feeling of remorse. Imagine that all of this negativity gathers onto your tongue in the form of a black mass. Light then radiates out from the enlightened body, speech, and mind of all those in the field of merit and hits this mass, purifying you as though your impurities were being washed away. To remedy this negativity, you then confess what you have done and pledge to refrain from committing such acts in the future. Next, without feeling envious, rejoice in all the relative and ultimate sources of virtue, those associated with samsara, nirvana, and the three paths. Request the buddhas of the ten directions and their offspring to turn the wheel of the Dharma, meaning the three vehicles of the listeners, solitary buddhas, and bodhisattvas. You should also implore them not to pass into nirvana until samsara is empty. Finally, dedicate all the virtue you have amassed throughout the three times, as represented by the virtue you have gathered here, to the cause of all beings attaining the state of buddhahood. Mindful of the seven branches outlined here, recite the liturgy a suitable number of times as you offer prostrations.

Supplication and Empowerment Attaining liberation and the state of omniscience depends on realizing the wisdom that is innate within your own mind. This realization, in turn, depends upon the blessings of your guru, which themselves are solely contingent upon the karmic link of devotion.

From the perspective of his or her qualities, your root guru is equal to the buddhas, yet in terms of kindness, your guru is superior. Having thoroughly grasped this fact, entrust your entire being to the guru, thinking to yourself, "From now until I attain enlightenment, in happiness or sorrow, in good times and bad, you will be my only guide. Please care for me, guru!" Place all your hopes and expectations in the guru, praying with such fervent devotion that you can no longer maintain your composure. With the hairs of your body standing on end, tears streaming from your eyes, and your mind so enthralled with the guru that you can think of nothing else, recite the prayers that begin, "Lord Guru Rinpoche, you are the embodiment . . ." and, "Apart from you, there is no one in whom I can place my hopes . . ."

After saying these prayers a number of times, combine your supplication with the yoga of invocation by reciting the Vajra Guru Mantra. The first three syllables of the mantra, OM AH HUM, are the seed syllables of the three vajras. VAJRA represents the dharmakaya since it cannot be swayed by the elaborations of concept and thought. GURU relates to the sambhogakaya, which is "heavy" with the qualities of the seven aspects of union that manifest out of the dharmakaya. PADMA signifies the nirmanakaya, the radiant awareness of discerning wisdom that manifests as the buddha family of enlightened speech. SIDDHI represents all the common and supreme spiritual attainments. Spiritual attainments are brought about through the force of supplication, which in this case refers to being mindful of the qualities of the great master of Oddiyana, who is inseparable from the three kayas, and supplicating him with heartfelt devotion, devotion being the natural expression of the basic nature of mind, freedom from elaborations. With HUM, you are saying, "Please bestow these attainments upon my mind stream this very instant!"

Keeping its meaning in mind, recite the Vajra Guru Mantra. At times, you can recite the mantra with the knowledge that the external environment is the palace of the Glorious Copper-Colored Mountain, all the beings that inhabit it are the assembly of the dakas and dakinis of Oddiyana, all sounds are the natural sound of mantra, and, secretly, that the movements of conceptual thought are self-liberated, leaving no trace like the path of a bird in flight.

To conclude, remind yourself of the sublime qualities of the root and lineage gurus and recite the lineage supplication, along with aspirations, with intense devotion. This will cause the retinue to dissolve into the guru, the embodiment of all sources of refuge. Visualizing as outlined in the liturgy, the guru then grants you the four empowerments, following which his enlightened body, speech, and mind merge inseparably with your own three gates. Once this has taken place, recite the mantra while maintaining the inner radiance of your own mind—the naked, empty awareness of the present moment.

To bring the session to a close, recite the lines that begin, "When my life has come to an end . . ." At the same time, dissolve the visualization as part of the completion stage. Your intense longing for the guru will then cause him to direct his compassion to you. Smiling and gazing upon you with affection, he sways slightly as a ray of warm red light streams out from his heart center, striking the heart center of your own body, still visualized as Vajrayogini. As soon as it strikes you, your body and mind are overcome with a feeling of bliss. At the end, you dissolve into red light—the essence of great bliss—and then transform into a sphere of light the size of a pea, the nature of which is the indivisibility of the energies and mind. The sphere of light then shoots up like a spark into the heart center of Guru Rinpoche. Once this merging has taken place, simply rest in the state that ensues.

When you arise from meditation, visualize your body and environment as described earlier, doing so instantaneously like a fish leaping out of the water. In addition, recite the supplication that begins, "O precious and glorious root guru, please dwell on the lotus seat in my heart." You should also recite general dedications and aspirations, as well as *The Secret Path to the Glorious Mountain: An Aspiration for the Glorious Copper-Colored Mountain.*

In between sessions, the general approach to adopt is the "three transformations" that were outlined above in the section on recitation and visualization. More specifically, however, you should respectfully offer the best portion of whatever you eat or drink as nectar and offer clothing as garments made of divine fabric. Whatever you perceive through the six senses, whether good or bad, positive or negative, do not get caught up in any ordinary thought patterns. Rather, simply maintain the flow of the radiant awareness of deity, mantra, and wisdom.

When you go to sleep at night, pray for the welfare of both yourself and all others, reciting *The Spontaneous Fulfillment of Wishes*, and especially *The Aspiration for Training in the Pure Realms of the Three Kayas*. When you are finished, imagine that the guru descends through your crown aperture to your heart, where he rests on a four-petaled lotus. He then emanates rays of light that fill your entire body. As you drift off to sleep, focus on the vivid clarity brought about by this practice, merging your own mind inseparably with the guru's enlightened mind and maintaining the flow of this union.

Alternatively, you can imagine that these light rays radiate out and strike the external environment, which you have visualized as the celestial palace. The palace then melts into light, like salt dissolving in water, and then merges with the sentient beings, whom you are visualizing as deities. These deities, in turn, dissolve into you, and you then dissolve into the guru at your heart center. Finally, purify the guru into a nonreferential state of luminosity and rest in naked, empty awareness, undisturbed by other thoughts; withdrawn, but not dull.

Should you awake, cut the flow of thought, whether your thoughts are linked with the pervasive spread of discursive thoughts, dreams, or anything else. Simply maintaining the expansive state of luminosity will allow you to grasp the luminosity of deep sleep and to recognize that you are dreaming during the dream state. When you wake up in the morning, practice the waking yoga and all the other elements as explained here in either four or some other number of sessions.

When you approach the time of death, practice the dissolution of the completion stage and merge your awareness with space. Resting in this way is the king of all forms of transference. If you are unable to bring about this transference, you will be liberated by recalling the three transformations in the intermediate state.

In short, by keeping your devotion and samaya vows completely pure, completing these preliminary practices will be enough to bring you to the Glorious Mountain of Chamara, even without engaging in the main practices of the Vajrayana path. In that pure realm, you will traverse the paths of the four masters of awareness and are sure to reach the state of Samantabhadra more swiftly than the course of the sun and the moon.

Once you have gained some experience of these preliminary practices, you may move on to the progressive stages of the main practice along with their subsidiary elements. The path of the vase empowerment is the development stage associated with the peaceful and wrathful masters of awareness. The path of the secret empowerment involves energetic practices and inner heat. The path of the knowledge/wisdom empowerment is the path of skillful means and the hidden meaning. The path of the fourth empowerment consists of the breakthrough and direct leap. Distill the essence of these practices and work diligently to actualize the unified state of the master of awareness in this very life!

This brief clarification of the various topics contained in The Sublime Path to Omniscience, *the preliminary practice liturgy of the Great Perfection of the Heart Essence of the Vast Expanse, distills the essence of these stages. It is meant to be used by those who do the preliminaries as a regular practice.*

Based on the topics outlined in the instruction manual and the oral instructions of my gurus, this work was composed by Khyentsé Wangpo, a loyal subject who has pleased his omniscient guru. It was written with the sole wish to benefit those fortunate individuals who are beginning to set out on this path. May the virtue created by this endeavor be a cause for all beings to swiftly attain the state of the immortal Pema Tötreng Tsel!

Advice on the Longchen Nyingtik Preliminary Practices

<svg>꧁꧂</svg>

DZONGSAR JAMYANG KHYENTSE RINPOCHE

INTRODUCTION

The Buddha's teachings aim to liberate us from all forms of delusion. That is what we call enlightenment. Liberation is not only a release from temporary forms of delusion, but also from the very root of delusion. In using the term "delusion," not only are we referring to some of the more gross forms of delusion, but also the subtlest forms of delusion. Even some things that we consider to be wise and virtuous are eventually the very things that need to be purified.

The Buddha taught numerous methods that we can use to release ourselves from delusion. Traditionally, the teachings speak of more than eighty-four thousand methods. Each of these is suited to the needs of a different kind of being and to the variations in motivation and determination that beings possess. Some individuals are determined to completely renounce samsara, for example. That is their main aim. For them, the Buddha taught the Shravakayana. Others are determined, not only to escape from samsara, but also to avoid dwelling in nirvana. In other words, their aim is to escape all extremes, not only for themselves, but also for the sake of all sentient beings. For them, the Buddha taught the Mahayana, or Great Vehicle. In either case, the methods the Buddha taught are intended to liberate us from delusion.

Escaping delusion is difficult because of the deeply ingrained habits that we have developed over countless lifetimes. One could say that the Buddhadharma is a systematic method that we can use to peel back the layers of these habitual patterns, which are like the skin of an onion. Through study and practice, we begin to peel off this skin. Each time we peel off a layer, we discover a new layer inside and think we've reached the core. Soon enough however, we realize that it is just another layer, and then we peel off *that* layer as well. The difficulty here is that we have the tendency to get stuck when we reach the inner layers. We do not immediately recognize that this is just a more stubborn and subtle form of delusion. This is why we need to train our minds.

Both the Shravakayana and Mahayana have a complete system of mind training. In the first, training the mind is based on physical, verbal, and mental discipline. This is accomplished through the whole structure of the vinaya, starting with shaving the head, wearing robes, and basically renouncing the worldly life in a physical sense.

Within the Mahayana there are two further approaches, one that takes the cause as the path and one that takes the result as the path. The latter of these two is also known as the Vajrayana. On this path, we train our mind, not only through renunciation and bodhichitta, but also by transforming impure experiences into pure perception. That is the forte of the Vajrayana; it is unique because of this difference in attitude.

The Vajrayana way of looking at the world is quite different. The shravakas see this samsaric world as something impure; this is what they call the "Truth of Suffering." Following this to its logical conclusion, the world is something to be gotten rid of and escaped from. That is the shravaka attitude. In the Mahayana, samsara is still thought to be imperfect, but instead of trying to escape, the aim is to practice compassion and bodhichitta. In the Vajrayana, we try to understand that all these seemingly impure phenomena are, in reality, pure and have been all along.

Ngöndro practice is rooted in the Vajrayana approach. Unfortunately, the term "ngöndro" has misled a lot of people. Literally translated, it actually means something like "preliminary practices." From this, we somehow develop the idea that this also means "not as important" or "not the main practice." We think of it as something that we have to do before we get to the "real" or "main" practice. This is quite sad because as our study deepens, we will realize that there is nothing more distinctively Vajrayana than ngöndro practice.

In the following explanation of these practices, I will focus on crucial points rather than technicalities. The visualizations and other such details can always be found in the great commentaries, such as *Words of My Perfect*

Teacher and the translations of Jigmé Lingpa's writings included here. Alternatively, you can also receive tips from students who are doing these practices, who can show you how to do prostrations and so forth.

The Structure of the Preliminary Practices

The preliminary practices begin with refuge and bodhichitta, after which there are the three practices unique to the Vajra Vehicle. Refuge is the first preliminary because it diverts one from the wrong path onto the right one. Within the right path, we have the Mahayana and the Shravakayana. To encourage practitioners to practice the first of these, we have bodhichitta, which embodies the entire Mahayana path.

When we use methods like visualization, substances, and mantras, which are not found in the Shravakayana and Mahayana traditions, we are practicing the Vajrayana. Included here are the practices of Vajrasattva mantra recitation and mandala offering, where we use substances as a support for practice. Finally, to dismantle the cocoon of delusion that surrounds us, we have the most profound path of guru yoga. These three—Vajrasattva, mandala offering, and guru yoga—are essential parts of the Vajrayana path. Thus, all three vehicles are contained within the ngöndro: refuge as Shravakayana practice, bodhichitta as Mahayana practice, and the rest as Vajrayana practice.

Ngöndro is not a kindergarten exercise; it is actually the main practice. As Patrül Rinpoche said, "In many ways, ngöndro is much more important than the main practice because it lays the foundation." Being with some of the great masters, such as His Holinesses Dilgo Khyentsé Rinpoche and Dudjom Rinpoche, I know this to be true from my own experience. If ngöndro were only a preliminary or prerequisite practice, one would think that clearly we would not find great masters practicing it. Surely a great master like Dilgo Khyentsé Rinpoche would not need to practice the Nyingtik ngöndro, for instance. But I have seen this with my own eyes; even toward the end of their lives, I found them practicing ngöndro. This alone should indicate why ngöndro practice is so necessary.

Theory and Pith Instructions

The distinctions between theory and the pith instructions are quite straightforward. To use an analogy, when learning to drive there is a driving manual that comes with the car. This manual is similar to the tantric texts and what we call theory. Such texts are very straightforward, logical, and rational. Pith instructions, on the other hand, are quite flexible and, at times, dramatic and outrageous.

Suppose there are fifty people wanting to learn how to drive, each with a different kind of paranoia and with different physical abilities. Perhaps some are unable to use their right foot properly, or have some other kind of abnormality. Each person has his or her own unique and distinct kind of physical and mental condition. When teaching someone to drive, the text itself, the driving manual, is standard. It is the same car, so each person gets the same materials. Some instructions are also standard. Everyone needs to know, for instance, that the car will go to the right when the steering wheel is turned right. Nonstandard instructions depend on the individual, on how much time one has to learn, for example. Some people may not care how fast they learn. Others may want a crash course.

Sometimes one might be taught something that appears to have absolutely nothing to do with the text. The teacher might say, "Drink a cup of coffee before you drive." The context could simply be that you have not woken up properly yet. The text, however, will never say, "You have to drink a cup of coffee before driving." That is just the teacher's own judgment. That is what we call a pith instruction. Such instructions are very versatile, colorful, unorthodox, and sometimes not so logical. Zen masters, for example, say, "What is the sound of one hand clapping?" On the face of it, this question seems completely ridiculous, but depending on when, where, and with whom the method is used, it may work on an individual basis.

Of these two, the ngöndro teachings are pith instructions. This may come as a surprise to some; they are not theory. For instance, the practices of prostrations and mandala offering are pith instructions. If you want to know their underlying theories, you have to study the *Guhyagarbha Tantra* or some other such text.[54]

It is even more important that we learn how to interpret theory. To return to our example of learning to drive, there must be some mention in the car manual of what you need to be cautious about. It probably says on the first page: "Exercise caution. Don't drink and drive, and remember to be alert." Theory is like that; it is not completely spelled out. You simply have to be careful when you drive. That is all the theory can say. "Be careful" is actually open to a lot of interpretation. Different people need to be careful in different ways.

With this in mind, you will see why doing one hundred thousand prostrations works for some, but not for others. For Milarepa, prostrations weren't necessary, because he was building a nine-storied house. To some students, the lama might say, "There is no need to do prostrations," because that person might be doing something else, like confirming the lama's flight tickets. Without this understanding, there is a danger of thinking that certain things are almost mandatory and that, as a Vajrayana student, one has to follow the Tibetan way of doing prostrations.

In other words, you would have developed the misunderstanding that every driver needs to drink a cup of coffee before they drive. It is very important to learn how to interpret what one reads on the first page of the manual. When it says that one has to be careful when driving, for one person this may mean, "drink a cup of coffee." Perhaps for someone else drinking coffee might make them nervous or agitated, so maybe a sip of a margarita is better to relax them . . . It could be the complete opposite!

It is also important to note that there are many different layers of pith instructions. Certain pith instructions are more generic in nature, such as "do one hundred thousand prostrations," and then there are exclusive pith instructions given to different individuals. In the explanation that follows, I will be referring to both the theory and some of the pith instructions. In terms of theory, the explanations will stay loyal to the actual ngöndro text and to the Vajrayana system in general. As for the pith instructions, most of the time I will be repeating what I have heard from my own teachers.

Three Pith Instructions

Every time we begin to practice, it helps not to plunge in right away. Instead, take a few moments to stop your ordinary chain of thoughts. This is especially relevant if you are very busy and have only five minutes for your daily practice, but even ordinarily we have this constant stream of thoughts. Suppose that just before practice you have a fight with your fiancé. This will probably trigger a chain of thoughts about what you want to say to your partner. If you start your practice in the midst of all this, it is not going to go so well. This is why it helps to put a stop to this chain of thoughts for just a few moments.

I have found this to be very, very useful. There are actually countless methods for stopping the chain of thoughts, but for me, before I practice, I just sit for a while. Every time a thought comes along, I try to stop it by cultivating a sense of renunciation, and I do this over and over again. I think about how I am now forty-years-old and, even if I live to be eighty, I only have half of my life left. I think that out of this forty years, I am going to sleep the equivalent of twenty years. So now there are only twelve hours a day that could actually be termed living. If we then factor in watching at least one movie a day, eating, and gossip, we have maybe five hours or so left. Out of forty years that means eight years remain, and most of that will go to indulging our paranoia, anxiety, and all that. . . . There is actually very little time for practice!

This should give you an idea of how to stop the chain of thoughts. Don't immediately throw yourself into the practice; instead, just watch yourself, watch your life, and watch what you are doing. If you are doing ten minutes of practice every day, you should try to stop the chain of thoughts for at least two to three minutes. We do this to transform the mind by invoking a sense of renunciation. When we think, "I am dying," "I am coming closer to death," and other such thoughts, it really helps.

Of the various traditional methods used to transform our ordinary perception, one very good one is what we call "expelling the stale breath." After doing several minutes of stopping the chain of thoughts, sit straight and breathe in quite strongly. You then block your right nostril as you breathe out from the left. On the out breath, visualize that all your passion and desire are expelled in the form of dark red light. Then you breathe in through the same nostril, thinking that all the buddhas' and bodhisattvas' wisdom and compassion is dissolving into you in the form of light. Then block the left nostril. As you breathe out, think that all your aggression flows out in the form of dark vapor, then breathe in as before. Finally, breathe in and out from both nostrils, this time thinking that all your ignorance is being dispelled in what looks like a dark cloud.

Do not linger too much on the details of the visualizations. Just think that whatever you are visualizing is actually happening. On this point, another pith instruction states that you should not linger on one form when visualizing by asking questions about its details. You shouldn't ask "What kind of white light is it?" or "What diameter is the light?" The whole purpose of Vajrayana visualization is to occupy the ordinary mind with extraordinary thoughts; *that* is the vital aspect here. If you focus too much on one detail, you are opening the door for more obstacles. As soon as you think it is fine, don't linger on it, just immediately go on to the next step of the visualization. This is one very common pith instruction.

The next step I strongly recommend. Suppose you are practicing at home, what you do is try to completely convince yourself that your environment is not just your ordinary residence; it is a pure realm. This is particularly important because the Vajrayana is a path that transforms impure vision into pure vision.

When we say "impure vision" this is not meant to imply that there is something dirty. It has nothing to do with that. Our vision is impure in the sense that we are stuck with all sorts of notions. For example, we might think, "One thousand people can't possibly fit into my bedroom," or, "*This* can't be used as a bedroom!" We have all these dualistic distinctions. We imagine that such and such can be used only for a certain purpose, or that it is too white, too dark, too hot, too cold, and so on.

Likewise, when we say "buddha realm," we are not talking about something you might see in some science fiction film, nor about some kind of really happy heaven. We are talking about a realm of nondualism. In itself, this is difficult to understand right now.

How does this nondual realm appear? For beginners, since this pertains to the Longchen Nyingtik ngöndro where Guru Rinpoche is the main figure, we can envision ourselves in the Realm of the Copper-Colored Mountain. Of course, this does not mean the ceilings and walls are made of copper. Basically, what we are doing here is getting rid of our ordinary perception. Just thinking, "This is not what I think it is" is enough to transform ordinary perception. That is the third of the three pith instructions we use to start the ngöndro.

The Theory of Visualization

The thought, "This does not truly exist the way I see it . . ." seems quite crazy from our ordinary point of view; it seems kind of irrational. From the theoretical point of view of the Vajrayana, however, this would be correct because everything you see is your own perception. If there are several people looking at the same girl, for instance, one person may be thinking, "That girl is beautiful" while the other may think that the very same girl is ugly. What they see is not what she is.

What we *see* is not what *truly is*. It is only our perception. That is the theory here. For now, the only way to practice this is through transforming our ordinary perception. So you see, the theory and the instructions always come together and complement each other.

When it comes to the visualizations, quite a few people tend to have problems. Once you begin to understand the theory in a little bit more depth, you will also become quite comfortable with the visualizations. The main purpose of visualizing is to purify our impure vision, our ordinary perception. If this is the case, what is pure perception? The principle of pure vision is not meant to teach that we have to see things just as they are painted in Tibetan thangkas. This is how many people think of pure perception. Yet that is not right, and not at all the point. In fact, if you manage to transform everything so that it duplicates a thangka, the problem will only get worse because in paintings they don't blink their eyes or have backs; they are flat, frozen, and their clouds do not move! Anyway, for me personally, Tibetan paintings and pictures have no real vibrancy.

The whole point here is to destroy impure perception. So what do we mean by impure perception? Impure perception is basically everything that we see, perceive, and label at the moment. It is not that something is wrong out there and that's why everything is impure. Instead, it is because, at the moment, whenever we perceive something, it is always filtered through our emotions, our desire, jealousy, pride, ignorance, and aggression. When we look at a person, we may see him or her through the filter of our passion, and will therefore see him or her as very desirable. We may look at another person through the lens of aggression, which will cause us to see him or her as very ugly and hideous. When perceiving others through our own insecurity, we make judgements, refer, and compare, and end up trying to defend or boost our pride, which all stems from ignorance. The list goes on and on.

All the different perceptions we have arise from our very own minds and are coming through these emotions. That is why everything we experience ends up being a disappointment. Regardless of whether it is felt in a big or a small way, the point is that there is always a little bit of disappointment. This is what we are trying to purify.

This all comes down to training the mind. In the Shravakayana tradition, one trains the mind through physical and verbal discipline; by shaving the head, begging for alms, wearing saffron robes, and refraining from worldly activities, such as getting married. In the Mahayana, on top of that one trains the mind by meditating on compassion, bodhichitta, and so forth. In the Vajrayana, over and above these two, we try to transform our impure vision into something pure.

We learn to do this by going step-by-step through the ngöndro. Our very first step is to stop the chain of thoughts. We then expel the stale breath along with a bit of visualization. Finally, we cultivate the notion that the very place where we are is no longer an ordinary place. With these steps, we have begun to transform this impure vision.

The Three Sacred Principles

The next three points are what Patrül Rinpoche taught as the three sacred principles. In whatever you do, and in whatever Dharma practice you might be engaged in, always begin with the motivation to benefit all sentient beings. When we say benefit, this not only refers to ordinary help, such as giving food or ordinary assistance, but also the wish to enlighten all beings. The first sacred principle is extremely important because without it our practice will become self-oriented; it will be just another act of selfishness. For this reason, you should always be thinking, "I shall practice for the sake of all sentient beings."

Even with a simple act of lighting a lamp, always begin with bodhichitta. Lighting a lamp simply to make a room beautiful represents a very ordinary, worldly kind of thinking. Doing so to accumulate merit and thinking that it will destroy samsara is a Shravakayana attitude. The Mahayana approach would be to light the lamp and think, "With this merit may all sentient beings achieve enlightenment!" With a tantric attitude, on top of that you would think: "This light is not an ordinary light. It is the light of wisdom that illuminates all sentient beings. As the light shines, may everything become the deity and mandala!"

In the midst of performing any good deed, or even as you practice the preliminaries, you should also remember that whatever you do is only an interpretation of the mind. This second sacred principle is what we call the practice of nonduality. You need to repeatedly convince yourself of this with the thought, "My mind is doing this. I am just imagining this. None of this truly exists."

Let's say you are doing prostrations. In the very act of doing them, you can think: "It seems like 'I' am here doing prostrations. 'I' feel that 'I' am experiencing some sort of pain, but in reality, this is all in my mind!" Since this will eliminate any clinging you may have toward your Dharma deeds, the benefit of thinking in this way is incredible. This will also directly counteract your pride and ego. The Dharma is supposed to be an antidote to our ego, yet it can also reinforce the ego if we get the idea that we are "good Dharma practitioners." Hence, whenever you practice, you should always try to recognize that everything that is happening is all in your own mind. You might then wonder, "If it is only my mind, does that mean there is no merit?" Even the notions "there *is* merit," and "there is *no* merit" are interpretations of our minds.

For the last point, at the end of our practice, we always dedicate the merit. The merit we have accumulated is not kept for ourselves. Instead, we dedicate it to all sentient beings. It is important to keep in mind that you can dedicate the merit you gather right away. It doesn't necessarily have to be at the end of a session. You can even dedicate the merit you may have forgotten to dedicate in all your past lives. You can say: "I dedicate this merit I have just accumulated, this merit that I am aware of, have seen, and can observe. I also dedicate all the merit of the past that I am not aware of, and all the merit that I will generate in the future." All of this can be dedicated. These three points are called "the three sacred principles."

THE UNIQUE PRELIMINARIES

Refuge

Next is the explanation of taking refuge. The longer-length Longchen Nyingtik ngöndro was compiled from the writings of the great Jigmé Lingpa and edited by Jamyang Khyentsé Wangpo.[55] In this version, after chanting, "*Think of me, o guru!*" we recite a truly beautiful *calling the guru from afar* song. With this prayer, not only do we call upon our guru, we also chant lines that reveal the weaknesses that we as Dharma practitioners may have. This is extremely valuable to read and comprehend.

You may think that this critical perspective reflects a cultural difference, but it does not. Certainly, in the West, people are used to being encouraged and hearing things like: "You are doing well. Keep it up!" While in Asian cultures, the outlook is more critical. With Buddhism originating in India, you might think that this critical reflection has been influenced by its roots in Asian culture, but this is not the case. The whole purpose of the Dharma is to dismantle the protective system of the ego. For this very reason, every word of the Dharma, and each and every method the Dharma employs, must go against the ego. Reciting and contemplating liturgies like Jigmé Lingpa's "Calling the Guru from Afar" will poke holes in the ego. This is what we call the "dawn of the Dharma practitioner."

Most of us, including myself, are not really Dharma practitioners; we are

Dharma students. We may be interested and inspired by Dharma, and the Dharma may make sense from time to time, but to be a practitioner of the Dharma is entirely different. A practitioner is someone who has seen the futility of the eight worldly pursuits, or is at least attempting to give them up. That is really, really difficult. Having said this, it is not unachievable. I have definitely seen it being achieved among Westerners. With only thirty or forty years of history in the West, the Dharma is quite new, so for me, it is quite a surprise. Yet for many of us, the Dharma is already poking some holes in our fixation on these eight worldly pursuits.

There is one immediate motivation that inspires us to take refuge. In the ordinary theistic way of taking refuge, that trigger is most often fear, which is usually very mundane and related to loss and gain in this life. The Shravakayana attitude to practice is triggered by a fear of samsara. We fear going to hell, and consequently take refuge in God or even the Buddha as we pray for the release of heaven, or something of a similar nature. Surprisingly, although we think we are Vajrayana in orientation, many of us actually take the shravaka approach. Very few of us are really practicing the Vajrayana.

Then again, if we have the shravaka attitude, we should consider ourselves lucky. Shravakayana practitioners are very high in the scheme of things. Their attitude is very sophisticated because at least they are completely revolted by samsara. I don't think we can say the same. On the contrary, we tend to be in love with samsara.

In this sense, Shravakayana practitioners are extremely precious. Their primary fear is being caught by and dwelling in samsara. Farmers are afraid that there will not be timely or sufficient rainfall, so out of fear, they go to the Buddhist temple and pray to the Buddha for rain. In the shravaka tradition, whether or not there is abundant rainfall makes little difference. Samsara is bad, and they are afraid of samsara.

For the bodhisattva, there is a higher fear: the fear of nirvana. In the Vajrayana, this gets even more sophisticated. Not only is there fear of samsara and nirvana, there is also fear of impure perception. The Vajrayana practitioner knows that as long as you have impure perception, the root of extreme duality will never be dismantled. These are the reasons we take refuge in the Buddha, Dharma, and Sangha.

Depending on the varying levels of fear, there are different ways of taking refuge. For the farmer, Buddha is the creator of rain or, you could say, the guardian against hail. That is what they pray for. It is the farmer's way of taking refuge, and it is a very obscured kind of refuge. For the Shravakayana practitioner, the Buddha is a tutor, a coach who will show them how to renounce samsara. This is much better than the theistic approach.

In the Mahayana and Vajrayana, the refuge is different. Of course, we say similar things when reciting the refuge liturgy: "I take refuge in the Buddha, Dharma, and Sangha." While in the Longchen Nyingtik, we say, "I take refuge in prana, nadi, and bindu. I take refuge in the guru, yidam deity, and dakini. I take refuge in the dharmakaya, sambhogakaya, and nirmanakaya." It doesn't matter how you take refuge. The most essential part of the theory of refuge exists in the Mahayana, and especially in the Vajrayana. When we say, "I take refuge in the Buddha," what we are ultimately saying is "I accept that I can be enlightened, that I have buddha nature."

This is very important to understand. Without knowing the essential theory, if you just follow the key instructions you may end up just like one of the many Vajrayana practitioners who think that the Buddha is "out there," and then prays with that mind-set. This approach is very theistic. When taking refuge this way, there is not such a big distinction between Christianity and Buddhism. After all, apart from the name differentiation of "Buddha" and "Jesus Christ," what is the difference? It is like treating the Buddha as a God. This is why you need to know the theory of refuge. When we say, "I take refuge in the Buddha," we mean, "I accept that I can be a buddha"; that "I am buddha," actually. Here we can see a degree of divergence. "*I can be buddha*" is the Mahayana attitude. "*I am buddha*" is the Vajrayana attitude.

When we wash a cup, although we say we are washing the cup, what is actually being washed off is the dirt. The key instructions that your mother gives you are, "Go and wash the cup." No mother or father would go through all the trouble of telling you that the dirt and the cup are different and that you should actually go and wash the dirt. They would never say this. Otherwise, there would be too much conversation, and it would be too confusing, so the key instructions are simple. What you need to understand from the theory side is that you are not washing the cup, you are actually washing the dirt. If you managed to truly wash the cup, the cup would disappear. This tells us that the cup and the dirt are two separate entities. It also tells us that the dirt will come off; that the dirt itself is not the cup.

This example highlights the quintessence of taking refuge. If you lack insight into the quintessential refuge, you will have no confidence when you take refuge in the Buddha. For example, when a mother with some experience in housekeeping tells her son or daughter to wash a cup, she has confidence. She knows the dirt and the cup are separate entities. That is why a mother or father has this confidence to say, "Go and wash the cup." Likewise, in the Vajrayana and Mahayana, the theory tells us that we are buddhas; that buddha nature is within us. This dirt that we have is only temporary. Accepting and knowing that is the quintessence of taking refuge. That is the theory of refuge.

So what are the key instructions? The key instructions are like a dishwasher. These instructions vary. For the shravaka, the key instruction is to take refuge in the Buddha as a tutor. The Mahayana is very similar, but we also have the idea that we too can be buddhas. There is also a different kind of fear. Not only is there fear of samsara, but also fear of nirvana.

In the Vajrayana, the key instruction is to visualize the guru. Most key instructions tell us we should visualize the guru as a buddha, or as Guru Rinpoche. Basically, we are advised to visualize the guru in some extraordinary form, not in his or her ordinary appearance. Of course, we also visualize the guru surrounded by all the retinue figures: the dakas, dakinis, buddhas, bodhisattvas, and all the other objects of the refuge tree. This is what you visualize in front of you.

Let me explain a bit more about the theory and key instructions so it is easier to distinguish between the two. Let us shift back to the theory. You may wonder why we visualize the guru as a buddha or in some other form, or why we visualize the guru at all. Why don't we visualize Shakyamuni Buddha? The reason is that we have a hard time relating the notion of buddha nature to ordinary human beings. Second, seeing the guru as a buddha is very difficult. The guru yawns and does everything that we think of as ordinary; sometimes our guru seems to be quite ignorant, or spaced out, and maybe even does things that seem absolutely irrational. At other times, we think the guru is okay. The guru seems sort of intuitive and so on and so forth.

In his explanation of guru yoga, Jamyang Khyentsé Chökyi Lodrö explains that in the Mahayana and Vajrayana, we believe that buddha nature is manifesting all the time. However, when not refined by merit, this manifestation is usually expressed as pride, jealousy, anger, aggression, or passion. On the other hand, when accompanied by merit, it is visible as devotion, compassion, love, understanding, and tolerance. This devotion, which is none other than our own perception, is actually like a reflection. Devotion is like a door through which we are able to see someone worthy of following. This someone we call "guru." This is entirely a production of the merit that accompanies your buddha nature.

Even though countless buddhas and bodhisattvas have come and gone, most of us lack the merit to meet them. Even if you were to encounter them, you wouldn't have sufficient merit to see them as buddhas and bodhisattvas. Take Devadatta, for example, who was a cousin of the Buddha. He lived with Shakyamuni Buddha all of his life, yet because he was constantly jealous of the Buddha, he didn't gain one good thing out of this relationship. What you shouldn't forget is that the guru is an expression of your devotion and merit. As a reflection of this merit and devotion, you see your teacher as someone worthy and wholesome.

At the same time, however, the guru is also someone who pokes holes in your pride and your ego. After all, this is our objective, isn't it? At the very least, as a Dharma practitioner you are supposed to want this to happen. Wanting to keep your ego intact while going ahead and asking a guru to destroy the ego is not only painful, it is also criminal. For that matter, it just won't work. Thus, in taking refuge, we are essentially saying, "From now until I attain enlightenment, not only will I destroy superficial delusion, I will go right to the core and completely uproot this delusion." And what is the root of delusion? It is the ego.

The person you ask to destroy your ego is the guru. This is why ngöndro teachings say:

> In terms of qualities, the guru is equal to the Buddha, but the guru's kindness is greater than that of all the buddhas of the three times.

So many buddhas have come and gone, yet you have not met them, nor have they talked to you, but this guru—this buddha—has talked to you, upset you, disappointed you, hurt your pride, and so on. Since this is what you need, there you have it. Theoretically, this is why the guru is so important.

There is one more point to add to this. We may still question why we have to visualize the guru as a Guru Rinpoche. We may think, "Shouldn't I just visualize him the way he is? Having seen and walked with him, it is much easier for me to think of him, since I have seen him with my own eyes. Yet in my entire life, I have never once laid eyes on Guru Rinpoche. The only thing I can refer to are these Tibetan paintings and statues. Why make things more difficult?"

There is a very important theory for this. First of all, the whole purpose of the Vajrayana is to transform impure vision into pure perception. The way you see and experience the guru now is your own impure perception.

This is one of the impure perceptions that we need to get rid of. If you can't immediately destroy the impure perception of "ceiling is ceiling," "wall is wall" and "floor is floor" that is fine. It is more important to discard the impure perception of the guru. This is first and foremost. It is all your own interpretation that he yawns, sleeps, has ordinary thoughts, or acts strangely. It is this perception that needs to be transformed.

Jamyang Khyentsé Chökyi Lodrö once said, "If you treat the guru as an ordinary person, and pray to him as such, you will have a corresponding result." So if you think of the guru as a good, compassionate person, you will get that much blessing. If you think of the guru as an arhat, you will receive the blessings of an arhat, and if you think of the guru is a great bodhisattva on the first or tenth bhumi, then that is the blessing you will receive. Similarly, by thinking that the guru is a buddha, you will receive the tremendous blessings that correspond to that particular attitude. It all depends on your outlook. In any case, it is all your own perception.

Many misunderstandings tend to develop around devotion and the guru-disciple relationship, so it is important to understand this aspect of guru devotion. Nowadays, many in the West have begun to think that this whole guru system is a bit like a dictatorship. In the East, where we tend to find societies that are often Confucianist in their way of thinking, there is a notion that the leader is always right. Even if the leader says, "this wall is black," when it is actually white, all the subjects, and the whole social group will have to agree that the wall is black. If you look at China, this kind of thing is still going on. Whatever the leader says goes. At least in the West we can laugh at our leaders, but in China, whatever the boss says is right and that is final.

The guru concept is beyond dictatorship. It goes beyond "what the leader says is always right." The guru principle is completely different from this notion, and by understanding the theory, it should really clear away many doubts. There is one very important point that clarifies this. Please make a mental note of this, highlight it, and constantly keep it in your head: *Never, ever in the Vajrayana practice will you see a guru yoga practice where the guru does not dissolve into you.* If you were to find such a practice, it would be wrong. I can confidently say it would either be wrong, a mistaken text, or something taught by a phony teacher. In the Vajrayana system, there would never be a practice that does not require the merging of oneself and the guru.

This tells us that the guru principle is beyond the concept of dictatorship and the Confucianist ideal of worshipping the leader. When you worship the leader, the leader is always the leader. They are better, while you are always secondary. In the Vajrayana, the whole purpose of guru yoga and guru devotion is to recognize that your mind is the Buddha. Your mind is the ultimate guru. To reach this understanding, we have an outer guru, then the dissolution, and finally the merging of your mind and the guru's mind.

There is no ultimate dictator "up there" directing your everyday life. This is absolutely an incorrect way to understand this principle. The most quintessential point you need to realize is that your mind is the Buddha. That is the theory here. That said, the guru that manifests as a reflection of one's devotion is unquestionably important. Thus, paying homage to a qualified master and honoring what they teach is also crucial. Nonetheless, it is important to keep the theory in mind.

PROSTRATIONS

When you prostrate, visualize the objects of refuge right in front of you. If you are unable to do the elaborate visualization, simply visualize your guru in the form of Guru Rinpoche or Vajradhara and do that as best you can. There is really no need to dwell too much on the details of the visualizations. Just have confidence that the guru is there along with all the buddhas and bodhisattvas, and that you are really in front of the objects of refuge doing prostrations.

Prostrations are an immediate method to take refuge and also a way to destroy pride. As a gesture of surrender, and as an expression of the intent to totally give up and expose our pride, we throw ourselves at the feet of the guru. To symbolize this, we prostrate, placing the five points of our body— our forehead, hands, and knees—down on the floor. That is the theory.

To return to the key instructions, the traditional approach is to do one hundred thousand prostrations. It is actually quite important to have this target, yet some people argue that keeping track of the amount doesn't matter. Our minds are very strange. Whenever it suits us, we manage to bring in the theory of nonduality with ideas like "counting doesn't matter," but this only shows that we have resistance to doing the practice. Counting does matter. For us, as ordinary human beings, counting is a way to encourage and discipline ourselves. This discipline is a necessary process.

If you are physically able and have the time, you should do this practice. The pace at which you complete the one hundred thousand prostrations is relatively unimportant. Finishing them faster than someone else does not necessarily mean you will achieve enlightenment sooner. More important is your attitude and motivation. As far as pace goes, if you were to do 150 prostrations a day, which usually takes about half an hour at most, then within three years you will finish 100,000 prostrations quite comfortably.

For many of us, being quite worldly people, the motivation to do prostrations does not come that readily. We might encourage ourselves by thinking, "well, I should do prostrations because it is good for my health." I certainly do not discourage this way of thinking. Basically, in this day and age, anything that takes you toward the practice of Dharma is quite important. Doing prostrations saves money since you don't have to go to the gym. It accumulates merit *and* muscles. So at the very least, have this kind of motivation.

While doing the prostrations, after every twenty-five prostrations, or even after every ten, you should regenerate your motivation and think, "I want to do this for the sake of sentient beings." By regularly bringing bodhichitta to mind, you are also taking care of the merit side of things.

As you take refuge, imagine that the guru is there before you, and visualize your friends, family, and countless sentient beings all around you. You should especially imagine that all the people you find annoying are right in front of you. All of you are doing prostrations together. This is a very Mahayana attitude. Not only do you take refuge, all sentient beings take refuge along with you.

Toward the end, if you are accumulating prostrations and want to end the session, dissolve the objects of refuge into yourself. Otherwise, if you are doing the ngöndro as a daily practice, what follows next is the cultivation of bodhichitta. If this is the case, you do not need to dissolve the refuge objects. You can let them just remain, since you will need a witness for the act of cultivating bodhichitta. As you finish your session, imagine that all the objects of refuge melt into light and then dissolve into you. Alternately, the refuge objects don't even have to dissolve into light. You can imagine that they come toward you slowly and then dissolve into you.

Many people have the idea that as the objects of refuge dissolve into them, somehow they are like a big bag, and the objects are like apples being put inside the bag. This is not the right mind-set. If you are like a bag, and the refuge objects are like apples, it is not really a true dissolution. The reason here is that the apple and the bag are still viewed as separate. Many people dissolve in this way. They think to themselves, "I am an ordinary, worthless, useless, ugly, stupid sentient being, and now the guru and the buddhas come and sit somewhere inside of this mess." It is not like that.

To better understand the concept of dissolution, take the example of a broken pot. Say we have a pot. Inside the pot there is space, and outside the pot there is space. If you break the pot, the space inside and the space outside become inseparable. You cannot really tell which is which. You cannot say "this" or "that" make up the space of the pot. It is impossible to distinguish between the two. Likewise during the dissolution, you and the object of refuge become inseparable. This understanding is extremely important.

Once you complete the dissolution, remain in the state that follows as much as you can. In the Vajrayana, this is considered to be the essential practice. Therefore, if you have time, you can redo the visualization and then dissolve it again, watching the dissolution over and over. Just observe the state of oneness between yourself and the objects of refuge over and over again.

What does this do? This is a bit like casting a fishing rod with some bait to hook wisdom. At first you think of yourself as a pathetic, ignorant sentient being, then all of a sudden the object of refuge is there, a wholesome, great, beautiful buddha. You and the objects of refuge merge inseparably; then you simply observe that state. This will definitely actualize your inner wisdom.

When doing this practice, first thing in the morning sit up and stop the chain of thoughts. Once you've done that, you can continue to sit for as long as you like. Next, invoke renunciation mind by reflecting on impermanence, the precious human body, the futility of this life, and the essenceless quality of the eight worldly pursuits. When you are ready, clear the stale breath in three sets of three, making nine exhalations total. After that, transform your ordinary surroundings into a pure realm. To assist in doing this, you can invoke Guru Rinpoche and recite the Seven-Line Supplication three times. Then sit up straight and rest for a while.

Next, recite the liturgy up to the refuge prayer, which you should recite three times. The refuge prayer should be memorized, because when doing prostrations one is supposed to simultaneously recite the lines of refuge. There are many ways to do this. You can recite the verses out loud or silently. If you like, instead of reciting it them, you can contemplate and meditate on their meaning.

Visualize the objects of refuge in front of you, with your guru in the form of Guru Rinpoche, surrounded by the entire retinue. There are buddhas, bodhisattvas, shravakas, deities such as Chakrasamvara and Vajrakumara, as well as dakinis and dharmapalas. Think that you are in front of all these objects of refuge, along with all sentient beings.

As you take refuge, recite the verses from the ngöndro liturgy and bring to mind the theory of refuge, knowing that the guru and objects of refuge are an expression of your buddha nature. In the presence of the objects of refuge, think that you are taking the vow to enlighten all sentient beings. With this mind-set, recite the prayer of refuge and bodhichitta.[56]

If you are doing ngöndro as a daily practice, you should focus on the practices one by one. Whatever part of the practice you are accumulating is where you spend more time. For example, once you have finished one hundred thousand prostrations and are focusing on Vajrasattva, you would recite refuge and bodhichitta three times each and then proceed to Vajrasattva, concentrating more on that part of the practice. Once you have completed Vajrasattva, you would repeat the one-hundred-syllable mantra seven times and then concentrate on the mandala. That's how it works.

In the long version of the Longchen Nyingtik ngöndro, not only do you prostrate when taking refuge, but also during guru yoga. After refuge, bodhichitta, Vajrasattva, and the mandala offering, you come to the guru yoga. In guru yoga, in addition to the Seven-Line Supplication there is also the Seven-Branch Prayer. Traditionally, as you recite the Seven-Branch Prayer, you should do another one hundred thousand prostrations. Keep in mind that though one hundred thousand prostrations may sound difficult, for most of us it is not all that hard.

In ngöndro practice, you will come across many important terms. There are, for example, many different terms for buddha nature. Each term is used in a slightly different way, yet this is very necessary. "Self-occurring awareness" is a term we use when the guru introduces the nature of the mind, whereas the term "buddha nature" is used when we are establishing the view. In other words, "buddha nature" is more of a theoretical term. When discussing the fruition, we tend to use the term "dharmakaya," and when giving key instructions, we use terms like "rigpa," "self-occurring wisdom," and so on. For different occasions, there are different terms.

INSPIRATION

Sometimes we don't feel inspired to practice. This is quite understandable. Even I, myself, although I am rolling around in the Dharma all the time, still forget about practicing; I still forget that I am getting closer and closer to death. Those who are tending to babies or have some other job to do have a much harder go of it. When we have the time to practice, we don't have the inspiration, nor do we put that much energy into having it. We don't even give it the same degree of attention that we would to a football game!

Many people say to me: "I am so lazy! Rinpoche, what should I do?" The general antidote for this situation is to read Dharma books and listen to the stories of the great masters of the past. This will certainly inspire you. Reading something like "Milarepa's Songs" really does evoke some inspiration. Eventually, however, your clever mind will know how to escape from that also. I have read Milarepa's songs many times, and on many occasions, it has worked, so you should definitely read "Milarepa's Songs," *Words of My Perfect Teacher*, and other such works. There are so many beautiful, inspiring books.

What I am saying is that you can't rely solely on this. If you rely only on these methods, after a while you will become jaded. This is how we end up becoming callous. If the Buddha Shakyamuni himself decided to spend one whole month with you, for the first week it would be quite inspiring. But perhaps after one week, he would start to get on your nerves. You might end up thinking, "He is too perfect!" or "He doesn't make any mistakes!" That alone would get under your skin. Every time you look at him, you see his perfection. Then, with the stupidity of an ordinary human being, you would inevitably start making comparisons: "He is so good. How come I am not like him?"

For this kind of problem, for laziness and the loss of inspiration, again we take refuge in the Buddha, Dharma, and Sangha. We say, "Please, protect me from the menace of laziness and the loss of inspiration!" Then, if it helps, you can also light incense or candles. Evoking a sense of inspiration is quite necessary. This is a basic key instruction on how to practice taking refuge.

VIEW, CONDUCT, AND SKILLFUL MEANS

We should be very strict with our actions, but at the same time we should adopt a Vajrayana-like view. The classic way of putting this is to say that we should take the outer form of the Shravakayana, the inner attitude of the Mahayana, and the secret practice of the Vajrayana. How can you do all of this at once? You should always take the highest view and apply it to the subtlest action. The subtlest, in this case, is the conduct found in the Shravakayana. For example, the shravaka emphasis on not harming others includes very wholesome actions like not eating meat or drinking alcohol. If people look at you and see your actions are wholesome, they will feel inspired by you. Along with this conduct, however, you should always have the Vajrayana view. Your conduct should not take over the view or vice versa.

Apart from the three nonvirtuous deeds of the mind, all other actions are allowed and encouraged if they are for the benefit of sentient beings. On top of not harming, but rather helping sentient beings, the Vajrayana practitioner must also be genuine. Sometimes we try to act and behave nicely, but the very act of inspiring people ends up becoming stifling. By placing so much emphasis on being an inspiration, we end up getting carried away by our conduct, and we become contrived. The act of inspiring may get tainted by one of the eight worldly pursuits, such as wanting praise and not wanting to be criticized. This is why Mahayana, and Vajrayana practitioners in particular, try to be as genuine and natural as possible.

The highest view must always be integrated with a variety of actions, including those that may be considered the lowest. Were you to apply only the highest view and the highest methods, you would not be able to get through to anyone. As a bodhisattva, you have to be able to effectively communicate with people, just as the Buddha was able to in his time. Nowadays, many people in the West have this idea that the Buddha was unfair to women since he is reputed to have spoken lowly of women in the Shravakayana teachings. In fact, this is a very good example of the Buddha having applied the highest view and the subtlest action. What you have to realize is the Buddha lived in India 2,500 years ago. India has long had a Brahmanic culture; there is a five-thousand-year history of Hindus dominating the country. There is also a strong caste system, with high castes, low castes, and untouchables.

In the Buddha's era, there was a strong cultural hierarchy between men and women. As a matter of fact, the Buddha is considered to be one of the great reformers. He was a revolutionary. He deconstructed the view of an ultimate, truly existing, permanent creator and refuted the notion of a caste system. In making his reforms acceptable to the public, these issues happened to be outwardly more important than sexism. Were he to have gone against all of these issues at the same time, nobody would have listened.

There is another relevant point here that many Westerners don't seem to understand. In the Vajrayana, the Buddha went beyond saying men and women are equal. In certain tantras, he even indicated that women are more important. This usually gets completely forgotten and ignored. One of the most important points in the Vajrayana is samaya. There are fourteen root samayas. These fourteen are the most crucial things that a Vajrayana practitioner must heed. The last of these fourteen samayas stipulates that women are the nature of wisdom, and that if you ignore this, you are breaking a Vajrayana vow, just as not holding bodhichitta and regarding the body as ordinary are also against Vajrayana principles.

This shows how skillful the Buddha was. Think about it. If you were a psychologist, how would you talk to your patients? Let's say your patient is addicted to coffee. Would you, as a skillful, compassionate psychologist, go and say, "No, don't drink coffee." Would you say that? Surely, you would say, "Maybe you should try decaf . . . how about that?" You have to slowly work through their clouded thinking. Only in the end can you say, "Coffee is bad for you." This is exactly what the Buddha did, although many Western Buddhists seem to miss this point.

Being people of a specific cultural upbringing, it's easy for Westerners to think that the Buddha was unfair, but keep in mind that we are talking about a society that existed 2,500 years ago. In particular, it was a Hindu society, where some people, referred to as the "untouchables," were even prohibited from standing up in certain places. It was believed that if they were to do so, the shadow they cast on the ground would make it an unclean place.

Even today, men dominate society more than women. It's very unequal. This is unfortunate, but that is the human mind. Societies have always looked down on women. In America, we find large organized groups fighting for women's rights and liberation, but despite all this, it is one of the only countries that has yet to place even one woman in a true position of power. The highest status that has manifested for a woman is secretary of state. In Asia, a region thought to look down on and even abuse women, women have held these high positions. Sri Lanka, for instance, was the first country to elect a female prime minister.

Bodhichitta

In the short liturgy of the Longchen Nyingtik ngöndro, refuge and bodhichitta are both included in one shloka, or stanza. However, be aware that bodhichitta is actually one of the main foundations of practice. Usually, when we refer to the "four foundations," refuge is counted as the first, bodhichitta as the second, then Vajrasattva, and finally mandala offering. When we talk about the "five foundations," we add guru yoga.

Contemplating bodhichitta is absolutely essential. Older Buddhists may consider themselves less at risk of being attracted to a mistaken view or path. Though many of us have this attitude, we have to be careful. Though we might not go against the Buddha or the Buddhadharma in any obvious way, falling prey to a mistaken view and getting attracted by a wrong path is quite easy. There are a number of reasons for this. First of all, most of us take a very theistic approach, owing to the habit of being theistic over many life times. This also ends up being an eternalistic approach, which is why we see Buddhists who are actually eternalists. Then there is the nihilistic approach, which we especially find among those who believe they have understood a little about emptiness. The problem is that with the wrong view, such people may appear to be Buddhists, but they are actually more like nihilistic atheists. They may think of themselves as Buddhists and not consciously go against the Buddha and his words, but still, it is a wrong path.

Another obvious issue that we should be cautious about, especially in the Vajrayana and Tibetan Buddhism in general, is the necessity of the view. This is a degenerate time, and there are many phony teachers around. Despite the many colorful methods they may use, there are certain teachings that neglect to teach the ground of the view. I have noticed many of us getting distracted by these colorful methods. Without being grounded in the basic view, there is a belief that the path is genuine. If you have taken this route, you are trapped on a wrong path. We may feel that we are seasoned Buddhists, but this danger is present every moment of every day.

Assuming that we have managed to divert our attention from the wrong path and are following the right one, there are three different approaches we can take. To enhance our determination to not only take the right path, but also the superior path, we practice bodhichitta. We are now talking about the Mahayana, which is a path of dwelling in neither samsara nor nirvana. The quintessence of the Mahayana path is bodhichitta. This is what makes it superior as a path.

Many of us have a vague idea about the Mahayana concept of bodhichitta, that it has something to do with kindness, tolerance, and humanitarianism. Although quite good, this understanding is really not enough. This is only one small aspect of bodhichitta. If your understanding of absolute bodhichitta is limited to the notion of kindness, compassion, tolerance, humanitarian charity work, or even the sacrifice of your own life for the sake of others, you still do not have a complete picture of bodhichitta.

To have a complete picture, we should not forget that there is relative *and* ultimate bodhichitta. At interreligious conferences, we have little choice but to speak diplomatically and say: "Christians talk about love and compassion. Judaism talks about love and compassion. We Buddhists talk about love and compassion. Therefore all religions talk about love and compassion. We all have the same goal, but different routes." This is what interreligious conferences are for; I am not trying to be chauvinistic. What I am saying is that

Buddhist compassion, and the Mahayana concept of compassion in particular, does not stop there. There is something further behind this compassion. It can be the same as the very love, compassion, and tolerance that makes you codependent and eventually backfires on you. Tolerance and compassion that do not have bodhichitta will victimize you in the end. You need a complete picture of bodhichitta.

When we talk about this "complete picture of bodhichitta," we are referring to ultimate bodhichitta. What is ultimate bodhichitta? It is an understanding of emptiness. It is extremely important that emptiness be in union with compassion. Actually, this is something we touched on briefly when talking about the three sacred principles. We discussed the necessity of beginning practice with a good motivation, with the wish to enlighten all sentient beings, and then the realization that whatever you do is the manifestation of your own mind.

Here, we are already approaching emptiness, in terms of the nonduality aspect. If we are missing nonduality, our every act will lead to disappointment. How far do you go, if you are a therapist trying to help an alcoholic or drug addict? If this person has somehow decided to become a drug addict for the next five thousand lifetimes, you, as a bodhisattva, must have the determination to be reborn wherever they are going to be reborn. You might, for instance, aspire to be reborn at the right time and place to be nearby him or her. Say for example, you are a bodhisattva and have been trying to help this drug addict for over two thousand lifetimes. Now, somewhere in an obscure place, their 2,042nd rebirth is going to happen. Although you need to appear for only half a day, in order to do that you have to actually be reborn there. It is almost a waste of a complete whole life, to be reborn there just to do something that will take only half an hour, or half a day, but as a bodhisattva you must do it. That is what we call the strength and quality of relative compassion.

Now we come to the real quintessence of bodhichitta. Why does a bodhisattva have this degree of compassion? Why don't they give up? What is the real basis of their confidence? The bodhisattva realizes that the notion of "drug addict," "problem," "healing," and "being healed," are all in their own mind. The bodhisattva knows that none of this exists "out there" somewhere, externally and truly. Based on this wisdom, the bodhisattva can develop compassion.

This understanding can really help. My own experience is like being a firefly in front of the sun. Even so, when I try to help people and things don't work according to plan, I say to myself, "How can I get frustrated?" In the first place, I myself have set up a certain goal based on my own interpretation. In helping a person, I imagine that he or she should reach a certain level, but this is entirely my own idea. After becoming obsessed with the idea of success, when the person is not there, I might lose hope and confidence in this person. Sometimes we do realize that it is all our own projection, but most of the time, we don't. Instead, we think: "This is how it should be. This is real success!" We don't realize that it is all our own interpretation. This is where we go blind. When you are helping, if you know that your so-called "help," "success," and "failure" are all in your own mind, you won't get worn out. Because you realize that it is all your mind's doing, you won't get tired. This is a very general and somewhat coarse example of ultimate bodhichitta. If you have this understanding, you have a complete picture of bodhichitta.

To reiterate, ultimate bodhichitta is an understanding of emptiness. Only when this is included is there a complete picture of bodhichitta. Most of the time, however, it is this aspect that is missing. When we talk about bodhichitta, usually we make reference to something simple, such as a kind compassionate heart, but that's not all. This is something many people have. It does not necessarily make you a bodhisattva. Of course, this is not to deny that there are very kind and compassionate people. There are people who may even sacrifice their lives for others, but still, they may not be bodhisattvas. In fact, they are in danger of acting out their obsession and could end up being victimized by their goal-oriented mind. Being too obsessed with a goal can produce a lot of side effects, such as thinking, "This is how it should work!" With this approach, a bodhisattva can lose hope and determination when things do not work out; they may even stop being a bodhisattva. Having said this, a bodhisattva should not just do things aimlessly.

For a bodhisattva, understanding emptiness does not mean simply to think, "Oh, this is emptiness," whenever something does not work out, and to stop there. As bodhisattvas, we carry on. Especially if we are just beginning as a bodhisattva, we carry on in accordance with the instructions, such as those found in the *Bodhicharyavatara*, as much as we can. Having this determination is part and parcel of relative bodhichitta. Relative bodhichitta and ultimate bodhichitta must always be brought together. In fact, they are two different aspects of the same thing.

Relative bodhichitta itself has two aspects, one being aspiration and the other application. Application bodhichitta has the sense of "entering" or "action," meaning to put bodhichitta into action with an act of generosity, discipline, or another one of the other six perfections. Aspiration bodhichitta is practicing or generating the motivation. It is the wish or aspiration.

One might think that aspiration bodhichitta seems quite lowly, with application bodhichitta superior and ultimate bodhichitta the highest. This, however, is not the case; they are equal in importance. In fact, lamas have said that for beginners like us, it's obvious that ultimate bodhichitta is only possible at an intellectual level. Most of the time, when we think about emptiness, in that moment we are creating something totally the opposite of what emptiness actually is. But at least we have some kind of intellectual understanding; this is a good start. Even application bodhichitta is difficult for many beginners. For instance, within the six perfections, generosity is probably the easiest to practice, but how much are we able to practice this? We are not endowed with enough wealth at either a spiritual or worldly level. We cannot feed and teach everyone, nor are we equipped with a tool for all situations. Maybe once in a while we can throw some coins at a beggar. To completely engage in application bodhichitta is difficult. Can you imagine cutting off your own limbs and feeding a hungry tiger, as the great bodhisattvas of the past have done?

For beginners like us, Jigmé Lingpa said that one must first learn and practice aspiration bodhichitta. This is something we can really practice. We can easily generate the aspiration, "I wish I were a king," for example, and then imagine ourselves to be a king giving everything away to beggars. There are all kinds of aspirations we can make, such as, "May all sentient beings have everything they need!"

As you read this, you may start to think: "That is just a wish. Wishing is well and good, but it doesn't really *do* anything." To belittle an aspiration in this way is unwise because the wishing or aspiring aspect is a very important part of the training. Why are we unable to perform active bodhichitta and ultimate bodhichitta? It is due to our lack of determination, to the weakness of our aspiration bodhichitta. It would seem that the only aspiration we have is when reciting prayers! Nevertheless, wishing to enlighten all sentient beings and wishing for everyone's happiness is something we can practice. So during bodhichitta practice, we place greater emphasis on "aspiring" bodhichitta. We aspire so that we are able to carry out "entering" and "ultimate" bodhichitta.

As you recite the bodhichitta liturgy, you can do all three aspects of bodhichitta together in your mind. Thinking, "May all sentient beings be happy!"

is aspiration bodhichitta. Then, to actually do prostrations for the sake of all sentient beings and to have sacrificed some of your precious time to recite prayers is the beginning of application bodhichitta. In sacrificing your time, you are practicing generosity. You are sitting up straight. Even if you do this for just a moment, what is happening? At least you are not harming anyone. Imagine the whole world, all of humanity, sitting straight everyday for five minutes. If this were to happen, 50 percent of the world's problems would disappear, just through sitting. So the sitting itself is discipline, as is cutting the chain of thoughts. Then, transforming your surroundings into a pure realm is samadhi. Thus, you can call this application bodhichitta. Lastly, toward the end of bodhichitta and refuge, you dissolve the field of merit into you and the two of you become inseparable. For however long it lasts, be it a few moments, minutes, or hours, you are watching the inseparability of the guru's mind and your own. You just watch. You watch and watch without any fabrication, and what is this? This is a way of meditating on ultimate bodhichitta. In this way, you are practicing all three bodhichittas together.

In generating bodhichitta, we really have to train our minds. For this, relative bodhichitta is the most crucial. What is bodhichitta mind? Certainly, it is not simply a matter of thinking, "Those poor men need help." Compared to bodhichitta, this humanitarian mind-set is of a much lower class.

Bodhichitta is the wish to enlighten all sentient beings. Helping sentient beings to dismantle their delusion is the best gift you could ever give. What better gift could you offer? Make sentient beings see their own true natures. Make them see this endless net of delusion. What could be better than seeing sentient beings released from this endless cocoon that they themselves have formed? As you can see, this mind-set is not merely a desire to help someone with a temporary problem.

During public gatherings, I have been asked on many occasions why Buddhists are not doing things to contribute in the same way that Christians are. Why are there no Buddhist hospitals, no Buddhist hospices? If answering in public, I would say, "Because Buddhists are lazy, and being lazy and selfish, Buddhists only talk about compassion." Indeed, this is partially true. In a more select group, I would say: "We should really rejoice for those Christians, Muslims, and Hindus, but even that we don't do!" Then, if speaking to a smaller, more selective group, there would possibly be a more detailed answer.

Suppose there is this religious group building thousands of childcare facilities or hospices. Again, this is a big generalization, because perhaps among them there is a bodhisattva as a Muslim, a Christian, or Hindu. But let's say that although these religious workers are doing a lot of caring work, there is no wish to enlighten sentient beings. Their aim is just to provide food and education. At the same time, imagine there is one hermit living somewhere in the mountains of the Himalayas who is doing none of this. In fact, within close range of him, there are a lot of babies dying, yet outwardly he is doing nothing about it. Inwardly, however, he is actually meditating, "May all sentient beings be enlightened!" and he continues to do this every day. Purely because of the enlightenment aspect, this person is worthier of homage than the first group. Why? Because it is so difficult to truly and genuinely wish for the enlightenment of others. It is much easier to give people food and educate them.

Most of us don't really appreciate this fact. We have never before genuinely wished for someone else to achieve enlightenment. Likewise, if someone were to come over and say to us: "Here you go, you have a ticket for enlightenment. There is only one ticket." I don't think we would even think about giving it to someone else! We'd grab it and go for it. Enlightenment is such a valuable thing.

Actually, enlightenment is much too large a subject, so let's not take that as an example. Instead, let's say someone comes along with a potion that promises you clairvoyance or omniscience. We would drink it ourselves, not even sharing half of it with others! Just think how often we are jealous when someone is a better practitioner. How often do we get jealous when someone receives a better or a higher teaching than we do? If you have genuine bodhichitta, you should be happy, shouldn't you? After all, isn't that what you wished for? Their getting enlightenment means your wish is at last coming true. Their receiving higher teachings, or becoming better practitioners, means that your aspiration is finally being fulfilled! But we don't feel this way, instead we feel jealous or envious. Some of us may be so-so Dharma practitioners, so we don't really feel jealous or envious, but we still feel left behind. Who cares? If you are a genuine bodhisattva, you shouldn't care about these things.

THE BODHISATTVA

There are three kinds of bodhisattva: the "kinglike" bodhisattva, the "boatmanlike" bodhisattva, and the "shepherdlike" bodhisattva. Among these, the most popular is the shepherdlike bodhisattva. The kinglike bodhisattva is a bodhisattva who wishes to become enlightened first and then to enlighten others. The boatmanlike bodhisattva is someone who wants to bring sentient beings to enlightenment together. The shepherdlike bodhisattva wishes to enlighten all sentient beings first and then, if necessary, get enlightened him- or herself. The third kind of bodhisattva is the one we should be aspiring toward.

Wishing to give the wisdom of enlightenment away is a mighty offering. Shantideva's *Bodhicharyavatara* discusses this at length. Out of the ten chapters found in this text, you should at least read the first eight. If you don't have that much time, however, you can read the first three chapters. This text contains some beautiful stanzas that explain why bodhichitta is essential. Bodhichitta is not merely a kind, compassionate, and humanitarian mind-set. It is much more than that. You can be compassionate, loving, and tolerant and yet still have ego. Bodhichitta, on the other hand, is a complete antidote for the ego. This is why it is so special.

If a social worker has this notion of destroying the ego, then this individual is doing social work with bodhichitta. But let's say a social worker is doing a lot of work to heal temporary pain, but has no bodhichitta, while at the same time there is a man in a cave doing nothing at all, or at least, he is not helping anyone in a physical sense. All he does is cultivate aspiration bodhichitta. As mentioned before, the man in the cave is more worthy of homage. Though of course, without appreciating the value of enlightenment, this idea is not easily accepted by a general audience. Shantideva addresses this point in the first chapter of the *Bodhicharyavatara*, where he says:

> Could our fathers or our mothers
> Ever have so generous a wish?
> Do the very gods, the rishis, or even Brahma
> Harbor such benevolence as this?

Who on this earth has given you enlightenment? Neither your father or mother, nor even the gods Indra and Brahma. Even they, compared to a bodhisattva, are not the kindest. If someone heals you temporarily from pain, while another is not doing much to heal you in a temporary sense but is genuinely planning on helping you permanently, it is this latter person you need to appreciate more.

You may think that doing humanitarian work will destroy the ego automatically, but this is not necessarily the case. It can also create a lot of ego. In fact, not only have many social workers not destroyed their ego, some have ended up abusing the very funds they collected to do humanitarian work!

The question is, "Which has greater value, one's view or one's actions?" It is the view that has to be valued more. Motivation as well is usually triggered by the view. Depending on what view you have, you will then have a corresponding motivation.

GENERATING BODHICHITTA

Two popular methods to generate bodhichitta are *tonglen*, or sending and taking, and what we call "the four immeasurables." In the short liturgy of the Longchen Nyingtik, bodhichitta is brief and condensed; there is no mention of these practices. While it is not as though you are missing something or have made a mistake by not practicing them, if you have time, it is a good idea to incorporate both.

Tonglen is well known and widely practiced. It is a great method to generate aspiration bodhichitta. As with other meditations, tonglen can be combined with a breathing exercise. On the out-breath, without any partiality, you give away all your happiness, virtue, and other valuable things to each and every sentient being. While breathing in, absorb the pain, suffering, problems, obscurations, and nonvirtues of all these beings, not just one or two of them. This is aspiration bodhichitta.

As a beginner bodhisattva, this is all we can do. Yet this is not to say aspiration bodhichitta is something simple. If you want to become courageous enough to cut off your limbs and give them to a hungry tiger, you have to begin by fine tuning your motivation, and tonglen meditation is a very powerful method for doing so.

The four immeasurables are another popular method. These may be combined with tonglen. For the first immeasurable, think, "May all sentient beings be happy, right now in this very moment!" Let's say that somewhere, in this very instant, someone is having a problem or is very depressed. Since the first immeasurable is loving-kindness, we can think, "May all sentient beings be happy!" With this thought, we imagine that somewhere, someone is receiving what he or she wants, what they wished for, that their expectations are fulfilled, and that they are freed from their fears. We also think, "May they have the cause of happiness," in which case we meditate and think, "May all sentient beings at this very moment have compassion and love." Hence, the first immeasurable thought is "May sentient beings have happiness and the causes of happiness." This differs from the ordinary humanitarian sense of giving because we are giving happiness and also its causes.

The second immeasurable thought is, "May all sentient beings be free from suffering." Suppose a number of people are suffering from depression. In this case, we can think: "May they be free from that depression. May they also be free from the causes of suffering: the emotions and all nonvirtuous thoughts and actions. May they be free of suffering in this very moment!" In addition, we think, "May sentient beings refrain from killing, stealing, lying, and be free from all negative emotions," because these are the causes of unhappiness. Here, you have given away happiness and the causes of happiness, and have also managed to separate them from unhappiness: from suffering and the causes of suffering.

As a result of all this, they experience joy. You then meditate on the third immeasurable thought, which is "May they remain in this joy forever."

The fourth immeasurable is equanimity. For this, think to yourself, "May all sentient beings be free from hope and fear. May all sentient beings be free from passion and aggression. Having discarded the dualistic notion of kin and enemies, may all become neutral. Being neither aggressive toward enemies, nor attached toward friends, may all become equal." You then remain with that.

Understanding the benefits and purpose of compassion and bodhichitta is extremely important. For this reason, please read *The Words of My Perfect Teacher*, especially the section where Patrül Rinpoche sings the praises of compassion and bodhichitta. In this book, Patrül Rinpoche presents some very good key instructions on how to arouse bodhichitta.

Bodhichitta is the cream of the Dharma. It is a shame that although we Buddhists talk about the greatness of bodhichitta and compassion a great deal, we don't always manage to put them into practice. In every situation, we should try to develop a good heart. After all, a good heart is the key to love, compassion, and bodhichitta. Without bodhichitta, every practice you do will reinforce the ego.

At the moment, the idea of engaging emptiness may be too complicated to really enter our heads. For now, the best antidote to ego is bodhichitta, the wish to enlighten each and every sentient being. If you have really developed the notion of enlightening all beings, wishing someone to be unhappy is almost impossible. Furthermore, though you are aiming for the highest form of happiness, you still rejoice even when sentient beings receive only a small form of happiness. You can see why this undermines the ego.

As the Kadampas repeatedly remind us, the practice of bodhichitta involves cultivating an attitude that prompts you to give gain to others and take loss for yourself. Some people might assume that this would cause one to lose confidence, yet the bodhisattva attitude of giving gain and happiness to others and not minding when loss or unpleasantness falls to oneself is not at all an attitude of low self-esteem. In fact, it's just the opposite. With this attitude one is actually creating confidence.

What does it mean to have low self-esteem? It means having a very, very large ego; this is why there is low self-esteem in the first place. There is too much ego, and it is this ego that always wants to be good and worthy. Feeling that your ego is not good is what we call low self-esteem. With the bodhisattva attitude, however, you give everything good to others and are not bothered if something bad happens to you. With this mind-set, there is no reference point, so it is confidence that grows, while low self-esteem never gets a chance to manifest. So don't be afraid of applying bodhichitta again and again!

During the practice itself, when you are coming to the end of a session, mix your own being with the guru's. Then simply watch what happens in that moment. If thoughts come, just watch the thoughts. As a beginner, you may get distracted. If you do, immediately revisualize the guru and merge again. You can watch this inseparability again and again. When I say watch, I am not asking you to recall what happened in your mind in the past, nor to plan to watch the mind in the future. I am talking about watching the mind in this very present moment. In order to do this, the key is to first dissolve the guru into yourself and then just observe what happens.

Many people get frustrated and wonder whether or not they're doing the practice the "right" way. The tip here is simple: just do it. Just dive in; after a while you will get the gist of it. When you are learning to drive, for example, you can go on talking about the breaks, gears, steering, and clutch forever, but somehow, sometime, you just have to drive, don't you? You just turn on the ignition, press gas, and go. You just have to do it. That is the key instruction.

It might sound like this just won't work right now. For a year or two, you might even go through a period where dissolving the guru into yourself is more like putting an apple into a bag. But that's the only way. After a while, it will be more like putting a glass of water into a bag. The bag might get a bit wet, yet you will also begin to understand the bag; you will already have gotten the gist of it. After some time, you will come to realize that merging with the guru is like breaking a clay pot and trying to find two separate, empty spaces.

Right now, this is the only practical tip that works. The fact is that we cannot help thinking that the guru, or the Buddha, is an independent entity and separate from ourselves. Recognizing this is actually an improvement. Remember that practicing Dharma is like peeling off a layer of skin. With this recognition, your theistic skin is about to be peeled off. At first, you have no choice but to practice in a theistic way, but a nontheistic attitude will gradually evolve. Then another layer of skin will be peeled off.

This sort of confusion is good. Of the many doubts that come up, not all are bad. Certain doubts are what we normally cherish as a discerning mind, so being critical can be helpful, especially where you find fault with your own ego's interpretation. This is a sign that the Dharma is entering your mind. We don't often adopt a critical attitude toward our ego's interpretation. Instead, we completely buy into it. When the Dharma is beginning to seep into our heads, we start feeling very critical about what we think; that's a good sign. That said, we shouldn't dwell on it. We should always try to go forward, to go further.

VISUALIZATION

Everything is an interpretation. This is not only the basis of Buddhist philosophy; it is also the reason why visualization works. When you refer to yourself as, "Louise," although you don't call it a visualization, actually, it is. Similarly, looking at your friend, "Lucinda," for example, is also a visualization. What you see is all stemming from your own imagination. Your Lucinda and my Lucinda may be completely different. It is on this basis that visualization works. It is a wonderful method.

Many people think that visualization is a Tibetan thing. Since very few teachers have put the effort into explaining the theory, this is understandable. Though we may assume that visualization is cultural or theistic, it is not. It is just that the method always seems to be emphasized at the expense of the theory. We are told to visualize this and visualize that, but never why it works, or why we should do it a certain way. This never gets explained, which is why we have such difficulty.

It is also on this basis that, as I mentioned earlier, visualizing Guru Rinpoche as we see him painted in a Tibetan thangka is pretty much a waste of time. Even if everyone were to use the same Tibetan thangka, as soon as each person looks at it, they have their own perception. Your perception is just that: *your* perception. What's more, your perception is probably not even close to what the original painter had in mind. For this reason, as you visualize Guru Rinpoche or any other deity, you might as well be a little bold in your visualization.

Guru Rinpoche is a superior, sublime being. In our ordinary minds, we think a sublime being has to look good, but what, exactly, does it mean to be "good looking"? Again, you have a certain interpretation of what it means to be good looking, and I have another. So you had better make use of your own interpretation. Surely, there is no need to learn mine! Even if you were to ask, "Rinpoche, what is your idea of good looking?" It would be you and your mind that would listen to my answer. You might think you have understood my version of "good looking," but actually you have not. Inevitably, you will end up with your own interpretation.

Visualization is really based on personal interpretation. Given this fact, your next question might be, "When visualizing Guru Rinpoche, since I like walkmans, digital cameras, and video cameras, is it okay if I visualize my Guru holding a digital camera instead of a vajra, and a laptop computer instead of a kapala?" This is where we would have a bit of a dispute. We are not really encouraged to make these sorts of innovations ourselves. Only when a qualified master—a tertön or contemporary treasure discoverer—reveals a teaching where Guru Rinpoche is holding a digital camera in his right hand and a laptop in his left, and we have received that transmission, could we visualize in this way.

It is not out of convenience that we place a vajra in his hand, nor is it because it looks beautiful. In fact, there is a lot of symbolism involved. Why does he have one face? Why not two? Why does he have a vajra in his hand? Why does he hold a kapala? Each aspect has its own significance, which is something that should always be kept intact; all the right attributes need to be there. Nevertheless, if you were to search the entire Tibetan Buddhist canon, you still wouldn't find anything that says, "This is exactly how Guru Rinpoche looks." Interestingly enough, there is a statue of Guru Rinpoche called the *Looks Like Me* statue, but there are a number of other statues that are reported to be close likenesses of Guru Rinpoche as well, and they all look different!

There is one further rule about visualization. Not only should the visualization be alive, vibrant, and clear, it should always be sealed with the idea of nonduality. During ngöndro teachings this is usually not emphasized, though it often comes up in teachings on actual sadhana practice. Anyhow, to give you some idea about how to get into this nonduality business, there are visualizations of Guru Rinpoche seated in his palace. The palace, however, is said to be as big as Mount Meru, or as big as the entire universe, while Guru Rinpoche is as small as a sesame seed. Even so, you neither find it to be an inconvenience, nor is it unaesthetic. The container is neither too big nor are the contents too small, nor is there a vast a gap between Guru Rinpoche and his palace. There are no such problems. Conversely, for that very visualization, and within that same state of meditation, you can also visualize the palace to be as small as a sesame seed and Guru Rinpoche as big as the whole universe. Yet Guru Rinpoche is actually inside this small sesame seed–sized palace. All of this is an exercise in nonduality. Visualization needs to have these qualities.

Vajrasattva

Before we begin to explain Vajrasattva practice, we should remember that the essence of practice, not only of the Longchen Nyingtik ngöndro, but also of any ngöndro, is training the mind. Generally speaking, the phrase "training the mind" refers to making our rigid minds more flexible. Why is the mind rigid? The mind is rigid because we fall prey to our emotions, and not only to the emotions, but also to the objects of the emotions: hope and fear. Almost everything we think and feel, or for that matter, almost everything interpreted by the mind, is based on hope or fear. For this reason, our minds are always bound by jealousy, pride, passion, aggression, ignorance, or some other emotion. We operate this way constantly and have done so for a very long time. This is why we have no control over our minds, why the emotions and their objects control our minds instead. This is what we mean by "rigid mind."

It is this rigid mind that we are trying to train, or to tame. There are many similar terms, such as "train," "tame," and "recognize," that are either applied at different stages, or used separately in the different vehicles. For instance, Shravakayana methods tend to use words like "tame." In this approach, this wild, rigid mind is viewed as something that must be tamed. The Mahayana, in contrast, would use the term "train." Rather than simply taming this wild, rigid mind, according to the Mahayana it can also be turned into something useful with the right training. In the Vajrayana, because of the view and determination, we go beyond "taming" and "training." Instead, we talk about "recognizing" the mind. So you see, each of the three vehicles has a slightly different approach. Yet these slight variations in approach actually make a considerable difference.

For now, let's refer to all that we are doing here as "training" the mind. The first and most important step in this process is to recognize the futility of samsara, to see the futility of worldly life and reflect on this again and again. As long as you place some value in this worldly life, there will always be a loophole in your Dharma practice. For this reason, we have to recognize that samsaric life is futile; we must truly invoke this mind-set. The traditional approach is to hear the preliminary thoughts over and over again. The Dharma is so vast, yet there is still merit in listening to these teachings again and again because it brings to mind the futility of samsara.

In the study of Buddhism, we talk about three kinds of wisdom: the wisdom that comes from hearing, the wisdom that comes from contemplation, and the wisdom that comes from meditation. In Tibetan, we call these three "*tö sam gom sum.*" The first word here, *tö*, means to listen and hear, yet it also has the meaning of study. I've noticed that many people seem to be missing this first element to some degree; either they haven't read very much about the Dharma, or they haven't listened to many teachings. From some of the questions that arise, it is apparent that people often take things quite literally.

The ability to understand the Dharma and its terminology from all angles is quite important. Even when it comes to the importance of understanding the futility of samsara, there will be some who read this and immediately think: "Oh, I know this. It is very true. My family life is useless and my job is pointless. I want to get out of this!" Some may actually try to abandon these things. What is not understood is that this itself can be a samsaric thought. This is not always the case, but it can be. It could be that you just want to have a long rest. You are tired of your present family situation, tired with this phase of life, and the Dharma happens to provide an excuse. Renunciation happens to be just the pretext to create another form of life. If you have understood renunciation in this way, you have either misinterpreted the teachings or not thoroughly understood them.

It's like this. Suppose you are dreaming, and let us imagine that your dream is a nightmare. You will obviously want this bad dream to end, but that in itself is not renunciation mind. Here, you just do not want the nightmare; you want a good dream. Renunciation mind, on the other hand, is knowing that it is a dream. That's it – period, full stop. We do not need to talk about whether something is good or bad. If it is bad, it is a dream; if it is good, it is a dream. To know *that* is renunciation mind. Sometimes life is tough, futile and tough. At other times, it is kind of nice, futile and nice. Whatever the case may be, we need to know that samsaric life is futile. That is what we call renunciation mind.

Whenever we have the slightest pain, it is easy for us to say: "Oh samsara, it's so terrible!" but we don't say this when we are happy. When you recognize that all of this is essenceless, changeable, and impermanent, no matter what happens in your life, whether it happens to be good or bad, it is then that you are beginning to become a Dharma practitioner, a spiritual person. Regardless of whether something is good or bad, as long as you know it is a dream, you will have no fear of waking up. More importantly, when you know it is a dream, you will be ready to give up both the bad and good equally. In one sutra, the Buddha said:

> If a young girl dreams of a boy coming into her life, she's happy. But within the same dream, if the boy meets with an accident and dies, suddenly she's very unhappy. Upon awakening, she will realize that her happiness when meeting the dream boy, and her unhappiness over the boy's death, were both but an elaborate dream.

The key point here is this: hearing and studying the teachings again and again help us to see the Dharma from every angle, not just in a one-sided way. Otherwise, our understanding will always be partial; it will be based on how we like to see things.

It is okay if you are not about to finish one hundred thousand prostrations. Not finishing your Vajrasattva on time is acceptable as well. The key point is to know that everything you have and aim for is futile and to try to get used to this notion on a daily basis, yet still go ahead with your practice. Until the dream is finished, you have to dream. Right now you simply do not have the power to wake up, so until the dream has ended, you will have to go through it. Once you know that it is a dream, it will not bother you, whereas if you do not know that it is a dream, the dream will bother you, tempt you, trap you, and bind you.

What makes us a beginner right now? Even though we may know that this is a dream intellectually, we still do not know how to wake up from it. Yet the ordinary people walking around in Paris and Munich at this very moment do not even have this intellectual understanding. As a rule, they truly believe that this is all real and terribly important. In contrast, we are somewhat more fortunate, since we know intellectually, or at least have heard, that this is a dream.

In what sense, then, are we practitioners? It is a bit like being on a battlefield surrounded by enemies, but with both your hands and legs chopped off. You cannot fight the enemy or run away. Even your tongue is cut out, so you cannot even verbally abuse the enemy! There is nothing you can do but watch. Nevertheless, this is still much better than what the people walking around in Paris and Munich experience. Surrounded by the enemy, they are cheated, trapped, and constantly assaulted, yet they do not even know what is happening. They do whatever the enemy says, and are continually defeated as a result. The enemy abuses them relentlessly, while at least our enemies are a little afraid of us. Though we are not able to do much about it, the enemy knows that we *know* they are the enemy. So it is very important that we cultivate this notion of the illusory nature of samsara. As Patrül Rinpoche said, doing so will bring about the dawn of the Dharma practitioner.

Cleaning the Vessel

Vajrasattva is a cleansing practice. In taking refuge, we divert our attention from the wrong path to the right one. With bodhichitta, we divert our attention from the shravaka path to the bodhisattva path. Having laid the foundation with these two practices, next we clean the vessel, meaning our body, speech, and mind. In the Mahayana and Shravakayana, the body is not regarded as a vessel, but rather a servant. In the Vajrayana, however, it is likened to a vessel, into which we pour the nectar of the Dharma. Outlining the first approach, the *Bodhicharyavatara* states:

> Slaves unsuitable for work
> Are not rewarded with supplies and clothing.
> This body, though you pamper it, will leave you—
> Why exhaust yourself with such great labor?
> So pay this body due remuneration,
> But then be sure to make it work for you.
> Do not lavish everything
> On what will not bring perfect benefit.

Here, we are advised to treat our body like a servant, to give it some wages, but not too much. We are advised to treat it as a bad master would treat a slave. If treated too well, the slave will only take control; likewise, we should only give our bodies a little bit of food and some clothes.

In the Vajrayana, however, the body is not likened to a slave, but to a vessel. This differs from the Shravakayana and the Mahayana, where only the mind is regarded as a vessel. In these approaches, it is the mind that needs to be tamed and trained, but in the Vajrayana even the body is a vessel. It, too, needs to be cleansed.

This brings us to the subject of bad karma and the obscurations, the defilements that need to be purified. The moment we hear the word "Vajrasattva," a little bell goes off in our heads, and we think of purification and cleansing. Using words like "cleansing" does imply that there is some sort of dirt or impurity present. In communicating between student and teacher, there is no other way to convey this better; we have little choice but to use words like "cleansing," "purification," "dirt," "defilement," and so forth. The problem is that when we practice Vajrasattva or talk about cleansing the defilements, it seems to trigger a lot of paranoia. It feels as though we are opening a can of worms that should be left alone. We do not want to talk about our dirt or defilements, or even to be reminded of them. We feel as though it all needs to be hushed up. In fact, we would much rather talk about our goodness instead.

This attitude stems from a certain misunderstanding, one that is present in both East and West. It is probably due to religious or cultural upbringing. In any case, the right attitude is this: When purifying the defilements, we are talking about uncovering our buddha nature. If there were no buddha nature, there would be no sense in purifying the things that keep it covered. This is an important point. When we purify defilements, we often get worked up with thoughts that we are bad, terrible, and dirty; that we are filled with anger, jealousy, and other emotions that need to be washed away. Instead of emphasizing such thoughts, we should put more energy into the idea that we are uncovering something. We need to think of the practice as a process of uncovering our buddha nature. All too often, people forget about the uncovering aspect, which is why there is an unwillingness to even talk about the dirt.

This process can be likened to washing a cup. When we wash a dirty cup, there is an implicit desire to see the cup clean. This is what drives us. As we soak the dirty cup in warm soapy water and clean away the dirt with a soft sponge, there is considerable enjoyment, especially when we see that it is becoming cleaner and cleaner. If the cup was going to remain dirty forever, if there were no sense that something is being uncovered, the process would be really painful. This uncovering business is the real purpose here. Buddhism, and particularly the Vajrayana, has nothing against the dirt, which in this case represents the emotions. What we want to recognize is the inner aspect. That is the rationale behind the process of uncovering.

GURU VAJRASATTVA

In the practice of Vajrasattva, you stay in your ordinary form and visualize the guru above your head in the form of Vajrasattva. The guru is a reflection of your devotion and merit, while devotion itself is a manifestation of buddha nature and merit. Without merit, you will not recognize the guru, as was the case with Devadatta. Devadatta was the Buddha's cousin, yet though they stayed together for a long time, Devadatta was unable to see even one good quality in the Buddha. Consequently, he did not receive any benefit from this relationship. For him the Buddha was just an ordinary person, a relative toward whom he was intensely competitive. Hence, merit plays an important role.

When taking refuge, the emphasis is protection. We are seeking protection from samsara, nirvana, impure vision, lack of devotion, lack of inspiration, and even from hail, storms, rain, bad health, and so on. Further, since in our dualistic minds we tend to think of Guru Rinpoche as a great protector, we visualize our guru in the form of Guru Rinpoche to protect us from all these things.

In Vajrasattva practice the guru has a different purpose. Of course, the power of protection is present as well, but Vajrasattva is associated primarily with purification. This is a bit like the different roles that your mother takes in life. Your mother is a daughter to her mother and a wife to her husband. Meanwhile, she may also be something entirely different when she goes to work. Different people perceive her in different ways. Likewise, all the buddhas and bodhisattvas are one in essence, but in our dualistic minds the variations in name, color, and appearance make a difference. Strictly speaking, you could visualize Guru Rinpoche and chant either the Vajrasattva mantra or the Guru Rinpoche mantra and it would still be cleansing.

Nevertheless, of all the incredible methods in the Vajrayana, Vajrasattva is known to be the supreme practice when it comes to purification. The power to purify is historically linked to the Buddha Vajrasattva. As a bodhisattva, Vajrasattva made the aspiration that upon becoming a Buddha, his name alone would be able to purify even the worst defilements. The subject of aspiration is quite important. Buddhas have different aspirations. Shakya-muni Buddha, for instance, aspired to be reborn in the human realm when human beings' life spans would be neither too short nor too long. In addi-tion, the fact that only four of the thousand buddhas in this eon teach the Vajrayana is also due to aspiration.

As you do the practice, visualize Guru Vajrasattva above your head. White in color and adorned with all the sambhogakaya ornaments, he embraces his consort and holds a vajra at heart level. With his left hand, he holds a bell, which rests on his left thigh. In the middle of his heart, visualize a small moon disc with the syllable HUM in its center. Think that both the letter HUM and Vajrasattva are the embodiment of all the buddhas, especially of buddha mind. Then supplicate Vajrasattva with the following words from the long ngöndro liturgy:

> Please grant me refuge and purify my negativity.
> With intense remorse, I confess all I've done!
> From now on I will be restrained, even at the cost of my life!

Next, chant the one-hundred-syllable mantra. As you chant the mantra, begin by imagining that many rays of light emanate out from the HUM in Vajrasattva's heart center. From this light, all kinds of offering substances manifest: flowers, incense, bath houses, mansions, gardens, peacocks, ele-phants, and whatever else you can imagine. These offering substances travel to the buddhas and bodhisattvas of the ten directions. The light then returns back, bringing with it the blessings of all the buddhas and bodhisattvas. These blessings all dissolve into the HUM syllable.

Next, nectar, in the form of light, begins to flow from the HUM syllable. Alternatively, you can imagine this nectar taking the form of a liquid, mer-curylike or milklike substance. Continue chanting the Vajrasattva mantra throughout this sequence. The nectar fills Vajrasattva's body, travels through his secret place, and enters the consort's body, completely filling hers as well. This nectar flows nonstop from the letter HUM, until it starts to overflow from every pore of both Vajrasattva and his consort. It then cascades like a waterfall, especially from their secret places, and dissolves into your head.

As the nectar slowly begins to fill up your forehead, it pushes down all the sickness, obscurations, defilements, and negative energies, to the point where all this comes out from your anus, your secret place, and your toes. These defilements are mainly related to physical acts, such as having killed someone in a past life, or other acts like stealing and sexual misconduct. This also includes headaches, stomachaches, and other forms of physical illness. All this is what we call "defilement of the *nadis*," the *nadis* being the chakras and channels inside your body.

Obscurations of the nadis can be caused by doing all kinds of odd things like killing people, or even by eating strange foods, associating with obscured beings, or staying in obscured places. Doing these sorts of things blocks your channels and chakras and they end up becoming very rusty. As a Vajrayana practitioner, you should concentrate more on cleansing the chakras and channels. This explanation is not usually given in ngöndro teachings.

As you visualize nectar continuously flowing from the letter HUM, keep in mind that you should be quite creative and flexible. What I do is imagine that even my body begins to change; as the nectar reaches my forehead, my body turns white from the top of the head to the forehead, while the rest of me stays a little bit dark. If it helps, you can do that. This just enhances the power of visualization.

As for all the details of the visualization, do not expect to do them all in one session, but if you are able to, then go ahead. From time to time, you should try to do the entire visualization in one session, or even with one round of the mala, or rosary. Let us suppose you are doing a Vajrasattva retreat or are at the stage where you are accumulating one hundred thousand Vajrasattva recitations. If this is the case, you can alternate how you visualize. For instance, one day you could chant the mantra of Vajrasattva and simply concentrate on his form above your head. That itself is very good. The next day, you could focus more on the letter HUM in his heart center while letting the rest remain a little bit unfocused. Then the following day, you could concentrate on the flow of nectar. On the fourth day, you could do all three.

If you have a lot of time you can continue to visualize the flow of nectar. For instance, you can visualize the nectar filling up the forehead for an extended period of time, perhaps for one month. During the second month, you could visualize the nectar flowing down to the throat. Alternatively, you could do half an hour to the forehead and half an hour to the throat, or you could try fifteen minutes, five minutes, or two minutes. It is entirely up to you, so please, be flexible.

It is really unnecessary to ask questions about this kind of thing. All these minor details can be endless: "How should the nectar travel through the body? What channel does it go through? Does it flow through the right channel or the left?" Sometimes I feel like answering, "Well, maybe it should travel by train!"

Also, though the main empowerment is part of guru yoga practice, you could also end by thinking that you are receiving the vase empowerment, as here we are purifying the physical defilements and the obscurations of the nadis. Similarly, as the nectar flows to the throat, imagine that you are receiving the secret empowerment, and as the nectar reaches the heart, imagine that you are receiving the third and the fourth empowerments, the wisdom and word initiations.

The nectar flowing down to the throat purifies all the defilements, but it mainly purifies speech defilements, which includes lying, cheating, using harsh words, gossiping, and making mistakes when you recite mantras by missing or adding extra words or not having the perfect pronunciation. It also purifies negative energy and disorders related to speech, such as when no matter what you say, people tend to misunderstand. For instance, if you say "right," people think you said "left." Or it might be that whatever you say annoys people, even when you say something with a good heart. Maybe your words and commands are not powerful enough, not seductive enough, or perhaps they are too seductive, so much so that it is annoying.

For Vajrayana students, it is especially important to cleanse problems related to *prana*. When we say "prana," we are talking about the winds; it is the stale air, or rather, the stale wind, that we cleanse. There are so many obscurations that damage our prana. We may have collected these obscurations by breathing bad air, smoking hashish, smoking cigars, drinking alcohol, or by slandering Vajrayana masters, saying impure things about the pure, or even by smelling the wrong incense. Each and every day we are inhaling so many obscurations! All of this needs to be cleansed.

Now again, to intensify the visualization you can visualize these things flowing down and then coming out in the form of black liquid from your anus, your secret place, or from your toes. You can visualize disease in the form of pus and blood, and negative energy in the form of all kinds of beings. For instance, you can visualize that the negative energy of prana and nadi takes the form of butterflies, scorpions, and various other insects and animals. You can even imagine that these creatures look partly like you and partly animal; you might perhaps visualize dogs that have your hands and your feet, and fleas or frogs that have your lips and so forth. Anyhow, it is bad energy coming out, so they all look hideous, or dirty, however you choose to elaborate on this.

To recap, there are many ways to be creative with the visualization. It is possible to go step by step from the crown chakra, to the forehead level, to the throat and so on; this is one way. Then again, if you prefer, you can also do it all in one go, whichever you choose. Yet another way is to visualize one day that Vajrasattva's nectar overflows, dissolves into you, and washes away all the dirt, pus, and blood, and that you receive only the vase empowerment. This purifies physical defilements and the obscuration of nadi. Then, on the next day, you purify the prana. It is up to you. Also, it is really not that important, but if it somehow bothers you or you are wondering where this dirt goes, you can imagine that it dissolves into the earth. Alternatively, you can even think that it all disappears into emptiness.

As you continue chanting the Vajrasattva mantra, the nectar descends to the heart level, cleansing all the defilements related to mind. This includes jealousy, competitiveness, aggression, selfishness, pride, covetousness, and the other forms of bad karma created by mind. Then there are things like wishing to harm others and having wrong or extreme views, such as believing that by killing human beings one will go to heaven.

This part of the practice also relates to the various forms of mental illness, including depression, anxiety, nervousness, and insecurity; being overly excited, overly amused, and overly nervous, or never amused, never anxious, and never nervous. This can even relate to lack of devotion, lack of inspiration, and the ridiculous endless sadness we feel sometimes, and also bulimia, which is a kind of mental illness, and the insane ambition and desire of wanting to be the best, wanting to get enlightened faster than anyone else. We have so many defilements!

As Vajrayana practitioners, on this third level we are trying to cleanse the defilements of *bindu*. We refer to bindu as drop, bodhichitta. At this point, it is difficult to go much further into the concept of bindu, and perhaps it's a bit untimely. I can only describe some of its outer aspects. Bindu is the domain of the mind and is also the most essential aspect. In Tibetan, this is called *tiklé*. To keep it as simple and unfabricated as possible, in tantric practice the blissful energy between female and male becomes very intense and very vast, but human beings complicate this tremendously and tend to fabricate this more and more. Let me give you one good example. In this age, one problem that human beings face is the need to be turned on. The oddity of needing to be aroused via chains and whips, for example, seems to be a bindu problem. Most of the ancient texts were written before the chain and whip problem, so it's hard to be sure about this. In such a situation, the bindu is so obscured that to evoke a certain experience, you have to do all kinds of strange things. It is this kind of age . . . who knows? Maybe in the next twenty years or so we will need chain saws to be turned on!

At this point, all I can do is introduce a few general things about bindu in a very metaphoric way, without going into much detail. If you want a more in-depth understanding, practice ngöndro for a year or two and then request teachings on a text like *Lamrim Yeshé Nyingpo* by Jamyang Khyentsé Wangpo and Chokgyur Lingpa, or *Tantra of the Secret Essence* and Vajraku-mara.[57] There are all kinds of ways to approach it, but once you do there is no way out. You will be like a snake in a tube. You will either go up or down.

Toward the end of the practice, you dissolve guru Vajrasattva into yourself. Actually, you can do this again and again. This is something very unique to Buddhism. You do not leave the deity "up there" as something pure, while you remain as something impure. Instead, you always merge with the deity at the end of the practice, so as to understand that you are also a buddha, and to know that you have been one from the beginning. To realize this insepara-bility, you dissolve into each other again and again during each session. You can even dissolve Vajrasattva into yourself whenever you feel like it, after you finish one round on the mala, for instance. Then, as you continue, you just revisualize Vajrasattva all over again. This is a very good approach to take. Then, at the end, Vajrasattva melts into you.

To conclude, just before you end the session, you supplicate to Vajrasattva as follows:

> Protector, under the sway of unknowing and ignorance
> I have transgressed my samayas and let them decline.
> Oh guru, protector, grant me refuge!
> Lord of mandalas, wielder of the vajra,
> Embodiment of great compassion,
> Lord of all beings, I go for refuge to you!

Once you have recited these lines, Vajrasattva dissolves into you, and you then become Vajrasattva as a result. As you remain in this state, observe your inseparability with Vajrasattva over and over again. You then chant OM VAJRASATTVA HUM, though this time you yourself *are* Vajrasattva.

To recap, this Vajrasattva practice has five main steps: First, we visualize Vajrasattva while reciting the liturgy. Second, we chant the one-hundred-syllable mantra with the four aspects mentioned above. Third, we pray to Vajrasattva. Fourth, Vajrasattva dissolves into us. Fifth, we remain as Vajrasattva while reciting the six-syllable mantra.

Mandala Offering

The fourth foundation practice is the mandala offering. In order to divert our attention from the wrong view, we take refuge. To divert our attention from the shravaka view, we practice bodhichitta. To cleanse our entire being, the vessel, we do Vajrasattva practice. Of the many methods of purification, Vajrasattva is supreme since in using the methods of visualization, chanting mantras, and so on, we are directly accessing our buddha nature. The next step is to become well equipped; to give ourselves the right equipment, the right tools. This is what we mean by the term "merit."

"Merit" can also mean ability. Patrül Rinpoche gave a good example for this. You may remember the story of the old lady and the dog's tooth. In this story, relics appeared because the old lady had the ability to think of a dog's tooth as though it were the Buddha's. Merit is an incredible thing. I don't have much experience, but the little that I have has taught me a lot. For example, try reading *Words of My Perfect Teacher* and then go and do one hundred thousand mandala offerings, not with a limited motivation, but as best you can. If you then go back and read *Words of My Perfect Teacher* again, your ability to understand and interpret each word will be completely different! Another way to test this is by doing shamatha meditation and seeing how much you can settle your mind, by observing how much it wanders. After you've done your mandala offerings, do the meditation again. You will notice a dramatic difference in your ability to stay focused.

Merit is ability. Take the word "impermanent," for instance. Right now, you have the ability to interpret this word only in terms of death, or on a very coarse level, like the change of seasons. Yet after generating a little merit, you will be able to interpret the meaning of impermanence on a much more subtle level. Let's say you're feeling happy right now. As the happiness arises, your understanding of impermanence will be there as well; you will be able to observe the changes in your emotions.

Lamas tell us that the Dharma is extremely precious, that it can cut through all kinds of dualistic nets, rocks, and fences like a diamond. We, on the other hand, are like destitute beggars, completely devoid of any enterprising mind-set. Suddenly, this diamond falls into our hands, and we do not know what to do with it. In our ignorance, we might even trade it for a hotdog or let it get stolen!

This sort of thing happens quite often. Where there is precious Dharma, there are also many obstacles. The presence of obstacles is actually a good sign. It means you are doing okay. The obstacles know it, which is why they have come. The obstacles are there because you are worthy of being obstructed. If you are not doing well, then you are your own obstacle. Why would anything want to bother you? The fact is that many obstacles are quite strong! They can really disturb you. At such times, you need the ability to take the offensive, to be defensive, to manipulate the obstacles, cheat the obstacles, seduce the obstacles, transform the obstacles, or just ignore the obstacles. There are many ways to deal with them, but the ability to take obstacles as a blessing – that is the highest!

To have this ability you need merit. There are numerous ways of accumulating merit, which are all wonderful and truly incredible. Yet for beginners like us, the most profound way of accumulating merit is the mandala offering. In Tibetan, the word for mandala is *kyil khor. Kyil* means dimension, meaning an all-inclusive dimension or circle. In this case, this refers to body, speech, and mind, and particularly, prana, nadi, and bindu. Of course, when making offerings, you want to offer something good, just as when you are giving someone a present. The most precious thing that you have is your prana, nadi, and bindu. Though we may be able to relate to these principles only on an intellectual level, what we are trying to do here is offer body, speech, and mind; our nadi, prana, and bindu, or buddha nature. We do this by envisioning all these realms, such as Mount Meru and the different planets, which are akin to a kind of container-mandala. We do not offer them as an ordinary realm, but as a buddha realm. All this is very much related to transforming the atmosphere, just as we do at the beginning of the practice.

When we make offerings, we detach from our body, speech, and mind and offer them in the form of more beautiful things. What we are really offering is not only our body, speech, and mind, but also prana, nadi, and bindu, and our buddha nature. How do we offer buddha nature? At the moment, our buddha nature is not visible, so to train our minds, we give it form.

If you want to practice Dzogchen in the future, or any practice that aims to accumulate merit, it is good to offer lamps. Offering has a lot to do with interdependent reality. In fact, the concept of offering is based on the Buddhist philosophy of interdependence. For instance, offering a lamp makes an auspicious interdependent connection since in doing so one understands that one's recognition of the true nature of mind will be enhanced. The mind itself is like a lamp, it knows everything and knows itself; it illuminates all and also illuminates itself. So there is an auspicious link between the mind and a lamp. The lamas tell us that offering lamps is very auspicious. Whatever you have is fine; you can offer many butter lamps, candles, or even electric lights. Whatever the case, this is a very good practice to do.

When it comes to the offering itself, again you should be quite creative. If the idea of Mount Meru, the southern planet, the eastern planet, does not come so easily to you, then offer a big mountain instead, or offer Asia, South America, North America, and Australia, adorned with all the beautiful places, all the national parks, and beautiful waterfalls. You can even include human wealth, such as banks and steel, the wealth of gods, like flying carpets and parasols, and the wealth of *nagas*, such as the conch that can wage war and the shell that can transform itself into places and palaces. You can offer wish-fulfilling trees and cows, or even beautiful ladies. All this is briefly mentioned in the explanation of the offering of the thirty-seven-heap mandala in *Words of My Perfect Teacher*. You can elaborate on this as much as you want. To enhance your visualization, you can use different substances, such as rice, which is frequently used by Tibetans. In addition to rice, you can also use coins, copper, gold, and silver.

To do the mandala offering, you will need a mandala plate. Although a small one is fine, according to Deshung Rinpoche it should be of a substantial size. It can be made of stone, sandalwood, copper, iron, steel, or even gold if you wish. It all depends on how much you can afford. As for the offering substances, some, like sandalwood powder and dried or fresh flowers, are readily available in the West, much more so than in places like Bhutan and Nepal.

All these things are simply intended to enhance the practice. They can also serve as a focal point to develop concentration. In fact, each and every grain of rice can be visualized as all the variety of things just mentioned: banks, palaces, bathhouses, and so on. Though it is a very Indian thing, personally, I always like to visualize bathhouses with dancing girls, or dancing boys, to be politically correct.

MANDALA OFFERING IN RETREAT

With this practice, one option is to do a Longchen Nyingtik retreat and do one hundred thousand mandala offerings in one go. Let's say you have taken leave from work and are aiming to finish in a month or two. This is quite good, actually, since this is the traditional approach. If this is the case, you will need two plates for your mandala. One of the mandala plates is placed on the shrine. Instead of seven heaps, this one should have five heaps to represent the five buddha families. This five-heaped mandala should be placed on the shrine, where it will function as the mandala in which your object of offering dwells.

Though the shrine was not mentioned in the context of refuge, bodhichitta, and Vajrasattva, with this practice you are beginning to accumulate merit. For this reason, you should have offering materials, including the seven offering bowls and the various offering substances. Of course, it depends on the situation. If you are doing a daily practice of one hundred mandala offerings and going to work in between, or if you are taking a long break and then restarting, it might be a little difficult to have a mandala on the shrine. If you are doing a long retreat, however, these things are necessary.

Once you start doing prostrations or mandala offerings, you should count however many you do. Even if you only do ten a day, you should write that down. Unless you happen to be a hidden buddha, you should count. We ignorant beings are usually motivated by goals. This is why it is good to count. I myself count; I'm trying to finish at least three hundred thousand prostrations in this lifetime. Either because I'm too busy or too lazy, I don't have much time to do them, so as I do prostrations, I pledge to myself, "If I do only twenty-five, it doesn't count, but if I do twenty-six or more, it's in the book!"

Patrül Rinpoche once wrote:

> When practicing the Dharma, you should follow the example of
> a horse being ridden hard by a rider. Whenever the horse sees one
> or two leaves of grass, it will eat.

In this example, the horse has very little time because its owner is whipping it constantly. It is forced to go on and on, so every time it gets a chance to eat, it eats. It doesn't have a designated time for lunch or dinner. That is how we should practice. Each time we practice, we should accumulate.

This sort of thing depends on the person. If counting does not encourage you, don't count. Nevertheless, counting is a major support for many of us. For me, it is very much an encouragement. Of course, the best approach is to do the practice until you experience certain signs, but this is very dangerous to judge. After all, we mostly interpret such signs incorrectly. Some people practice for one day and after hearing a crow make a noise they think, "Ah, there's a sign," and then they stop! Then there's what we call the indicator of time, which is usually something like: "I will practice until I die." This is good too, but it is second best because there are still a lot of loopholes. You tend to relax a little too much. The last method is to count.

Many practitioners combine the second and the third methods, which helps create discipline. In other words, they rely on the time aspect as well as counting. When you think to yourself, "I have to finish one hundred thousand," you have a goal. Without such a target, you might end up just doing whatever you like. On the other hand, for some people a target is completely unnecessary, because they would practice anyway. If that is the kind of person you are, there is no need to count.

HOW TO DO THE MANDALA PRACTICE

If you are doing a mandala retreat, you would have two mandala plates, with the five-heaped one for the shrine. The mandala on the shrine can be left for a long time; it does not need to be changed daily. For this reason, you should mix the grains with some butter or something that glues them together. This can be changed once in a while. If the retreat is going to take one year, for instance, it should be changed periodically.

With the offering that you are making and visualizing, you should have some saffron water or rose water. There is no need to chant the Vajrasattva mantra. Some traditions do chant the Vajrasattva mantra at this point, and in the West these different approaches often get mixed up. It seems that in every Dharma center, there is the habit of first chanting the Vajrasattva mantra when cleaning the mandala plate. Nevertheless, if you do this, it does not do any harm.

As you clean the plate, use your wrist without adding any water, while visualizing at the same time. If you want more detail, imagine that you are cleansing all the offering substances. The real offering substances are your body, speech, and mind, so that is what you are really cleansing.

Imagine that Guru Rinpoche and his retinue are in front of you as the objects of your offering. If you want to elaborate further, you can visualize the entire refuge tree that is described in the long version of the Longchen Nyingtik ngöndro: Guru Rinpoche is in its center. In front of him are the buddhas, to his right the bodhisattvas, behind him the Dharma texts, and so on. The object of offering is one and the same here, though we use different names. During refuge we call this the "object of refuge," whereas with bodhichitta, we call it the "witness of bodhichitta," and now during the mandala offering, we say the "object of offering."

At this point, you may also sprinkle a bit of scented water on the mandala plate. As you do, you should think about applying bodhichitta, meaning that you offer the mandala for the sake of all sentient beings, for their enlightenment. That is bodhichitta. Adding the "moisture of bodhichitta" symbolizes the profundity of this Vajrayana practice and helps us get past the idea that we are merely throwing rice on a plate or a stone. Practically speaking, it also helps the rice stick to the plate.

Then we have the seven heaps, which is what we accumulate. First, we place one heap in the center. There are two ways to place the next heap. One is to put it between you and the first heap and the other is to put it in front of the central heap. You can do whichever is more convenient. For those who prefer the first option, the third heap is then placed on the left. This heap is termed "the heap of Jambudvipa," referring to the planet on which we reside. The sixth should be next to the fifth, between the piles in the middle and on the left. If you prefer the second option, in which the second heap is placed in front of the central heap, Jambudvipa is at the three o' clock-position and the sun is next to that (between the piles in the middle and on the right). The sun and the moon are the sixth and the seventh heaps, respectively.

With the exception of the sun and moon, each of these heaps represents a planet, with the third heap representing the earth. In addition to these seven, I usually include an eighth heap that symbolizes all wealth, including that of the gods. Once you finish placing the heaps, you simply brush them off and start over.

To understand the symbolism here, you need to learn Buddhist cosmology, but do not get too hung up on details and techniques! Visualization is the most important factor. I myself have some problem with Buddhist cosmology; there is no need to think too much about this. What you need to know is that all of this is a concept of the universe: The central heap represents Mount Meru, which is said to be made up of four kinds of jewels. Its basis is square shaped, and it is in the center of the ocean, with half above water and half below. At the very top is the palace of king Indra. Somewhere in the middle of Mount Meru is the palace of the demigods. On the right, to the eastern side of Mount Meru, is the planet "Purvavideha." It is believed that the people there have a different color, shape, and appearance. At the southern side of Mount Meru is "Jambudvipa," which is our planet. We are, of course, familiar with how we look, so there is no need to go into that.

As for the other planets, to the west is "Aparagodaniya," and in the north is "Uttarakuru." Each of these planets is actually accompanied by two smaller planets, so there are many more, but this should give you some idea of what these heaps are.

If you are doing the extended Longchen Nyingtik ngöndro and want to do it in the conventional way, the approach is slightly different. The traditional method is to first place five heaps, then three heaps, and finally one heap. In any case, this is what you offer. Each time you finish, you brush off the rice; that is counted as one. You then do this one hundred thousand times. It is easy. For me, Vajrasattva is the most difficult. When chanted properly and with the right pronunciation, it seems as though you will never finish. Doing prostrations and mandala practice might sound and look difficult, but actually they are not.

Each time you finish one hundred mandala offerings, or perhaps every twenty-five times, you should offer one thirty-seven-heap mandala. I offer the thirty-seven heaps after completing one hundred shorter offerings. There is a diagram that shows where to place the thirty-seven heaps, but I don't know how much time should be spent scrutinizing the drawing, then looking at the mandala and not getting it right. I would just chant the long liturgy and simply place thirty-seven heaps on top of one another.

The rings that are used in mandalas are a Tibetan invention; you can use them if you like, but they are not crucial. Personally, I never use the rings. Their whole purpose is to make the offering look good, there is no other reason. It does look beautiful, however. Certain Tibetan customs have nothing to do with the Dharma; they are just cultural.

Some people are more Tibetologists than Buddhists, so you should be careful. Aside from the Dharma, Tibetans are well known for teaching their garbage too. They may teach you how to be Tibetan and maybe even how to have Tibetan emotions!

In any case, when you offer the thirty-seven heaps, you always do so in a clockwise manner. At the end of the session, dissolve the object of offering into you, then remain in that state as long as you can.

In essence, it is your mind that imagines the continents, wealth, prosperity, and all the other offerings. For ordinary beings like us, if asked to offer our minds, how would we do that? To help with this, we give it a certain form. We visualize flowers and all of the other numerous offerings. There is really no contradiction here because whenever you think of flowers, it is *your* mind that is creating *your* flowers. You can even offer your compassion.

Everything is mind: the height, length, and width of Mount Meru, the entire universe . . . everything; all of this is mind.

We should tell this to the physicists. The mandala is a very good study of physics and of the big bang theory. Basically, we are saying that even the big bang is one's own mind. In this case, it is some physicist's mind. As long as the mind is there, it is the mind that is creating all these distinctions: the universe, the atmosphere, the stars, the moon, planets, and everything else. Nevertheless, for the most part, we only know this on an intellectual level.

As mentioned earlier, there is theory and there are key instructions. According to the theory, as soon as you know everything is mind—that your own mind is dharmakaya, sambhogakaya, and nirmanakaya—you are finished; you are enlightened. Since that is difficult, however, there are key instructions as well. When you learn to drive a car, for example, your teacher might tell you to drink a cup of tea, which has nothing to do with driving, nothing at all. That is exactly the point. In a sense, we can say that rice and coins have nothing to do with enlightenment, but at the same time, there is obviously a connection. After all, who made the coins precious in the first place? It is all in our minds. Through education and habit, our minds have been taught to believe that money and gold are precious.

For this reason, you can offer everything—body, speech, mind, and even attachment. After all, when you offer your mind, it comes in a package. Moreover, since the Vajrayana teaches that the basic essence of attachment is discriminating wisdom, and the basic essence of aggression is mirror-like wisdom, nothing is bad. It is actually good.

Like everything else, it is possible to do this practice with the wrong attitude. As I mentioned before, there are three different attitudes: First, we have the farmer-like attitude; we see an expression of this in Thailand, Bhutan, and India, where people pray to Buddha and take refuge for a good rainfall. This attitude is wrong. At the very least, it is extremely limited in scope. It may give you some good results, but you should aim for a higher attitude. At the very least, you should aim for the shravaka attitude.

Offering of the Simple Beggar

In the long version of the Longchen Nyingtik ngöndro, the mandala offering is followed by the offering of the simple beggar, or kusali offering. This is both a preparation for guru yoga, as well as a sort of inner mandala offering.

The short ngöndro composed by Jamyang Khyentsé Wangpo, on the other hand, is quite condensed and doesn't contain this practice. For those doing the long ngöndro, the kusali practice is part of the liturgy and cannot be ignored, but even if you are using the short text, it is a good idea to integrate it into your practice. The kusali practice is an excellent method for accumulating merit, one of the best in fact; it is much better than the outer mandala offering. The kusali practice is a tsok, a fire puja, and also what we call "paying the karmic debt," as is *sur* (smoke offering).

Kusali practice also helps create the right atmosphere for the practice of guru yoga, in which you visualize yourself as Vajrayogini. At the beginning of the kusali practice, you say P'ET and envision a complete separation of body and mind. Here, you are actually doing *powa*: you eject your consciousness from the body, which is left behind, sitting there in front of you in a collapsed state like a discarded empty bag. The body lies motionless; there is no blinking of the eyes, no movement, and no breathing. It is a completely lifeless body. At that moment, you should remain in a state of nongrasping.

The Four Maras

In Buddhism, we talk about the four maras, or four demons. These four are the child of god mara, the mara of death, the mara of the defilements, meaning all the emotions, and finally, the mara of the aggregates. The moment you say P'ET and the body falls down in a heap, your consciousness ascends upward, no longer with any form. Looking down at your body, you see a completely alien, rotten, useless body. With this perspective, you understand that this body is not the most important thing.

Usually, pride is developed based on two factors: our minds and bodies. Since we have a body, we have pride. Destroying the body, therefore, leads to the destruction of pride. This is a victory over the first mara. In other words, having no attachment to your body is the destruction of the child of god mara. This stage of practice dismantles the body, yet the mind continues on; it is not like turning off a lamp or snuffing out a candle. Hence, the very fact that consciousness remains is victory over death.

It is this victory over the mara of death that we also call Vajrayogini. At this point, you take the form of Vajrayogini or, according to the Longchen Nyingtik, Krodhikali. Krodhikali is a beautiful black woman, adorned with all the heruka ornaments. These ornaments include a crown and bracelets crafted out of bone and tiger-skin skirts. She is naked and holding a curved knife, which symbolizes the destruction of the third mara, the mara of emotion. Vajrayogini is red. Otherwise there is no real difference between these two figures.

Finally, she has to destroy the mara of the aggregates. To do this, she starts to dismember the body, like Hannibal Lecter would: She slowly cuts the skull away from the inanimate body. This is your skull, of course. After this, she lifts the kapala, or skull cup, with your hair still intact. If it is blond, see it as blond; if brunette, see it as brunette; if long, see it as long; if dyed, it is dyed; and if punk-style, it's punk-style. As you pick it up, the skull cup becomes enormous, as big as the three worlds. In doing so, you are making this a practice of nonduality.

At this point, you also visualize a tripod of three human skulls, representing the three kayas—the dharmakaya, sambhogakaya, and nirmanakaya. You place the kapala on top of the tripod formation, and then return to cut the hands and fingers, as well as slowly flaying the skin and removing the lungs, liver, and blood. Not a drop should be spilled, as it is so precious. Extract each of these body parts with the edge of the curved knife, right down to the lips, teeth, nose, and eyes. Then place it all inside the kapala.

THE FEAST

As you stand next to the kapala in the form of the dakini, imagine a great wisdom fire blazing forth from beneath the hearth of three heads. Then, as you chant OM AH HUM, visualize the body, or rather, what is now your ex-body, melting and boiling. For a more vivid image, the next time you are making chicken or beef stew, take a look at the ingredients bubbling away in the pot and that should help. Of course, that is for the first part only. After a while, you are supposed to visualize every drop as having the power of nectar. Each and every drop contains all the pleasurable things you can imagine, such as lakes, gardens, food, and drink. Since it is wish-fulfilling nectar, it becomes whatever one wants it to be. This nectar is first offered to the buddhas, bodhisattvas, and especially to Guru Rinpoche; they are the VIPs.

If you want to do a more elaborate version, you can think of the offering as a banquet party. Once you start cooking, you can send out invitation cards, usually in the form of light coming from your heart. First, of course, there are the VIP cards to the Copper-Colored Mountain, the realm of Amitabha, and the realm of Akshobya, as well as to all the other pure realms. All the guests promptly arrive in their limousines, looking elegant in their finest. You can roll out the red carpet and all the trappings when they arrive, in whatever way you wish. Next, send forth invitations to the six realms. Some of the guests come riding on bicycles, some arrive on a broomstick, while others come via public transport or hitchhiking. They all take their seats.

Once everyone is assembled, the first portion should be offered to the VIPs. In this case, VIP means those who have destroyed the ego, which includes arhats up to the Buddha. In return, you receive the common and unique spiritual attainments. Common spiritual attainments include such things as long life and freedom from obstacles and sickness, which is why this practice is good to do when you are ill. Unique spiritual attainments include love, compassion, diligence, and devotion, as well as the power to recognize the nature of mind.

Once the VIPs have been taken care of, you can make offerings to the beings of the six realms. Each time these beings drink, eat, lick, chew, swallow, or suck at these offerings, imagine that all their suffering disappears. Not only that, they also give rise to love, compassion, bodhichitta, and devotion, allowing them to help many other sentient beings as well.

There are also two special groups of guests. One group includes all those who have been bothering you, or those you think of as your enemies. Giving them an offering makes them feel that the score has been settled. The other group is made up of those to whom we owe a karmic debt; these guests are the largest in number. We have karmic debts with many people. When we sit down to receive a teaching and block someone else's view, for example, it creates a karmic debt. I myself receive a karmic debt every time I walk into a room and people stand up. If I were an enlightened being, the more this would happen the better. Actually, it is good to pay respect to someone else, even to unenlightened beings, but from my end, this means I will have to return the favor for roughly five hundred lifetimes. Whenever the person who stood up for me comes into a room, I myself will have to rise to my feet. If I walk into a room and fifty people stand up, then this five hundred lifetimes gets multiplied by fifty, so I would be standing up for these people for twenty-five thousand lifetimes. We are all paying off our karmic debts.

As the party draws to a close, foods and presents are distributed until nothing remains. The special thing about this party is that the guests do not leave. Instead, they all dissolve into you. As always, the buddhas and bodhisattvas dissolve into you, but here all the sentient beings dissolve into you too. The host, the guests, and the feast all become inseparable. Knowing that all of this is the creation of your mind, simply rest for some time.

The kusali practice is included in the long version of the Longchen

Nyingtik preliminaries. Doing it brings a great deal of blessings. Although it is said you can offer a mandala using just dust, the kusali practice was originally intended for practitioners who are quite poor, for those who cannot afford mandala plates, offerings, or all the other special substances. As Patrül Rinpoche points out in *The Words of My Perfect Teacher*, "kusali" literally means "beggar," which is why it is called the poor person's practice. From a mundane point of view, this practice is made for less fortunate people, but from a spiritual point of view, it is a higher teaching. There is one important point to understand: practices that seem to be inferior or ones that seem outrageous and use controversial language and methods are considered to be high teachings in the Vajrayana.

The kusali practice provides a very good transition. In this practice, you leave your ordinary state and become Vajrayogini. You then construct the guru mandala, which works much better since you have already transformed yourself. For this reason, you can also incorporate this practice into the short Longchen Nyingtik sadhana.

There are two parts to the practice, one involves cutting and the other the actual offering. What you accumulate is six hundred thousand repetitions of the syllables OM AH HUM, which is quite easy to do. If you have the time, this is probably a six-day job, or about twelve days if you are going slowly.

As mentioned earlier, here the practitioner is visualized as a deity. In the short text, however, this is not mentioned because the text is concise and all the details are concealed. Nevertheless, if you want to practice guru yoga seriously, it is important to transform yourself. From refuge and bodhichitta up to Vajrasattva and the mandala offering, you remain an ordinary person. With the kusali practice, however, you have become slightly more than ordinary, as represented by this transformation into Vajrayogini or Krodhikali. As a one of these dakinis, you try to mix your mind with the guru's.

In effect, what you are trying to mix is already that much more sublime. In fact, the sole purpose of guru yoga is to recognize the nature of mind. At this stage you are trying to become a vessel for the guru's blessings. By visualizing yourself in a more sublime form, an auspicious interdependent connection is formed. This, in turn, makes it easier to invoke the blessings. As always, toward the end of the session you dissolve the visualization. Either you dissolve or the guru dissolves into you.

You may wonder why we visualize ourselves as a female dakini. When we speak of transforming ourselves into the feminine, we are not really talking about gender; we are referring to the qualities of emptiness and clarity. The quality of emptiness is always symbolized by the feminine, whereas clarity, or what is also described as compassion and method, is symbolized by the masculine. Ultimately, however, we are transforming into something beyond form, color, shape, and identity; beyond gender and nationality.

Guru Yoga

The most profound yoga is guru yoga. Ngöndro practice includes the outer guru yoga. Practicing the outer guru yoga will prepare you for the inner and secret yogas, for which you must receive certain empowerments. These days, since both lamas and disciples seem to have limited time for Dharma practice, we find many guru practices being done in a short period of time. This might not be so advisable to do, however, unless you happen to be a disciple of superior faculties or have encountered a guru who is a mahasiddha, meaning that he or she is able to transform everything.

Of course, it all depends. The guru may not be that "qualified" and the disciple may not have "superior faculties," but if there is at least genuine devotion, this kind of short cut might work. On the other hand, if you are not a person with strong devotion and do not have any of these superior faculties, in the end, it will be much more rewarding to take a gradual approach. This is the safest and most comfortable approach to take.

In essence, guru yoga is not about worshipping a guru. It is not a mundane, ordinary practice of viewing the guru as a teacher or guide, nor does it involve seeing the guru as some sort of dictator. In a more profound sense, the guru has to be taken as a path, not only as a teacher. In Tibetan, this is what we call "Lama lam khyer"—taking the guru as the path. This is most essential. The word "guru" does not only refer to the outer guru, but also to the inner and secret gurus.

Samsaric life is like a carefully crafted box, one made by such a great carpenter that the joints are almost invisible. Since we cannot see any joints or cracks, it may not even occur to us that the box can be opened. Our samsaric life is carefully crafted in exactly the same way. Day by day, year by year, and lifetime after lifetime, our lives are fashioned by our experienced ego. The notion that this box might have joints, not to mention the idea that we may actually be able to open it, does not occur to us at all. We do not stop to take the time to inspect the box; this thought never enters our heads.

Once you locate the joints of the box and manage to move them a bit, the whole system gets disrupted. Similarly, when you disrupt your samsaric life, you are half a step closer, maybe even one step closer, to enlightenment. Though not entirely opened, the box has become disjointed. Once that starts to happen with your samsaric life, amazing things can occur. If you have the merit, devotion, and pure perception, they can happen anytime and anywhere. They can be triggered by the most ridiculous of situations, though they tend to come about through a remark, comment, gesture, or even a message from the guru.

One such experience is called "great spontaneity." This is a Dzogchen term, actually, so perhaps it is a bit early to introduce this principle. Personally, I have read books about Dzogchen and the experience of spontaneity and heard many teachings on the subject. But the thing is, with many lamas, especially the younger ones, I do not have much pure vision. Just looking at some of the lamas and disciples intoxicated with words like "spontaneity" and "unfabricated" is a bit of a laughing matter. We don't even know what spontaneity is! For us, it just means being more effortless . . . that's about it. Yet, this term carries great meaning. When everything stops, once there is no more fixation, that is spontaneity. One is no longer stuck with an idea.

Right now, however, we can only infer what this might be like. It is as though we are attempting to describe what lies on the other side of a mountain. Using some kind of reference point, we *imagine* there must be some trees and towns, but there is no direct cognition.

A story about Nyoshul Lungtok, one of Patrül Rinpoche's main disciples, is quite telling. This story took place after he had become a great master himself. Nyoshul Lungtok had a disciple who was completely illiterate. This disciple had never read any of the great Dzogchen texts, not even one. He did not even know how to read. The only thing he really knew was how to chant the mantra of Padmasambhava: OM AH HUM VAJRA GURU PADMA SIDDHI HUM. Of course, he was also very devoted to his master. He practiced year after year, but still nothing happened, yet his devotion remained unshakable. When his guru Nyoshul Lungtok died, in fact, he still did not have any kind of meditative experience. Still, his devotion never wavered.

Then one day he was making tea and a burning hot ember suddenly hit his hand. He felt the sharp pain of the fire burning into his flesh and shouted out loud, "A tsa!" shaking his hand vigorously. At that very moment, as Nyoshul Lungtok had experienced, everything stopped. Previously, the old man had always been very fussy about tea; he needed the exact number of tea leaves, and the water had to be heated just right. Yet from then on, it no longer mattered to him. Someone could have put cow dung in his tea, and he would have felt the same way. Everything stopped for him.

This phrase "everything stopped" also indicates a new beginning. It is as though once the ordinary world stops, the extraordinary world begins. But right now, formulating a precise picture of this is difficult. It is something we can only talk about and vaguely imagine.

This great Vajrayana method is not found in either the Shravakayana or Mahayana. The Buddha himself said, "As times degenerate, the teachings, especially the higher ones, will have an even greater effect." So while we may be going through a time of degeneration, it is also an age where some of the great methods, such as Dzogchen, Mahamudra, and the nonduality of samsara and nirvana, work better than ever before. Our negative emotions have reached their highest level, and people do all kinds of negative things with great intensity. Yet, this is also the age where the teachings of the Buddha, especially the Great Perfection teachings, resonate with great force. Never before have these methods worked so effectively. Now *that* is something quite encouraging!

What we are trying to do here is break the box of our samsaric existence. If we can't do it completely, we should at least try to make it a little disjointed, so we can no longer be locked in. This is what we call "understanding the nature of mind." Nowadays, how often do we hear the words, "rest in the nature of the mind"? Though easily enough said, this can actually be quite difficult. At first it may seem simple enough, after all, when we say "rest-in-the-nature-of-mind," there are just six words. Yet in truth, these words are not readily understood. What do we mean by "rest," for example? It is easy to gaze out into the sky and blankly declare, "rest in the nature of the mind." Then we sit there, basically wasting two minutes, or maybe even twenty, of our precious human life! It is the biggest waste of time. What does it mean to rest? Is it something like plunging onto our bed and stretching our legs out? And what is meant by "in the"? Likewise, we surely don't appreciate the term "nature" in any real sense, and we definitely don't comprehend what mind is. So in the end, this term "rest in the nature of mind" has almost no meaning at all.

Nonetheless, we see people going along to meditation centers and when the lama says "rest in the nature of the mind," most of the students make some kind of futile attempt to do so. I cannot help but ask myself, what are they doing? It is almost an embarrassment to see this kind of thing. But my belief in karma has improved quite a lot as a result. It's a bit similar to how leaders like Jiang Zemin, the former president of China, can announce something and billions of Chinese then believe whatever he said. In our case, the guru says, "Rest in the nature of the mind," and somehow the disciple also buys it. Most of the time, however, neither the disciple nor the teacher have a clue what they are talking about.

Having said that, I should add that this is just my own skepticism and impure vision. From an entirely different vantage point, it is very encouraging just to have heard the words, "rest in the nature of the mind." Even if they are only recited like a parrot, just to have this phrase alive and kicking in the world shows that we, as Dharma practitioners and followers of the Vajrayana path, have a great deal of merit.

In relation to merit, I would like to share an analogy made by His Holiness Dilgo Khyentsé Rinpoche. One time in Bodhgaya he said something incredible concerning merit. "Suppose there are five hundred arhats from the shravaka tradition and they need to go somewhere. Though they have a chariot, there is no horse to pull it. Now remember that arhats are enlightened beings; having destroyed the ego, they no longer have to return to samsara. Should the Buddha happen to be passing by, he might consider dragging the chariot with his toe, but these five hundred arhats would not have sufficient merit to allow the Buddha to do such a thing. But suppose there is also one *ordinary* human being who has heard the word of bodhichitta," Rinpoche continued. "Were this person to suddenly get into the chariot, his or her merit would be so great that the Buddha would have to drag the chariot with his own neck."

Nowadays, during this degenerate time, it is really quite astonishing that we can even hear profound phrases like "rest in the nature of the mind." Even to have this phrase coming from the lips of masters from time to time is incredible. Regardless of whether it remains in your heart for a moment or not, just to have had this experience is very fortunate.

As mentioned earlier, the main purpose of all the Buddha's teachings is to train the mind. At this point, we have finally reached a level where we try to rest in mind's nature; this is the highest form of training. Here we aim not only to recognize the nature of mind, but also to dwell in it, and by dwelling in the nature of mind, to manifest from within it. This is what we are trying to do. A complete recognition of the mind is what we call nirvana.

All the buddhas, bodhisattvas, mahasiddhas, and gurus of the past have taught that there are only two ways to recognize the nature of mind: through merit and through the blessing of the guru. Without one of these, even if we engage in years and years of contemplation, let alone a detailed study of Buddhist philosophy, the nature of mind will still remain a mystery to us. Intellectual academic studies will only serve to give you a vague idea. They do not give you the real picture. It is more like a picture of a picture, or a hundredth-generation photocopy. The real picture comes when you meditate. For these very reasons, the accumulation of merit and the blessings of the guru are the two most important methods.

How, then, do we accumulate merit? In the Vajrayana, there are two supreme ways to do this: to have compassion toward sentient beings or devotion to the guru. The latter of the two, guru devotion, is much more practical and feasible. We might feel compassionate for one or two days, or one or two hours, but for ignorant beings like ourselves, it is difficult to be compassionate all the time. To have devotion toward the guru, to one single person, or to two or three, is much more feasible.

Some say that a practitioner should have only one guru. Sometimes, however, what initially starts out as advice somehow becomes a tradition, which is not so good. On certain occasions a lama may say, "It is better to have one path and follow one guru." This advice must be given to certain people. For instance, there are certain people who tend to do a little bit more window shopping than necessary, certain people who do not have much time. For them, it may be better to stick with one guru, but some opportunists use this advice as propaganda. It becomes a kind of campaign, where they tell their particular group, "We had better follow only our guru, and our lineage." In such circumstances, advice becomes a political tool.

I can assure you with a great deal of confidence, however, that you can follow as many gurus as you like. Jamyang Khyentsé Wangpo had one hundred and fifty gurus; Jamgön Kongtrül Lodrö Thaye had almost as many, and Chogyur Lingpa, the same. Jamyang Khyentsé Chökyi Lodrö boasted more than seventy gurus. I myself, though I have no special realization, have studied with over twenty teachers.

On the other hand, if you wish to have only one guru, that is also fine. This was the common approach in India. Indian masters would have only one guru and one deity practice, yet they would still manage to achieve attainments. In fact, Atisha criticized Tibetans on this point. "In India," he said, "practitioners can achieve hundreds and thousands of attainments with one deity, whereas in Tibet, practitioners end up getting destroyed by the one hundred deities." So this is a bit of a Tibetan habit.

THE GURU PRINCIPLE

To accumulate merit, devotion toward the master and the teachings is crucial. What do we mean by guru devotion? To whom is our devotion directed? First of all, we should understand that the guru principle contains three levels: the outer, inner, and secret guru. As the great Sakya master, Könchog Lhundrup, said:

> The outer guru is the embodiment of all the buddhas; this is the guru you can see, talk to, and communicate with, and also the one you receive teachings and instructions from. The inner guru is the nature of the mind. The secret guru is the emptiness of all phenomena.

Another quotation was given by Deshung Rinpoche, one of my Sakya masters. He said:

> First we try to meditate that the outer guru is a buddha. Second, we see the guru as a buddha. Third, we see, or recognize, our own mind to be the buddha.

These outer, inner, and secret gurus are actually one and the same. This is the speciality of the Vajrayana teachings.

The principle of the outer guru is very vast. As deluded beings, even this level of the guru is somewhat beyond us, as are the outer and inner gurus. Though we may be able to get a vague intellectual understanding, to truly understand, we need a bridge between ourselves and the inner and the secret gurus. That bridge is the outer guru.

The outer guru is the tangible, visible guru with whom we can share our experiences. By and large, the outer guru is entirely a manifestation of devotion. Should you approach the outer guru with your ordinary perception, naturally, this person will seem to be just a normal human being. Maybe he or she likes pizza with anchovies or strong coffee, yawns when tired, or gets angry when you make a mistake, or who at least *seems* to get angry. Not having come from your home town, the guru might also be quite exotic, the more foreign the better. It is even preferable if the guru has a different skin color altogether. We expect someone with these kinds of qualities. This is especially true if you happen to be quite gullible or naïve when it comes to colors, shapes, and races, be they Tibetan, Asian, or otherwise.

The guru must be slightly more special than you. He or she has to know the Dharma, be more learned, and have more experience in meditation. The guru should have greater intuition, a little clairvoyance, and a certain degree of power to get things done. From his or her own point of view, however, the guru can't afford to be *too* special. Suppose you have a guru and invite him to a restaurant. What if he were to come floating through the door? Or what if he were able to order without looking at the menu, without going through the pretense of not knowing what wine to choose? If this were to happen, we wouldn't like it one bit. When the guru is completely omniscient and manifesting in an enlightened way, we don't like it. We prefer our gurus to be slightly human. Of course, we think our guru should be more special than an ordinary human being, but at the same time, we also hope that he or she is not *too* special. Otherwise we find it very annoying.

When we do certain things behind the guru's back, it's comforting to think he doesn't know. Just imagine having a guru who knew every single thing you do! What if he knew everything: from how many times you have masturbated on sacred days, right down to what size underwear you wear, or how many moles you have on the top of your penis? It would be terrible. You don't want him to have that kind of knowledge. It would feel so uncomfortable to be with such a person.

It feels uncomfortable to be with a perfect being. It's a bit like being a thief in a large prison complex where all the other prison cells are empty, as if you are the only thief in the world, and you have been caught. You feel so bad and guilty, not because you have stolen something, but just because you are the only one there. Suddenly the prison door opens and in comes another thief, and you feel much better. "Ah, well I'm not the only guilty person," you think. In a similar way, we like it when the guru makes mistakes sometimes. This is how complicated our human lives and minds are.

It is amazing to watch great masters, such as Dilgo Khyentsé Rinpoche. He would occasionally say, "Oh, I didn't know that." It was astounding that he actually got the flu from time to time, or that he even got sleepy. We knew that His Holiness hardly slept at night; he just kept going day and night, but now and then, during pujas he would appear to be sleeping. It's inspiring, actually, because his sleepiness was such an immense display of compassion. He would not really lie down, or stretch out his legs and sleep. When we went to him in the middle of the night, perhaps at two in the morning, he was either meditating or writing something. This made us feel bad. "Wow, I shouldn't go back and sleep," we would think. When he would doze off during the day, it made us feel okay to be sleepy. This is the kind of mind we have.

In the context of the mandala offering, I quoted Jigmé Lingpa as saying, "Even meditating for the time it would take to drink a cup of tea will really penetrate your mind." But he then went on to say, "Years of meditation is good, but this is nothing compared to recalling the outer guru for just a moment." As you can see, in the Vajrayana, the guru is a really big deal.

On this point, I will give another example from the perspective of the guru lineage. We can think of the guru lineage as something similar to a staircase. Usually, right at the top of the guru lineage is the primordial Buddha, or Adi Buddha. For the Nyingmapas, this is Samantabhadra, while for the Kagyüpas, Gelukpas, and Sakyapas it is Vajradhara. Who is this blue guy? The primordial Buddha is actually a symbol of the nature of mind. The guru lineage is the staircase that leads you toward your own nature; it is the very first step and the most important. That first step is the outer guru.

In this sense, the outer guru is like a boat, bridge, or staircase that takes you to your destination. When you finally get there, you will realize that the outer guru is none other than your own mind and none other than the emptiness of all phenomena. At that point, you will not have the burden of someone watching over you, of someone breathing down your neck. No longer will there be any notion of someone correcting you, criticizing you, or dictating what you should do in life. You will then know that all this is your own mind. This is what we are trying to achieve. Right now, on the path, we call this mingling our own mind with the guru's mind.

If we lack a proper understanding of the guru principle, we may think of the guru as a dictator at times. In the end, however, what we need to know is that the outer guru is not an independent, truly existent entity outside of our own minds. To think of the guru as a perfect being, or as someone who is something you can never be, or could even dream of being, is not the right attitude to have. As my teacher Deshung Rinpoche said, the purpose of guru yoga is to understand the nature of the mind. This is the forte of the Vajrayana.

In the quotation given above, the first thing Deshung Rinpoche said was, "First we try to meditate that the outer guru is a buddha." This means we have to fabricate; it means we have to pretend, make believe, or imagine. At this point, the path is a little bit contrived; it is slightly fabricated and forced. All the same, this is a necessary step.

The effort that goes into thinking of the guru as a buddha is extremely important. The question is, "Are we just faking it?" The answer is no, and there are many reasons for this. First, the very nature of the outer guru *is* buddha, but for now recognizing this takes a bit of discipline due to our delusion. It takes effort to think that our guru has four arms rather than two, that the guru is green and has extra eyes, or that the guru is Guru Rinpoche, as is the case in the Longchen Nyingtik. All this is necessary so long as we are on the path, yet in reality the guru actually *is* a buddha; that is the nature of the guru. In this sense we are not faking it.

The second reason applies not only to the guru, but to every perception we have. When you look at something and see imperfection, that imperfection is not "out there." It is a creation of your mind. Whether you see someone as beautiful, ugly, imperfect, or perfect, all this is simply created by your mind. From a philosophical point of view, all this dualistic perception is a fabrication. This obviously applies to the guru as well. If you see the guru as someone imperfect, as someone who makes mistakes, has too big a nose, or as too short or too tall, you must know that it is all your own perception. In reality, the guru is adorned with the thirty-two major and eighty minor marks. He or she is the Buddha. This is why we contemplate this way over and over again and try to visualize and meditate on our guru as a buddha.

This practice purifies a great deal of defilement. As the defilements diminish, your perception, your slant on things, will also change. You will slowly come to see the guru as a buddha. By then, you will already have reached the second stage, yet you still will not see yourself in this way. Why? Because the notion that there is an "I" seeing "a guru" as "a buddha" will remain. In other words, you will still see the guru as a separate entity.

In the third stage, even that differentiation disappears. By then, all the defilements will have been purified. As a result, you will see things from a completely different angle, and there will no longer be an independent external guru "out there." It is then that you see the nature of mind as the buddha. Again, this is the forte of the Vajrayana.

Keep in mind that merging with the guru is more than just a feeling in the heart or a sense of connection. These are not the only things we are after. The very concept of connection means there is another being to connect with. When we talk of connection and think in this way, we are still bound by the notion of separate entities. Feelings, moreover, are very fickle. They are just another skin that we will eventually have to peel off. Realizing the inseparability of your own being and the guru's, by contrast, is something that can never be peeled off. This is the real you; you have seen the inner and secret guru. Feelings, on the other hand, are only temporary.

On the path, it seems as though the guru is a separate being, yet the path itself also reminds us that this is not the case. This is the skillful aspect of the path. It is not the path's fault that we tend to think of the guru as a separate entity. This duality is created by the mind. It is a habit. If we unequivocally understood the inseparability of the guru and our own being, guru yoga would be unnecessary.

The guru is like a mirror. To see the buddha within—the true nature of mind—we use the outer guru as a mirror. As part of this process, we use devotion to keep this mirror clean. What is devotion? Saraha once said, "Devotion is trust in cause, condition, and effect." This kind of trust in cause, condition, and effect naturally occurs when you cook an egg, for example. There only needs to be a certain amount of water, heat, and cooking time; these factors combined will determine whether the egg will be cooked or not. That is devotion. Devotion is not make-believe. It is not like placing an egg on a plate and leaving that plate on the table, all the while pretending that the egg will be cooked without water or heat. That is what we call idiot devotion.

Devotion is trust in cause, condition, and effect. As can be inferred from the example of cooking an egg, where there is a good understanding of karma, an awareness of devotion will also increase. If you lack a thorough understanding of karma, however, you might erroneously believe the principle of karma and devotion to be contradictory. You may say certain things like, "Oh, it's my karma. There is no point in having devotion." If the right causes and conditions are in place, the egg will be cooked. In this example, you are the egg, not the shell and all of that, but the cookable aspect. If simply left alone, nothing will get cooked, but with the right causes and conditions, you are cookable. We also refer to this as the ultimate form of taking refuge. This probably contradicts certain Christian principles. For instance, were you to believe in original sin, Buddhists would say you are not cookable. It is important to understand that we all have the capacity to change.

The fact that we are cookable is quite significant. If we were not cookable, devotion wouldn't work. Were we uncookable, nothing would work; we would be stuck. Yet in reality, we are not stuck. After all, the sole reason an egg can be cooked is simply because it's cookable; that is the cause. The conditions themselves are water and fire, or in our case, renunciation.

Prostrations, mandala offerings, compassion, and devotion—all of these factors are also conditions. The effect is the act of being cooked.

This is where the egg comes in. Whether the egg is cooked or not, an egg is still an egg, isn't it? The Buddha said, "Whether the buddhas of the past, present, and future come or not, the nature of phenomena will remain as it is." This is a great quotation. It is not as though everything became emptiness after Shakyamuni Buddha came to this earth and taught. Everything has been emptiness right from the very start, regardless of whether the Buddha came and said, "Everything is emptiness" or not.

Jigmé Lingpa said, "It is extremely important to examine the guru." As long as the vajra master is qualified and has the authentic blessings of a lineage, guru devotion works. The problem is the term "qualified." What do we mean by that? At the very least, a guru must have compassion. What this means is that the guru must work for you, not for him- or herself. Nevertheless, by the time you truly know the guru is qualified, you will already be quite advanced. Thus, as we can see, this path is quite confusing! What's more, a qualified master is very rare. Even Jigmé Lingpa himself lamented the rarity of qualified masters, and this was several hundred years ago.

Nowadays, in this very, very degenerate era, everyone seems to have his or her own personal agenda. The catchphrase "to have an agenda" is actually quite important when it comes to examining the guru. The guru must be interested in your enlightenment. If you happen to meet a person who can teach a little, maybe not so much, but a little bit, and this person is genuinely interested in enlightening you, then you are quite safe. On the other hand, were you to encounter a guru very learned in the sutras, shastras, and mantras, but not very interested in your enlightenment, that would be an entirely different story. If the guru's interest in you is mainly for the sake of expanding disciple membership, for your wealth, for your looks, for your skill, or for your ability to slave away at some project, then there is considerable danger.

Having an agenda can be really problematic from both sides. For instance, if a student approaches a guru just wanting the guru's attention, not for the sake of enlightenment, and yet the guru is interested only in the enlightenment of the student, the guru's methods will not work. The guru might even do something that will end up driving away a potential practitioner, especially if the guru is not skillful. It is an even sorrier story when a student pursues the guru's attention or some sort of personal relationship, with no interest in the actual enlightenment, while at the same time, the guru is merely interested in publicity, fame, power, and money. This may actually work, but it is very sad. It works because they feed each other's egos.

Undoubtedly, it would be much simpler if we could say, "These are the qualifications of the guru, and these are the steps you should follow." What is really required is a much deeper process of reflection, and we should especially rely on the wisdom that comes from hearing, contemplating, and meditating. Of these three, the wisdom born of hearing is especially important. It is wonderful to hear and study the teachings over and over again.

Long before modern civilization celebrated free speech, the Buddha himself stressed great respect for reasoning and emphasized that a path should be examined rather than followed blindly. While it is important to examine the path and its authority figures, we must also watch out for the cultural baggage that accompanies this process. The world is becoming much smaller, and democracy, in particular, tends to make things more transparent. In the West, the behavior of Tibetan lamas is often criticized. At first glance, this might make us feel defensive, but there is some truth here. Tibetan lamas, for example, often say to their Western students, "You Westerners are so materialistic!" To this, critics respond, "Well, what about you guys? You come to the West, rake in the money, then go back to Nepal or India and buy the latest cars and watches."

It is very true that this kind of thing is happening. According to the critics, spiritual materialism has now reached its highest level; it is even to the point where the Dharma has become something of a commodity. From a very narrow perspective, one might even say that if some of the high lamas were to sell their silver and gold teacup holders, it would surely feed five hundred children in Ethiopia for an entire month. We should try not to forget the other side of this, however. What appears to be simplicity and humility can instead be another form of hypocrisy. There are some, not only lamas but laypeople as well, who are paralyzed by the idea of losing their image of being simple and humble, so much so that it becomes a major source of suffering. From this point of view, I find those people who simply do what they want to do more admirable, those who simply go ahead and wear four Rolex watches, one on each ankle, and one on each arm. In other words, one should not come to a conclusion based on any old rational system.

In the tradition that I was raised in, we have great examples like His Holiness Dilgo Khyentsé Rinpoche, who was a great buddha in my eyes. When I reflect on him and his qualities, it is amazing to think that his feet truly touched this earth; to think that, at some time or another, he actually walked through such and such an airport. Once, for example, while we were waiting in a transit lounge at an airport in Germany, the pilot and airline staff all came over and asked us if they could just touch his hand or feet or something. Yet despite his greatness, he never claimed to be something special. He always said he was worthless. For me, that was the highest teaching. While it was obvious that he was a living buddha, he shunned all praise and recognition. Most of us, in contrast, cannot wait to show off whatever positive qualities we may have.

Guru Yoga Visualization

If you are continuing on from the kusali practice, simply sustain the confidence of being Vajrayogini. In the short sadhana, however, guru yoga practice comes right after the mandala offering, so in this case it would be best to remain seated and instantly visualize yourself as Vajrayogini or Vajravarahi after a brief pause. In the long Longchen Nyingtik liturgy, it mentions that Vajrayogini is red in color, but you can actually visualize yourself either way. Except for the fact she is red in guru yoga and black in the kusali practice, these two are one and the same.

As you look around, imagine your surroundings to be the Copper-Colored Mountain; transform everything into a pure realm. This is similar to what we referred to earlier as "transforming the atmosphere," but in this case, we are doing it in a more elaborate way. Envision yourself holding a curved knife in your right hand and a kapala, or skull cup, in your left hand. Semiwrathful, beautiful, and slender, you have three eyes and are adorned with exquisite ornaments, including a tiger-skin skirt and bone ornamentation. You are standing as though you had been walking and suddenly stopped, just like you are about to take a step forward. Gazing up into the sky with your three eyes, you can see a lotus with one hundred thousand petals, on top of which are sun and moon discs.

Seated on the moon disc is your root guru—lord of the Sangha, embodiment of all objects of refuge, essence of all the buddhas, and leader of all the bodhisattvas. In essence, he is your own root guru, but in form he is Padmakara, the Lotus-born. His complexion is white, and his cheeks are tinged slightly red. He is not old, wrinkled, and ordinary. On the contrary, he is young, majestic, vibrant, and dressed like royalty. He is sitting in the manner of a king, with his right hand holding a vajra and his left holding a kapala. In the crook of his left arm, he cradles a khatvanga, which symbolizes his consort Mandarava. Since this is ngöndro, Mandarava is temporarily hidden in the form of one of his implements. Upon completing the outer guru yoga, it is possible to begin the secret guru yoga, at which point the form of Mandarava becomes explicit.

Visualize Guru Rinpoche sitting amidst millions of spheres of rainbow light. Guru Rinpoche is within the biggest sphere, and in the space around him are his twenty-five disciples, with King Trisong Deutsen at the forefront. In the space above Guru Rinpoche are all the mahasiddhas of the Dzogchen lineage, including Vimalamitra, Jnanasutra, Shri Simha, and Prahevajra, or Garab Dorje. All the remaining space is filled with all kind of deities of the different lineages, as well as dakinis and dharmapalas. Imagine that your surroundings, especially the space in front of you, are entirely filled with the objects of refuge, like a thick cloud.

As you behold the objects of refuge, imbue your perception with the notion that though their appearance is completely clear and vivid, none of them has an objective, truly existent nature. It is like looking at a lake during a full moon, the reflection of the moon is clear, vivid, and very vibrant, yet it is just a reflection. Likewise, all the refuge objects of the guru yoga are seated before you like the reflection of the moon in water. As you visualize all this, give rise to strong, heartfelt devotion and chant the Seven-Line Supplication. Then, after a while, you can chant OM AH HUM VAJRA GURU PADMA SIDDHI HUM.

There is one tradition of doing the Seven-Line Supplication alone one hundred thousand times. When it comes to the Vajra Guru mantra, it is one hundred thousand *times* one hundred, which equals ten million. This, however, is quite easy. If you have the time, it tends to be a two-month job.

As you chant the Vajra Guru mantra, concentrate on the mandala. Simply gaze at Guru Rinpoche's face as he sits there in a sphere of light. When you get tired of this, move your eyes downwards to King Trisong Deutsen, who is seated like great Manjushri, yet in the form of a Tibetan king. When you find yourself getting distracted, notice the beautiful lady Yeshé Tsogyal sitting to the right, and so on and so forth.

Keep in mind, however, that you should not view these figures as ordinary teachers that you can see and feel. If you want to visualize the Dalai Lama, for example, rather than visualizing him in an ordinary way, imagine him above Guru Rinpoche in the form of Avalokiteshvara. This is much better, because even when it comes to the Dalai Lama, his ordinary form still has an impure aspect. He is aging, for instance, and he is not fluent in

Spanish; he has limitations such as these. What's more, you should also be aware that even Avalokiteshvara, in all his greatness, is only but a teardrop of Amitabha.

In the Vajrayana, to release ourselves from this endless cycle of delusion, the key is to understand the nature of mind. To do so, there are only two choices: we either receive the blessings of the guru or we accumulate the merit. There are also two main ways to accumulate merit. One approach is to have impartial compassion toward sentient beings, and the other is to have pure devotion toward the guru. All of this tells us that guru yoga is the most essential practice in tantra.

In a very general sense, one could say that guru yoga is a devotional practice, for it is the mingling of one's own mind and the guru's that lies at the very heart of the practice. This practice of mingling, not only extends to the mind, but also to your entire being, from your identity and form, right down to your sense of taste. You are merging the entire dimension of your being with that of the guru.

The term "mingling," in fact, is quite misleading. It gives the sense that there are two things to mix. Nonetheless, we have no choice but to make use of this language. As Samantabhadra once said, "In aiming to express some of the highest truths, the words and phrases of human beings are simply insufficient."

The essence of mind is emptiness; this is actually the very essence of everything. Thus, while we may speak as though there are two separate entities, the outer guru is none other than a reflection of your devotion. Thus, the merging that takes place in guru yoga is much more than mixing. It is the understanding that these two have never been apart. The outer, inner, and secret gurus are none other than the nature of your own mind.

For beginners like us, however, the path is such that we cannot help but have someone there as a role model. We need someone to be a source of inspiration, an object of refuge and offering, and even an object to whom we can express our emotions. Whining, complaining, supplicating, begging, and praying—these are the only ways we know how to communicate. Yet, it is fine to use such methods.

Always remember that, in the Vajrayana, confusion is accepted as the path, and the path is confusion. Thus, eventually, the path as well is something we need to discard. Of course, we try to offer our devotion, admiration, and unchanging pure vision to the outer guru, until slowly, step by step, we are ready to mingle our being with the inner and secret gurus. We then come to realize that our inner and secret gurus have never been apart from us; they are there all the time.

In discussing how to relate to the outer guru, we can talk about form and appearance, yet the secret and inner gurus need to be discovered, though of course, reading and receiving teachings certainly helps.

What you need to realize is that whatever you hear, read, or contemplate will create some understanding in your mind, yet whatever this understanding might be, it is actually just a patch. Sooner or later this patch is going to fall off. In a way, even this fixation presents no problem because sooner or later it too will fall away, but you should be aware that such fixation will greatly prolong your path. Given that you may have only twenty more years, and that what you have understood is actually nothing but a patch, are you prepared to spend another ten years believing it to be reality? You should always be prepared to peel off this outer skin. As you come to see the next layer, you may think that you have found the real fruit, but always be ready to accept that it is only another layer of skin. This not only applies to hearing, contemplating, and reading, it is even more relevant when you meditate. This is the real meaning of the saying, "experience is like morning mist."

Since guru yoga carries such great blessings, it will also stir up your mind. It can alter your mood, and even mix up your life. You should be prepared for such things. More than anything else, however, it invokes *nyam*, experiences. "Experience" may not actually be the best translation for this term, but it will have to do.

There are three varieties of experience. Sometimes you may feel very blissful, in which case there is a sense that you can accept anything and everything, no matter what happens. In the same way a saucer fits a cup, everything fits just right, you may even feel as if you could place a table on the cup. In other words, everything is acceptable and tolerable. Should you hear some news like, "The world is upside-down right now!" your reaction would be, "Sure, why not?" There is complete acceptance and, on a physical level, a great deal of bliss. That is one kind of *nyam*. Most of us do not experience this, but still we want it. The fact that we long for *nyam* is quite sad and pathetic.

Another kind of *nyam* is the experience of nonconceptuality. This may go on for a few minutes or hours, and sometimes, even for days. With this experience, you will have no thoughts, no aggression, no obvious passion, no judgmental attitudes, no comparison, and no insecurity, yet everything will appear to be vividly present. It is better not to describe this in too much detail, otherwise you will idealize this experience. You have to discover it for yourself.

The third experience is clarity, in which everything manifests with crystal clarity. This feels as though you could almost tell how many leaves a tree has, or what is going on in someone else's head.

All of these experiences are what we call *nyam*. The great masters of the past have told us that *nyam* is like mist; sooner or later it will dissolve. In other words, these experiences are not our final destination. For many of us, even having a good dream is something we wish for, yet we should really be prepared to give all this up.

It is the secret guru, meaning emptiness, that we must discover within our own awareness. We must let the greatness of our own buddha nature grow; we must give it a chance. Right now, our buddha nature does not even have the opportunity to wiggle its toes because we are invariably preoccupied with other things. Nonetheless, though we constantly busy ourselves with this and that, our buddha natures remain vibrant. Everything is intact, including all the thirty-two major and eighty minor marks of buddhahood.

The masters of the past have said that we are like beggars living in a shantytown. Though we have been living in a slum, sleeping in an old worn-out bed in a very poor household for twenty years, all we have to do is dig two inches beneath our bed and we will find a cache of diamonds. Yet because we are preoccupied with our task of begging, we are entirely oblivious to the presence of this treasure. This is how we are at the moment. It is as though we are not giving our buddha nature the chance to function. Through practice, however, we create an opening for it to manifest.

In the practice of guru yoga, one practical piece of advice is that your own being can be mingled with the guru's being over and over again. When you visualize Guru Rinpoche sitting before you and chant OM AH HUM VAJRA GURU PADMA SIDDHI HUM, let Guru Rinpoche dissolve into you every ten, twenty, or hundred mantras . . . the more the better. Simply let Guru Rinpoche dissolve inseparably into you and then simply watch what happens. It is not a good idea to spell out the details here, but something will happen when you do this. This key will open up a whole new world. It's like a television with one thousand channels! Needless to say, this will stir up your life a little as well. After all, some of these channels will probably show horror movies, won't they?

Jigmé Lingpa once said, "We have watched this show for so many life-times . . . Enough!" This cycle is so boring: We eat our breakfast, lunch, and dinner, go to a job in between, then come back to our husbands and wives. How many billions of times have we done all this? All this eating of our own children and parents as fish and prawns. Sometimes we eat them grilled, sometimes barbecued, sometimes chopped up and stir fried. Enough is enough! Let's watch another show, one that costs much less. Why don't we watch our own minds instead? The key to doing this is to mingle your own mind with the guru's again and again. This is vitally important.

Despite knowing this, I myself do not do it often enough, but when I do it's amazing. When I am riding the escalator to catch the subway in London, for instance, I might promise myself, "I will mingle my mind with the guru's until I reach the end of the escalator." This only takes a few moments to do. Then, of course, I go back to watching movies and all the other important things I have to do. If you take these little moments to mingle your mind with the guru's mind and then observe what happens for a few minutes, everything else will become less of a big deal.

Mind you, this should be done without expecting immediate results, so don't be impatient. Due to your habitual patterns, hang-ups, and distrac-tions, nothing may happen in the beginning. If you complain, however, it would be like putting an egg on a table and then complaining that it's not getting cooked. The egg needs to be placed in water, and the flame must be turned on for at least a few minutes, depending on the strength of the fire. How can you complain if you've only put the egg into the pot for a few moments, or haven't even done that much?

This kind of outlook indicates a misunderstanding of causality. Of all people, those living in the West should be the last to complain. After all, it was the Western world that first put a man on the moon and the first to real-ize that the world is round. We Tibetans still think it's flat! Since Western culture is dominated by the scientific worldview, and since science is very much a doctrine of causality, it is just a matter of diverting one's attention into the inner world.

Causality should always be taken into consideration. It may indeed take some time to see an effect. When compared to the billions and billions of lifetimes spent without even having taken this egg out of the carton, a few years is not long at all. At long last, you now know that there is an egg that needs to be taken out. This is already quite an improvement. Simply having this information involves a great deal of merit.

Besides being patient, it is also important to pray. This is almost a theistic approach, except for the fact that, as Buddhists, our fundamental view is the view of emptiness. Prayer, however, is good and it works. As you are chanting OM AH HUM VAJRA GURU PADMA SIDDHI HUM, for example, you can also imagine your guru seated at the crown of your head and pray:

Bless me guru so that my mind enters the Dharma, and so that the Dharma enters my mind.
Bless me so that my Dharma practice won't meet with such a bumpy ride.
Bless me so that the defilements of the path are cleared away.
Bless me so that all this confusion and delusion may arise as wisdom.
Bless me guru so that all these nondharmic thoughts stop right this instant.
Bless me so that love, compassion, and bodhichitta will grow in my being.
Bless me so that relative and ultimate bodhichitta will grow in my being.
Bless me so that genuine devotion will also grow in my being.
Bless me so that I will not lose inspiration.
Bless me so that the next distraction, whatever it might be, will not distract me.
Bless me so that I will not be overpowered by past karmic deeds and habits.
Bless me so that I will not be deceived by a seemingly good result.
Bless me so that I have the good health to be able to help many people.
Bless me so that regardless of whatever thought enters my mind, it eventually leads to the Dharma.

This last wish is particularly beautiful. Here you are saying, "Even with those thoughts and actions that appear to be very mundane and nondharmic, bless me so that these too may eventually lead to something meaningful." Such a thought could start out with an impulse to go out for a pint of a beer. Perhaps you are thinking of an Irish Guinness and have a strong desire to pursue this impulse. Although it may initially lead you to a bar, it could also bring about something completely unexpected. Maybe you'll meet up with a stranger, for example, and end up discussing the Dharma. This conversation, in turn, may spark an interest in the person. Perhaps you'll mention the name of a particular Dharma center. At the end of the day, you will have been instrumental in creating a karmic link between this person and the Dharma.

If these prayers become a little boring, imagine yourself beneath Guru Rinpoche and, as you continue to chant OM AH HUM VAJRA GURU PADMA SIDDHI HUM, visualize an uninterrupted stream of nectar flowing down and dissolving into you. You can also visualize Guru Rinpoche seated on a lotus in your heart, though this method is usually applied when retiring at night. If you are encountering some sort of obstacle, such as a family dispute, depression, or sadness, you can visualize Guru Rinpoche above your shoulder and imagine that he becomes very wrathful, even to the point where fangs start to emerge from his mouth. While envisioning this wrathful form of Guru Rinpoche, imagine that fire and scorpions flow out of his vajra and move toward you, your obstacles, and obscurations. These scorpions snap at all the obstacles and swallow them up, until each and every obscuration is destroyed. There are endless methods such as this.

Another technique can be used when you feel as though you are approaching death. If this is the case, visualize Guru Rinpoche in an Amitabha-like form, red in color, but with his usual attributes. Although Guru Rinpoche is holding a kapala in the usual way, he is none other than Amitabha. You should then transfer yourself into his heart over and over again.

When doing these practices, there is a tendency for boredom to set in after a while. We are never happy with just one channel; we always end up switching to the next. So here you can switch. You can imagine that Guru Rinpoche is everywhere, for example, that he is filling every inch of space. As you continue to chant the mantra, look around in all directions and imagine that everything transforms into Guru Rinpoche. If there are people around you, for instance, transform them all into Guru Rinpoche. Pens, pencils, watches, books, handkerchiefs, diapers, and whatever else you see . . . transform them all into the form of Guru Rinpoche. When you look outside, imagine the trees, mountains, and lakes in the form of Guru Rinpoche. Even if you feel hot and suddenly a breeze comes along to cool you down, imagine this to be a manifestation of Guru Rinpoche. When we wonder how to take the guru as the path, it is a matter of taking everything to be none other than Guru Rinpoche. You should even hear the sounds of coughs and farts to be Guru Rinpoche's voice, mainly in the form of mantra OM AH HUM VAJRA GURU PADMA SIDDHI HUM.

These methods might sound very theistic, but there is an important distinction to keep in mind. In the theistic mind-set, what is missing is the notion of mingling one's own mind with the guru's. The real guru is the inner nature of mind, which is emptiness. This is what makes these two mind-sets different. When you have the view of emptiness as a base and then go ahead with these theistic methods, it works.

For those who can accept emptiness, everything is possible. Take the example of the mirage. If you see what appears to be water in a desert and know that it is a mirage, it will be completely up to you how to take it. Whether you approach it or go around it will be of little consequence. If you approach, it will not be because you think there is real water there. Similarly, if you divert your path, it will not be due to the nonexistence of water, but simply because you know there is a mirage there. The nonexistence of water and the mirage are different. Here, nonexistence means that the water once existed and then became nonexistent, yet the water in the mirage never existed, neither as mirage nor water. The water is a complete illusion.

If you do not have a particular practice, this ngöndro can be your main practice. It is fine to go to different teachings, but if you want to attend an initiation, you had better ask whether doing page after page of a sadhana is a requirement. If the answer is yes, you should definitely think twice. You might even be told that the commitment is not too much, but in reality, these commitments can add up quickly. If you have the time, however, then of course please go ahead. This is a wonderful path. If receiving empowerments and collecting various commitments makes you feel good, and you are the type of person who does not particularly feel guilty about not keeping them, then fine!

At first, practitioners are usually eager to follow the path. After practicing for some time, however, they get slightly bored. This is the human mind. It is like eating an omelette every single day. Eventually, you will end up wanting fried eggs. There are obstacles along the way as well. Actually, what is happening is that you are slowly beginning to master the path. As you draw near, you may get bored and want to change. Naturally, a new practice may be inspiring for a few days, but what you do not realize is that you are going back to square one, for this new exciting practice will itself eventually become boring.

My suggestion is this: meet as many lamas, and hear as many Dharma teachings, as possible. If you truly want to pursue the Dzogchen path, and the Longchen Nyingtik in particular, it is especially good to do this. It is also good to meet people from the same lineage. I would also suggest that you do not allow yourself to get distracted by the scores of attractive practices that are out there. Once you have finished the ngöndro, there are many masters you can go to if you want to receive teachings on Dzogchen.

THE FOUR EMPOWERMENTS

In the Mahayana, the principle of buddha nature is usually introduced through philosophical and contemplative analysis in a thorough and gradual manner. At first, we may get just a glimpse of buddha nature, though we will not have discovered it in any absolute sense. We then try to contemplate and practice to discover it more fully. In the Mahayana, this discovery, prompted by our practice of the six perfections, unfolds over three countless eons.

The Vajrayana path, in contrast, allows us to practice the six perfections and other such factors in a single session. It is this contrast in method that distinguishes the Vajrayana way of introducing buddha nature from that of the Mahayana. This is not to say that one approach is good and the other bad. Nonetheless, there is a significant distinction to be made here. For the Mahayana practitioner, the mind is the sole emphasis, but in the Vajrayana, it is not only the mind that we are concerned with, but also our body and speech.

Buddha nature is introduced at the outset of the Vajrayana path via the first door of the tantric path: empowerment. Through empowerment, body, speech, and mind are all introduced as a manifestation of our own buddha nature. Empowerments tell us that we have buddha nature. To express this, we use different names like Tara and Manjushri. Based on merit, which is created by devotion, we discover this buddha nature for ourselves via the guru's introduction.

What actually happens in an empowerment depends on the recipient of the empowerment, the one who gives it, and the connection between these two. The recipient of the empowerment may have unshakable trust in the one who gives the empowerment and in the path itself, but to have such devotion is not easy. I often tell practitioners that, while they may think they have devotion toward their guru, most of the time it is more like admiration. Though admiration is necessary to begin with, true devotion is not simply a matter of liking someone.

The question is this: how do we go beyond admiration and develop real devotion? First, the most important factor is motivation. Your motivation should be for the sake of enlightenment. For a moment, let us forget about enlightening all sentient beings. At the very least, you should be motivated to seek your own enlightenment.

For many of us, however, enlightenment is not our motivation when approaching the guru. Why is it that so many students suffer when the guru ignores them? It is because their motivation is to have the guru's unwavering attention, not to attain enlightenment. When the guru, this poor guru with five hundred students, eventually directs his attention to someone else, the student ends up suffering. To have the correct motivation, therefore, is incredibly important.

If you are interested in enlightenment, then 50 percent of your problems are resolved, if not 90 percent. You can get what you need, meaning the teachings and instructions, and then say farewell until next time. The dilemma comes when we are told to hang around. Interpreting a piece of advice is not always easy. The instructions we receive, moreover, cannot always be taken in black and white terms. The predicament we find ourselves in is that we do not know how real it all is. We may think the guru is testing us or doing something for a specific reason.

In many instances, however, the lion's share of these gurus are quite often as passive and inert as a vegetable! Despite the fact that the guru is not doing anything at all, students create their own paranoia with thoughts like, "Oh, oh . . . he knows!" or "Oh, oh . . . she's testing me."

All too frequently, students think that I myself am omniscient. I must confess that, on many occasions, I let them think so. Sometimes, however, I categorically reply, "No, no, I didn't know that." I actually tell them outright. Yet the more I say, "I didn't know," the more they say, "Oh, you are so humble." The guru, it seems, is in a win-win situation. In any case, the main factor is your motivation. The rest you will learn as you progress along the path. You should seek out the guru to attain enlightenment, not for their attention, to feel included, or anything else.

The term "empowerment" derives from the Sanskrit word "abisheka." Sanskrit is an exceptionally rich language, especially when it comes to the nuances of each individual word. Since one word can contain several levels of meaning, we can end up with different interpretations. That is the beauty of Sanskrit.

The term "empowerment" has two primary meanings. In Tibetan, we refer to these two meanings with the words *torwa* and *lugpa*, which can be translated as *dismantling* and *pouring*, respectively. In this case, "dismantling" refers to dismantling the cocoon, or shell, of ignorance. "Pouring," on the other hand, refers either to pouring the blessings, or pouring/discovering buddha nature.

When it comes to understanding the implied meaning of empowerment, however, the terms we use can actually be misleading. To interpret the word "empowerment" to mean "pouring" and "discovering," and even when we use the expression "receive an empowerment," can inadvertently lead us to think we are being given a power that was previously not in our possession. The term "empowerment" almost has the connotation of conferring something, not unlike a knighting, for instance.

This interpretation is far from the true spirit of the tantric initiation. In being empowered, one is being introduced to something within oneself, albeit something that has gone unrecognized. Activating this recognition is what we mean by the term "empowerment."

There are various empowerments with numerous divisions, yet according to the highest yoga tantra, there are four main types. Each of these four, referred to as the "four empowerments," is designed to dismantle one of the four defilements. These four are the defilements of *nadi*, which relate to the veins, chakras, or channels; the defilement of *prana*, which coincides with speech, or wind-energy; and the defilement of *bindu*, which is a defilement of mind. There are two ways to explain the fourth defilement: one is to say it is the residue of the three combined or, in other words, something similar to *alaya*. Alternatively, it can be described as "the ground of everything," but this second way of explaining it is quite difficult to understand.

The empowerment ritual utilizes symbolic implements and substances. First, the guru will place a vase on your head and then pour some liquid into your hand, saying, "Drink this saffron water." Next, the guru will use a *kapala*, which is traditionally filled with nectar. This substance is actually a mixture of the father and mother consort's essence. These days, however, most of lamas use Bordeaux or Chianti if the empowerment is given in Europe, or tequila if it is being given in America. With the third empowerment, the substance is related to the consort. Nowadays, lamas will flash a picture of a dakini or something similar. Finally, for the fourth empowerment, which is referred to as the word empowerment, a substance like crystal is sometimes used, though technically speaking this is no longer a necessity. The crystal symbolizes the nature of mind.

Each individual part of the empowerment can be very elaborate. We could talk for ages about the mechanics of the vase empowerment alone. Take the use of water, for instance. To start, the Buddhist teachings originated in India, where it is customary to use water for purification. Yet even in our ordinary lives, we habitually associate washing with cleansing. At the very least, we understand that we are not making more dirt when we wash something.

There are many reasons that justify the use of water as a tantric substance. First of all, the Vajrayana always incorporates ordinary human habits into the path. If you have an article of clothing that needs washing, you would not think to wash it with soil; you would use water. The Vajrayana uses this habitual pattern. From the Vajrayana perspective, one would say that what we call "water" has many manifestations. When water is in the sink, it is washing water. When in the toilet bowl, it is dirty water. When flowing out of a shower nozzle, it is clean washing water. Similarly, when placed in an offering bowl, it then becomes offering water. Even though there is only one entity called water, by associating certain attributes with it, our perception changes. We have drinking water, washing water, bottled water, and natural water. These days, we even have carbonated and noncarbonated mineral water, giving us the choice of having our water with or without bubbles. Given that we perceive it in such a variety of ways, why shouldn't the Vajrayana incorporate water into the tantric path?

This use of logic is grounded in the approach of the Prasangika Madhyamaka, a school of Buddhist philosophy that uses the internal logic of its opponent's beliefs to dismantle all conceptual views. You can never tell a Vajrayana practitioner, "This is just superstition!"

Were you to say such a thing, they would only respond, "These apparent superstitions are actually based on the logic that you yourself created!" Rightly so, all the responsibility will end up on your own shoulders. They will then ask, "Why can't I use water as an empowerment substance? You could use this very same water in at least ten different ways, couldn't you?"

It is, after all, our own logic that leads us to perceive water as either pure or ordinary. When water is bottled and packaged properly, you might pay a considerable price for it. Yet if you were to go to Bhutan and explain that in some places you have to *buy* water, let alone mention the price, they would already find it very strange.

In the course of an empowerment, and within tantric practice in general, we use many different methods. Not only do we use various substances, we also employ mantras, mudras, and samadhi. The water in the vase, for instance, is packaged very well. In fact, it is much better than expensive bottled water like Evian. Millions of cities are visualized within every drop. Here we are talking about entire cities like Frankfurt and London, and also vast cities of dakinis. Though this use of samadhi is already quite extensive, this is only one aspect of the packaging. We also bless the water with sacred gestures called mudras.

The principle of empowerment probably sounds very complicated, long-winded, or maybe even ritualistic. There is some good news, though. In the Longchen Nyingtik, or in any ngöndro, for that matter, it is possible to take all four empowerments while reciting a single stanza and doing the visualizations found in the guru yoga. Actually, in the long version of the Longchen Nyingtik ngöndro, the explanation of the four empowerments is quite elaborate.

For this reason, you can supplement the short ngöndro by inserting the long version of the self-empowerment. Self-empowerment mainly involves visualization and meditation. The visualization itself is not that compli-cated. The earlier discussion concerning the intricate details relating to the five buddha families and the use of water was all theory. What we find in the Longchen Nyingtik ngöndro are the key instructions, which are made as simple and practical as possible.

While empowerment usually comes at the end of the guru yoga prac-tice, you can take the self-empowerment over and over again as you chant the vajra guru mantra. You may do so each time you complete one round of the rosary, for instance. To begin, you visualize a white letter OM at the forehead of the guru. If you are unable to get a clear image of these letters, that is fine. Simply imagine that a strong, vibrant, majestic white light issues from the guru's forehead and dissolves into your own. As is the case in Vajra-sattva practice, this cleanses all your defilements. The white light cleanses the defilements of the body, as well as the obscurations and karmic deeds created primarily by the body. It also cleanses the obscurations of the *nadis*, such as the three channels and five chakras.

As this light fills your body, imagine that the seed of the nirmanakaya is implanted within your being. You should also think that the guru's body and your own body become inseparable. Another way of putting this is to think that your body becomes an indestructible vajra body. With this first visualization, you can say that you have received the vase empowerment.

This empowerment also opens the door to the meditations of the development stage.

The four empowerments can be taken one after another in a single session. Alternatively, you can also concentrate on each empowerment one by one, dedicating about a year to each. I've seen my father using this approach when teaching his students in Eastern Bhutan.[58] In the first year, for instance, you visualize this white light, then during the second year, you focus on the light coming from the guru's throat, and so forth. This latter approach is very thorough.

For the second empowerment, visualize the letter AH at the throat of the guru. From this letter AH, brilliant rays of red light stream forth and dissolve into your throat, thereby cleansing the defilements of speech, or what we also refer to as the defilements of *prana*. As this red light dissolves into you, your speech becomes vajra speech, inseparable from the guru's. The seed of the sambhogakaya is also implanted in your being and you receive the secret empowerment. In addition, this second empowerment opens the door to the meditations of the completion stage.

In the Vajrayana, there are two main forms of meditation practice: the development stage and completion stage. In the development stage, you imagine yourself, along with every phenomenon, to be a deity. In the completion stage, this deity is dissolved. That is the most straightforward way to explain these two stages. In developmental meditation, you will find various methods, such as imagining oneself to be a deity, visualizing lotuses, sun and moon discs, as well the projection and reabsorption of light rays. All of these are basically tantric in nature.

There are two kinds of completion stage. One is referred to as completion meditation with form, and the other as formless completion stage meditation. The completion stage with form involves *anuyoga* practices, such as meditating on the chakras and channels and controlling the *prana* by trying to insert it into the central channel, the *avadhuti*. This also includes dream yoga, bardo, and kundalini practices. All of these fall under the completion stage with form. The formless completion stage is the highest form of vipashyana, or insight.

With the third empowerment, visualize the letter HUM at the center of the guru's heart, out of which comes a dazzling blue light that dissolves into your own heart center. This light expels all the defilements of mind or, rather, the obscurations of *bindu*. It also opens the door to *trekchö* practice, the first of the two formless completion stage meditations. In receiving this empowerment, the seed of the dharmakaya is planted in your mind, transforming it into vajra mind. In other words, your mind is now inseparable from the guru's mind.

For the fourth empowerment, visualize another round of blue light projecting out from the letter HUM at the guru's heart. This blue light dissolves into your entire body, your forehead, throat, and heart, thereby dispelling all defilements, their residues, and any remaining habitual patterns. Through this, you receive the word empowerment, which destroys the alaya, meaning the mind, basically. You also receive the blessings of the guru's entire body, speech, and mind. As a result, your own being merges inseparably with the entire being of the guru. Once this merging has taken place, simply observe what happens.

PRACTICE IN DAILY LIFE

In the traditional approach, we are reminded to practice the Dharma again and again. Lamas tend to repeat these preliminary ideas to the point where it becomes almost painful for the student. There are few ways to get sidetracked with these concepts. The exotic elements that we find in the main teachings are decidedly absent. There are no colorful visualizations, no exercises with *prana* and *nadi*, and so forth. In fact, all of these details can become almost a trip. Just hearing about these practices is exciting. Nevertheless, as all the lamas of the past have taught, we should not pay less attention to these preliminary thoughts. For beginners like us, this is what will drive our minds toward the Dharma.

Not being able to imbue our minds with the Dharma is a common problem. Quite a few of us, including myself, have been in the Dharma for a long time, and yet our minds are still very rigid. Some mundane factor might make us happy, but when we are faced with the most trivial, ridiculous of circumstances, we still end up feeling hurt. That is not a good sign! It means the Dharma is going in one ear and out the other, that it is not affecting us the way that it should. The Dharma has to penetrate our hearts.

Another point to remember is that you do not necessarily have to go somewhere else to practice. You should not get discouraged and think, "I will never be able to practice the Dharma properly because I can't go live in a cave for three or six years." It has nothing to do with that. There are people who have lived in Kathmandu for thirty years and are still the same! In fact, some of these people have become even more rigid. Not only do they have all the ordinary mundane human garbage, they are also wearing a disguise, the camouflage of a Dharma practitioner. Once others begin to see through this camouflage, these so-called Dharma practitioners find it unbearable; they really lose it.

Dharma practice has nothing to do with chanting more mantras or spending more hours sitting. Rather, it concerns simple, everyday things. In this era, it is our worldly, day-to-day lives that we really have to watch. We need to bring the Dharma to mind when things are not turning out as we planned, or if our mood suddenly changes.

Our minds are very fickle. One minute we are okay, and the next minute some ridiculous circumstance stirs up all kinds of past emotions. After bringing up all these things we have done or regret, we brood for days, perhaps even cry. Not only do we cry and brood to ourselves, we also long for attention and end up exhibiting our feelings to others. This person—our friend, relative, or whomever we end up calling—ends up getting disturbed as well.

What's the point of all this? As bodhisattvas, if we want to suffer, we should suffer alone! Why drag another person into it? This is even more true if we are tonglen practitioners, in which case we are supposed to take on other peoples' suffering, not seek someone to share our own suffering with. So, for older Dharma practitioners like myself, it is about time that we let the Dharma sink in. Don't ever let the Dharma become something you can pin an excuse on.

I recite Jamgön Kongtrül Lodrö Thaye's *Calling the Guru* every day. This is a wonderful prayer. Every time I recite it, I try to dwell on at least one stanza. This is very penetrating; it feels like my flaws are constantly being exposed. The Dharma is like that, especially pith instructions. As Patrül Rinpoche says, if it feels like a certain piece of advice is revealing some of the worst things inside of you, it is a good sign. It means the pith instructions are working.

Nowadays, it is hard to tell whether teachings are Buddhist or New Age. Listening to New Age teachers, and even some Buddhist masters, may make you feel good. It will validate your ego and confirm your feelings. If that is what you want, you might as well do something more tangible. Go have a good massage or listen to a piece of nice music, like Beethoven's Fifth. These things will cheer you up.

Pith instructions, on the other hand, should make you feel bad. When you read the *Words of My Perfect Teacher*, the more it depresses you, the more you are beginning to understand the Dharma. *Words of My Perfect Teacher* is a depressing book; it is a book that rattles you. What it tells us is disconcerting, and that is quite important.

In any case, not all forms of depression are bad. Without ever letting such states to the surface, we would be oblivious to them. We would not even be aware that they are problems. Without this knowledge, how could we even begin to be motivated to purify them? This process should really bring things out in the open.

The Dharma should penetrate our minds. As Kongtrül Rinpoche wrote, "Our Dharma practice should really bear fruit." This has nothing to do with good dreams, a certain sensation after sitting for a long time, or even some sort of ecstatic feeling, clairvoyance, or enhancement of intuition. These outcomes are not the results we are looking for. What Kongtrül Rinpoche meant was that, as we practice, we begin to place less emphasis on some of the things that had previously seemed to be such a big deal. That is the fruit of Dharma practice.

In the past, receiving a compliment may have easily moved us. "Your hair looks good! The color is so nice," someone might say, and for half a day, this intoxicates us. Later in the day, however, someone else might say that our hair doesn't look that good, throwing us into a state of depression. After doing some Dharma practice, if this sort of thing no longer makes any difference to us, our Dharma practice is bearing fruit. This is more preferable than millions of good dreams, even one where the Buddha himself appears and places his hand on the top of your head to bless you!

It is difficult to tell whether such dreams are good or bad signs. Their occurrence may cause a practitioner to think that he or she has reached some level of attainment and block the urge to practice further. For these reasons, Patrül Rinpoche said that good dreams can actually be what he calls a "devil's manifestation." He also said that if you dreamt last night that the Buddha was having dinner with you, you should treat the dream as you would the saliva you spit on the ground. You should not even give it a second thought. When we spit, do we check to see where it landed or how much is there? Likewise, you should never mention your dreams or even write them down. Otherwise, when you notice that your compassion toward sentient beings is growing a little, or that devotion toward the path and the teacher is increasing, you might just become more relaxed.

One of the lines in Kongtrül Rinpoche's prayer reads: "Kyoshey tingney kyewar jingyi lob." Chögyam Trungpa termed this "a genuine heart of sadness," and I think this is quite a good phrase. This "genuine heart of sadness" is really important. Let's say that you are having a good dream. Despite the fact that you are enjoying the dream, deep down, somewhere in your mind, you know that sooner or later you are going to wake up. That is what we call the "genuine heart of sadness." Sooner or later, our relationships, our health, and all the other circumstances we face will change. None of this is going to last.

Change is inevitable. While it may not be obvious, this "genuine heart of sadness" is always there. It is as though someone were chasing you, or like a race against time. For this reason, Dharma practice should never be set aside with the thought, "I will do it some other time." More often than not, when we say, "I will practice this weekend," it just doesn't happen.

Dharma practice has little to do with sitting and chanting; it is more a matter of confronting your ego and pride, and accepting things as they are. That you can do at any time. You may be on a beach looking at the sunset, and though there is nothing terribly wrong, an alarm bell suddenly goes off in your head, saying "ding, ding, ding . . . time to practice the Dharma!" At that very moment, you can always think: "I'm looking at this sunset, but I'd better take a good look, because I might never see one again. This might be the last sunset of my life. Who knows, in the next life I might be an insect, a being that has no knowledge of sunsets and sunrises, let alone the capacity to comprehend this idea." By then, you will have a totally different interpretation of what a sunset is.

Later in the same prayer, Kongtrül says: "Bless me so that I remember death from the depths of my heart!" Death, dying, and the fact that we are constantly getting closer and closer to death—we need to bring these to mind again and again. We also need strong trust, belief, and devotion toward causality. On this one we may need prompting from time to time, otherwise we forget about it completely.

Just listen to your complaints. We complain to the Buddha, to the guru, to our husbands and wives, and to our friends. If you listen to your complaints and contemplate them, you will realize that most are based on not understanding causality. It is a bit like this: imagine that you are driving toward a cliff. The road is really bad, and you have been warned that it is dangerous. Going ahead with this course is fatal, and you know it. What is more, despite having been told not to drink, you go ahead and drink anyway. You then speed recklessly toward the cliff and fall off it, and still you complain.

We are the same way. If you think back, you will see that the causes and conditions for what you experience have been systematically organized by you alone! For years you have learned, practiced, and gathered these causes and conditions so carefully, but when the unpleasant result occurs, you complain. This is usually how it is. Another illustration of this failure to understand causality is a lack of conviction in the Three Jewels—the Buddha, Dharma, and Sangha.

Dharma Is Not Therapy

These are what we call preliminary thoughts. One time I received teachings from His Holiness Dilgo Khyentsé Rinpoche every day for seven months in a row, with no weekend breaks. He would teach one subject in the morning, another in the afternoon, and one more at night. Whatever the subject was, he always began with these preliminary thoughts, spending at least forty-five minutes to an hour talking about them. The main teaching usually lasted five to ten minutes, or half an hour at the longest. Indeed, it is quite important to hear the preliminary thoughts again and again. We find this unsettling, yet this is the purpose of Dharma.

Never think that you will be able to settle your life down by practicing the Dharma. The Dharma is not therapy. In fact, it is just the opposite. The purpose of the Dharma is to really stir up your life. It is meant to turn your life upside down. If that is what you have asked for, why complain? If it is not turning your life upside down, on the other hand, the Dharma is not working. That kind of Dharma is just another one of these New Age methods; the Dharma should really disturb you.

If you really want to practice the Dharma, it means that you aim to achieve enlightenment. Striving to be happy or to be a good person is not your main objective. Of course, it is not as though you intend to be unhappy or become a bad person. As a rule, in wanting to fit into society, you try to be polite and gentle. You act respectfully and with the proper etiquette. Many people think that, as Dharma practitioners, we should act a certain way. When we look at another who may seem to be doing things a little inhumanely, we think: "How can he be a Dharma practitioner! He is so arrogant!" Yet it is very difficult to judge another person, because for a genuine Dharma practitioner, fitting in is not really the point.

If a great master from the past, like Tilopa or Naropa, were to walk into our room right now, we would not allow them to enter! We would see them as homeless, street beggars, or maybe even intruders. Imagine Tilopa, almost completely naked and perhaps partially covered with something resembling a g-string if we are lucky. His hair has never been shampooed, and there is a live fish protruding from his mouth, with its tail still quivering. "He is supposed to be a Buddhist," we would think, "how can he do such a thing?"

We tend to have a very theistic, judgmental mind. Our attitude is very Shravakayana, actually. Of course, Shravakayana judgment is already quite good, but we are talking about the Vajrayana here. We are talking about going beyond all conceptions. Milarepa, for instance, was considered one of the worst looking, most annoying of people. Since he had a habit of going around naked, his sister gave him a piece of cloth, hoping that he would make some clothing. Instead of making a proper shirt or pants, however, he sewed the cloth to fit his penis like a sock! He made socks to fit his hands, his feet, and his penis. He wasted the whole cloth! He didn't even do it deliberately. From an ordinary point of view, we would regard such a person either as completely childish or as inhuman.

We should really have this aspiration. We should pray that one day we reach a stage where we have enough courage to become just like these eccentric people. Right now, we can only afford to be slightly nonconformist. A little bit of craziness is okay. It is kind of a character-building activity. We are very scared of going beyond that, however, because we would become outcasts.

We should pray that someday we really become crazy, but not in the sense of becoming something like a lunatic in an asylum. The craziness we are referring to means going beyond the eight worldly pursuits. Truly not caring whether you are being praised or criticized is the ultimate craziness. From the mundane, worldly point of view, whenever you are praised, you are supposed to be happy; when you are criticized, you are expected to be unhappy. However, sublime beings are not moved; that's why we think they are crazy. This is what you should aim for.

Do not do this right now, however, because it will backfire on you. Just aspire. If you tried doing this now, it would not only fail to help your practice, it would also upset others. So continue in a way that any decent human being would want you to behave. But at the same time, let this alarm continuously sound in your head: "All of this is useless."

Finally, always pay attention to the three sacred principles. That will make the practice complete. As I said earlier, practicing does not necessarily mean sitting down and reciting mantras, meditating, or something like that. Rather, we should try to turn everything we do into something beneficial.

If not for the sake of sentient beings at this very moment, at least we should have the aspiration that whatever we do will benefit sentient beings at some time in the future. Whatever you do, always do it with the motivation of helping sentient beings. This is the first of the three sacred principles, which are also known as the three supreme methods.

When it comes to Dharma practice, we need to be ambitious in generating the proper motivation. It is not enough to settle for simple kindness or a good attitude. We should try to have bodhichitta mind. Even with a minor act like offering a small candle, try to remember to do it with the wish to enlighten all sentient beings. As His Holiness Dudjom Rinpoche said: "Dharma practice is quite easy. It's all a matter of motivation." It all comes down to our attitude. The only problem is that on many occasions, we just don't remember these crucial instructions. On top of that, we always end up trying to do something more complicated, which is totally unnecessary. So when you are offering a candle, or perhaps offering a bouquet of flowers to your teacher, at that very moment, you should try to seal it with the motivation of bodhichitta.

Begin everything with the motivation of bodhichitta. This motivation, moreover, should be permeated with the attitude of nonduality. This can be a little difficult in the beginning. Though we may not be able to constantly meditate on emptiness, we should at least have the notion that this is just our own perception. Even with the most simple act, be it lighting a candle or doing three prostrations, you should understand that, although you are accumulating merit and doing something good, it is just your mind that is doing it. As I advised right from the start, you need to get used to this idea. Try to know that whatever you are offering or doing, whether it is Dharma practice or a simple good deed, all this is something your mind is interpreting. There is no truly existing holy act. It's just your mind.

This will release you from countless defilements. For one, it will release you from the pride of having done something. Should the person to whom you are offering a bouquet of flowers squash them instantly, or discard them without a second glance, you will not care so much. If, however, you lack this attitude of nonduality, you will remain attached to the object you are giving away. You will still want to know how this person is going to use or not use it. Things like this indicate a strong clinging toward your actions. To conclude, dedicate the merit you have accumulated to all sentient beings.

These are the three supreme methods and they are critically important. If you can remember these three in all your actions, in your day-to-day life, very soon you will become a great Dharma practitioner. It won't take long, just a month or two. Even if you are a seasoned Dharma practitioner, always remember that in order to make an action worthwhile and beneficial, these three principles are crucial.

Three very important points mentioned in Jamgön Kongtrül's prayer relate to the principles of abandoning, transforming, and knowing, three pieces of practical advice that clearly define the three yanas, the Shravakayana, Mahayana, and Vajrayana. Let's say there is a person who is experiencing desire or aggression. According to Jamgön Kongtrül's instructions, there are three principal ways to deal with the situation. According to the Shravakayana, we abandon the emotion by suppressing, dismantling, and discouraging it. Basically, we get rid of the emotion.

In the Mahayana, the method is to transform the emotion. With this approach, we are not necessarily abandoning it, nor are we allowing the emotion to manifest as it likes, in a wild, untamed, and harmful way. Rather, it is transformed.

The Vajrayana approach is simply to know the essence of the emotion. This method is perfected by not doing anything, at least not in the sense of either abandoning or transforming the emotion, as we do in the first two yanas. In the Secret Mantrayana, we do not fabricate anything, and in this unfabricated situation, we aim to simply recognize the emotion's essence. That is how the Vajrayana deals with this situation.

In the Shravakayana, whenever desire, passion, or aggression arises, you try to discourage and abandon it. You summon to mind the futility of samsaric life and then analyze the results that this passion or aggression is likely to bring. It is a matter of knowing the emotions are only going to result in pain. Falling prey to these emotions does not lead to any real pleasure in the end. For this reason, we cultivate renunciation by giving rise to a sense of revulsion.

Much of the passion and aggression that we go through creates pain right from the start. Quite often, an emotion will bring us pain and suffering when it first begins. At other times, certain emotions may not seem painful at first, though they will eventually lead to suffering. Emotions such as desire might well bring us bliss, or satisfaction, but that experience is only going to breed more hope and fear. In the end, suffering is what we end up with.

To deal with this situation, a Shravakayana practitioner would abandon these emotions by meditating on impermanence and ugliness. As desire develops toward an object you consider beautiful, for example, here you would look at it and try to see the reality of it. For example, if you happened to be looking at someone and developed desire, you would analyze this person in a step-by-step manner. Mentally, you would go through and break down each and every particle of their existence, from their hair, skin, blood, pus, and mucus, right down to the intestines.

You will soon learn that there is not a single entity out there that can escape this kind of analysis. Moreover, by carefully analyzing in this way, you will no longer feel that this particular object is something inherently precious. This is what we call ugliness meditation. Not only is it helpful, it is also a path that is free of risk because it deals with raw truths.

Feelings of infatuation are usually anchored in vague notions like, "I really like her" or "I really like him." This is how it was in the story of Utpala, a famous nun during the Buddha's time. She was so beautiful that she was named after the Utpala, an exquisitely beautiful flower.

Owing to her beauty, one man was so attached to her that he would follow her everywhere she went. Finally, Utpala asked him, "Why do you chase me all the time?"

"I think I'm infatuated," the man said, "I'm madly in love with you!"

Utpala responded by asking, "Which part of me is it that you like the most?"

The man thought about it for a while, before finally answering, "I find your eyes the most attractive."

Utpala then said, "Well, that's easy," and she took out her eyes and gave them to him. It was because of this that she became blind. As she offered her eyes to him, she said, "Take these. After all, these are what you like the most." Yet he got so revolted by the two dead, staring eyes in his hand that he developed renunciation. Later he became an arhat, a realized being.

This practice of revulsion is based on the shravaka attitude, the mindset of individual liberation. It poses no risk. The shravaka teachings, in fact, are in many ways more appropriate for us than the Secret Mantrayana, or Vajrayana, which poses many risks. The Shravakayana is not only simple, straightforward, and honest, it also deals with day-to-day truths. Nothing can change the reality that life is impermanent and every emotion is painful. These are facts.

When Shakyamuni Buddha traveled outside his palace, he saw death, old age, and sickness for the first time. Never before had he experienced such things, nor had he known of the misery in the world. Up to that point, he had lived in seclusion in a beautiful palace. In fact, his father made sure that he was sheltered from the ugliness of the world. Since he was fairly naive and inexperienced, when he first saw death, old age, and sickness, he asked his chariot driver, "What is this?"

"This is death, old age, and sickness," the driver answered.

Innocently, Prince Siddhartha then asked, "Is this going to happen to me, too?"

To which Chana, his chariot driver, said, "Yes, your majesty, this will also happen to you."

This is a Shravakayana teaching. Whether we like it or not, death is something that is going to happen to all of us. This approach is very profound. In the shravaka teachings, emotions are dismantled by completely discouraging their causes and conditions.

In addition to the praktimosha method of dealing with the emotions, however, the Mahayana emphasizes the method of transformation. How are the emotions transformed? They are transformed by generating the proper motivation, by aspiring, "May the jealousy of all sentient beings come to me. May all beings be free of jealousy!" By giving good things to others and bringing bad things to oneself, emotions are transformed. It is an incredible method.

As Buddhists, we have surely heard that aggression is bad. Thus, when we encounter aggression our immediate reaction is to think: "I don't want this." When we experience jealousy or aggression, because we are in love with this self, we do not want to have this negativity, right? According to the Mahayana, with its more expansive view, such an attitude is considered a weakness. If we do not want the bad and only want the good, we are still stained by the ego; we still cling to the self.

In the Mahayana approach, we would say, "This is bad. It really is terrible, but all sentient beings also suffer in this way. May the aggression, jealousy, and pride of all sentient beings come to me!" From the relative point of view, what happens when we do this? First of all, it goes against the ego. It is the ego that wants to be a holy person. Ego wants to be the best, a sublime being, and to go beyond. It is ego that wants to boast, "I have no desire. I have no jealousy."

This method completely undermines the ego. By continually applying it, the ego will become smaller and smaller, until it will finally have no place to live at all. Once that has happened, what is left of the emotions? By then, the emotions will have become as unreal as a scarecrow, like a mirage. It is like asking, "What would you do if there were no you?" If there were no "you," and no "I," then just imagine, what would become of passion? What would you do with it? That is the great transformation.

On an ultimate level, a bodhisattva knows that emotions are compounded phenomena and will exhaust themselves. Likewise, since emotions do not truly or permanently exist in and of themselves, it is true to say that they are characterized by emptiness. Essentially, these emotions are also something that can be transformed. Without this quality of emptiness, emotions would be real, and there could be no transformation. The bodhisattva understands these facts. Armed with this knowledge, bodhisattvas are able to transform the emotions.

In the Vajrayana, both the Shravakayana and Mahayana methods are accepted, but on the top of that, what does a Vajrayana practitioner do? Nothing. When the emotion comes, we simply observe it. This is where many people are misled. When an emotion arises, you are not supposed to fabricate, but what does that mean? To put it in very simple terms: you stop everything. This does not mean that you immediately come to a halt if you happen to be walking down the street. "Do not fabricate" does not mean you stop walking, plonk yourself down on a bench, sit cross-legged, and then watch. It has nothing to do with that.

In the Mahayana, and especially in the Shravakayana, whenever an emotion comes along, we also observe it. Yet ordinarily, most of us do not really watch, we just let go and get swept away by the emotion. Desire comes and we identify the desire, then anger comes and we identify the anger.

After receiving some teachings, we may develop a habit of watching, yet we tend to think, "where does it comes from?" or "why is it here?" To search for an emotion's source can be misleading, however, because it is a fabrication. When we ask: "Why was I angry?" there are a hundred thousand reasons, and we are always right. The reasons we pinpoint tend to confirm our beliefs. "I have a right to get angry," we will say, "I was in the right. I have to get angry or these people are going to walk all over me!" Because the fabricating is so intense, none of the methods will be able to work with this situation, not the wisdom of the Vajrayana, the transformation of the Mahayana, or even the rejection of the Shravakayana.

Instead, do not fabricate anything; just watch. The moment you observe them, the emotions disappear right on the spot. For beginners, they will reappear, but the fact that they disappeared to begin with is more important. Even if only for a split second, that very disappearance of the emotion is also the arising of wisdom. Recognizing this naked awareness is the third approach, that of knowing.

Knowing an emotion is to understand that it has no root, that there is nothing there. The emotion does not linger. It is not as though these desires are some sort of hideous, satanic, evil being that has decided to come and take up residence within you. It is not like that. Even the word "disappear" is not really the right term, but for now, we have no choice but to use this sort of wording. The moment you experience anger, just watch. Do not observe the cause of the anger, or the result of the anger; just watch the emotion itself. As you watch, you will find there is nothing that you can point to and say, "that is anger." This understanding is wisdom.

All three of these principles must be practiced at the same time. For example, should you be walking down the street and suddenly experience some sort of aggression, you can abandon, transform, and know the emotion simultaneously. How is this possible? First you have to understand that aggression is not good, that it will only lead to more suffering. Furthermore, since the emotion is all your own perception, there is no point in getting angry. With this understanding, this brief moment of realizing the futility of your emotion, you are practicing the shravaka approach. Second, you think, "May the anger of all sentient beings come to me. May all beings be free of anger!" This is the practice of the Mahayana. Third, you observe the emotion. As you do, you are practicing the Vajrayana.

When it comes to the Vajrayana, you may have a karmic relationship with a particular deity. To explain, buddha nature has five immediate manifestations. When these five manifestations are not recognized, they appear as passion, aggression, jealousy, pride, and ignorance. Let's say that you are angry, or aggressive by nature. If this is the case, you would also tend to create karma linked to aggression. If you were to get inspired and moved by the Dharma in one of your lifetimes, that would create a certain amount of merit. Due to the coming together of this merit and your personal defilement, aggression, you would be more suitable for a practice like Vajrakumara.

This is a complicated procedure. For instance, let's say that you are connected to a deity of the vajra family, such as Akshobya. Were you to end up practicing Amitabha, a deity of the padma family, it would be fine to go ahead with this practice. Later, through the blessing of Amitabha, you will be led to Akshobya. This does not mean, however, that you should not search for the right karmic connection. You should still search. Having said that, do not stop your practice to dedicate your time to searching. Just go ahead and continue to practice. This is itself a way to begin searching. That will lead you to your definitive connection.

These days in the West, people meet together to practice quite frequently. It is not unlike a weekend football game, or a weekend picnic. Weekend ngöndro they call it. On weekdays, we might have Wednesday evening Chenrezig practice, and that kind of thing. Nonetheless, group practice is meant to inspire individual practice. If you have the time, you should do ngöndro in a retreat setting, practicing three or four sessions a day. Otherwise, you may do it as a daily practice.

You can also count the numbers and accumulate if you so desire. Prostrations come first. When you complete the required amount of accumulations, you then go on to the next practice. If you like, you may take a different approach. You could do twenty thousand prostrations, for example, and then focus on Vajrasattva. Later, after doing perhaps twenty thousand Vajrasattva mantras, you could go back to prostrations. Alternatively, you can do all the foundations together. It is a personal choice. In any case, I would suggest adding more meditation to the period of dissolution. After merging your mind with the guru's, simply remain in that state as long as you can.

Meditating in this way is extremely important. Tibetan monks tend to skip the meditation. They love chanting and reading, but they never sit still and meditate; this is a really bad habit.

Meditating for just a short time, however, can be incredibly powerful. With this in mind, if you want to get rid of your resistance to doing thousands and thousands of prostrations, you should meditate between prostrations. Then prostrating becomes about being clear and present. If you meditate in this way, the time goes very quickly, just like reading a good novel. If you can be clear and present through one tonglen meditation, for instance, the time will fly by.

This may take a little while, but after a month or two you will get the hang of it. Until you are introduced to some of the higher Dzogchen meditations, you will have to keep this up, or you will lose it. It's a bit like exercise. A recognition of the nature of the mind, however, will not be lost. Once you get a taste for it, the world will open up more and more.

The Sublime Path to Omniscience

— ❧ —

A Liturgy for the Preliminary Practices of the
Heart Essence of the Vast Expanse

COMPILED BY JIGMÉ TRINLÉ ÖZER

Blessing of Speech

OM AH HUM

Emerging from the syllable RAM, fire consumes my tongue,
Turning it into a vajra of red light with three prongs.
In its center is the essence of dependent origination,
Strung like a string of pearls around the Sanskrit alphabet.
An offering of light flows out to the buddhas and their heirs.
Pleasing them it returns, bringing all blessings and siddhis,
And purifying verbal obscurations into vajra speech.

Recite the following seven times each:

A A II U U RI RI LI LI E AI O AU AM AH

KA KHA GA GHA NA CHA CHA JA JHA NA TA TA DA DHA NA TA TA DA
DHA NA PA PA BA BHA MA YA RA LA VA SHA SHA SA HA KSHA

OM YÉ DHARMA HETU PRABHAVA HETUN TESHAN TATAGATO
HYAVADAT TESHAN CHA YO NIRODHA EVAM VADÉ MAHASHRAMANAH
SVAHA

Essence of all the buddhas throughout the three times, embodiment of the
four kayas, glorious guru, I pray to you!
Please grant your blessings that I may receive empowerment!
Please grant your blessings that the extraordinary realization of this
profound path may take birth in my being!
Please grant your blessings that I may realize the view of the true nature
of original purity!
Please grant your blessings that I may perfect the wisdom of the
spontaneously present four visions!

*Though you have been a buddha from the very beginning, your emanations
appear ceaselessly to guide beings according to their needs.*
*You display various illusory manifestations, yet are free from dualistic fixation,
the aggregates, sense sources, and elements.*
*Though you appear in human form, in truth you are a buddha, radiating
with a thousand light rays of wisdom and love.*
*I rely on you as my refuge forever, not only for this life! Please grant me your
blessings!*

*Enclosed herein is the liturgy for the Great Perfection preliminary practices of
the Heart Essence of the Vast Expanse.*

I. GURU SUPPLICATION

*To begin, recite the following words three times to arouse the glorious guru's
wisdom mind:*

Think of me, o guru!

Then offer the following prayer with intense feeling:

From the blossoming flower of faith in my heart,
Rise up, o kind guru, my sole source of refuge!
I am plagued by my karma and the kleshas it creates.
O guru, please protect me from this terrible plight!
Remain upon my crown on the chakra of great bliss.
With all my mindful awareness, to you, my guru, I pray!

I am not in hell or in the realm of spirits or animals,
A long-lived god, barbarian, or someone with wrong view.
This is not a realm without buddhas, nor am I mentally impaired.
Indeed, now I am free from these eight restricted states.

I am human with all my senses; I have been born in a central place.
My way of life is not corrupt, and I have faith in the Buddhadharma.
These five personal riches I now possess in their entirety.
A buddha has come and taught the Dharma; it survives and is practiced.
Likewise, I am now cared for by a true spiritual guide.
These five circumstantial riches I now possess as well.
Yet when some unforeseen circumstance will be my end, I do not know.
One day this life will be over, and it will be time for me to move on.
Think of me, Guru Rinpoche, turn my mind toward the Dharma!
Omniscient masters, don't let me stray onto wrong or inferior paths!
Think of me, kind root guru, you who are one with these masters!

If I don't do something worthwhile now that I have this human life,
In the future such a support for liberation will not be found.
Once the merit that led me to this pleasurable state has run out,
After death I will find myself wandering as a being in the lower realms.
Not knowing virtue from vice, nor hearing the sound of Dharma,
I won't meet my spiritual teachers; what fate could be worse than this?
To think of the classes of sentient beings, and how numerous they are,
Is to know that the chances of getting a human body are slim to none.
And when I see all the people living immoral, unspiritual lives,
It is clear that a truly spiritual life is as rare as a star in the day.
Think of me, Guru Rinpoche, turn my mind toward the Dharma!
Omniscient masters, don't let me stray onto wrong or inferior paths!
Think of me, kind root guru, you who are one with these masters!

Though I've made it to the sanctuary of this precious human life,
This sublime form will not be fit to serve as a basis for liberation
Should the mind that dwells within it be completely out of control.
Especially if I'm gripped by demons, with the five poisons raging inside,
When negative karma overwhelms me, or laziness distracts my mind,
If I fall under another's control, if my practice is superficial or fear based,

Or if I am simply ignorant; these circumstances that can suddenly strike—
Should these eight restricted states befall me, blocking my Dharma
    practice,
Think of me, Guru Rinpoche, turn my mind toward the Dharma!
Omniscient masters, don't let me stray onto wrong or inferior paths!
Think of me, kind root guru, you who are one with these masters!

If I am not fed up with samsara, or if I lack the jewel of faith,
If I am bound by my own attachment, or behave like a degenerate,
When I don't shy away from evil and my way of life is corrupt,
With vows completely broken and samaya torn to shreds—
All of these factors will cut my mind off from the Dharma.
Should these eight restricted states befall me, blocking my Dharma
    practice,
Think of me, Guru Rinpoche, turn my mind toward the Dharma!
Omniscient masters, don't let me stray onto wrong or inferior paths!
Think of me, kind root guru, you who are one with these masters!

Right now I'm not stricken with illness or plagued with suffering,
I'm not beholden to another, in servitude, or with another such fate.
So now that I have the right conditions and my freedom of choice,
If I waste these freedoms and riches in a state of indolence,
Not only will I lose my wealth and family, my friends and all I hold dear,
I will part with my own body, which I treasure above all else!
One day it will be taken from bed and thrown in some desolate spot,
Where wolves, vultures, and dogs will devour it piece by piece,
As I wander the intermediate state, experiencing horror beyond
    compare.
Think of me, Guru Rinpoche, turn my mind toward the Dharma!
Omniscient masters, don't let me stray onto wrong or inferior paths!
Think of me, kind root guru, you who are one with these masters!

Led by the ripening of my virtuous and negative deeds,
I may one day wake to find myself reborn on the planes of hell:
On a ground of molten iron, I'll be decapitated with weapons,
Dismembered by saws and beaten by hammers blazing with fire;
Imprisoned in a doorless iron house, screaming for my life,

Impaled on red hot skewers, boiled alive in molten bronze,
Or trapped in a raging inferno in one of the Eight Hot Hells.
I may wind up in snowy mountains filled with glacial ravines,
Terrifying landscapes engulfed by blizzards and driving snow.
There my youthful body, defeated by the biting cold and wind,
Will break out in terrible blisters and burst into festering sores.

No end will be heard to my screaming, to my cries of agony,
As I experience a feeling of suffering that defies the imagination.
The last bit of strength having left me, like a patient about to die,
I will let out a long, deep groan through teeth clenched tightly shut,
As the cracks in my skin and flesh grow deeper in the Eight Cold Hells.
I could end up on the Plain of Razors, with my feet cut to shreds,
Or in the Forest of Swords, where my body will be cut and sliced,
Slipping into a swamp of rotting corpses or a pit of burning ash,
In the Neighboring Hells that surround the Hell of Incessant Torment.
Perhaps it will be my fate to be used and abused in a transitory state—
As a door, pillar, hearth, rope, or otherwise, stuck in the Ephemeral Hells.
It is intense anger that causes these Eighteen Hells to occur,
So when this emotion arises, when anger wells up from within,
Think of me, Guru Rinpoche, turn my mind toward the Dharma!
Omniscient masters, don't let me stray onto wrong or inferior paths!
Think of me, kind root guru, you who are one with these masters!

Likewise, I may end up reborn in a horrible and destitute realm,
Where even the words "food," "drink," and "enjoyment" are unknown,
As a spirit who goes without sustenance for months and years on end,
With a body so weak and emaciated that I'll lack the strength to stand up.
It is greed that leads to rebirth as one of the three kinds of spirits.

Perhaps I'll be born as an animal, in terror of being preyed on or killed,
Or used and abused till exhaustion, not knowing right from wrong.
Ignorance is the seed of the boundless suffering in situations like these,
So when I myself am wandering in a state of deep ignorance,
Think of me, Guru Rinpoche, turn my mind toward the Dharma!
Omniscient masters, don't let me stray onto wrong or inferior paths!
Think of me, kind root guru, you who are one with these masters!

I've set out on the path of Dharma, yet I can't control my negative deeds.

Though I've entered the gate of the Mahayana, I don't think of helping
   others.

I've received the four empowerments, yet I don't meditate on the two
   stages.

O guru, I pray that you free me from the error of my ways!

Though I haven't realized the view, I act with reckless abandon.

Though distracted from meditation, I arrogantly cling to my ideas.

Though my conduct is off track, I remain oblivious to my own flaws.

O guru, please free me from becoming a jaded practitioner!

I may end up dying tomorrow, yet I'm obsessed with my home, clothes,
   and wealth.

The days of my youth are long gone, but renunciation and weariness
   I do not have.

The teachings I've heard are few, yet I pride myself on knowing
   a great deal.

O guru, please free me from being such an ignorant fool!

Though I get lost in circumstances, my mind is busy and dreams of
   pilgrimage.

I may stay in isolated places, yet my mind is as hard as wood.

I act calmly and speak with decorum, yet passion and anger remain.

O guru, please free me from the eight worldly concerns!

O guru, please wake me from this dense slumber I'm in!

O guru, swiftly free me from this dark dungeon!

With this fervent plea, arouse the compassion of the guru.

II. TAKING REFUGE

In the true Three Jewels—the Buddha—and Three Roots; ⁸

In nadi, prana, and bindu, with the nature of bodhichitta; ⁸

In the essence, nature and compassion mandala, ⁸

I take refuge until the heart of enlightenment is attained. ⁸

Recite this stanza three times.

III. AROUSING BODHICHITTA

Oh!
Dazed by myriad appearances, like the moon's reflection in water, ፧
Beings wander endlessly through the cycles of samsara. ፧
So they may rest in the space of luminous self-awareness, ፧
I arouse bodhichitta imbued with the four immeasurables. ፧ (3x)

Recite this stanza three times.

IV. THE MEDITATION AND RECITATION OF VAJRASATTVA

AH ፧
On the crown of my head, in my ordinary form, ፧
Upon a white lotus and a moon disc seat, ፧
Appears guru Vajrasattva from a syllable HUM. ፧
Brilliant and white, with sambhogakaya ornaments, ፧
He embraces Vajratöpa, holding vajra and bell. ፧

Please grant me refuge and purify my negativity. ፧
With intense remorse, I confess all I've done! ፧
I will restrain myself from now on, even at the cost of my life! ፧

Resting on the full moon in his heart center ፧
Is the syllable HUM, surrounded by the mantra. ፧
Reciting the mantra invokes his wisdom mind, ፧
Causing clouds of bodhichitta nectar to flow ፧
From the union of the consorts' blissful play, ፧
Raining down like a shower of camphor. ፧

May this purify the karma and afflictions that create suffering, ፧
Both my own and those of all beings throughout the three realms. ፧
May it refine away all illness, along with harmful forces, ፧
Our negativity, obscurations, misdeeds, and broken vows! ፧

OM VAJRASATTVA SAMAYA ፧ MANUPALAYA ፧ VAJRASATTVA TVENOPA ፧
TISHTA DRIDHO MÉ BHAVA ፧ SUTOSHYO MÉ BHAVA ፧ SUPOSHYO MÉ

BHAVA ⁑ ANURAKTO MÉ BHAVA ⁑ SARVA SIDDHIM MÉ PRAYACHA ⁑
SARVA KARMA SU CHA MÉ ⁑ CHITTAM SHREYAM KURU HUM ⁑ HA HA
HA HA HOH ⁑ BHAGAVAN ⁑ SARVA TATAGATA ⁑ VAJRA MA MÉ MUNCHA ⁑
VAJRI BHAVA MAHA SAMAYA SATTVA AH ⁑

*Once you have recited this mantra as many times as possible, recite the following
lines:*

Protector, under the sway of unknowing and ignorance ⁑
I have transgressed and impaired my samayas. ⁑
Oh guru, protector, grant me refuge! ⁑
Lord of mandalas, wielder of the vajra, ⁑
Embodiment of great compassion, ⁑
Lord of all beings, I go for refuge to you! ⁑

I confess all lapses of the subsidiary and main samayas of enlightened body,
speech, and mind, both my own and those of all sentient beings. Please
purify and cleanse this whole host of impurity, all our negativity, obscurations, faults, and misdeeds!

To this supplication, Vajrasattva responds, "Fortunate child, all of your
breaches and transgressions of samaya are now purified!"

OM VAJRASATTVA HUM ⁑

After repeating this mantra as many times as possible, rest evenly in meditation.

V. MANDALA

OM AH HUM ⁑
The third-order thousandfold universe with its billion realms, ⁑
Filled with the seven jewels and the wealth of gods and men, ⁑
In offering all this, along with my very own body, ⁑
May I attain the ability to turn the wheel of Dharma! ⁑

The Richly Arrayed Supreme Realm of great bliss, ⁑
With its five certainties and piles of the five families, ⁑
Filled with immeasurable clouds of pleasurable offerings— ⁑
With this offering, may I enjoy the sambhogakaya realm! ⁑

The youthful vase body, the purity of all that appears and exists; ༔
Adorned with unceasing compassion, the play of reality itself— ༔
Completely purified of any fixation on the kayas and bindus, ༔
With this offering, may I enjoy the dharmakaya realm! ༔

VI. GATHERING THE ACCUMULATIONS OF THE SIMPLE BEGGAR

P'ET ༔
Casting aside my treasured body, I conquer the demon of the divine child. ༔
My mind shoots out from the aperture of Brahma, projected up into space, ༔
Then transforms into Tröma, conquering the demon of the Lord of Death. ༔
With a hooked knife in my left hand conquering the demon of affliction, ༔
I slice off the skull of my corpse, conquering the demon of the aggregates. ༔
With my right hand I take this skull cup, enacting enlightened activity, ༔
Placing it on a trikaya hearth, fashioned from three human heads. ༔
Inside it I place the corpse, now big enough to fill one billion worlds. ༔
Melted into amrita by the AH stroke, it flows down from the syllable HAM, ༔
Purified, multiplied, and transformed by the power of the three syllables. ༔

OM AH HUM ༔

Once you have repeated these three syllables as many times as possible, recite the following:

P'ET ༔
Fulfilling my sacred bond with the offerings to the guests above ༔
Completes the accumulations, bringing siddhis, common and supreme. ༔
Pleasing the samsaric guests below, all karmic debts are now paid, ༔
While malicious and obstructive forces in particular are appeased. ༔
Illness, negative energies, and obstacles recede into space. ༔
Adverse circumstances and ego clinging are reduced to dust. ༔
In the end, all the offerings, recipients and the one making offerings, ༔
Dissolve into the Great Perfection, the basic nature of simplicity, AH. ༔

VII. GURU YOGA

Ah! ৪

I appear in the midst of a buddha realm, the Glorious Copper-Colored
   Mountain, ৪

Self-manifest, spontaneously present, infinitely pure, and perfectly
   arrayed. ৪

As my physical support, I appear in the form of Vajrayogini, ৪

Brilliant red with one face and two arms, holding a curved knife and skull
   cup. ৪

My two legs are poised as in stride and my three eyes gaze into space. ৪

On my crown is a lotus flower with a thousand petals, along with a sun
   and a moon. ৪

Upon it sits my root guru, in whom all sources of refuge converge, ৪

Inseparable from the nirmanakaya, at one with Padmavajra. ৪

He appears in the form of a youth, his skin white with a reddish glow, ৪

For clothing he wears a robe, as well as a shawl, cloak, and cape. ৪

His body, with one face and two arms, sits in the pose of a reveling king. ৪

In his right hand he holds a vajra; in his left, a skull cup and vase. ৪

His head is adorned with a hat, lotus petals upon its sides. ৪

A three-pronged khatvanga he cradles in the crook of his left arm, ৪

The supreme bliss-emptiness partner, taking her hidden form. ৪

He dwells in an expanse of light, filled with rainbow-colored spheres. ৪

Surrounding him in a beautiful web composed of five colored lights ৪

Are the twenty-five emanated disciples, the king and his subjects, ৪

With panditas, siddhas, and vidyadharas from both India and Tibet, ৪

Yidams, dakinis, dharmapalas and the oath-bound gathering like clouds. ৪

I visualize all them before me, the great equality of clarity and
   emptiness! ৪

HUM ৪

In the northwest of the land of Oddiyana, ৪

In the center of a blooming lotus flower, ৪

Is the one with supreme, wondrous siddhi: ৪

The renowned Lotus-Born Padmakara, ৪

Surrounded by a vast retinue of dakinis. ৪

Following in your footsteps, I pray: ৪

Please come and bestow your blessings! 𑁋
GURU PADMA SIDDHI HUM 𑁋

HRIH 𑁋
I bow down in prostration, with my body multiplied 𑁋
As many times as there are atoms in the entire universe. 𑁋
As the offering mudra I give all that appears and exists as a gift— 𑁋
Offerings arranged before me and those imagined in meditation. 𑁋
All the things I've done wrong with body, speech, or mind 𑁋
I confess within the state of the luminous dharmakaya. 𑁋
I rejoice in all virtue, the great gathering of positive deeds, 𑁋
Both those that are included in the ultimate and relative truths. 𑁋
I beseech you to turn the wheel of Dharma of the three vehicles 𑁋
To those in need of guidance with three different potentials. 𑁋
Until samsara has been emptied, for as long as that may take, 𑁋
I beseech you to remain with us. Do not pass into parinirvana! 𑁋
All the roots of virtue gathered throughout the three times 𑁋
I now dedicate to the cause of great enlightenment. 𑁋

Lord Guru Rinpoche, you are the embodiment 𑁋
Of the compassion and blessings of all the buddhas. 𑁋
You are the sole protector of all that lives and breathes. 𑁋
My body and all my wealth, my very own heart and mind 𑁋
Without the slightest hesitation, I offer them to you! 𑁋
From this moment on, until enlightenment is won, 𑁋
When I'm happy or sad, good or bad, high or low, 𑁋
O Padmakara, my precious master, keep me in your heart! 𑁋

Apart from you, there is no one in whom I can place my hopes. 𑁋
O Guru dark times have now fallen upon us degenerate beings. 𑁋
We are mired in a swamp of suffering, unbearable though it may be. 𑁋
Please come to our rescue Great Master! Protect us from this plight! 𑁋
Please grant us the four empowerments, O Guru with your blessings! 𑁋
Please transfer your realization to us, O Guru out of your compassion! 𑁋
Please purify the two obscurations, O Guru with your might and power! 𑁋

When my life has come to an end, 𑁋
May I end up on the Glorious Mountain of Chamara. 𑁋

In this self-appearing realm of emanated union, ⁸
May my physical support, the form of Vajrayogini, ⁸
Transform into a sphere of shimmering light, ⁸
And merge with you, master Padmakara, ⁸
Attaining buddhahood as we unite as one! ⁸
From the play of this great wisdom, ⁸
The miraculous display of emptiness-bliss, ⁸
Please revive me, master Padmakara, ⁸
As a realized guide to lead the beings ⁸
That live throughout the three realms! ⁸
I pray to you from the depths of my heart, ⁸
Without merely mouthing these words! ⁸
Please bless me and grant my wishes ⁸
From the expanse of your wisdom mind! ⁸

OM AH HUM VAJRA GURU PADMA SIDDHI HUM ⁸

VIII. LINEAGE SUPPLICATION

How wondrous! ⁸
In a pure realm unrestricted and unconfined in any way, ⁸
Is the dharmakaya buddha Samantabhadra and his display— ⁸
The sambhogakaya Vajrasattva, like a moon reflected in water, ⁸
And the nirmanakaya Garap Dorje, with all the signs of buddhahood. ⁸
To all of you I now pray: Please grant me blessings and empowerment! ⁸

Shri Simha, treasury of the ultimate teachings; ⁸
Manjushrimitra, universal ruler of the nine yanas; ⁸
Jnanasutra and great scholar Vimalamitra; ⁸
To all of you I now pray: Please show me the path to liberation! ⁸

Padmasambhava, sole ornament of this world; ⁸
King, subject, and partner—his supreme heart children; ⁸
Longchen Rabjam, who revealed an ocean of mind termas; ⁸
Jigmé Lingpa, entrusted with the space treasury of dakinis; ⁸
To all of you I now pray: Please grant me the fruit of liberation! ⁸

[*Chatral Rinpoche Sangyé Dorjé's addendum to the lineage prayer:*

Jigmé Gyalwé Nyugu, who followed the system that ends phenomena;
Orgyan Chökyi Wangpo, whose twofold wisdom burst forth from
the expanse;
Lungtoke Tenpé Nyima, who arrived at the royal domain of the
primordial state;
Pema Ledrel Tsel, who found the realized state of the four enlightened
kayas;
Root guru, whose incomparable kindness I can never hope to repay;
To all of you I now pray: Please show me my own true nature, the
original state!]

With disgust for samsara and the determination to be free, 8
May I meaningfully serve my vajra guru as though he were my own eyes. 8
Carrying out the guru's command, may I never be inconsistent 8
In accomplishing these profound practices with great diligence. 8
Through this, may the blessings of the guru's mind be transmitted to me! 8

Samsara and nirvana, all that appears and exists, has been Akanishta from
the start, 8
Purified, perfected, and matured as deity, mantra, and dharmakaya. 8
Beyond all moral judgments, the Great Perfection requires no effort or
strain 8
The radiance of awareness transcends mind-made experience and analysis. 8
May I directly perceive this reality, may I see it nakedly! 8

Divested of conceptual constructs in the inner space of rainbow light, 8
May the visible experiences of the kayas and bindus evolve. 8
May the expression of awareness expand fully as sambhogakaya realms. 8
May I attain buddhahood, transcending mind and exhausting
phenomena. 8
May I gain the eternal stronghold of the youthful vase body! 8

If I haven't made the practice of Atiyoga a living experience 8
And the coarse body has not been freed into pure space, 8
When the constituents of this life begin to unravel, 8
May death dawn as luminosity, the dharmakaya of original purity! 8

May the apparitions of the intermediate state be freed as sambhogakaya! 8
Completely mastering the paths of the breakthrough and direct leap, 8
May I be liberated like a child leaping onto its mother's lap! 8

With this great secret luminosity, the supreme pinnacle of all yanas, 8
Buddhahood is not sought elsewhere; the dharmakaya's true face
   manifests. 8
Yet if this does not bring liberation into the primordial state, 8
By taking the supreme path of five dharmas, buddhahood without
   meditation, 8
May I be born in one of the five realms of the natural nirmanakaya. 8
I especially wish to take birth in the Palace of Lotus Light, 8
Surrounded by an ocean of vidyadharas, led by Padmakara. 8
As they celebrate their sacred feast of the great and secret Dharma, 8
May I be revived in their presence, reborn as their most favored child, 8
And become whatever it is that all sentient beings may need! 8

Through the blessings of the ocean of vidyadharas and victorious ones, 8
And by the truth of the dharmadhatu, which surpasses the imagination, 8
May I use these freedoms and riches to perfect, mature, and purify, 8
And actualizing this interdependence, may I attain buddhahood! 8

With these words, offer sincere and heartfelt prayers.

IX. TAKING THE FOUR EMPOWERMENTS

Between the eyebrows of the guru is an OM, dazzling like a crystal. From it
a ray of light streams out and penetrates the crown of my head. This purifies
all my physical karma and the obscurations of my nadis. The blessings of
vajra form infuse my being and I obtain the vase empowerment, becoming
a vessel for the development stage. The seed of the matured vidyadhara is
implanted in my being, and I now have the potential to attain the level of
nirmanakaya buddha.

From the syllable AH in his throat, blazing like a ruby, a second light streams
out and penetrates my throat center. This purifies my verbal karma and the
obscurations of prana. The blessings of vajra speech infuse my being and
I obtain the secret empowerment, becoming a vessel for the practice of

mantra recitation. The seed of the vidyadhara with power over longevity is implanted in my being, and I now have the potential to attain the level of a sambhogakaya buddha.

From the sky-blue HUM syllable in his heart center, light streams out and penetrates my own, purifying mental karma and the obscurations of bindu. The blessings of vajra mind infuse my being and I obtain the knowledge-wisdom empowerment, becoming a vessel for bliss-emptiness, the practice of yogic heat. The seed of the vidyadhara of the great seal is implanted in my being, and I now have the potential to attain the level of a dharmakaya buddha.

Like a shooting star, a second HUM syllable then shoots out from the HUM in his heart center and merges inseparably with my own mind, purifying karma of the universal substrate and cognitive obscurations. The blessings of vajra wisdom infuse my being and I obtain the empowerment in which the absolute is indicated through words, becoming a vessel for the Great Perfection of original purity. The seed of the spontaneously present vidyadhara is implanted in my being, and I now have the potential to attain the ultimate result, the level of a svabhavikakaya buddha.

Recite these words in tandem with the visualization as you receive the path empowerments. When you are finished, recite as follows:

Warm, red light suddenly shoots out from the guru's heart. The moment it reaches my own heart, my body, still visualized as Vajrayogini, transforms into a small sphere of red light the size of a pea. Dissolving into the heart of Guru Rinpoche, we become inseparable, merging in one taste.

Rest in meditation, beyond all reference points, ideas, and expressions.

When you arise from meditation, recite the following:

O precious and glorious root guru,
Please dwell on the lotus seat in my heart.
Accept me with your immense kindness,
Grant me siddhis of body, speech, and mind!

O glorious guru, may I not harbor wrong views
Toward your example for even a moment.
With devotion, may I see all you do as sublime.
May the guru's blessings infuse my mind!

In all lives, may I not part from the true guru,
Forever enjoying the richness of Dharma.
Perfecting the qualities of the paths and levels,
May I swiftly attain the state of Vajradhara!

X. DEDICATION

Through this virtue may all beings
Perfect the accumulations of merit and wisdom
And achieve the two sacred kayas
That arise from merit and wisdom!

Whatever virtue beings may possess,
What they've done, are doing, and will do,
May they all attain the stages of perfection
Just like the bodhisattva Samantabhadra.

As the courageous Manjushri understood,
And just like Samantabhadra as well,
I completely dedicate all this virtue,
Following their example, one and all!

As all the buddhas of the three times
Have praised dedication as supreme,
I now dedicate all my virtues as well
So that all may engage in sublime deeds!

XI. SPECIFIC ASPIRATION

In all of my lives, wherever I may be born,
May I have the seven qualities of the higher realms.
May I meet with the Dharma as soon as I am born
And have the freedom to accomplish it correctly!

May I please my precious guru
And practice the Dharma day and night.
Realizing the Dharma and its innermost meaning,
May I cross over the ocean of existence in that life!

May I then teach the sacred Dharma in samsara
And never tire of working to help others.
Without bias, benefiting others on a vast scale,
May we all attain buddhahood as one!

This liturgy for the Great Perfection preliminary practices of the Heart Essence of the Vast Expanse, The Sublime Path to Omniscience, *was written by the great tantric yogi Jigmé Trinlé Özer, one nurtured by the kindness of the vidyadhara Jigmé Lingpa and other true masters and who holds samaya in high regard.*

May the virtue involved in composing this work result in the followers of this tradition seeing their guru as the buddha. Through this, may they actualize self-awareness, realizing their own basic nature to be Samantabhadra, and enact an endless stream of beneficial activity for the ocean of beings and worlds!

THE SUBLIME PATH
TO ENLIGHTENMENT

— ❧⊪❧ —

A Concise Liturgy for the Longchen Nyingtik Preliminary Practices

JAMYANG KHYENTSÉ WANGPO

REFUGE AND BODHICHITTA

Namo
I and all beings take refuge
In the Three Roots 'til enlightenment is won.
To attain enlightenment for the benefit of others,
I cultivate aspiration, application, and ultimate bodhichitta.

THE MEDITATION AND RECITATION
OF VAJRASATTVA

AH
Upon a lotus and moon disc on the crown of my head,
Sits guru Vajrasattva and his consort.
A stream of nectar descends from the mantra in his heart,
Purifying illness, malevolent forces, misdeeds, and obscurations.

Then recite the hundred syllables:

OM VAJRASATTVA SAMAYA MANUPALAYA VAJRASATTVA TVENOPA
TISHTA DRIDHO MÉ BHAVA SUTOSHYO MÉ BHAVA SUPOSHYO MÉ
BHAVA ANURAKTO MÉ BHAVA SARVA SIDDHIM MÉ PRAYACHA SARVA

KARMA SU CHA MÉ CHITTAM SHREYAM KURU HUM HA HA HA HA HOH
BHAGAVAN SARVA TATAGATA VAJRA MA MÉ MUNCHA VAJRI BHAVA
MAHA SAMAYA SATTVA AH

Vajrasattva melts into light and dissolves into me.

MANDALA OFFERING

Pure realms of the three kayas and wealth,
Clouds of outer, inner, and secret offerings
I offer to the Three Jewels and Three Roots.
Please accept them and bestow supreme and ordinary siddhis!

OM AH HUM GURU DEVA DAKINI SAPARIVARA RATNA MANDALA PUJA
MEGHA AH HUM

GURU YOGA

In the space before me, in an expanse of rainbow light,
Is Tötreng Tsel, embodiment of all sources of refuge—
My root guru, surrounded by a virtual ocean
Of vidyadharas from the three lineages.

*Next, recite the Seven-Line Supplication and the approach Vajra Guru Mantra
with enthusiasm:*

HUM In the northwest of the land of Oddiyana,
In the center of a blooming lotus flower,
Is the one with supreme, wondrous siddhi:
The renowned Lotus-Born Padmakara,
Surrounded by a vast retinue of dakinis.
Following in your footsteps, I pray:
Please come and bestow your blessings!

OM AH HUM VAJRA GURU PADMA SIDDHI HUM

Conclude with the following stanza:

From the light of the seed syllables in the three places,
I attain blessings, empowerment, and siddhis.
The guru melts into light and dissolves into me.
Inseparable and uncontrived, I rest at ease.

And then dedicate the merit.

Appendix I

— ❧ ∥ ❧ —

Learning to Visualize

EXCERPT FROM *NOTES ON THE DEVELOPMENT STAGE*
BY KUNKHYEN TENPÉ NYIMA

Start out by placing a painting or statue before you, using one made by a skilled artisan and with all the appropriate characteristics. Next, arrange offerings before it and practice the preliminaries. You can do the latter in a brief form or a more extensive one; either is acceptable. Then, according to the oral instructions of Jamyang Khyentsé Wangpo (which he taught from the Condensed Realization of the Gurus), visualize a throne on the crown of your head. It should be held up by snow lions and piled with lotus, sun, and moon disc seats. Upon this throne imagine your kind, precious root guru in the form of the guru Vajradhara, the embodiment of all sources of refuge. Then, with great devotion, pray to him as the very essence of all the buddhas throughout the three times and offer him your body and all your possessions. Supplicate him to bless your state of being and, in particular, request his blessings so that the true absorptions of the development stage will arise in your mind this very moment. Imagine that your guru is pleased by this and smiles. He then dissolves into red light and dissolves into your crown. Once your ordinary mind and his enlightened mind have merged inseparably, rest for a while.

Once this is finished, gaze at the painting or statue placed before you. Then close your eyes and visualize the image immediately, transferring it to your own body. Train by alternating between these two steps. Once you've gotten used to the visualization, you can refine your ability by changing its size, increasing or decreasing the number of figures, visualizing the central deity and then the retinue, and so forth. You can also alternate periods of simultaneously visualizing the complete form of the deity with periods where you only focus on certain parts or ornaments.

Whichever you do, start out by focusing solely on the central deity. Starting at the tip of its crown and working your way down to the lotus seat, try to develop a clear visualization of each element: the color of its body, its face, hands and ornamentation, its clothing, the pupils of its eyes, the shape of its arms and legs, the appearance of the marks and signs, the radiation and absorption of light rays, and so on . . . work at visualizing all of these in minute detail.

The figure you are visualizing should not be a corporeal entity. It shouldn't be flat like a painting or protrude like a carving, in other words. On the other hand, it should not be a mindless entity either, like a rainbow. Rather, it should be clearly defined in every respect—its front and back, left and right sides, proportions, and so forth. Yet at the same time, it should be devoid of any sense of materiality. You should train as though it is a body of clear light, as if a deity with the wisdom of omniscience, love, and power had actually arrived.

Once you have a handle on this aspect of the practice, you can move on to sequentially visualizing its other elements—the retinue, celestial palace, the layout of the pure realm, and the protection circle. At times you can focus on the visualization as a whole, while at others focusing on specific elements.

The term "clear appearance" refers to the point at which every aspect of the supporting and supported mandala circles arise in your mind with a sense of vivid clarity. This is one of the primary functions of the development stage; it is a unique method that allows one to practice calm abiding by focusing the mind on the deity. For this very reason, it is important to meditate by purposely keeping your awareness on the visualized form of the deity. Once you are familiar with this process, the five meditative experiences will sequentially arise.

APPENDIX II

⟨❂⟩

Retreat in the Longchen Nyingtik Lineage

In Tibet, dedicated meditators often spend extended periods in strict retreat, where they do nothing but practice the Buddha's teachings for months and years on end. In the following pages, I will give a brief overview of a traditional Longchen Nyingtik retreat as practiced in the lineage of Chatral Rinpoche, a renowned yogi who oversees numerous three-year retreat centers throughout the Himalayas.[59]

THE THREE-YEAR RETREAT CURRICULUM

The traditional three-year retreat is broken up into three phases: the preliminary practices, development stage, and completion stage/Great Perfection. The first phase begins with a one-hundred-day retreat. For the duration of the retreat, four three-hour meditation sessions are practiced each day. In the first hundred days, two hours of each session are spent contemplating the topics contained in the outer preliminary practices (for the first fifty-two days) and various bodhichitta-style contemplations (for the last forty-eight days). In the third hour of each session, the practitioner accumulates the prayers of refuge and bodhichitta. By the end of the one-hundred-day retreat, the retreatant will have spent eight hundred hours contemplating and accumulated one hundred thousand refuge prayers and thirty thousand bodhichitta prayers.

Once these practices have been completed, the meditator accumulates one hundred thousand recitations of the one-hundred-syllable mantra. For the mandala practice, one must accumulate thirty thousand three-kaya mandala offerings (the mandala offering spelled out in the Longchen Nyingtik ngöndro liturgy), followed by seventy thousand four-line mandala offerings, such as the stanza that begins, "The earth is perfumed with scented water . . ." The offering of the simple beggar[60] is also practiced at this point, though there is no specific requirement for this practice aside from the visualized offering of one's own body. The final segment of the preliminary practices is guru yoga. The requirement for this practice is to offer one hundred thousand full-body prostrations, which are performed while reciting the seven-branch offering, and twelve million vajra guru mantras. When practiced properly in four daily sessions of three hours each, this last step will take over one year to complete. Thus, the outer and inner preliminaries will take nearly two years to complete altogether, totaling nearly nine thousand hours of practice.

Next is the development stage, in which the student receives teachings on Jigmé Lingpa's *Ladder to Akanishta* and Patrül Rinpoche's *Four Stakes That Bind the Life-Force,* and practices the following sadhanas: *Gathering of the Masters of Awareness,*[61] *Great Compassion: The Self-Liberation of Suffering,*[62] and *Tiklé Gyachen*[63] as the inner, secret, and extremely secret guru practices; *Gathering of Great Glorious Ones*[64] as the yidam practice, and *Yumkha Dechen Gyalmo*[65] as the dakini practice.

In the third and final phase of practice, the retreatant practices vase breathing, yogic heat, and physical yogas for the completion stage with symbolic attributes. For the Great Perfection, the student receives teachings on the *Yeshé Lama* and practices the breakthrough and direct leap.

DAILY SCHEDULE

The first formal meditation session begins at 3 a.m. and lasts until 6 a.m. Immediately upon waking, the retreatant assumes the proper meditation posture and then expels the stale breath in three cycles of three breaths. Next, is the blessing of speech, in which one recites various sounds and mantras to purify obscurations of speech and increase the power of one's recitations. Following this, one forms the correct motivation for practice and cultivates bodhichitta. To conclude, one invokes the blessings of the guru by reciting the guru supplication from the beginning of the Longchen Nyingtik ngöndro and then envisioning the bestowal of the four empowerments. These vital points of body, speech, and mind constitute the preparatory steps for each meditation session. One then continues on to the main practice, which will vary depending upon the year of the retreat.

Following the early morning session, one should perform the smoke offering Riwo Sangchö and then eat breakfast. The next session begins at 7 a.m. and ends at 10 a.m. After this session, the retreatant performs a brief torma offering and water offering, performs one hundred prostrations, and then eats lunch. After lunch there is short break, during which one may read practice manuals or biographies of Buddhist masters. The afternoon session begins at 1 p.m. and ends at 4 p.m., following which one makes offerings to the Dharma protectors and recites various aspirations, and then eats dinner. The final session of the day starts at 6 p.m. and ends at 9 p.m. Following this session, one practices a short chöd practice, adapted from *The Bellowing Laugh of the Dakinis*, the main chöd practice of the Heart Essence of the Vast Expanse. The day ends with the recitation of various prayers and aspirations.

In addition to the various practices performed during and in between sessions, there are also meditations for the moments before sleep. When practicing the preliminary practices, one visualizes the guru on the crown of one's head while lying in bed. Next, one imagines that the guru travels from the top of one's head to the heart center in the central channel, at which point light emits out from the guru's body. At first, this light fills one's body, then the surrounding area, and finally the entire universe. Falling asleep in this way facilitates lucid dreaming and recognizing the luminosity of the state of deep sleep. When practicing the development stage, one visualizes the revolving mantra chain in one's heart center of whichever yidam deity one is practicing, and then falls asleep while reciting the corresponding mantra. In the final stage of Great Perfection practice, one falls asleep while practicing the key instructions for "gathering phenomena into the vase."

APPENDIX III

⊰⊱

The Fourfold Heart Essence

In the fourteenth century, Longchen Rabjam compiled the Nyingma tradition's most famous collection of Great Perfection teachings, the Fourfold Heart Essence. This massive compilation spans thirteen volumes and contains hundreds of individual titles. It is perhaps the most thorough presentation of the Heart Essence teachings ever put down in writing. Over the centuries, the greatest scholars and meditators of the Nyingma school have looked to these sacred texts for guidance on the profound meditative practices of Vajrayana Buddhism. Later works on the Great Perfection, such as Jigmé Lingpa's renowned *Supreme Wisdom*, draw heavily from its lucid explanations and pith instructions. Its texts are even used as a primary source of information by Tibetan historians.

The Fourfold Heart Essence contains five sections: the Heart Essence of Vimalamitra (Vima Nyingtik), the Heart Essence of the Dakinis (Khandro Nyingtik), the Guru's Quintessence (Lama Yangtik), the Quintessence of the Dakinis (Khandro Yangtik), and the Profound Quintessence (Zabmo Yangtik).[66] The first two sections contain the Heart Essence teachings of Vimalamitra and Padmasambhava, respectively. The following three sections contain the writings of Longchenpa: The Guru's Quintessence contains his commentaries on Vimalamitra's teachings; the Quintessence of the Dakinis contains his clarifications of the Heart Essence of the Dakinis; and the Profound Quintessence deals with the teachings of both. In the following passage, the Third Dzogchen Rinpoche gives a brief overview of the contents of the Fourfold Heart Essence:

The import of the Three Classes, the Ninefold Expanse, and all the other key instructions of the Great Perfection were condensed by the Kashmiri scholar Vimalamitra and codified in the Secret Heart Essence, the Sangwa Nyingtik. These teachings came to be known as the vast Heart Essence of Vimalamitra, or Vima Nyingtik. Padmasambhava, the master from Oddiyana, codified the Heart Essence of the Dakinis, or Khandro Nyingtik. His teachings came to be known as the profound Heart Essence of Padma, or Pema Nyingtik. The omniscient Longchenpa then wrote brief clarifications on the first set and more extensive commentaries on the second. The former are collectively referred to as the Quintessential Wish-Fulfilling Jewel, which is also known as the Guru's Quintessence, or Lama Yangtik, and the latter as the Quintessence of the Dakinis, or Khandro Yangtik. All of these teachings were then gathered into one compilation, thus condensing both the transmitted teachings and treasures. This collection is referred to as the Fourfold Heart Essence, the Nyingtik Yabshi.[67]

The Fourfold Heart Essence covers a wide range of Buddhist practices. Its two main sections, which contain the teachings of Vimalamitra and Padmasambhava, respectively, each constitute a complete path to liberation. Both cycles contain a series of instructions on the outer, inner, and unique preliminary practices, as well as on the various meditations that make up the main body of tantric practice. As might be expected, the two core Heart Essence practices, breakthrough and direct leap, receive the most attention. Yet though the emphasis is clearly on these two stages, there are also numerous texts that relate to other forms of Vajrayana practice, such as the development and completion stages.

The Fourfold Heart Essence devotes far less attention to the development stage than the completion stage, especially in the teachings of Vimalamitra. Moreover, its few sadhana practices are presented in a style and format that sets them apart from the more complex and lengthy development stage sadhanas of the Mahayoga tradition. The usual sadhana divisions of lama, yidam, and dakini are also absent. Instead, the majority of its ritual practices concern Dorjé Yudrönma, Sokdrup Nakmo, Danglha, and other Dzogchen Dharma protectors.

In terms of completion stage practice, a diverse range of approaches is represented. The Fourfold Heart Essence includes texts on the practices of yogic heat, luminosity, transference, yogic union, as well as extensive instructions on the various intermediate states, or bardos. Though these practices are not unique to the Great Perfection, they are often integrated into this path as methods that prepare the student for the fruitional practices of the Heart Essence.

The Fourfold Heart Essence's most outstanding contribution to the Great Perfection tradition is its extensive treatment of the breakthrough and direct leap, the fundamental practices of the Heart Essence tradition. Longchenpa's collection contains scores of texts that relate to these two stages. These include detailed instructions on the unique Heart Essence preliminary practices, as well as elegant poems and detailed treatises intended to lead the meditator first to a recognition of the *originally pure* nature of mind, and then to an experience of its *spontaneously present* manifestations.

In contrast to Longchenpa's Seven Treasuries, which outline the philosophical underpinnings of the Great Perfection, the texts of the Fourfold Heart Essence are short and to the point. They are not intended to be theoretical expositions, but practical guides to the subtleties of meditation. As such, they are often pithy and evocative, and many are just a few pages in length.[68] Not all of its texts deal strictly with practice, however. As with many treasure cycles, the teachings contained in the Fourfold Heart Essence center on a number of tantras.[69] There are also numerous biographies of lineage masters, detailed lineage histories, and instruction manuals that explain how to bestow the empowerments of the Great Perfection.

THE HEART ESSENCE OF VIMALAMITRA

The Heart Essence of Vimalamitra contains the Dzogchen teachings that Longchenpa received from his own root guru, Kumaradza (1266–1343). The Indian master Vimalamitra first gave these teachings in secret to five disciples during his sojourn to Tibet. As mentioned in the previous section, these teachings were then passed on as an oral transmission and also written down and hidden as treasures by Vimalamitra's student Nyang Tingdzin Zangpo (eighth–ninth centuries). Centuries later they were revealed by Dangma Lhungyal and propagated by Chetsün Sengé Wangchuk (eleventh–twelfth centuries). Though the Heart Essence of Vimalamitra combines the lineages of the transmitted teachings and revealed treasures, it is often cited as belonging to the tradition of the transmitted teachings.

The first grouping of texts in this collection is divided into four categories: the *Golden Lettered,* the *Conch Lettered*, the *Turquoise Lettered*, and the *Copper Lettered* and *Ornamented Letters*, which are grouped together. Of these four, the aptly entitled *Golden Lettered* group forms the core of the Heart Essence of Vimalamitra. It contains a lengthy inventory of the contents of the collection, a root tantra, as well as a lengthy commentary on this tantra composed by Garap Dorjé.

The *Golden Lettered* collection also includes a series of teachings called "last testaments." The first group of last testaments includes three teachings transmitted by the buddha Vajradhara to Garap Dorjé. These three are called the *Three Last Testaments of the Buddha*. The next set, entitled the *Four Last Testaments of the Masters of Awareness*, consists of four posthumous teachings transmitted by the very first Great Perfection masters. These four texts contain what are, perhaps, the most famous Heart Essence teachings in the entire Great Perfection lineage: Garap Dorjé's *Three Statements That Strike the Vital Point*, Manjushrimitra's *Six Experiences of Meditation*, Shri Simha's *Seven Nails*, and Jnanasutra's *Six Methods of Resting*. A fifth testament by Vimalamitra is also included.

The remaining volumes of the collection contain a wealth of material on the intricacies of Great Perfection practice. Many of the texts are filled with annotations that flesh out the cryptic root verses. Many are quite brief, with some just a few pages long. The majority of these texts deal with the Great Perfection's breakthrough and direct leap practices, and there is a notable absence of ritual-based sadhana literature.[70] There are, however, nearly two hundred pages devoted to the various empowerments of the Vima Nyingtik, as well as a lengthy lineage history and numerous biographies of important lineage masters.

Longchenpa's commentaries on the Heart Essence of Vimalamitra fill two volumes. Collectively, these commentaries are entitled the Guru's Quintessence, though they are more popularly known as the Quintessential Wish-Fulfilling Jewel, or Yangtik Yizhin Norbu. Of all Longchenpa's writings—which remain unrivaled as comprehensive presentations of Great Perfection thought and practice—this collection is held in especially high regard. It was this body of writings that the great master himself directed his

students to consult when in doubt concerning their Great Perfection meditation. Shortly before he passed away, Longchenpa told his students:

> Those of you who are able to benefit others should do so without
> any sense of attachment. Bestow upon your fortunate students
> whatever empowerments, tantric teachings, and key instructions
> they wish to receive. Those of you who are focusing on practicing
> the sacred Dharma, do not let yourself get caught up in mundane
> activities. Instead, rest evenly in the nature of the breakthrough
> and direct leap. When there are things you do not understand,
> consult *The Quintessential Wish-Fulfilling Jewel*. This work of
> mine is like a wish-granting gem, so you should study it in great
> detail and meditate on what you learn. This will bring an end to
> samsara and allow you to reach the state of nirvana.[71]

The commentaries that constitute the Guru's Quintessence are based primarily on a Dzogchen tantra entitled the *Garland of Pearls*. This precious
tantra is one of the Seventeen Key Instruction Class Tantras, each of which
addresses various aspects of the view, meditation, and conduct of the Heart
Essence teachings. According to Longchenpa, the unique contribution of
the *Garland of Pearls* is the series of skillful key instructions it employs to
bring about liberation.[72] Elaborating further, the Third Karmapa, Rangjung
Dorjé, explains that the *Garland of Pearls* shows the practitioner how to
develop his or her meditation by fully integrating the fruitional state, and
how to recognize the various experiential signs that herald the onset of true
realization.[73]

As with the other sections of the Fourfold Heart Essence, the Guru's
Quintessence covers a broad range of topics. It opens with an inventory of
its contents, a lineage history, and supplications and offering rituals meant to
serve as preliminary practices. Next, we find a series of texts for the empowerments associated with this collection, followed by nearly 540 pages on the
main and subsidiary practices of the Heart Essence. The compilation concludes with a series of sadhana practices for the main protectors of the lineage.

HEART ESSENCE OF THE DAKINIS

The most treasured cycle of Padmasambhava's Great Perfection teachings is
the Heart Essence of the Dakinis. This is not only an exhaustive presentation

of Dzogchen theory and practice, but also one of the clearest. Its texts lay out straightforward guidelines for each and every stage of the Heart Essence, starting with the common preliminary practices, and then progressing through the unique Dzogchen preliminaries, the various stages of tantric practice, and finally to the practices of breakthrough and direct leap.

Padmasambhava sought out the Heart Essence teachings after receiving a prophecy from the dakini Vajravarahi, who told him that his destined teacher was Shri Simha. Once he found this master, he dwelt in the charnel grounds of ancient India for twenty-five years studying and practicing the teachings he received. At the close of the eighth century, the Dharma king Trisong Deutsen invited Padmasambhava to Tibet to help construct Samye Monastery. While there, he taught the entire range of Buddhist teachings and helped plant the Dharma firmly in Tibetan soil.

Padmasambhava transmitted the Heart Essence teachings in secret to a few close disciples. He first taught the Heart Essence of the Dakinis to Yeshé Tsogyal at the cave complex of Zhotö Tidrö in central Tibet, and later at Samyé Chimpu. The following passage from the *Precious History of the Treasure* recounts how this transmission took place:[74]

> One time the master Padmasambhava was practicing at Zhotö Tidro Trak along with his spiritual partner, Lady Tsogyal of Kharchen. While they were there, wisdom dakinis exhorted Yeshé Tsogyal with the following prophetic declaration: "The enlightened mind of this great master, the nirmanakaya buddha, holds a set of profound key instructions called the Heart Essence of the Dakinis. These direct instructions bring buddhahood in three years and cause the corporeal aggregates to disappear in this very life. You must request these teachings!"
>
> Hearing this, Yeshé Tsogyal offered a great tantric feast and requested the teachings. "Great master," she said, "please give me the direct instructions that will cause the aggregates to disappear and bring buddhahood in this very life. Please bestow upon me the key instructions of the Heart Essence!"
>
> With this supplication, she made innumerable prostrations and circumambulations, upon which the great master replied, "Tsogyal, your request is an excellent one, for I possess instructions that are unlike those I have given you in the past. These teachings lie beyond the nine vehicles and are the very pinnacle of them all.

Just seeing these key points is enough to destroy all intellectually fabricated beliefs and meditations. With this approach, the levels and paths are perfected without any need for effort. Without correcting or changing anything, the afflictions are freed on their own; there is no need to use antidotes. This fruition is not produced by causes, but is perfected in and of itself, for the wisdom mind is spontaneously present and arises instantaneously. In this very life, the corporeal, flesh and blood aggregates will be freed into the luminous sambhogakaya. Within three years, you will venture forth to the Supreme Realm and be able to seize the stronghold in the realm of the spontaneously present dharmakaya. These instructions I will now teach you!"

The great master then revealed the true mandala of the peaceful and wrathful deities in the great feast hall, empowering and offering instructions to a hundred thousand wisdom dakinis, headed by the lady from Kharchen. He taught them all the Seventeen Tantras, with the *Tantra of the Clear Expanse of the Sun* as the eighteenth, along with a great many key instructions. All these teachings were then grouped into two categories. The first set contained key instructions on the vastness of the tantras, while the second collection was composed by the master himself and contained cycles for simple yogis. Each was then committed to writing and cataloged by the master and Yeshé Tsogyal.

It was at this time that the king extended an invitation to the master and his spiritual partner to visit Chimpu. The two then set off, accompanied by the king, the queen, and the royal children. Once there, they began a series of 108 tantric feasts. During the course of these feasts, a young, eight-year-old princess named Pemasel, the daughter of the noble Queen Changchup Men of the Drom clan, passed away. Seeing her body, the king burst into tears and fell to the floor unconscious. Yeshé Tsogyal then covered him with a white sash and sprinkled him with sandalwood water, upon which the king regained consciousness.

The master then spoke:

"Alas, noble king, worldly affairs are but a dream.
By their very character, conditioned things are illusory.
Politics, too, are like last night's dream,

And wealth and subjects, like the drop of dew on a blade
    of grass.
Life is as impermanent as a bubble about to burst,
And all conditioned things are subject to decay.
All that comes together must part in the end—
This is the nature of all conditioned things.
Nothing whatsoever is stable and permanent,
So do not believe the impermanent to be permanent.
Instead train in the nature of the birthless dharmakaya!"

To these words of advice, the master added many prophecies concerning future events and told the king about the series of incarnations that Princess Pemasel was to take. At the conclusion of all this, he prophesied the coming of Tsultrim Dorjé and Trimé Özer. The princess was commanded to be the guardian of the profound Heart Essence teachings, and they were then concealed as a profound treasure. Later, just as the master had prophesied, these teachings were revealed by the omniscient Tsultrim Dorjé and spread far and wide by Trimé Özer.[75]

As noted here, the Heart Essence of the Dakinis was hidden as a treasure and then revealed by the reincarnation of Princess Pemasel, Pema Ledrel Tsel. Longchenpa was the immediate reincarnation of Pema Ledrel Tsel. He came into contact with the treasure revelations of his previous incarnation, and also received the Heart Essence teachings directly from Padmasambhava and Yeshé Tsogyal in a visionary state.

The texts of the Heart Essence of the Dakinis follow a similar, though slightly different, structure than those of the Heart Essence of Vimalamitra. The collection opens with an inventory of the treasure's contents and a short presentation of the lineage history. The next section contains the *Six Essence Tantras That Liberate Upon Wearing*, which begins with the root tantra, *Essence Tantra That Liberates Upon Wearing*. These six tantras are accompanied by six short commentaries. A series of three testaments follows, which are nearly identical to the *Three Last Testaments of the Buddha* found in the Heart Essence of Vimalamitra. The *Four Last Testaments of the Masters of Awareness*, however, are absent in this collection. Following these testaments, there is a more lengthy commentary on the six essence tantras, entitled *Essential Instructions on the Essence Tantras That Liberate Upon*

Wearing. This grouping of texts, which forms the core of the Heart Essence of the Dakinis, contains some of the most frequently cited literature in the entire Great Perfection tradition.

The next two texts are the main sadhana practices of this cycle, the *Outer and Inner Sadhanas of the Sugatas.* Following these two concise ritual practices is an extensive series of texts that present the various levels of empowerment. The following passage gives an overview of these empowerments and their relationship to Heart Essence practices:

> To begin, novice practitioners should be granted the vase empowerment and instructed to practice the approach of the threefold ritual of the yidams of the five buddha families. They should then meditate on these yidams until the experiential signs of success have manifested in their entirety. Next, bestow the secret empowerment and instruct them to meditate on a suitable yogic heat practice until all the experiential signs of success for this practice have manifested. Once this has come to pass, grant the knowledge-wisdom empowerment and have the students utilize a mudra until the bindu is workable and there is some degree of facility concerning the nature of bliss-emptiness. Then bestow the word empowerment and instruct them to meditate on the breakthrough stage until its nature has been recognized. Following this, bestow the empowerment into the display of awareness and introduce the direct leap, instructing them to meditate until the four visions have reached a point of perfection. There is nothing wrong with bestowing all of these empowerments and instructions simultaneously, but doing so in a gradual manner is particularly effective.[76]

A number of practice-related teachings follow this series of empowerment texts.

The second volume of the Heart Essence of the Dakinis begins with a text entitled *Questions and Answers: A Rosary of Golden Amrita.* This wonderful composition contains a dialogue between Yeshé Tsogyal and Padmasambhava, in which Yeshé Tsogyal requests clarifications concerning the view, meditation, and conduct of the Great Perfection. Following this are a number of completion stage writings, including pith teachings on the practices of yogic union, the intermediate states, luminosity, yogic heat, and the extraction of essences. The volume continues with texts related to the protector practices of the cycle; outer, inner, and secret guru yoga practices; short texts on the breakthrough and direct leap practices; writings on various usages of the cycle's tantras; writings on the intermediate states; and various prophecies, supplications, and lineage histories. Summarizing the unique contribution of this cycle, Terdak Lingpa writes:

> Generally speaking, in other classes of tantra found in the Vajrayana, the meaning is concealed using vajra words. In contrast, this meaning is taught explicitly in the Seventeen Tantras and the commentaries that elucidate their essential meaning. In particular, the style and approach of the *Six Essence Tantras That Liberate Upon Wearing*, the *Three Last Testaments of the Buddha*, and the key instructions on these teachings composed by the Great One of Oddiyana and his spiritual partner are in harmony insofar as they all teach the innermost realization of the buddhas. This eminent and supreme path, the profound and secret Great Perfection, is what we now know as the "Heart Essence of the Dakinis." In this tradition, symbolic representations are used to point out the true, fundamental nature of things. For those fortunate individuals with a karmic connection to these teachings, this provides an unsurpassed avenue for bringing about a swift realization of this true nature.[77]

Longchenpa's commentaries on the Heart Essence of the Dakinis span three volumes. Of all his works, this collection receives a unique level of praise as a unique contribution to the practice literature of the Great Perfection. In terms of its length and systematic structure, it is certainly one of the most comprehensive presentations of Heart Essence practice ever composed, yet its true contribution lies in the seemingly limitless pith instructions it contains and its marvelously clear instructions on the subtleties of Great Perfection meditation practice. Commenting on the unique status of this collection, Dudjom Rinpoche writes:

> It is clear that in the land of snow mountains all the other writings on the [Heart Essence], those which are considered to be

profound, contain not even a fraction of the profound points which are elucidated in this ocean of indestructible reality, the mind treasure of this second Samantabhadra.[78]

As might be expected, the circumstances surrounding the composition of these texts were far from ordinary. In fact, though its contents are commentaries, the Quintessence of the Dakinis is also considered a mind treasure.[79] Longchenpa received the transmission of the Heart Essence of the Dakinis directly from Padmasambhava and Yeshé Tsogyal in a visionary state, an encounter that is said to have lasted six days. The following passage relates the wondrous circumstances that surrounded these transmissions:

> One winter, in the Year of the Female Wood Rabbit, Longchenpa was practicing at Chimpu Hill in Rimochen Cave, along with eight of his fortunate male and female students. As he was giving them the empowerments and explanations of the Secret Heart Essence, many protectors and dakinis suddenly arrived and exhorted him to begin teaching the Heart Essence of the Dakinis. He then sent the yogi Özer Kocha to fetch the texts.
>
> When they gathered together later, the practitioners there could actually see all the innumerable gatherings of dakinis that were taking place. At night, the din of the dakinis' natural sounds could be heard in every direction, as could various instruments. The yogis and yoginis, each and every one, had neither dreams that indicated that they were asleep, nor anything that showed they were wide awake. Instead, everyone remained in a state of blissful, clear, and thought-free wisdom day and night for an entire month. When introductions were given, everyone beheld the light of deep, pervasive blue, as well as the light of the fivefold wisdom. When instructions were given, and during the course of all the supportive teachings, the entire sky would fill with rainbows. This went on for an entire month.
>
> When Longchenpa composed the treatises of the great Heart Essence commentaries that have come to be known as the Quintessence of the Dakinis, various wondrous omens occurred. A great many beings were brought to the state of liberation and omniscience through the empowerments, explanations, and instructions of the Heart Essence.[80]

As in the other cycles of the Fourfold Heart Essence, the first two texts in this collection are an inventory of the cycle's contents and a lineage history. Following this is a lengthy empowerment text, a series of writings on various preparatory practices, and finally two groups of three texts on the breakthrough and direct leap.

A single five-hundred-page treatise takes up almost the entire second volume. Entitled *An Ocean of Clouds of the Profound Reality*, this vast text is the longest composition in the Fourfold Heart Essence. It offers a comprehensive presentation of Great Perfection thought and practice, from descriptions of the ground of reality to practical instructions on tantric practice, all the way up to the fruition of Great Perfection meditation. This is a rare example of Great Perfection literature that gives equal attention to both the theoretical grounding of the Heart Essence and its practical implementation, treating both in an incredibly detailed manner. It also covers related topics such as the lineage history of the Great Perfection and the various samaya vows associated with the four empowerments.

The third and final volume of the collection contains a great number of practice-related texts. It includes texts on the development stage, completion stage, and of course Heart Essence practice proper: the breakthrough and direct leap. There are also various texts associated with a sadhana of the five buddha families, as well as various rituals and Dharma protector practices.

The fifth and final component of the Fourfold Heart Essence is the Profound Quintessence, which constitutes the final two volumes of the collection. As mentioned earlier, this compilation contains instructions that relate to the teachings of both Vimalamitra and Padmasambhava. This collection contains further instructions and clarifications of the teachings contained in the preceding sections of the Fourfold Heart Essence. One interesting addition is a short text on the direct leap practice of dark retreat.[81] The Profound Quintessence is not as comprehensive or systematically organized as the other components of the Fourfold Heart Essence and contains no inventory.[82]

Appendix IV

⊰›||‹⊱

The Nine Yanas

In the Nyingma school, the spiritual journey is framed as a progression through nine spiritual approaches, which are typically referred to as "vehicles" or "*yanas.*" The first three yanas include the Buddha's more accessible teachings, those of the *Sutrayana*, or Sutra Vehicle. The latter six vehicles contain the teachings of Buddhist tantra and are referred to as the *Vajrayana*, or Vajra Vehicle.

Students of the Nyingma teachings practice these various approaches as a unity. Lower vehicles are not dispensed with in favor of supposedly "higher" teachings, but rather integrated into a more refined and holistic approach to spiritual development. Thus, core teachings like renunciation and compassion are equally important in all nine vehicles, though they may be expressed in more subtle ways. In the Foundational Vehicle, for instance, renunciation involves leaving behind "worldly" activities and taking up the life of a celibate monk or nun, while in the Great Perfection, renunciation means to leave behind all dualistic perception and contrived spiritual effort.

Each vehicle contains three distinct components: view, meditation, and conduct. The view refers to a set of philosophical tenets espoused by a particular approach. On a more experiential level, the view prescribes how practitioners of a given vehicle should "see" reality and its relative manifestations. Meditation consists of the practical techniques that allow practitioners to integrate Buddhist principles with their own lives, thus providing a bridge between theory and experience, while conduct spells out the ethical guidelines of each system.

The following sections outline the features of each approach. Keep in mind, however, that each vehicle is a world unto itself, with its own unique philosophical views, meditations, and ethical systems. This array of new concepts and terminology can be bewildering to the novice practitioner. The following presentation is meant as a brief introduction to these rich traditions.

THE SUTRA VEHICLE

The Sutra Vehicle, or *Sutrayana*, contains two distinct approaches: the Foundational Vehicle, or *Hinayana*, and the Great Vehicle, or *Mahayana*. The former contains the most basic teachings of the Buddhist tradition, including the Four Noble Truths, impermanence, and interdependence. The Great Vehicle expands the view and scope of the Foundational Vehicle with concepts like bodhichitta and emptiness. In this approach, the outcome of spiritual practice is the attainment of buddhahood, whereas the end point of the Foundational Vehicle is a lesser level of realization known as the state of the foe destroyer, or *arhat*.

The Foundational Vehicle is broken down further into the Vehicles of the Listeners and Solitary Buddhas—the Shravakayana and Pratyekabuddhayana. The basic mind-set of these vehicles is the same, in that both approaches focus on individual liberation, rather than the liberation of all beings. There are, however, subtle differences when it comes to the level of realization and the style of practice espoused by each system.

The Foundational Vehicle

As stated above, practitioners of the Listener Vehicle are primarily motivated by a desire to free themselves from the suffering of samsara. The starting point in this approach is the Four Noble Truths, the Buddha's very first teaching. The first two truths highlight the unsatisfactory nature of samsara and the factors that generate suffering. As an alternative to this cycle of ignorance and misery, the last two truths present the possibility of the cessation of suffering and the path that leads to this cessation.

The view of the Listener Vehicle focuses on the absence of self. More specifically, practitioners of this approach aim to realize that there is no independent, unitary, and lasting identity to be found in any aspect of our physical or mental existence. Through analysis and direct observation, they come to see the mind and body as an ever-shifting constellation of individual components, none of which constitutes a "self."

This realization is limited, however, insofar as the individual components of the mind and body are believed to truly exist. According to this system, body and mind are composed of indivisible particles of matter and discrete moments of mind. These instances of matter and consciousness, moreover, are believed to be indivisible and ultimately real. According to more advanced vehicles, this belief indicates a subtle level of clinging and ignorance, and it is precisely this subtle ignorance that blocks the attainment of complete buddhahood.

In Tibet, the views of the Foundational Vehicle are typically studied via the philosophical tenets of two Buddhist schools: the Vaibashika, or Particularists, and the Sautrantika, or Followers of Sutra. The Particularists base their views primarily on the Abhidharma teachings, an incredibly detailed presentation of the mind, mental events, and the laws of the natural world, as seen through the lens of Indian Buddhist cosmology. According to this presentation, both the mind and physical objects can be broken down into constituent parts. All such coarse phenomena, therefore, do not truly exist; they constitute the relative truth. Once mind and matter have been thoroughly dissected, however, one will find the indivisible particles and instants of mind noted above. As these are held to truly exist, they are said to constitute the ultimate truth.

The Sutra Followers have a slightly different view. According to this school, the primary sources of suffering are the mistaken concepts we have about ourselves and the world around us. These notions do not actually perform the same functions that their real-world counterparts do, however. The concept "cup," for example, does not function as a real cup does. Unfortunately, we constantly mix up our ideas about things and the things themselves, thus creating an endless cycle of confusion. Our biggest mistake, of course, is to think that there is an "I" or "self" somewhere in the psycho-physical components of our existence. This is a classic example of our tendency to conflate theory with reality. In light of this process, the Sutra Followers hold that the relative truth consists of all that does not truly function—meaning the realm of concept and imputation—while the ultimate truth refers to that which does.

As with the other eight vehicles, meditation in the Listener Vehicle involves two forms of meditation: tranquility and insight, which are also known by their Sanskrit names—*shamata and vipashyana*. Tranquility is designed to pacify destructive emotional patterns and bring the mind to a point of stillness, while insight elicits an understanding of the nature of the focal point of one's meditation. All the various approaches to Buddhist practice employ these two forms of meditation, yet there is a great degree of variability when it comes to specific techniques. In the Foundational Vehicle, there are many forms of tranquility meditation, which may involve focusing on the breath, absorbing oneself in states of love, compassion, joy, and equanimity, or concentrating on the physical body, sensations, the mind, and phenomena. Insight meditation relates primarily to realizing the various facets of the Four Noble Truths, and basic principles like impermanence and the absence of self, in particular.

The ethical code of the Listener Vehicle stresses strict discipline and nonviolence. Followers of this approach often take various sets of vows to ground their ethical practice. These vows range from relatively straightforward lists of five or eight precepts, all the way up to the incredibly detailed monastic rules of fully ordained monks and nuns that number in the hundreds. In addition to such vows, they also pledge to live by the principle of nonviolence. In practical terms, this means abstaining from the "ten forms of vice": (1) killing, (2) stealing, (3) sexual misconduct, (4) lying, (5) sowing discord, (6) idle chatter, (7) harsh speech, (8) malice, (9) envy, and (10) distorted beliefs.

In the following passage, Vimalamitra summarizes this approach:

> The Vehicle of the Listeners has seven principles: First, the *gateway* to this approach is the four truths: suffering, its source, its cessation, and the path. Second, the *view* that is realized pertains to the two selves. With this approach, individual selflessness is realized, while the selflessness of phenomena is not. To elaborate, the individual self is realized to be empty and devoid of a self. In terms of phenomena, however, objectively apprehended objects and the subjective mind that perceives them are believed to ultimately exist in an extremely subtle form. Third, the *meditation* of this approach consists of employing solely the tranquility of cessation to bring the objects of the six collections to a point of cessation. Fourth, its *conduct* involves engaging in the ten virtues for one's own benefit alone. Fifth, its *result* is the level of a foe destroyer, which is the culmination of progressing through the

four pairs and eight levels of attainment. Sixth, according to the general approach of this vehicle, in terms of *duration* it is believed to take two, three, or more lives to attain the result of becoming a foe destroyer. Superior individuals attain this result in one hundred eons; mediocre individuals do so in two hundred; and those who are inferior do so in three hundred eons. Seventh, in terms of its *benefit* for oneself and others, this approach entails applying oneself solely to methods that pacify one's own afflictions and the five poisons.

The Vehicle of Solitary Buddhas is very similar to the Listener Vehicle. Both share the same basic motivation of liberation for oneself, and both lead to the result of the foe destroyer (though there are subtle distinctions between the foe destroyer of the listeners and the foe destroyer of the solitary buddhas). There are, however, differences between the two. In terms of view, the solitary buddhas are said to have a slightly more sophisticated understanding of the absence of self. Whereas the listeners only realize the absence of self in relation to the person, the solitary buddhas also realize that the "partless particles" of matter are also devoid of any essential identity. Nonetheless, followers of this vehicle fall short in terms of the subjective mind, which they hold to consist of truly existent moments of mind, a belief they share with the listeners. In terms of meditation, the solitary buddhas focus on the twelve links of interdependence, while their ethics are similar to those of the listeners. The solitary buddhas are referred to as such because they do not need to rely upon a spiritual teacher in their final birth and because, in some instances, they dwell and practice alone.

On this approach, Vimalamitra writes:

> There are seven principles in the Vehicle of Solitary Buddhas: First, the *gateway* to this approach is the twelve links of interdependent origination. When these twelve links occur in their usual manner, samsara occurs, whereas nirvana results once this process has been reversed. The Vehicle of Solitary Buddhas elicits an understanding of this process. Second, the *view* of this approach relates to the two truths. The outer relative truth holds the twelve links of interdependent origination to be illusory. In terms of the ultimate, their view concerning individual selflessness is equivalent to the listeners'. In terms of phenomena, they assert external

objective perceptions to be empty, while believing the internal subjective mind that perceives them to be ultimately existent. Third, *meditation* in this approach consists of meditating on the emptiness of the aforementioned twelve links in their reverse order. Fourth, its *conduct* emphasizes those activities that benefit oneself, though there are also some, such as miraculous physical displays, that benefit others. Fifth, the *result* of this path is the attainment of the wish-fulfilling state of bliss. Sixth, the *duration* it takes to reach this level of attainment is equivalent to that of the listeners. Seventh, the *benefit* for oneself and others enacted by this approach was discussed in the context of conduct.

The Bodhisattva Vehicle

The Bodhisattva Vehicle, also known as the Great Vehicle, or *Mahayana*, builds upon the renunciation and insights of the Foundational Vehicle. One distinct feature of this approach is the principle of *bodhichitta*—the wish to bring all beings to the state of buddhahood and the activities engendered by this wish. Unlike the Foundational Vehicle, in which practitioners strive to liberate only *themselves* from the suffering of samsara, adherents of the Bodhisattva Vehicle work to awaken *all* beings. Those who have pledged to do so are known as *bodhisattvas*—enlightened warriors.

The two truths, another hallmark of the Great Vehicle, offer a model of reality that encompasses both the distorted perceptions of ordinary beings and the Buddha's deep insight into the true nature of existence. The *relative truth* refers to the confused minds of ordinary beings and all that they perceive through the distorted lens of dualistic fixation, the belief that self and other truly exist. The *ultimate truth*, on the other hand, refers to reality itself and the wisdom that beholds this reality once the mind has been divested of ignorance.

In terms of view, the Bodhisattva Vehicle stresses the importance of realizing emptiness, or *shunyata*. In realizing emptiness, one comes to see that all phenomena, both the external material world and the mind that perceives it, lack any essential existence. No basic building blocks of matter or eternal mind can ever be found. In other words, the seemingly solid and stable world around us, and even our own minds, are utterly ephemeral and illusory. Nevertheless, this does not mean that there is nothing at all, for while we may not find anything when we take the time to investigate, the entire range of relative appearances still manifests. In fact, it is precisely because these appearances have no true existence that they can manifest at all. If they truly existed, they would be fixed and static, stuck with an essence that is immutable and incapable of change.

Another principle in this approach is *sugata-garbha*, or buddha nature. The theory of buddha nature stipulates that all sentient beings possess the innate potential to achieve perfect and complete awakening. From this point of view, there is no essential difference between buddhas and ordinary beings. Though buddhas have actualized this potential and ordinary beings have not, the fundamental nature of both remains the same. Buddha nature does not get worse in samsara, nor does it improve in nirvana. Rather, the process of awakening is simply a matter of removing the destructive emotions and habitual patterns that block the radiance of this innate nature, like removing mud from a piece of gold.

There are two main philosophical schools in the Great Vehicle: the Mind Only School and the Middle Way. The Mind Only School has its roots in the works of Vasubhandu and his older brother Asanga, two Indian masters who lived in the fourth century CE. Asanga experienced visions of the future buddha Maitreya and transcribed a number of teachings on the view and practices of the Great Vehicle. The Mind Only School, which grew out of these teachings, holds that all the various appearances that we experience as the "external" world are nothing more than the mind's projections. True reality, they hold, is devoid of perceiver and perceived. Thus, the Mind Only School understands emptiness to be the absence of duality within consciousness itself, which they hold to be ultimately existent.

The Middle Way takes this critique even further. According to masters like Nagarjuna and Chandrakirti, two Indian pioneers of the Middle Way teachings, even the view of a truly existing nondual consciousness is untenable. Just like external phenomena, the mind cannot be found when subjected to examination. In fact, the Middle Way takes issue with every theoretical model that is meant to present an accurate snapshot of reality. While it is fine to speak in conventional terms about our day-to-day lives, language and theory are held to be utterly inadequate when it comes to the true nature of reality. All one can say, according to the Middle Way, is that reality transcends all conceptual formulations.

In terms of meditation, once again we have the two core practices of tranquility and insight. As in the Foundational Vehicle, tranquility serves to concentrate the mind and provide a solid foundation for the cultivation of insight. In this approach, insight involves realizing that all phenomena are unreal and illusory, and that both subject and object lack inherent existence. In other words, one gains insight into the empty nature of the entire universe and its inhabitants.

In postmeditation, one uses the six perfections, or *paramitas*, to work for the welfare of all beings. These six—generosity, discipline, patience, diligence, meditative stability, and knowledge—are the main practices of the bodhisattva. The sixth perfection, knowledge, is of particular importance because all the remaining five perfections become transcendent when linked with the knowledge of emptiness.

Summarizing this approach, Vimalamitra writes:

> There are also seven principles in the Vehicle of the Bodhisattvas: First, the *gateways* to this approach are the two truths and six perfections. Second, the *view* of this approach involves realizing that both the individual and phenomena are devoid of self and empty, divesting them of the obscuring overlay of ignorance. Third, *meditation* here consists of cultivating a nonconceptual state of concentration, the union of tranquility and insight. Fourth, its *conduct* entails refraining from the ten forms of nonvirtue for one's own benefit and practicing the ten forms of virtue for the benefit of others. In this way, this vehicle emphasizes the pursuit of altruism. Fifth, the *result* of this approach is the gradual progression through the ten levels, culminating in the eleventh, the level of complete illumination. Sixth, the *duration* it takes to reach this level is three incalculable eons. Seventh, in terms of the *benefit* for oneself and others, one's own benefit is brought to a point of culmination, and one works solely for the welfare of others via the six perfections.

THE VAJRA VEHICLE

The Vajra Vehicle contains the tantric teachings of the Buddhist tradition. On the surface, the practices and philosophies of the Vajra Vehicle seem a world apart from the accessible teachings of the Foundational and Great Vehicles. These differences, however, are merely superficial. The end result of both vehicles is the state of complete awakening—buddhahood. Renunciation and bodhichitta, moreover, are indispensable elements of both approaches, as are the view of emptiness and the enlightened potential of buddha nature.

The two approaches do diverge, however, in terms of technique. The methods of the Vajra Vehicle speed up the process of spiritual growth, and at the same time involve less hardship than the practices of the Sutra Vehicle. They are so efficient, in fact, that it is said that the Vajra Vehicle enables the practitioner to attain in a single life and single body what would otherwise take three immeasurable eons to accomplish—the state of buddhahood itself.

The supreme efficiency of the Vajra Vehicle lies in its willingness to use all the various facets of human existence as aids on the spiritual path. Whereas emotions and sense pleasures are often viewed as impediments in the Foundational and Great Vehicles, the Vajra Vehicle harnesses their power and channels it in a more constructive direction. This open attitude allows the Vajrayana practitioner to skillfully use all activities and experiences—even negative thoughts and emotions—as fuel for the fire of awakening.

Though there are many different styles of practice in this vehicle, the development stage and completion stage are often viewed as the hallmarks of tantric practice. The development stage uses visualization, mantra recitation, and deep states of concentration to disrupt the habitual tendency to view the world and its inhabitants as impure and truly existent. The imaginary process of visualizing oneself as a deity in a pure realm, for example, allows the practitioner to experience directly the fluid, ethereal nature of perception.

The completion stage has two components: the conceptual completion stage and nonconceptual completion stage. The first aims to harness the subtle energies of the body and consciously bring them into the central channel. These practices, which often involve intense yogic postures, focus on the link between the energetic body and the mind, the idea being that by controlling the former one will be able to undo the negative conditioning of the latter. The nonconceptual completion stage, by contrast, is an effortless approach. Often associated with the Great Perfection and Mahamudra, this form of completion stage practice emphasizes recognizing the nature of mind and experiencing its pure expressions without the filter of dualistic fixation.

The gateway to tantric practice is empowerment, or abhisheka. Conferred by a guru, empowerments authorize students to practice the teachings of the Vajra Vehicle. Each lineage and style of practice has its own unique empowerments, which are said to "ripen" the students' entire being and prepare them for tantric practice. The commitments of each empowerment are known as samaya vows.

The Nyingma and Sarma schools formulate the various approaches to Buddhist tantra in slightly different ways. In the Sarma schools, the Vajra Vehicle is commonly broken down into the four classes of tantra: Kriya Tantra, Upa Tantra, Yoga Tantra, and Anuttarayoga Tantra. Anuttarayoga Tantra is then broken down further into Mother Tantra, Father Tantra, and Nondual Tantra. In the Nyingma school, a different approach is taken. Instead of this fourfold classification, the various tantras are categorized into two groups: the three outer tantras and three inner tantras. The three outer tantras correspond to the first three mentioned above. The three inner tantras—Mahayoga, Anuyoga, and Atiyoga—correspond roughly to Father Tantra, Mother Tantra, and Nondual Tantra, respectively.

The Three Outer Tantras

KRIYA TANTRA

Kriya Tantra, or Activity Tantra, is the first of the three outer tantras. The view of this approach concerns the ultimate and relative truths. In terms of the ultimate, Kriya stresses the inseparability of appearance and emptiness, and that all phenomena are essentially beyond arising and cessation. In terms of the relative, these same phenomena are viewed as divine forms.

Kriya stresses the vital role of meditation in spiritual practice, as do all Buddhist traditions. What sets this approach apart is its use of purification rituals, ablutions, and specific requirements concerning diet and clothing. Such activities are linked with tantric meditations, such as the visualization of deities and mantra recitation. In Kriya meditation, the deity is regarded as superior to oneself, whereas in later approaches the deity is considered an expression of the nature of one's own mind.

Explaining the Kriya approach, Vimalamitra writes:

There are seven principles in the Kriya Vehicle: First, the *gateways* to this approach are ablutions and acts of ritual purity. Ablutions include using water to cleanse externally, as well as the cultivation of nonconceptual states to cleanse internally. Ritual purity involves acts like partaking of the three white foods and the three sweets. Second, the *view* of this approach involves realizing ultimate reality, free of the four limitations of the genuine. In terms of the relative, by virtue of realizing the ultimate, [all phenomena] are viewed as the deities of the three buddha families and asserted to appear as such. Third, *meditation* in this approach consists of viewing oneself (as the samaya being) and the deity (as the wisdom being) as master and servant. Fourth, its *conduct* entails working for the welfare of both oneself and others by following the five root and two subsidiary principles laid out in the treatises of this tradition. Fifth, the *result* of this approach is the attainment of the level of a vajra holder of the three families. Sixth, the *duration* it takes to reach this level is either sixteen or seven lifetimes. Seventh, in terms of *benefit*, one carries out the four forms of enlightened activity for the welfare of both oneself and others.

UPA TANTRA

Upa Tantra, or Practice Tantra, is the second of the three outer tantras. This approach is also referred to as Dual Tantra, or Ubhaya Tantra, because it links the view of Yoga Tantra (the third outer tantra) with the practices of Kriya Tantra. Thus, it is essentially an amalgam of Kriya Tantra and Yoga Tantra. In contrast to the previous approach, here the deity is viewed as a friend or companion, rather than one's superior.

Summarizing this approach, Vimalamitra explains:

There are also seven principles in Upa Tantra: First, the *gateways* to this approach are mantra, mudra, and concentration, in addition to ablutions and acts of ritual purity. Second, the *view* of this approach is in harmony with that of the Yoga Vehicle. Third, *meditation* in this vehicle consists of familiarizing oneself with the four actualities. One meditates on the actuality of the self as the samaya being, on the actuality of the deity as the wisdom being, on the actuality of the syllable as the seed syllable at the heart center of both the samaya and wisdom being, and on the actuality of verbal recitation as emanation and absorption of light rays from oneself and the wisdom being. Fourth, its *conduct* is equivalent to that of the previous section. Fifth, the *result* of this approach is the attainment of the level of a vajra holder of the four families. Sixth, the *duration* it takes to reach this level is either five or seven lifetimes. Seventh, in terms of *benefit*, this approach is the same as the previous vehicle. It enacts the welfare of both oneself and others.

Yoga Tantra

The last of the three outer tantras is *Yoga Tantra*, the Tantra of Union. Unlike the first two outer tantras, this approach does not place as much emphasis on acts of ritual purity. In terms of the view, *Yoga* practitioners see the ultimate truth as the pure wisdom of reality itself, while in terms of the relative truth, they see all phenomena as the expression, or luminosity, of the ultimate. In meditation, practitioners of this vehicle view themselves as inseparable from the deity and practice a formless meditation that involves immersing oneself in the ultimate nature of reality itself.

Vimalamitra explains further:

> The seven principles of *Yoga Tantra* are as follows: First, as the *gateway* to this approach, concentration is emphasized. Second, the *view* of this approach has two aspects: The ultimate is viewed as the sphere of reality, naturally pure wisdom. The relative is held to be the result of realizing this ultimate, namely, the assembly of deities of the five families, or of the vajra family. Third, *meditation* in this vehicle consists of meditating on the deity via the manifest enlightenment that involves images, and settling continually in the state of reality itself, which transcends images. When meditating on the deity, moreover, oneself (as the samaya being) and the deity (as the wisdom being) are treated as companions. Fourth, in terms of *conduct*, one must act in harmony with the scriptures of this tradition, such as maintaining the vows of the five buddha families. Fifth, the *result* of this approach is the actualization of wisdom, which is pure inside and out, and the subsequent attainment of the level of the pure, rich array. Sixth, the *duration* it takes to reach this level is either five or three lifetimes. Seventh, in terms of *benefit*, this approach utilizes the four forms of enlightened activity to work for the welfare of both oneself and others.

The Three Inner Tantras

The three inner tantras—*Maha*, *Anu*, and *Ati*—are typified by their use of the various development and completion stage yogas. While all three approaches involve both forms of practice, each emphasizes one particular form of meditation. *Mahayoga*, or Great Yoga, emphasizes the deity visualizations and mantra recitations of the development stage, while *Anu* and *Ati* focus on the completion stage. Within the completion stage, *Anuyoga* is primarily associated with the subtle body practices of the completion stage with symbolic attributes. *Atiyoga* is synonymous with the Great Perfection, the completion stage without symbolic attributes.

One of the unique features of the inner tantras is their use of the four empowerments. Each of the four empowerments—the vase, secret, knowledge-wisdom, and word empowerments—prepares the student for a different form of tantric practice, helps dispel a particular obscuration, and forms a karmic link with a particular aspect of enlightenment. The vase empowerment prepares the student to practice the development stage, dispels physical obscurations, and forms a connection with the nirmanakaya, the embodied aspect of buddhahood. The secret empowerment prepares the student to practice mantra recitation, dispels verbal obscurations, and forms a connection with the sambhogakaya, the luminous aspect of buddhahood. The knowledge-wisdom empowerment prepares the student to practice the subtle body practice of yogic heat,[83] dispels mental obscurations, and forms a connection with the dharmakaya, the empty aspect of buddhahood. Finally, the word empowerment prepares the student to practice the Great Perfection, dispels the obscurations to full realization, and forms a connection with the svabhavikakaya, the unified aspect of buddhahood.

MAHAYOGA

Mahayoga, or Great Yoga, is the first of the three inner tantras. This approach to practice is intended for those whose dominant emotional pattern is anger and who are inclined to a more elaborate form of meditation practice. In terms of view, this vehicle stresses the inseparability of the two superior truths. The superior ultimate truth is the sphere of reality itself, along with the various forms of wisdom and embodiment that constitute the state of buddhahood. The superior relative truth consists of the universe and its inhabitants, which are manifestations of the ultimate.

As noted above, *Mahayoga* stresses the visualizations and mantra recitations of the development stage. The meditative liturgies of this approach, moreover, are extremely elaborate, with detailed visualizations that may involve hundreds of figures. The three absorptions, or three *samadhis*, form the framework for *Mahayoga* meditation. With these three steps, the meditator immerses the mind in emptiness, compassion, and then the union of these two—expressed as a seed syllable—before moving on to the complex visualizations and mantra recitations of development stage proper.

Like all tantric practice, the ethical component of *Mahayoga* revolves around the various tantric pledges, or *samaya*, that one commits to when receiving an empowerment. There are a vast number of *samaya* vows, but the simplified approach stipulates that the tantric practitioner must view all experiences as expressions of deity, mantra, and wisdom: all appearances are to be seen as divine forms, all sounds as mantra, and all thoughts and mental events as wisdom.

Summarizing this approach, Vimalamitra writes:

> There are seven principles in Mahayoga: First, as the *gateway* to this approach, one trains in the union of development and completion, the inseparability of skillful means and knowledge. Second, the *view* of this approach is to realize reality itself; to see all phenomena, whether of samsara, nirvana, or the path, as one's own awareness, the enlightened mind—empty, illuminating, and free of all elaborations. Third, *meditation* in this vehicle emphasizes absorbing the mind in the deity, either through complete perfection or the threefold ritual, and resting in the completion stage that constitutes the nature of the deity—the state of reality itself, beyond conceptual mind and devoid of elaborations. Fourth, in terms of *conduct*, one practices the Three Roots, the twenty-five subsidiaries, union and liberation, and being free from concepts and all moral judgments. Fifth, the *result* of this approach is the attainment of the essential five kayas and the actualization of the level of the lotus endowed. Sixth, the *duration* it takes to reach this level is, for diligent practitioners who maintain their *samayas*, a single lifetime. Seventh, in terms of *benefit*, this approach utilizes the four forms of enlightened activity to work for the welfare of both oneself and others.

ANUYOGA

Anuyoga, or Subsequent Yoga, is the second of the three inner tantras. This approach to practice is intended for those whose dominant emotional pattern is passion and who are inclined to a simpler form of meditation practice.

In terms of view, this vehicle aims to realize the indivisibility of emptiness and bliss, which are referred to as the mandalas of Samantabhadri and Samantabhadra, respectively.

In terms of meditation, the hallmark of this approach is its use of the various completion stage yogas, and especially those that involve harnessing the energies of the subtle body and redirecting them into the central channel. Though this system does employ deity visualizations, here visualization is simpler and more direct. Here the meditator is advised to manifest the visualization in a single instant, rather than construct an elaborate environment and the deities that dwell there one element at a time. This process is often likened to a fish leaping out of water.

As with *Mahayoga*, *Anuyoga* also has numerous *samaya* vows that must be maintained once one has received empowerment. In addition, the ethics of this system stress the importance of utilizing sense experiences as an avenue to awakening. In other words, one is advised not to discriminate or make moral judgments that reinforce a dualistic perspective.

On this approach, Vimalamitra writes:

> The seven principles of *Anuyoga* are as follows: First, the *gateway* to this approach is the inseparability of the sphere of reality and wisdom, through which the natural mind itself is experienced. Second, in terms of *view*, in this approach one realizes all dualistic phenomena of both samsara and nirvana to be one's own awareness, the sole sphere of the dharmakaya, beyond all elaborations and with the supreme of all aspects. Third, *meditation* in this vehicle does not involve a progressive approach, nor one that uses rituals and other causes to bring about a specific result. Rather, in this system development is perfected through an instant of mindfulness, or simultaneous perfection. All of the energetic channels, elements, and centers are meditated upon as being primordially the mandala of the deity. Fourth, the *conduct* of this approach is in accord with that of *Mahayoga*. In addition, one works with the energies and yogic heat, the yoga of the blazing and melting of blissful warmth. Fifth, as the *result* of this approach, the wisdom of indivisible means and wisdom actualizes the level of the great mass of the wheel of syllables. Sixth, in terms of *duration*, elevated by extraordinary methods, this level is attained in a single lifetime. Seventh, in terms of *benefit*, within a view and meditation that

require no effort or exertion, one accomplishes the four activities as a byproduct and thereby tames beings.

ATIYOGA

Atiyoga, or Supreme Yoga, is synonymous with the Great Perfection. This system is intended for those whose dominant emotional pattern is ignorance and who are inclined to an extremely simple form of meditation practice, in which the sole focal point is the pure, luminous essence of mind. Known as the Supreme Vehicle, it involves a level of directness and profundity that far surpasses the other eight vehicles, transcending cause and effect.

The Great Perfection is divided into three classes: the Mind Class, Space Class, and Key Instruction Class. All three focus on the essence of mind, yet each has its own unique orientation. The Mind Class points out that all appearances are manifestations of the mind. The Space Class, by contrast, focuses more on emptiness, emphasizing purity and innate liberation. The Key Instruction Class shows that these two are, in fact, inseparable. In other words, this approach does not overemphasize either appearance or emptiness, and instead teaches that the swiftest path to buddhahood entails working with both.

The Key Instruction Class is itself divided into four categories: the Outer, Inner, Secret, and Extremely Secret Unsurpassed Cycles. This last division, the Extremely Secret Unsurpassed Cycle of the Key Instruction Class, is more commonly referred to as Nyingtik, the "Heart Essence" of the Great Perfection. The Heart Essence teachings present the most profound and direct path to spiritual awakening. In contrast to the elaborate philosophies of the sutra tradition, and even the complex development and completion stage practices found in other forms of Buddhist tantra, this approach is grounded in the understanding that the enlightened state is directly accessible each and every moment.

According to this system, our own awareness is already pure and pristine; it always has been. This fundamental state is termed *original purity*.[84] The mind's pure nature is not a void or blank state, however, but luminous and capable of manifesting spontaneously. This *spontaneous presence*[85] is the second main principle of the Heart Essence.

The principles of original purity and spontaneous presence relate to the practices of the breakthrough[86] and direct leap.[87] Together, these two form the core of Heart Essence practice. With the view of breakthrough, the guru introduces the student directly to the mind's fundamental nature of original purity. From that point on, the student's sole task is simply to sustain recognition of the mind's true nature. For those who are unable to master the breakthrough view instantaneously, the meditations of the direct leap may be utilized to speed up the process of realization, assuming that one is already grounded in the nature of mind. In this approach, one uses physical postures and gazes to directly experience the manifestations of reality itself.

Summarizing the core principles of the Great Perfection, Vimalamitra states:

> The seven principles of *Atiyoga* are as follows: First, the *gateway* to this approach is a spontaneous state of carefree effortlessness in which there is nothing to be done. Second, the *view* that one must realize is emptiness—ineffable, without reference point, and beyond the intellect. Third, *meditation* in this approach does not employ focal points or imagery. Rather, it is an uncontrived and fixation-free innate lucidity, a spontaneously present and completely perfect equality, a rootless transparency. Fourth, in this approach *conduct* is spontaneous, free of conscious action, and beyond moral deliberations; in essence, it is a unified play. Fifth, the *result* of this approach is the so-called "level of supreme wisdom," which is not something that can be eliminated or attained; it is a primordial, spontaneous, and vast perfection. Sixth, in terms of *duration*, there is no distinguishing between the three times. This attainment is innate and occurs on its own, originally and primordially. Seventh, this enacts the twofold *benefit* effortlessly, as a vast, all-encompassing, primordially perfect, spontaneous presence.

Appendix V

❧❦❧

Longchen Nyingtik Ngöndro Literature

Tibetan Literature on the Longchen Nyingtik Ngöndro

► The liturgy for the Longchen Nyingtik ngöndro:
  rNam mkhyen lam bzang by 'jigs med 'phrin las 'od zer (Jigmé Trinlé Özer)

► In addition to the liturgical arrangement itself, the primary texts for this practice were written by Jigmé Lingpa:
  Thun mong gi sngon 'gro sems sbyong rnam pa bdun gyi don khrid thar ba'i them skas

  rDzogs pa chen po klong chen snying thig gi thun mong gi sngon 'gro khrid kyi lag len la 'debs lugs

  rDzogs pa chen po klong chen snying thig gi thun mong ma yin pa'i sngon 'gro'i khrid yig dran pa nyer gzhag

► Other important works are:
  Klong chen snying thig gi sngon 'gro'i ngag 'don gyi 'bru 'grel rnam mkhyen lam sgron by chos kyi grags pa (Chokyi Trakpa)

  sNgon 'gro kun las 'dus pa by g.yu khog bya bral ba chos dbyings rang grol (Yukhok Chatralwa)

  sNgon 'gro'i ngag 'don rnam mkhyen lam bzang gsal byed by mkhyen brtse dbang po (Jamyang Khyentsé Wangpo)

  sNgon 'gro'i khrid yig thar lam gsal byed sgron me by 'gro 'dul dpa' bo rdo rje (Adzom Drukpa)

  sNgon 'gro'i rnam bshad mtshungs med bla ma'i byin rlabs 'char rgyun by theg mchog rdo rje (Thekchog Dorje)

  sNgon 'gro'i dmigs rim bsdus pa by dpal sprul O rgyan chos kyi dbang po (Patrül Rinpoche) *sNgon 'gro'i dmigs rim zab don bdud rtsi'i nying khu* by mkhyen brtse dbang po (Jamyang Khyentsé Wangpo)

rDzogs pa chen po klong chen snying thig gi sngon 'gro'i khrid yig kun bzang bla ma'i zhal lung by dpal sprul O rgyan chos kyi dbang po (Patrül Rinpoche)

rDzogs pa chen po klong chen snying thig gi sngon 'gro'i khrid yig kun bzang bla ma'i zhal lung gi zin bris by Mkhan chen ngag dbang dpal bzang (Khenpo Ngawang Pelzang)

Translated Literature on the Longchen Nyingtik Ngöndro

▸ Print publications:

Jamyang Khyentsé Wangpo. 1996. *An Elucidation of the Path to Excellent Omniscience.* Halifax: Vajravairochana Translation Committee.

Jamyang Khyentsé Wangpo, et al. 2006. *A Guide to the Practice of Ngöndro.* Roqueredonde, France: Rigpa Publications.

Khenpo Ngawang Pelzang. 2004. *A Guide to "The Words of My Perfect Teacher."* Translated by the Padmakara Translation Group. Boston: Shambhala.

Longchenpa, and Jigmé Lingpa. Forthcoming. *Dzogchen Mind Training.* Translated by Cortland Dahl. Ithaca, N.Y.: Snow Lion Publications.

Patrul Rinpoche. 1994. *The Words of My Perfect Teacher.* Translated by the Padmakara Translation Group. San Francisco: HarperCollins.

Tulku Thondup. 1982. *Dzogchen: Innermost Essence Preliminary Practice.* Dharamsala, India: Library of Tibetan Works and Archives.

▸ Internet publications:

Chökyi Drakpa. *A Torch for the Path to Omniscience: A Word by Word Commentary to the Longchen Nyingtik Ngöndro.* http://www.lotsawa-house.org.

Chöying Rangdrol. *Ngöndro Compendium: A Commentary on the Longchen Nyingtik Preliminary Practices.* http://www.lotsawahouse. org.

Jamyang Khyentsé Wangpo. *Illuminating the Excellent Path to Omniscience: Notes on the Longchen Nyingtik Ngöndro.* http://www.lotsawa-house.org.

Jamyang Khyentsé Wangpo. *The Excellent Path to Enlightenment.* http:// www.lotsawahouse.org.

Patrül Rinpoche. *A Brief Guide to the Stages of Visualization for the Ngöndro Practice.* http://www.lotsawahouse.org.

Abbreviations

BT   *Treasury of Knowledge: Systems of Buddhist Tantra*. Jamgön Kongtrul.
      Ithaca, N.Y.: Snow Lion Publications, 2005.

CCM   *dPal gsang ba'i snying po de kho na nyid nges pa'i rgyud kyi 'grel pa phyogs
      bcu'i mun pa thams cad rnam par sel ba*. Klong chen rab 'byams. In *rNying
      ma bka' ma rgyas pa*, vol. 26, pp. 1–629, compiled by bDud 'joms 'jigs bral
      ye shes rdo rje. Kalimpong, India: Dupjung Lama, 1982–1987.

CG   *bsKyed pa'i rim pa cho ga dang sbyar ba'i gsal byed zung 'jug snye ma*. dGe
      rtse ma h'a pandita tshe dbang mchog grub. Odiyan, Calif.: Dharma Pub-
      lishing, 2004.

DMW   *Deity, Mantra and Wisdom: Development Stage Meditation in Tibetan
      Buddhist Tantra*. Jigme Lingpa, Patrul Rinpoche, and Getse Mahāpaṇḍita.
      Ithaca, N.Y.: Snow Lion Publications, 2006.

DR   *rDzogs rim chos drug bsdus don*. dPal sprul O rgyan 'jigs med chos kyi
      dbang po. Chengdu, China: Si khron mi rigs dpe skrun khang, 2003.

DZ   *The Practice of Dzogchen*. Tulku Thondup. Ithaca, N.Y.: Snow Lion Publi-
      cations, 1989.

EM   *Empowerment*. Tsele Natsok Rangdröl. Kathmandu, Nepal: Rangjung
      Yeshe Publications, 1993.

GP2   *Great Perfection, Volume 2: Separation and Breakthrough*. The Third Dzog-
      chen Rinpoche. Ithaca, N.Y.: Snow Lion Publications, 2008.

HE   *Zab mo snying thig gi gnad thams cad bsdus pa'i don khrid lag len gsal ba*.
      bKra shis rgya mtsho. In *Rin chen gter mdzod chen mo*, vol. 90 (si), pp.
      1–96. Paro, Bhutan: Ngodrup and Sherab Drimay, 1976.

JL   *bsKyed rim lha'i khrid kyi rnam par bzhag pa 'og min bgrod pa'i them skas*
      (Dodrupchen edition). 'Jigs med gling pa. Dodrupchen Monastery, n.d.

KG   *dPal sgrub pa chen po bka' brgyad kyi spyi don rnam par bshad pa dngos grub
      snying po*. 'Ju mi pham rgya mtsho. Chengdu, China: Si khron mi rigs dpe
      skrun khang, 2000.

KJ   *mKhas pa'i tshul la 'jug pa'i sgo.* 'Ju mi pham rgya mtsho. Chengdu, China:
      mTsho sngon mi rigs dpe skrun khang, 2003.

KN   *rDzogs pa chen po mkha' 'gro snying thig gi khrid yig thar lam bgrod byed
      shing rta bzang po.* Nges don bstan 'dzin bzang po. Chengdu, China: Si
      khron mi rigs dpe skrun khang, 1997.

KR   *bsKyed rim gyi zin bris cho ga spyi 'gros ltar bkod pa man ngag kun btus.* Kun
      mkhyen bstan pa'i nyi ma. Delhi: Chos Spyod Publications, 2000.

LW   *Light of Wisdom, Volume 2.* Padmasambhava and Jamgön Kongtrul. Kath-
      mandu, Nepal: Rangjung Yeshe Publications, 1986.

MV   *dBus dang mtha' rnam par 'byed pa'i bstan bcos kyi 'grel pa 'od zer phreng ba.*
      'Ju mi pham rgya mtsho. Paro, Bhutan: Lama Ngodrup and Sherab Demy,
      1984.

ND   *Lam zhugs kyi gang zag las dang po pa la phan pa'i bskyed rdzogs kyi gnad
      bsdus.* Kong sprul blo gros mtha' yas. Publication data unknown.

NO   *Yon tan rin po che'i mdzod kyi 'grel pa zab don snang byed nyi ma'i 'od zer.*
      mKhan po yon tan rgya mtsho. Kathmandu, Nepal: Shechen Monastery,
      n.d.

NS   *The Nyingma School of Tibetan Buddhism.* Dudjom Rinpoche. Boston:
      Wisdom Publications, 1991.

ON   *gSang 'grel phyogs bcu'i mun sel gyi spyi don 'od gsal snying po.* 'Ju mi pham
      rgya mtsho. Chengdu, China: Si khron mi rigs dpe skrun khang, 2000.

SD   *dPal gsang ba'i snying po de kho na nyid nges pa'i rgyud kyi rgyal po sgyu
      'phrul drwa ba spyi don gyi sgo nas gtan la 'bebs par byed pa'i legs bshad
      gsang bdag zhal lung.* Lo chen Dharma shri. Kathmandu, Nepal: Shechen
      Publications, n.d.

SG   *Theg pa lam zhugs kyi bshags pa'i rtsa 'grel bsdus pa thar lam sgron me.* Nges
      don bstan 'dzin bzang po. Chengdu, China: Si khron mi rigs dpe skrun
      khang, 1997.

SS   *Srog sdom gzer bzhi'i dmigs pa gnad 'gags khams gsum rol pa tshangs pa'i sgra
      dbyangs.* dPal sprul O rgyan 'jigs med chos kyi dbang po. Chengdu, China:
      Si khron mi rigs dpe skrun khang, 2003.

ST   *Srog sdom gzer bzhi'i zin bris kun mkhyen brgyud pa'i zhal lung.* mKhan
      chen ngag dbang dpal bzang. Publication data unknown.

TC   *Theg pa'i mchog rin po che'i mdzod.* Klong chen rab 'byams. Gangtok, Sik-
      kim: Sherab Gyaltsen and Khyentse Labrang, 1983.

TD   *Bod rgya tshig mdzod chen mo.* Krang dbyi sun, editor. Chengdu, China: Si
      khron mi rigs dpe skrun khang, 1988.

TK   *Shes bya kun khyab mdzod.* Kong sprul blo gros mtha' yas. Kathmandu,
      Nepal: Padma Karpo Translation Committee, n.d.

TS   *rDzogs pa chen po gsang ba snying thig ma bu'i bka' srol chu bo gnyis 'dus kyi
      khrid yig dri med zhal lung.* Kong sprul blo gros mtha' yas. In *rNying ma*

bka' ma rgyas pa, compiled by bDud 'joms 'jigs bral ye shes rdo rje. Kalimpong, India: Dupjung Lama, 1982–1987.

WC   *Zab bsang bdud rtsi'i sgo 'byed skal bzang kun dga'i rol ston.* Dil mgo mkhyen brtse. Kathmandu, Nepal: Shechen Publications, n.d.

YD   *Theg pa chen po'i man ngag gi bstan bcos yid bzhin rin po che'i mdzod.* Klong chen rab 'byams. Gangtok, Sikkim: Sherab Gyaltsen and Khyentse Labrang, 1983.

YT   *Yon tan rin po che'i mdzod las 'bras bu'i theg pa'i rgya cher 'grel rnam mkhyen shing rta.* 'Jigs med gling pa. Kathmandu, Nepal: Shechen Monastery, n.d.

ZD   *Zab don rgya mtsho'i sprin.* Klong chen rab 'byams. Darjeeling, India: Talung Tsetrul Pema Wangyal, 1976.

GLOSSARY

―――――――――――――― ❦ ――――――――――――――

Absolute bodhichitta (*don dam byang sems*) – The wisdom that directly realizes
EMPTINESS. [TD 1304]

Absorption (*ting nge 'dzin*) – "To truly grasp," meaning that within this mental state
one is able to focus one-pointedly and continuously on a given topic or on the
object one is examining. [TD 1027]

Accomplished master (*grub thob*) – An individual who has actualized the unique
realizations of the path and achieved both supreme and mundane SPIRITUAL
ATTAINMENTS. [TD 403]

Accumulation of merit (*bsod nams kyi tshogs*) – The accumulation of positive, virtuous activities, such as making offerings, that involve a conceptual reference
point. [TD 3051]

Accumulation of wisdom (*ye shes kyi tshogs*) – The accumulation of nonreferential
WISDOM is the accumulation of the undefiled virtue that enacts the attainment
of the DHARMAKAYA, the fruitional wisdom in which EMPTINESS is embraced
by BODHICHITTA. [TD 2594]

Active wisdom (*bya grub ye shes*) – The form of WISDOM that involves the enlightened form, speech, and mind spontaneously working for the welfare of sentient
beings. [YT 431]

Afflicted mind (*nyon yid*) – A neutral, obscured state of mind characterized by fixation on the self; this form of consciousness, which continues to function until
the paths of realization have been attained, observes the UNIVERSAL GROUND
CONSCIOUSNESS and continually takes it to be a self. [TK 2, 197]

Affliction (*nyon mongs pa*) – A factor that upsets or disturbs the mind and body and
produces fatigue. [TD 971]

Afflictive obscurations (*nyon mongs pa'i sgrib pa*) – Thought patterns, such as avarice, that obstruct the attainment of liberation. [TD 970]

Akanishta (*'Og min*) – See SUPREME REALM.

Akshobya (*Mi bskyod pa*) – As one member of the FIVE BUDDHA FAMILIES,

Akshobya represents the VAJRA family and the principle of enlightened mind, indivisible EMPTINESS and compassion. [BT 408]

Amitabha (*'Od dpag med*) – As one member of the FIVE BUDDHA FAMILIES, Amitabha represents the lotus family and the principle of enlightened speech, the source of all the Buddhist teachings. [BT 408]

Amitayus (*Tshe dpag med*) – A buddha of the lotus family associated with longevity.

Amoghasiddhi (*Don yod grub pa*) – As one member of the FIVE BUDDHA FAMILIES, Amoghasiddhi represents the karma family and the principle of ENLIGHTENED ACTIVITY, which is carried out by venerating the buddhas and working for the welfare of sentient beings. [BT 408]

Amrita (*bdud rtsi*) – See NECTAR.

Anuttarayoga Tantra (*rnal 'byor bla na med pa'i rgyud*) – Literally, "Unsurpassed Union Tantra." The fourth and highest of the FOUR CLASSES OF TANTRA. In the NEW SCHOOLS, this system consists of the FATHER TANTRAS, MOTHER TANTRAS, and NONDUAL TANTRAS. In the NYINGMA SCHOOL, this class of tantra is equated with the THREE INNER TANTRAS of MAHAYOGA, ANU-YOGA, and ATIYOGA. Ju Mipam explains the uniqueness of this system: "From the perspective of this approach, not only is the CAUSAL VEHICLE of the per-fections a 'long path,' but the OUTER TANTRAS are as well. In other words, this is the true 'swift path' and 'FRUITIONAL VEHICLE.' All other approaches are taught according to the mind-sets of disciples to lead them to this vehicle. Here, in contrast, the ultimate, DEFINITIVE MEANING is revealed explicitly, just as it is seen by the WISDOM of the BUDDHAS." [KG 37]

Anuyoga (*rjes su rnal 'byor*) – Literally, "Concordant Yoga." Anuyoga is the eighth of the NINE VEHICLES found in the tantric tradition of the NYINGMA SCHOOL. To enter this system, one first receives the thirty-six supreme EMPOWERMENTS, which include ten outer empowerments, eleven inner empowerments, thirteen practice empowerments and two SECRET EMPOWERMENTS. Next, one trains in the Anuyoga view until one has come to a definitive understanding of the essence of the threefold MANDALA of SAMANTABHADRA. In the meditative system of this tradition, one practices the PATHS OF LIBERATION and SKILL-FUL MEANS. The former involves settling in a nonconceptual state that is in harmony with REALITY ITSELF or, in accordance with letters, reciting MAN-TRAS to visualize a mandala of DEITIES. The latter entails arousing coemergent WISDOM by relying upon the upper and lower gates. In terms of conduct, one understands all appearances and mental events to be the play of the wisdom of great bliss, and with this understanding, uses the direct cause of being beyond acceptance and rejection to attain the fruition of this path. Here, the fruition involves the five yogas (which are in essence the FIVE PATHS), the completion of the ten levels, and the attainment of the state of Samantabhadra. [TD 3120]

Application bodhichitta (*'jug pa'i byang chub kyi sems*) – To develop BODHICHITTA by actually engaging in certain activities, such as the SIX PERFECTIONS, with the express aim being to bring all sentient beings to the state of buddhahood. [TD 905] This consists of committing oneself to the cause of enlightenment, in contrast to ASPIRATION BODHICHITTA, where one commits oneself to its fruition. [YT 475]

Application of mindfulness (*dran pa nyer bzhag*) – "Mindfulness" here refers to KNOWLEDGE, meaning to know the characteristics of phenomena as they are, unmistakenly. Hence, this aspect relates to INSIGHT. "Application" refers to the placement of attention one-pointedly on the analytic process that one's knowledge is engaged in. Hence, this aspect relates to TRANQUILITY. Most commonly, there are said to be four applications of mindfulness, which are the four focal points used when cultivating insight. These are (1) the application of mindfulness to the body, (2) the application of mindfulness to sensation, (3) the application of mindfulness to the mind, and (4) the application of mindfulness to phenomena. These four partially constitute the THIRTY-SEVEN FACTORS OF ENLIGHTENMENT. [TD 1322]

Approach and accomplishment (*bsnyen sgrub*) – The four phases of tantric practice: approach, close approach, accomplishment, and great accomplishment. Ju Mipam explains: "Approach and accomplishment subsume all the various practices that utilize the unique methods of the SECRET MANTRA tradition to achieve whatever SPIRITUAL ACCOMPLISHMENTS one desires, whether supreme or mundane." [ON 534]

Aspiration bodhichitta (*smon pa'i byang chub kyi sems*) – To commit oneself to attaining the fruitional [state of buddhahood], meaning that one is oriented toward the attainment of enlightenment and, consequently, engages in its related practices. [YT 475]

Atiyoga (*shin tu rnal 'byor*) – Literally, "Supreme Yoga." Atiyoga is the highest of the NYINGMA tradition's NINE VEHICLES. In the textual tradition of this tantric system, Atiyoga is equated with the GREAT PERFECTION of one's self-occurring WISDOM. This wisdom is free from elaborations and not subject to any sense of partiality or limitation. As such, it is considered the very pinnacle of all the various vehicles, since it contains all of their significance. Within this Great Perfection, all the various phenomena of samsara and nirvana, all that appears and exists, arise as the play of this self-occurring wisdom, apart from which nothing exists. The fundamental basis of existence, in this tradition, is this self-occurring wisdom. In terms of the path, there are two forms of practice: the BREAKTHROUGH stage of original purity and the DIRECT LEAP stage of spontaneous presence. Through these two practices, the four visions are brought to a state of culmination, and one attains the result of this process, liberation within the very ground, the attainment of the permanent state of the YOUTHFUL VASE BODY. [TD 3118]

Avalokiteshvara (*sPyan ras gzigs*) – As a YIDAM DEITY, Avalokiteshvara is considered to be the unified essence of the enlightened speech of all the BUDDHAS and the embodiment of compassion. [TD 1674]

Awareness mantra (*rig sngags*) – A MANTRA that is used to accomplish the activity of a DEITY and which emphasizes the VAJRA WISDOM of the enlightened mind. [TD 2681]

Bardo (*bar do*) – See INTERMEDIATE STATE.

Blissful One (*bde bar gshegs pa*) – An alternate term for the BUDDHAS, who, by relying upon the path of bliss—the VEHICLE OF THE BODHISATTVAS—progress to the blissful fruition, the state of perfect buddhahood. [TD 1368]

Blood (*khrag*) – As a symbolic representation used in DEVELOPMENT STAGE practice, blood is often visualized filling a SKULL CUP, representing the conquering of the FOUR DEMONS.

Bodhichitta (*byang chub kyi sems*) – This mind-set comes about by taking the welfare of others as one's focal point and then orienting oneself with the desire to attain total and perfect enlightenment. This unique frame of mind forms the core of the GREAT VEHICLE path. It can be divided into ASPIRATION BODHICHITTA and APPLICATION BODHICHITTA. [TD 1869]

Bodhisattva (*byang chub sems dpa'*) – Literally, "heroic being of enlightenment." Individuals who train in the GREAT VEHICLE and are so-called because they do not become discouraged in the face of the long duration it takes to attain great enlightenment, nor in giving away their own head and limbs out of generosity. [TD 1870]

Bön (*bon*) – A religious tradition founded by Shenrap that flourished in Tibet prior to the advent of the Buddhist teachings. [TD 1870]

Breakthrough (*khregs chod*) – Along with DIRECT LEAP, breakthrough is one of two stages of practice found in the GREAT PERFECTION's KEY INSTRUCTION CLASS. This practice is designed to liberate those prone to laziness in an effortless manner. In this approach, one first identifies, and then sustains recognition of, one's own innately pure, empty awareness. This practice is the essence of Great Perfection practice. [DZ 67]

Buddha (*sangs rgyas*) – One who has cleared away the darkness of the TWO OBSCURATIONS and in whom the two forms of KNOWLEDGE have blossomed. [TD 2913]

Causal Vehicle (*rgyu'i theg pa*) – An alternate name of the Vehicle of Characteristics, or VEHICLE OF PERFECTIONS, so-called because it takes the factors that cause the attainment of perfect buddhahood, such as the thirty-seven factors of enlightenment, as the path. [TD 580]

Central channel (*rtsa dbu ma*) – The central channel is the main energetic channel in the body. It runs vertically through the center of the body. Its upper end is located at the cranial aperture on the crown of the head, while its lower end is found in the secret place (the perineum). [TD 2212]

Chakra (*'khor lo*) – (1) In terms of the energetic body, the chakras are circular conglomerations of energetic channels that are supported by the CENTRAL CHAN-
NEL. [TD 2209] (2) As a symbolic implement used in DEVELOPMENT STAGE
practice, the chakra is a circular instrument that symbolizes cutting through the
AFFLICTIONS. [KR 51]

Channels, energies, and essences (*rtsa rlung thig le*) – These three factors function as
the support for consciousness, ensuring that the life remains stable and the life-
force uninterrupted. Of these three, the channels are said to be like a house, the
essences like the wealth contained therein, and the ENERGIES like their owner.
[TD 2213]

Charya Tantra (*spyod rgyud*) – Literally, "Performance Tantra." The second of the
THREE OUTER TANTRAS; the view of this tradition is similar to that of YOGA
TANTRA, while its conduct is equated with that of KRIYA TANTRA. For this
reason, it is also known as "Dual Tantra." [NS 271] This is the second of FOUR
CLASSES OF TANTRA found in the NEW SCHOOLS.

Chöd (*gcod*) – A spiritual tradition founded in Tibet by the female saint Machik
Lapdrön. [TD 747]

Cognitive obscurations (*shes bya'i sgrib pa*) – The conceptualization of the THREE
SPHERES, which obstructs the attainment of total omniscience (the state of
buddhahood). [TD 2860]

Completion stage (*rdzogs rim*) – Tantric practice is divided into two phases, the
DEVELOPMENT STAGE and the completion stage. Explaining these two, Lochen
Dharmashri writes: "To summarize, the development stage involves transform-
ing impure appearances into pure ones and meditating on the MANDALA circle.
In the completion stage, the aim is to realize the WISDOM of bliss–EMPTINESS."
The latter, he continues, can be divided further into the completion stage with
symbolic attributes and completion stage without symbolic attributes. He
writes: "In this stage, one either meditates conceptually on the ENERGIES,
CHANNELS, AND ESSENCES, or nonconceptually by absorbing oneself in REAL-
ITY." [SD 325] Ju Mipam summarizes this phase as follows: "All the various
forms of completion stage practice bring about the manifest appearance of pure
wisdom by bringing the karmic energies into the CENTRAL CHANNEL, though
this may be brought about either directly or indirectly." [ON 417]

Conditioned phenomena (*'dus byas*) – That which has arisen or been constructed
due to the coincidence of multiple causes and conditions; the phenomena that
collectively constitute the five aggregates. [TD 1408]

Dakini (*mkha' 'gro ma*) – (1) A yogini who has attained the extraordinary SPIRI-
TUAL ACCOMPLISHMENTS; (2) a female divinity who has taken birth in a PURE
REALM or other similar location. [TD 298]

Definitive meaning (*nges don*) – To specific disciples, it is taught that the profound
nature of all phenomena is EMPTINESS, free from arising, cessation, and every
other elaboration, and that the actual condition and nature of things is one of

LUMINOSITY, which is beyond anything that can be thought or put into words. The definitive meaning refers to this nature, as well as to the scriptures that teach it and their related commentaries. [TD 655]

Deity (*lha*) – See YIDAM DEITY.

Desire realm (*'dod khams*) – One of the THREE REALMS that constitute SAMSARA; sentient beings in this realm are attached to material food and sex, primarily because they sustain themselves through the five sense pleasures. This realm is referred to as such because it is home to desirous sentient beings. [TD 1414]

Development and completion (*bskyed rdzogs gnyis*) – The DEVELOPMENT STAGE and COMPLETION STAGE constitute the inner tantric path to liberation. According to Khenpo Ngaga: "All the various categories of TANTRA relate to the two stages of development and completion." [ST 6] Explaining the function of these two approaches, Lochen Dharmashri writes: "The development stage purifies [the idea that] the environment and its inhabitants are real entities with their own characteristics, while the completion stage purifies the subtle cling- ing that can occur while meditating that these are all illusory, as is the case in development stage practice." [SD 325]

Development, completion, and Great Perfection (*bskyed rdzogs gsum*) – In the NYINGMA tradition, the system of the INNER TANTRAS is said to comprise three avenues of practice—the DEVELOPMENT STAGE, the COMPLETION STAGE, and the GREAT PERFECTION. These three, in turn, are associated with MAHAYOGA, ANUYOGA, and ATIYOGA—the THREE INNER TANTRAS. As Dilgo Khyentsé explains: "Development and Mahayoga are like the basis for all the teachings, completion and Anuyoga are like the path of all the teachings, and the Great Perfection of Atiyoga is like the result of all the teachings." [WC 773]

Development Stage (*bskyed rim*) – Along with the COMPLETION STAGE, the devel- opment stage is one of two phases that constitute Buddhist practice in the INNER TANTRAS. This form of practice purifies the habitual tendencies associ- ated with the four types of birth by meditating on ordinary appearances, sounds, and thoughts as deity, mantra, and wisdom. [TD 184] Explaining further, Ju Mipam writes: "The phases of development stage practice correspond to the way in which conventional existence develops.... Practicing with this approach purifies the habitual patterns of samsara, perfects the fruition of nirvana, and matures the practitioner for the completion stage." [ON 416] This practice is discussed extensively in DMW.

Dharma (*chos*) – Most commonly, the word "dharma" is used to refer either to the BUDDHA's teachings or as a general term meaning "phenomena." As the Great Dictionary notes, however, this word has ten traditional usages, all of which relate to something that "holds its own essence." These ten are (1) know- able objects, (2) spiritual paths, (3) the transcendence of suffering, (4) mental objects, (5) merit, (6) life, (7) the sublime words of the Buddha, (8) temporal progression, (9) regulation, and (10) systems. [TD 825]

Dharmakaya (*chos kyi sku*) – One of the THREE KAYAS. When classified into two forms, the state of buddhahood is divided into the dharmakaya and RUPAKAYA (the form of reality and the embodied forms). The dharmakaya benefits oneself and results from the culmination of abandonment and realization. [TD 829]

Dharma protector (*chos skyong*) – A protective deity that is bound under oath to protect the Buddhist teachings. [TD 830]

Direct leap (*thod rgal*) – Along with the BREAKTHROUGH stage, direct leap is one of two phases of practice found in the GREAT PERFECTION's KEY INSTRUCTION CLASS. In contrast to breakthrough, which focuses on emptiness and original purity, the direct leap emphasizes spontaneous presence and the active manifestations of reality itself. This approach is directed toward diligent individuals who liberate themselves through meditation. [YT 689]

Discerning wisdom (*so sor rtogs pa'i ye shes*) – The inner state of clarity in which all that can be known is understood in a distinct manner. [ZD 78]

Dissolution phase (*bsdu rim*) – A concluding ritual in which one dissolves the visualization of the DEVELOPMENT STAGE into the nonreferential sphere. [TD 1488]

Dominant result (*bdag po'i 'bras bu*) – One of a fivefold classification of results; a result whose arising is entirely dictated by a particular cause that "dominates" its corresponding result, such as when virtuous activities cause a rebirth in a positive location. [TD 1358]

Dual Tantra (*gnyis ka rgyud*) – An alternate name for CHARYA TANTRA.

Dzogchen (*rdzogs chen*) – See GREAT PERFECTION.

Early Translation School (*snga 'gyur*) – See NYINGMA SCHOOL.

Eight collections of consciousness (*rnam shes tshogs brgyad*) – The six collections of consciousness plus the AFFLICTED MIND and the UNIVERSAL GROUND CONSCIOUSNESS. [TK 1, 50]

Eight freedoms (*dal ba brgyad*) – Freedom from the eight restricted states: the hell, spirit, and animal realms; the realm of long-life gods, borderlands, being born dumb, having wrong views, or living in a dark age. [TD 1254]

Eight Great Sadhana Teachings (*sgrub pa bka' brgyad*) – MAHAYOGA is traditionally divided into two sections: the TANTRA SECTION, which includes the *GUHYAGARBHA TANTRA*, and the SADHANA SECTION. The latter division contains the Eight Great Sadhana Teachings, which constitute the ritual practices and instructions associated with eight divinities—five transcendent deities and three mundane deities. The five wisdom deities are MANJUSHRI Yamantaka (embodying enlightened form), Padma HAYAGRIVA (embodying enlightened speech), Vishuddha (embodying enlightened mind), Vajramrita Mahottara (embodying enlightened qualities), and VAJRAKILAYA (embodying enlightened activity). The three classes of worldly divinities are Matarah (liberating sorcery), Lokastotrapuja (mundane praises), and Vajramantrabhiru (wrathful mantra). [NS 283] These teachings have been maintained and practiced in both

the TRANSMITTED TEACHINGS OF THE NYINGMA SCHOOL and the TREA-
SURE tradition. In the former, the primary source is a cycle titled The Fortress
and Precipice of the Eight Teachings: The Distilled Realization of the Four
Wise Men. There are a great many related teachings in the treasure tradition.
The most important, however, are found in the revelations of Nyang Ral Nyima
Özer, Guru Chöwang, and Rigdzin Gödem. [WC 777]

Eight masters of awareness (*rig 'dzin chen po brgyad*) – These eight masters of
awareness were Indian gurus entrusted with the Eight Great Sadhana Teachings: Vimalamitra, Humkara, Manjushrimitra, Nagarjuna, Padmasambhava,
Dhanasamskrita, Rambuguhya-Devachandra, and Shantigarbha. These individuals are also referred to as the "eight great ACCOMPLISHED MASTERS" (*grub
pa'i slob dpon chen po brgyad*). Details on the lives of these masters can be found
in NS 475–483.

Eight mundane spiritual attainments (*thun mong gi ngos grub brgyad*) – See MUN-
DANE SPIRITUAL ATTAINMENT.

Eight restricted states (*mi khom pa brgyad*) – The hell, spirit, and animal realms; the
realm of long-life gods, borderlands, being born dumb, having wrong views, or
living in a dark age. [TD 2064]

Eight worldly pursuits (*'jig rten chos brgyad*) – The eight factors that, through
minor beneficial or harmful effects, bring about happiness and unhappiness,
respectively: gain and loss; fame and infamy; praise and insult; pleasure and
pain. [TD 895]

Empowerment (*dbang*) – In a general sense, an empowerment is a tantric ritual that
matures the student and allows her or him to engage in specific tantric practices.
There are a great many divisions and descriptions pertaining to empowerment,
such as those of the ground, path, and fruition. There are also unique empowerments associated with each tantric lineage and vehicle. Concerning the meaning of the term "empowerment," Jamgön Kongtrül explains that the original
Sanskrit term has the literal meaning of "to scatter and pour." The meaning, he
explains, is that empowerments cleanse and purify the psycho-physical continuum by "scattering" the obscurations and then "pouring" the potential of WIS-
DOM into what is then a clean vessel, the purified psycho-physical continuum.
[TK 3, 54] Stressing the importance of the empowerment ritual, Tsele Natsok
Rangdröl writes: "Unless you first obtain the ripening empowerments, you are
not authorized to hear even a single verse of the tantras, statements, and instructions. (Unauthorized) people who engage in expounding and listening to the
tantras will not only fail to receive blessings, they will create immense demerit
from divulging the secrecy of these teachings. A person who has not obtained
empowerment may pretend to practice the liberating instructions, but, instead
of bringing accomplishment, the practice will create obstacles and countless
other defects." [EM 39]

Empowerment into the display of awareness (*rig pa'i rtsal dbang*) – In the ATIYOGA tradition, those with the fortune to do so may enter into the MANDALA of ULTI-MATE BODHICHITTA right from the beginning, without having to rely upon the symbolic wisdom of the first three empowerments. The empowerment that allows one to do so is the empowerment into the display of awareness. Quoting the master Manjushrimitra, Jamgön Kongtrül writes: "The profound, supreme, and true empowerment / Is the attainment of the empowerment into the display of awareness. / It is an empowerment because one realizes the nature of mind." [TK 3, 103]

Emptiness (*stong pa nyid*) – The manner in which all phenomena are devoid of inherent existence; their true nature. In certain contexts, sixteen or eighteen forms of emptiness are listed: (1) internal emptiness, (2) external emptiness, (3) internal and external emptiness, (4) the emptiness of emptiness, (5) great emptiness, (6) ultimate emptiness, (7) conditioned emptiness, (8) unconditioned emptiness, (9) emptiness that transcends extremes, (10) emptiness without beginning or end, (11) unrelinquished emptiness, (12) natural emptiness, (13) the emptiness of all phenomena, (14) the emptiness of particular characteristics, (15) unobservable emptiness, and (16) the emptiness of the essential lack of entities. When eighteen are listed, the following two are added: (17) the emptiness of the lack of entities, and (18) emptiness of the very essence. [TD 1110]

Energy (*rlung*) – One element of the triad ENERGIES, CHANNELS, AND ESSENCES. This factor has the nature of the five elements and completely pervades the energetic channels. [TD 2734]

Enlightened activity (*'phrin las*) – One aspect of the fruitional state of buddhahood. The most common presentation of enlightened activity contains four divisions: pacifying, enriching, magnetizing, and wrathful activity. To these four, a fifth division is sometimes added, that of spontaneous activity. [TD 1771] According to Ju Mipam, enlightened activity can also be divided into supreme and mundane. The former, he writes, involves "planting the seed of liberation in the minds of others by granting EMPOWERMENTS, and through MANTRAS, MUDRAS, and so forth, while the latter functions to bring others more temporary forms of happiness." [ON 559]

Essence kaya (*ngo bo nyid sku*) – As discussed in the Perfection of Knowledge literature, the essence kaya is one particular facet of buddhahood. In particular, this refers to the kaya of the perfection of the sphere of reality, in which there are two forms of purity, natural purity and incidental purity. [TD 663]

Faith (*dad pa*) – Generally, three types of faith are discussed in the scholastic tradition: lucid faith, inspired faith, and the faith of conviction. The first entails a lucid frame of mind that arises in reference to the Three Jewels. The second concerns the desire to engage the third and fourth noble truths and reject the first two noble truths. The third involves having conviction in the principle of karmic causality. [YD 607]

Father Tantra (*pha rgyud*) – Father Tantra emphasizes both the methods of the

DEVELOPMENT STAGE and the energetic practices of the COMPLETION STAGE. In the NEW SCHOOLS, the Father Tantra includes the five stages of the Guhyasamaja Tantra. [ST 6] In the NYINGMA tradition, Father Tantra is equated with MAHAYOGA, the seventh of the NINE VEHICLES. [DZ 24]

Five acts of immediate retribution (*mtshams med lnga*) – (1) To kill one's father, (2) to kill one's mother, (3) to kill a foe-destroyer, (4) to create a schism within the Buddhist community, and (5) to maliciously draw blood from the body of a buddha. [TD 2311]

Five buddha families (*rigs lnga*) – The five buddha families function as the support for the FIVE WISDOMS. The relationship between these two groups is as follows: The WISDOM OF THE SPHERE OF REALITY is linked with the BUDDHA family and the buddha VAIROCHANA, ACTIVE WISDOM with the karma family and the buddha AMOGHASIDDHI, the WISDOM OF EQUALITY with the jewel family and the buddha RATNASAMBHAVA, DISCERNING WISDOM with the LOTUS family and the buddha AMITABHA, and MIRROR-LIKE WISDOM with the VAJRA family and either VAJRASATTVA or AKSHOBYA. [TK 2, 80]

Five degenerations (*snyigs ma lnga*) – (1) The degeneration of life span, (2) the degeneration of the afflictions, (3) the degeneration of sentient beings, (4) the degeneration of time, and (5) the degeneration of the view. [TD 1001]

Fivefold certainty (*nges pa lnga*) – The five certainties of the SAMBHOGAKAYA: the certain place is the Richly Arrayed SUPREME REALM, the certain form has all the MARKS AND SIGNS of buddhahood, the certain retinue consists solely of realized BODHISATTVAS, the certain teaching is that of the GREAT VEHICLE alone, and the certain time is the duration of SAMSARA. [TD 656]

Five perfections (*phun sum tshogs pa lnga*) – The perfect teaching, the perfect time, the perfect teacher, the perfect place, and the perfect retinue. [TD 1718]

Five substances that come from cows (*ba byung lnga*) – Cow urine, dung, milk, butter, and curd that have not touched the ground. [TD 1802]

Five visions (*gzigs pa lnga*) – The five visions beheld by the Victorious One Shvetaketu [the name of Shakyamuni as he dwelt in Tushita Heaven before taking birth for the final time]: (1) his birthplace, Kapilavastu; (2) his royal caste; (3) his descent from the Shakya clan; (4) his mother, Mayadevi; and (5) the era into which he was born, that of the fivefold degeneration. [TD 2495]

Five wisdoms (*ye shes lnga*) – According to Jigmé Lingpa, wisdom can be divided into twenty-five categories, as there are five different forms of wisdom present in each continuum of the FIVE BUDDHA FAMILIES. [YT 431] More commonly, however, five forms of wisdom are taught. Dudjom Rinpoche explains that the WISDOM OF THE SPHERE OF REALITY is that which realizes how things really are, whereas the four subsequent wisdoms—MIRROR-LIKE WISDOM, the WISDOM OF EQUALITY, DISCERNING WISDOM, and ACTIVE WISDOM—in their function of supporting and depending upon the former, constitute the wisdom that comprehends all that exists. It has also been explained that the first wisdom mentioned above refers to the ultimate, while the latter four relate to the relative. [NS 140]

Foe-destroyer (*dgra bcom pa*) – One who has destroyed or conquered all of his or her foes, here referring to the FOUR DEMONS. [TD 464] This is the fruition of the FOUNDATIONAL VEHICLE.

Formless realm (*gzugs med khams*) – The four spheres of perception, from that of boundless space up to the peak of existence. In these spheres, there is no coarse form, only clear mental forms. The beings in these realms are free of attachment to form but are attached to the state of formlessness. [TD 2503]

Form realm (*gzugs khams*) – The abodes of the first through fourth states of ABSORPTION, which are located in the space above Mount Meru. The inhabitants of this realm have bodies of light that are clear by nature. Although they are free from passion, they still cling to form. [TD 2499]

Foundational Vehicle (*theg pa dman pa*) – The vehicle of the LISTENERS and SOLITARY BUDDHAS. [TD 1183] See also SUTRA VEHICLE, VEHICLE OF LISTENERS, AND VEHICLE OF SOLITARY BUDDHAS.

Four absorptions (*bsam gtan bzhi*) – Four states of increasingly refined concentration associated with the FORM REALM.

Four Classes of Tantra (*rgyud sde bzhi*) – The four classes of tantra are KRIYA TANTRA, CHARYA TANTRA, YOGA TANTRA, and ANUTTARAYOGA TANTRA. These four divisions are commonly presented in the NEW SCHOOLS and subsume all tantric teachings. Although this classification system is also found in the NYINGMA SCHOOL, that tradition more often groups the tantras into the THREE OUTER TANTRAS and THREE INNER TANTRAS.

Four demons (*bdud bzhi*) – The demon of the AFFLICTIONS, the demon of the aggregates, the demon of the lord of death, and the demon of the divine son. [TD 1364]

Four empowerments (*dbang bzhi*) – The VASE EMPOWERMENT, SECRET EMPOWERMENT, KNOWLEDGE-WISDOM EMPOWERMENT, and PRECIOUS WORD EMPOWERMENT. [TD 1935]

Fourfold Heart Essence (snying thig ya bzhi) – A collection of GREAT PERFECTION teachings compiled by Longchen Rabjam. This compilation contains five primary divisions: (1) the HEART ESSENCE OF THE DAKINIS (Khandro Nyingtik), the Dzogchen teachings of Padmasambhava; (2) the Quintessence of the Dakinis (Khandro Yangtik), a collection of Longchenpa's commentaries on Padmasambhava's teachings; (3) the HEART ESSENCE OF VIMALAMITRA (Vima Nyingtik), the Dzogchen teachings of Vimalamitra; (4) the Quintessence of the Guru (Lama Yangtik), a collection of Longchenpa's commentaries on Vimalamitra's teachings; and (5) The Profound Quintessence (Zabmo Nyingtik), a collection of Longchenpa's commentaries that apply to both Padmasambhava's and Vimalamitra's teachings.

Four forms of fearlessness (*mi 'jigs pa bzhi*) – (1) Fearlessness in the face of perfect realization, (2) fearlessness in the face of perfect abandonment, (3) fearlessness in the face of teaching obstructive phenomena, and (4) fearlessness in the face teaching the path of certain release. [TD 2068]

Four fundamental and naturally negative deeds (*rang bzhin gyi sdig pa'i rtsa ba bzhi*) – (1) Taking life, (2) stealing, (3) sexual activity, and (4) dishonestly proclaiming one's spiritual achievements. See also FOUR FUNDAMENTAL PRECEPTS.

Four fundamental precepts (*rtsa ba bzhi*) – The fundamental precepts associated with the vows of INDIVIDUAL LIBERATION: restraining from taking life, stealing, sexual activity, and dishonestly proclaiming one's own spiritual achievements. These four are the fundamental vows of ordained individuals. If they are allowed to degenerate, one's vows will be completely destroyed. [TD 2210]

Four immeasurables (*tshad med bzhi*) – Immeasurable love, immeasurable compassion, immeasurable joy, and immeasurable equanimity; these four mind-sets are held by practitioners of the Great Vehicle and are so called because one meditates by focusing on sentient beings without any sense of limitation, and because they bring an immeasurable amount of merit. [TD 2260]

Four kinds of enlightened activity (*phrin las rnam pa bzhi*) – See ENLIGHTENED ACTIVITY.

Four obscurations (*sgrib pa bzhi*) – (1) The obscuration of desire, (2) the obscuration of the NON-BUDDHISTS, (3) the obscuration of the inferiority of the listeners, and (4) the obscuration of the inferiority of solitary buddhas. Alternately, the four are (1) the afflictive obscurations, (2) cognitive obscurations, (3) desirous obscurations, and (4) obstructive obscurations. A third enumeration gives (1) karmic obscurations, (2) afflictive obscurations, (3) cognitive obscurations, and (4) obscurations of meditative equipoise. [TD 612]

Four seals that mark the Buddha's teachings (*bkar btags kyi phyag rgya bzhi*) – (1) All conditioned phenomena are impermanent; (2) all that is defiled is suffering; (3) all phenomena are empty and devoid of self; and (4) nirvana is peace. [TD 828]

Four types of generosity (*sbyin pa rnam bzhi*) – (1) The outer generosity of giving material goods; (2) dharmic generosity; (3) the generosity of protection, or fearlessness; and (4) the generosity of love, the wish that all beings achieve a state of perfect happiness. [YT 486]

Four ways of attracting students (*bsdu ba'i dngos po bzhi*) – (1) Practicing generosity, both in terms of the Dharma and in a material sense; (2) offering helpful advice; (3) acting meaningfully, or in accordance with the wishes of those in need of guidance; and (4) acting appropriately, that is, in accordance with the behavior of those in need of guidance. [TD 1487]

Fruitional Vehicle (*'bras bu'i theg pa*) – An alternate term for the VAJRA VEHICLE; Ju Mipam explains: "This vehicle is referred to as such because the essential FRUITION is seen to be present within the very ground, whereas in other systems it is believed to be something that must be attained. Hence, in this system, the FRUITION is taken as the path in the present moment." [KG 40]

Geluk school (*dge lugs pa*) – A tradition of Buddhist study and practice founded by Tsong Khapa and his followers. [TD 454]

Glorious Magical Web (*sGyu 'phrul drva ba*) – See TANTRA OF THE SECRET ESSENCE.

Great Compassionate One (*thugs rje chen po*) – Mahakaruna; a form of the BODHISATTVA AVALOKITESHVARA.

Great Perfection (*rdzogs pa chen po*) – This term is used in the tantric tradition of the NYINGMA SCHOOL, where it refers to the DHARMAKAYA (the nature of the mind lacking an essence), the sambhogakaya (self-illumination), and the nirmanakaya (pervasive compassionate resonance). Thus, in the great perfection, all the qualities of the THREE KAYAS are spontaneously perfect, and since this is the way all phenomena really are, it is great. [TD 2360]

Great Vehicle (*theg pa chen po*) – The VEHICLE OF THE BODHISATTVAS, so called because it is superior to the FOUNDATIONAL VEHICLE of the LISTENERS and SOLITARY BUDDHAS in seven ways. [TD 1183]

Ground, path, and fruition (*gzhi lam 'bras gsum*) – The view, meditation, and fruition of each vehicle. The ground consists of coming to a definitive understanding of the view; the path involves familiarizing oneself with this through meditation; and the fruition is the attainment of enlightenment. [TD 2421]

Guhyagarbha Tantra (*rGyud gsang ba snying po*) – See TANTRA OF THE SECRET ESSENCE.

Guru (*bla ma*) – A spiritual teacher; according to Clarifying the Practice of the Heart Essence, there are three types of guru: (1) the external guru who introduces one to meanings and the symbols that represent them; (2) the inner guru of understanding and experiencing the way things are; and (3) the secret, true guru of realization. The text goes on to explain, "for the novice practitioner, the outer guru is of paramount importance." [HE 16]

Guru Yoga (*bla ma'i rnal 'byor*) – A meditative ritual in which the practitioner meditates on his or her root guru as the union of all the buddhas. [TD 1914]

Hayagriva (*rTa mgrin*) – Literally, "Horse Neck." Hayagriva is a wrathful divinity of the LOTUS family and one of the YIDAM DEITIES of the EIGHT GREAT SADHANA TEACHINGS.

Hearing lineage (*snyan brgyud*) – Key instructions that have been transmitted orally through a succession of spiritual teachers. [TD 996]

Hearing lineage of people (*gang zag snyan brgyud*) – The transmission of teachings in the human realm [SD 70]; the lineage that has been gradually passed down since the eighth century, when the master Padmasambhava and the great scholar Vimalamitra directly taught their students the key instructions of the three yogas of the INNER TANTRAS. [TD 343]

Heart Essence (*snying thig*) – The KEY INSTRUCTION CLASS of the GREAT

PERFECTION contains various divisions, the most profound of which is termed Nyingtik, or Heart Essence. In the Heart Essence, the first stage of practice is the breakthrough of original purity, or *kadak trekchö*. *Kadak* is original purity, meaning the primordially pure nature of awareness. Breakthrough refers to the process resolving the nature of emptiness by breaking past or cutting through all levels of conceptuality, even the experiences of meditation. The second stage of practice is called the direct leap into spontaneous presence, or *lhundrup tögal*. This term conveys the sense of leaping straight into the immediate experience of original wisdom. Here, the quality of vivid clarity is emphasized, the spontaneously present, luminous nature of mind. This phase is likened to crossing over a mountain pass directly, rather than climbing in a more methodic, step-by-step manner. [GP2 xviii]

Heart Essence of the Dakinis (*mKha' 'gro snying thig*) – A collection of instructions from the NYINGMA tradition that the master Padmasambhava directly taught the DAKINI Yeshé Tsogyal and which were subsequently revealed as a TREASURE by Pema Ledrel Tsel. [TD 297] This is one division of the FOURFOLD HEART ESSENCE, a collection of Great Perfection instructions compiled by the master Longchenpa.

Heart Essence of the Vast Expanse (*Klong chen snying thig*) – The mind TREASURE of Rigdzin Jigmé Lingpa. [TD 48]

Heart Essence of Vimalamitra (*Bi ma'i snying thig*) – The GREAT PERFECTION teachings of Vimalamitra, which were compiled by Longchenpa and included in the FOURFOLD HEART ESSENCE.

Heruka (*he ru ka*) – 1) A blood drinker; 2) Chakrasamvara; 3) a general name for wrathful deities. [TD 3069]

Hinayana (*theg pa dman pa*) – See FOUNDATIONAL VEHICLE.

Individual liberation (*so sor thar pa*) – The liberation from the lower realms and samsara that those who maintain discipline [practitioners of the Foundational Vehicle] attain for themselves. [TD 2959]

Inner Tantras (*nang rgyud*) – See THREE INNER TANTRAS.

Insight (*lhag mthong*) – Along with TRANQUILITY, insight is one of the common denominators and causes of all states of ABSORPTION. It entails the observation of the specific distinguishing nature of a given object. [TD 3092]

Interdependent origination (*rten 'brel*) – The fact that all phenomena arise due to the interdependent relationship of their own specific causes and conditions. [KJ 18]

Intermediate state (*bar srid/bar do*) – The bardo, or intermediate state, typically refers to the state that occurs between DEATH and a future rebirth. It can also, however, refer to the transitional periods that constitute the entire stream of existence, inclusive of birth, dreaming, meditation, death, REALITY itself, and transmigration. Concerning the specific COMPLETION STAGE practice that relates to this state, Dza Patrul writes (referring to the three intermediate states of death, reality itself, and transmigration): "In the first intermediate state, one brings LUMINOSITY onto the path as the DHARMAKAYA. In the second, union is brought onto the path as SAMBHOGAKAYA. And in the third, rebirth is taken onto the path as NIRMANAKAYA." [DR 445]

Jonang school (*jo nang lugs*) – A lineage founded by Yumo Mikyö Dorjé, and later propagated by Tukjé Tsöndru, Dolpopa Sherap Gyaltsen, and Taranata. [TD 878]

Kadampa school (*bka' gdams pa*) – A Buddhist school founded by Atisha and Dromtön that believed that each and every teaching of the Buddha should be understood as a practical instruction. [TD 72]

Kagyü (*bka' brgyud*) – See TAKPO KAGYÜ and SHANGPA KAGYÜ.

Kalachakra (*dus kyi 'khor lo*) – An ANUTTARAYOGA TANTRA; 2) a YIDAM DEITY of the nondual tantras. [TD 1267]

Kama (*bka' ma*) – See TRANSMITTED TEACHINGS OF THE NYINGMA SCHOOL.

Kangyur (*bka' 'gyur*) – The Three Collections of teachings given by the Buddha and the Four Classes of Tantra, all of which were translated into Tibetan and compiled into a 104- or 108-volume collection. [TD 69]

Karma (*las*) – The nature of action; a mental factor that propels the mind toward a concordant object and causes it to fluctuate. [TD 2769] See also PRINCIPLE OF KARMIC CAUSALITY.

Kaya (*sku*) – An honorific term for body, which is often used to refer to the "body" or "form" of buddhahood, in all its various aspects. See also NIRMANAKAYA, SAMBHOGAKAYA, DHARMAKAYA, and ESSENCE KAYA.

Key Instruction Class (*man ngag sde*) – The third and most profound division of the Great Perfection teachings, along with the Mind Class and Space Class. This category is further divided into outer, inner, secret, and extremely secret unsurpassed cycles. The latter refers to the Heart Essence teachings of the GREAT PERFECTION. This refers primarily to the HEART ESSENCE OF THE DAKINIS (the key instructions that were taught by the master of Oddiyana, Padmakara) and the HEART ESSENCE OF VIMALAMITRA (the lineage of the great scholar Vimalamitra). [TD 2056] See also THREE CLASSES OF THE GREAT PERFECTION.

Khandro Nyingtik (*mkha' 'gro snying thig*) – See HEART ESSENCE OF THE DAKINIS.

Knowledge (*shes rab*) – Knowledge is the factor that focuses on a specific entity, examines this object, and is then able to distinguish its essence and individual features, its general and specific characteristics, and whether it should be taken up or abandoned. Once perfected, it functions to dispel doubt. "Knowledge" is synonymous with the terms "total awareness," "total understanding," "awakening," "thorough analysis," "thorough understanding," "confidence," "intellect," "mental functioning," and "clear realization." [TD 2863]

Knowledge–wisdom empowerment (*shes rab ye shes kyi dbang*) – The second of the

THREE HIGHER, SUPREME EMPOWERMENTS, which is bestowed upon the student's mind in dependence upon the MANDALA of the FEMALE MUDRA. This purifies mental impurities and, in terms of the path, empowers the student to train in the COMPLETION STAGE. As the result of this empowerment, a causal link is formed that leads to the attainment of the DHARMAKAYA. [TD 2865]

Kriya Tantra (*bya rgyud*) – Literally, "Activity Tantra." First of the THREE OUTER TANTRAS. The view of this system, in terms of the ultimate, relates to the self-purity of all phenomena, while relatively one gains SPIRITUAL ACCOMPLISHMENTS by being blessed by the pure DEITY. Practice in this tradition focuses on the WISDOM BEING and MANTRA recitation. Its conduct involves various forms of ritual purification and asceticism. [KG 34]

Kusali (Offerings of) (*ku sa li'i tshogs gsog*) – See SIMPLE BEGGAR (OFFERING OF).

Liberation (*thar pa*) – To be freed from that which binds; in terms of samsara, that which binds is KARMA and the AFFLICTIONS. Hence, these are the factors that need to be eliminated for liberation to occur. Synonyms for "liberation" include "freedom," "true goodness," "immortality," "the ultimate," "the immaculate," "complete freedom," "elimination," "purity and freedom," "enlightenment," "NIRVANA," "peace," and "the absence of rebirth." [TD 1153]

Listener (*nyan thos*) – An individual who has entered into the VEHICLE OF THE LISTENERS, one of the THREE VEHICLES. These are individuals who do not focus on practicing the teachings associated with the GREAT VEHICLE, but are so called because they "listen" or hear the teachings from the BUDDHA and so forth, and then repeat what they have heard to others. Hence they are also known as "those who listen and then repeat." [TD 933]

Longchen Nyingtik (*klong chen snying thig*) – See HEART ESSENCE OF THE VAST EXPANSE.

Lower existence (*ngan 'gro*) – A general term used to refer to the three lower realms, where beings experience nothing but intense suffering as the result of the great number of nonvirtuous acts they committed in the past. [TD 646]

Lower realm (*ngan song*) – Synonymous with LOWER EXISTENCE. [TD 649]

Luminosity (*'od gsal*) – Though the term "luminosity" literally means "light which is able to dispel darkness" [TD 2535], it is also commonly used in reference to WISDOM, the subjective counterpart to REALITY. As the practitioner progresses along the various paths and levels, the manner in which luminous wisdom perceives its object, REALITY, becomes more and more refined. [NO 4, 17]

Magical Web (*sGyu 'phrul drva ba*) – See *TANTRA OF THE SECRET ESSENCE.*

Mahamudra (*phyag rgya chen po*) – (1) "Mahamudra" is the term given to the ultimate fruition, the SUPREME SPIRITUAL ACCOMPLISHMENT. (2) The term can also refer to one of the FOUR MUDRAS taught in the YOGA TANTRA tradition. In this context, the practice of Mahamudra relates to the enlightened form. As such, it eliminates the temporary confusion of the UNIVERSAL GROUND

CONSCIOUSNESS and actualizes its nature, MIRROR-LIKE WISDOM. [TD 1732] Also a fruitional teaching of the Kagyü and Geluk schools that emphasizes the nature of mind.

Mahayana (*theg pa chen po*) – See GREAT VEHICLE.

Mahayoga (*rnal 'byor chen po*) – Mahayoga is one of NINE VEHICLES found in the NYINGMA tantric tradition. In this system, one begins by maturing one's state of being with the eighteen supreme EMPOWERMENTS: the ten outer, beneficial empowerments; the five inner empowerments of potentiality; and the three profound, secret empowerments. In the next step, one comes to a definitive understanding of the VIEW, which relates to the indivisibility of the superior two truths. In terms of meditation, the development stage is emphasized—the THREE ABSORPTIONS form the structure for this stage of practice, while its essence consists of a threefold process: purification, perfection, and maturation. This is then sealed with the four stakes that bind the life-force. In the COMPLETION STAGE practice of this system, one meditates on the CHANNELS, ENERGIES, ESSENCES, and LUMINOSITY. Then, as the conduct, one relies upon the direct cause, which can be either elaborate in form, unelaborate, or extremely unelaborate, and then attains the fruition of this process—the completion of the FIVE PATHS (which are subsumed under the FOUR MASTERS OF AWARENESS). This state of fruition is known as the unified state of the VAJRA HOLDER. [TD 2052]

Male and female spiritual partners (*yab yum*) – In the SECRET MANTRA VEHICLE, male and female DEITIES are said to embody key Buddhist principles and are visualized in this capacity. Getse Mahapandita explains: "Subjective appearances relate to the masculine principle of SKILLFUL MEANS. In contrast, the object, meaning EMPTINESS, relates to KNOWLEDGE, the feminine principle. The indivisible unity of these two is the great primordial union of all that exists." Discussing further, he writes: "Emptiness can be witnessed based on appearance, while appearances arise unhindered as the display of emptiness, which itself manifests as causality. Since the truth of this is undeniable, the two truths are in union; they do not conflict with the principle of INTERDEPENDENT ORIGINATION. You cannot attain the perfect result of NIRVANA by utilizing just one of these while abandoning the other. Therefore, the way to bring this onto the path is to meditate on the male and female deities in union, which symbolizes the indivisible union of skillful means and knowledge." [CG 50]

Mandala (*dkyil 'khor*) – Explaining the meaning of this term, Ju Mipam writes: "Manda means 'essence' or 'pith,' while la has the sense of 'to take' or 'grasp.' Hence, together this term means 'that which forms the basis for grasping essential qualities.' Alternately, when this word is translated literally as a whole, it means 'that which is wholly spherical and entirely surrounds.'"

Concerning the various types of mandala, Mipam continues: "There are three types of mandala: those of the ground, path, and fruition. The natural mandala of the ground refers to the universe and its inhabitants being primordially present as divinities, both in terms of the support and supported. . . . In terms of the path, there is the mandala of meditation, of which there are the two forms: the symbolic mandala (such as paintings, lines, arrangements, and those made from colored powder) and the true mandala that is represented by these forms (enlightened form, speech, and mind). . . . The mandala of the ultimate fruition is composed of the ENLIGHTENED FORMS and WISDOMS that occur once the path has been completely traversed and one has attained the state of SAMAN-TABHADRA." [ON 494] The term "threefold mandala" is used to refer to the physical mandala of the DEITY, the verbal mandala of MANTRA, and the mental mandala of concentration. [KN 94]

Manjughosha (*'jam dpal gzhon nur gyur pa*) – The "Gentle, Glorious, and Youthful One"; see MANJUSHRI.

Manjushri (*'jam dpal dbyangs*) – The "Gentle, Glorious, and Melodic One"; a BODHISATTVA and YIDAM DEITY that personifies perfect knowledge. He is "gentle" in the sense of having totally eliminated any trace of coarse negativity and glorious in that he is in the form of a sixteen-year-old youth at all times. [TD 888]

Mantra (*sngags*) – Mantras are formations of syllables that protect practitioners of the VAJRA VEHICLE from the ordinary perceptions of their own minds. They also function to invoke the YIDAM DEITIES and their retinues. [TD 707] Explaining the etymology of the term, Dudjom Rinpoche writes, "Mana, which conveys the meaning of mind, and traya, which conveys that of protection, become 'mantra' by syllabic contraction, and therefrom the sense of protecting the mind is derived." [NS 257] See also SECRET MANTRA VEHICLE.

Marks and signs (*mtshan dpe*) – The excellent marks and signs that signify a fully realized being. [TD 2306]

Master of awareness (*rig pa 'dzin pa*) – In this term, "awareness" refers to DEITY, MANTRA, and the WISDOM of great BLISS. One who has "mastered" these three with profound and SKILLFUL MEANS is a "master of awareness." [TD 2683]

Meditation (*sgom pa*) – See VIEW, MEDITATION, CONDUCT, AND FRUITION.

Middle Way (*dbu ma*) – A body of literature and a philosophical school that teaches profound emptiness. [TD 1939]

Mind Class (*sems sde*) – See THREE CLASSES OF THE GREAT PERFECTION.

Mind lineage of the victorious ones (*rgyal ba dgongs brgyud*) – In this lineage, the victorious one SAMANTABHADRA transmits realization to the regents of the FIVE BUDDHA FAMILIES. These five, in turn, transmit this realization to their simultaneously arisen retinue, the BODHISATTVAS and so forth. [SD 69]

Mirror–like wisdom (*me long lta bu'i ye shes*) – An aspect of WISDOM, its self-illumination and unobstructed capacity to manifest. [ZD 78]

Mother Tantra (*ma rgyud*) – In the Mother Tantra, the COMPLETION STAGE associated with the subtle essences is emphasized, in which case one relies either upon the body of another or one's own body. In the NEW SCHOOLS, the Mother Tantra includes Naropa's Six Dharmas. [ST 6] In the NYINGMA tradition, Mother Tantra is equated with ANUYOGA, the eighth of the NINE VEHICLES. [DZ 24]

Mudra (phyag rgya) – Most commonly, the term "seal," or "mudra," refers to physical gestures that embody certain Buddhist principles. According to Ju Mipam, however, the Sanskrit term "mudra" carries the meaning of "a stamp, symbol, or seal that is difficult to move beyond." Explaining further, he writes, "What this means is that these are unique factors that symbolize the enlightened form, speech, mind, and activities of realized beings. Once something has been 'sealed' with one of these, it is difficult to stray from the factor that is being represented." [ON 568]

Mundane spiritual attainment (thun mong dngos grub) – In addition to the SUPREME SPIRITUAL ATTAINMENT, there are eight mundane SPIRITUAL ATTAINMENTS: (1) the sword that enables one to travel through the sky and space, (2) pills that allow one to be invisible and shift shape, (3) eye salve that allows one to see any worldly form as nonexistent, (4) swift-footedness, (5) the ability to extract and sustain oneself on the essences of plants and minerals (which includes the practice of alchemy), (6) the ability to travel to celestial realms, (7) invisibility, and (8) the ability to extract treasures from the earth and provide beings with what they desire. [TD 675]

Natural nirmanakaya (rang bzhin sprul pa'i sku) – According to Jamgön Kongtrül, the "natural NIRMANAKAYA" is like a reflection cast by the SAMBHOGAKAYA, and encompasses the five PURE REALMS, KAYAS, WISDOMS, Dharmas, and other elements that appear to tenth-level BODHISATTVAS. In particular, this refers to the five nirmanakaya realms: the SUPREME REALM (Akanishta, the realm of the buddha family and the buddha VAIROCHANA), Complete Joy (Abhirati, the realm of the vajra family and the buddha AKSHOBYA), the Glorious (Shrimat, the realm of the jewel family and the buddha RATNASAMBHAVA), the Realm of Bliss, or Lotus Mound (Sukhavati/Padmakuta, the realm of the LOTUS family and the buddha AMITABHA), and Accomplishment of Supreme Activity (Karmaprasiddhi, the realm of the karma family and the buddha AMOGHASIDDHI). [TK 1, 84]

Nectar (bdud rtsi) – A substance that allows one to conquer death. [TD 1362]

New Schools (gsar ma) – This appellation is applied most commonly to the Sakya, Kagyü, and Geluk traditions. More specifically, it refers to those who uphold the Tantras of the SECRET MANTRA that were brought to Tibet in a period that began with the work of the great translator Rinchen Zangpo (tenth century CE). [TD 3008] See also NYINGMA SCHOOL.

Ngöndro (sngon 'gro) – See PRELIMINARY PRACTICE.

Nine vehicles (theg pa dgu) – The nine vehicles constitute the path of the NYINGMA SCHOOL of the Early Translations, the Ngagyur Nyingma. The first three vehicles are those of the SUTRA VEHICLE, the exoteric Buddhist teachings: (1) the VEHICLE OF THE LISTENERS, (2) the VEHICLE OF THE SOLITARY BUD-DHAS, and (3) the VEHICLE OF THE BODHISATTVAS. The next set constitutes the THREE OUTER TANTRAS: (4) the Vehicle of KRIYA, or Activity Tantra; (5) the Vehicle of UBHAYA, or Dual Tantra; and (6) the Vehicle of YOGA, or Union Tantra. The final set of three represents the inner tantric tradition: (7) the Vehicle of MAHAYOGA, or Great Yoga; (8) the Vehicle of ANUYOGA, or Concordant Yoga; and (9) the Vehicle of ATIYOGA, or Supreme Yoga (also known as the GREAT PERFECTION). [NS 164]

Nirmanakaya (*sprul pa'i sku*) – (1) A form of buddhahood that arises from the empowering condition of the SAMBHOGAKAYA; an embodied form that comes into existence and appears to both pure and impure disciples, working for the benefit of these beings in accordance with their mental predispositions. (2) A name applied to the reincarnations of great lamas. [TD 1689]

Nirvana (*mya ngan las 'das pa*) – (1) To be liberated from suffering; (2) peace. [TD 2126]

Non-Buddhist (*mu stegs pa*) – Those whose religious persuasion does not involve maintaining that the Three Jewels are a source of refuge or accepting the FOUR SEALS THAT MARK THE BUDDHA'S TEACHINGS. [TD 2101]

Nondual Tantra (*gnyis med rgyud*) – The third of three divisions that constitute the ANUTTARAYOGA TANTRA; Nondual Tantra stresses the view of the PATH OF LIBERATION. In the NEW SCHOOLS, this includes the Six Applications of the Kalachakra Tantra. [ST 6]

Nyingma school (*rnying ma'i lugs*) – This tradition, which consists of NINE VEHI-CLES, is also referred to as the SECRET MANTRA school of the Early Transla-tions. The teachings of this school were first translated into Tibetan during the eighth century reign of King Trisong Deutsen and spread by the master Padma-sambhava and his followers. [TD 992]

Nyingtik (*snying thig*) – See HEART ESSENCE.

Nyingtik Yabshi (*snying thig ya bzhi*) – See FOURFOLD HEART ESSENCE.

Oath-bound protectors (*dam can*) – Worldly protective spirits that have taken a sacred oath [to safeguard the Buddha's teachings]. [TD 1245]

Outer tantras (*phyi rgyud*) – See THREE OUTER TANTRAS.

Path and Fruition (*lam 'bras*) – A profound teaching from the Sakya school that was originally transmitted by the siddha Virupa in ancient India, and later brought to Tibet by Drogmi Lotsawa. [TD 2767]

Performance Tantra (*spyod rgyud*) – See CHARYA TANTRA.

Precious word empowerment (*tshig dbang rin po che*) – The precious word EMPOW-ERMENT is one of the three higher supreme empowerments. This is bestowed upon the student's ordinary body, speech, and mind in reliance upon the MAN-DALA of ultimate BODHICHITTA. It purifies the impurities associated with the THREE GATES, along with their related habitual patterns. In terms of the path, it empowers the student to train in the natural GREAT PERFECTION. As its result, a causal link is formed that leads to the attainment of the ESSENCE KAYA, VAJRA WISDOM. [TD 2271]

Preliminary practice (*sngon 'gro*) – An activity that must be completed prior to beginning the main practice. [TD 716]

Principle of karmic causality (*las rgyu 'bras*) – The causes and results associated with virtuous and negative actions, such as the fact that suffering results from engaging in negative activities. [TD 2773]

Provisional meaning (*drang don*) – Teachings that emphasize the worldly perspective and which are given in order to guide ordinary disciples. This type of teaching employs various forms of verbal and conceptual expression to analyze and reify "individuals," "sentient beings," "the aggregates," "sense fields," and so forth, as well as their "birth," "cessation," "comings," and "goings." This also includes the Buddhist treatises and commentaries that are used as vehicles to express this level of meaning. [TD 1319]

Pure perception (*dag snang*) – The perception that all that appears and exists, the entire universe and its inhabitants, are a PURE REALM and the play of the KAYAS and WISDOM. [TD 1237]

Pure realm (*zhing khams*) – A pure land where BUDDHAS and BODHISATTVAS abide, such as the REALM OF BLISS. [TD 2388]

Rainbow Body (*'ja' lus*) – The liberation of the aggregates into a body of light. [TD 892]

Ratnasambhava (*Rin chen 'byung ldan*) – As one member of the FIVE BUDDHA FAMILIES, Ratnasambhava represents the buddha family of enlightened qualities, the source of all that is desirable. [BT 408]

Reality (*chos nyid*) – (1) The character or nature of something; (2) the empty nature of things. [TD 836]

Realm of Bliss (*bde ba can*) – The pure realm of AMITABHA. [TD 1368]

Refuge (*skyabs 'gro*) – To rely upon and supplicate one's GURU and the THREE JEWELS, placing one's faith and trust in them, to be protected from temporary and ultimate fears and suffering. [TD 142]

Relative bodhichitta (*kun rdzob byang chub kyi sems*) – All forms of bodhichitta that arise from coarse conceptual designations. [TD 24]

Renunciation (*nges 'byung*) – The desire to be free from all planes of SAMSARA, liberated from the prison of the THREE REALMS, and delivered to the blissful state of NIRVANA. [TD 658]

Result of disengagement (*bral ba'i 'bras bu*) – One division of a fivefold classification of results; the result that ensues once the power of knowledge has brought about the exhaustion of the element it is meant to eliminate, as when the afflictions are eliminated by meditating on the path of realized beings. [TD 1904]

Result of individual effort (*skyes bu byed pa'i 'bras bu*) – One division of a fivefold classification of results; a result that depends upon the efforts of a living being or individual, such as a harvest that results from planting crops or the wealth that is created through a business transaction. [TD 164]

Result that resembles its cause (*rgyu mthun gyi 'bras bu*) – One division of a five-fold classification of results; a result that is identical to, or which resembles in form, its own cause, such as VIRTUE arising from virtue. These results, which are caused by both omnipresent causes and causes of equivalent status, can take two different forms, one behavioral and one experiential. The first refers to propensities that carry across lifetimes, such as having the desire to engage in negativity as a result of having done so in a previous life. The second refers to corresponding experiences, such as when one acts generously in one life and experiences wealth in a future life as a result. [TD 564]

Richly Arrayed Realm (*stug po bkod pa'i zhing*) – A SAMBHOGAKAYA realm located above the seventeen levels of the FORM REALM. [TD 1103]

Ripened result (*rnam smin gyi 'bras bu*) – One division of a fivefold classification of results; a result that emerges from the ripening of either defiled VIRTUE or vice, such as the defiled, perpetuating aggregates. [TD 1574]

Rupakaya (*gzugs kyi sku*) – This refers to the NIRMANAKAYA, the emanated form that has attachment, and the SAMBHOGAKAYA, the form of perfect enjoyment that does not. These KAYAS manifest in an embodied manner for the benefit of others. They appear to the perception of impure and pure disciples, respectively, once the referential ACCUMULATION OF MERIT has been perfected. [TD 2499]

Sadhana (*sgrub pa/sgrub thabs*) – As Mipam explains, a sadhana is "that which enables one to attain or accomplish a desired end." In terms of tantric practice, he writes, this refers to "all the various practices that utilize the unique methods of the SECRET MANTRA tradition to achieve whatever SPIRITUAL ACCOMPLISHMENTS one desires, whether supreme or mundane." [ON 534]

Sakya school (*sa skya*) – A Buddhist lineage established in Tibet by Khön Könchok Gyalpo. [TD 2889]

Samantabhadra (*Kun tu bzang po*) – (1) That which is virtuous and good in every way, completely perfect; (2) the SPHERE OF REALITY, the DHARMAKAYA; (3) a general term for buddhahood; (4) a particular TATAGATA; (5) a particular BODHISATTVA; and (6) the SAMBHOGAKAYA of the Bön tradition. [TD 18]

Samantabhadri (*Kun tu bzang mo*) – The female counterpart of SAMANTA-BHADRA; representing WISDOM, Samantabhadri embodies the empty nature of all phenomena, the "pure spacious expanse." [NS 284]

Samaya being (*dam tshig sems dpa'*) – The samaya being is one of the three beings set forth in DEVELOPMENT STAGE practice. This is the deity that one visualizes in conjunction with the ritual of whichever YIDAM DEITY is being practiced. [TK 3, 45] According to Jamgön Kongtrül, the samaya being corresponds to the luminous, enlightened mind. This, in turn, is inseparable from the WISDOM BEING, the DHARMAKAYA of all buddhas. [LW 62]

Samaya vow (*dam tshig*) – Along with the vows of INDIVIDUAL LIBERATION found in the FOUNDATIONAL VEHICLE and the BODHISATTVA precepts of the GREAT VEHICLE, the samaya vows are one of three sets of vows that form the basis for Buddhist practice. These vows are associated specifically with the VAJRAYANA. Jamgön Kongtrül explains: "The word samaya means 'pledged commitment,' 'oath,' 'precept,' etc. Hence, this refers to a vajra promise or samaya because one is not to transgress what has been pledged. Samaya vows involve both benefit and risk because, if kept, samaya vows become the foundation for all the trainings of MANTRA. If not kept, however, all these trainings become futile." There are innumerable divisions of the samaya vows found in the various tantras. At the most fundamental level, however, one pledges to continually maintain the view of the enlightened form, speech and mind of the buddhas. [LW 46]

Sambhogakaya (*longs spyod rdzogs pa'i sku*) – One of the FIVE KAYAS; while not wavering from the DHARMAKAYA, this form appears solely to those disciples who are noble BODHISATTVAS. It is also the basis for the arising of the NIR-MANAKAYA and is adorned with MARKS AND SIGNS. [TD 2818]

Samsara (*'khor ba*) – Literally, to revolve in a cyclic manner; the abode of the six classes of existence or, said differently, the five defiled and perpetuating aggregates. [TD 316]

Sarma schools (*gsar ma*) – See NEW SCHOOLS.

Secret empowerment (*gsang dbang*) – The secret EMPOWERMENT is the first of the three higher supreme empowerments (the other two being the KNOWLEDGE-WISDOM EMPOWERMENT and the PRECIOUS WORD EMPOWERMENT). This is bestowed upon the ordinary speech of the student by relying upon the MANDALA of relative BODHICHITTA of the MALE AND FEMALE SPIRITUAL PARTNERS in union. This purifies the impurities of ordinary speech. In terms of the path, this empowers one to meditate on the energetic practices and recite MANTRA. In terms of the FRUITION, a link is formed to the attainment of the SAMBHOGAKAYA and VAJRA SPEECH. [TD 3006]

Secret Mantra (*gsang sngags*) – Secret Mantra is the WISDOM of great bliss, which protects the mind from subtle concepts through the union of empty KNOWL-EDGE and compassionate SKILLFUL MEANS. It is referred to as such because it is practiced in secret and not divulged to those who are not suitable recipients of these teachings. [TD 3002] See also SECRET MANTRA VEHICLE.

Secret Mantra Vehicle (*gsang sngags kyi theg pa*) – An alternate term for the VAJRA VEHICLE. Ju Mipam explains: "This system is 'secret' insofar as the profound MANDALA of the victorious ones' enlightened form, speech, and mind is present as the innate nature of all phenomena. Nevertheless, this is inherently hidden from those who are confused and must be revealed skillfully. It is not revealed explicitly to the inferior practitioners of the lower approaches but is transmitted secretly. Hence, it is not part of the range of experience of ordinary disciples. The term 'MANTRA' indicates that, in order to practice the MANDALA of these three secrets, this nature is presented as it actually is; it is not hidden or kept secret." [KG 38]

Self-occurring wisdom (*rang byung ye shes*) – The primordially indwelling awareness present within the mind streams of all sentient beings, the indivisibility of space and wisdom. [TD 2650]

Seven aspects of union (*kha sbyor yan lag bdun*) – The nature of a sambhogakaya buddha possesses these seven aspects of union: (1) complete enjoyment, (2) union, (3) great bliss, (4) absence of nature, (5) completely filled with compassion, (6) being uninterrupted, and (7) being unceasing. [TD 204]

Seven branches (*yan lag bdun*) – Seven practices that allow one to gather the accumulations and that function as a preliminary to practicing the Buddhist teachings. [TD 2554] These seven are (1) prostration, (2) offering, (3) confession, (4) rejoicing, (5) requesting to teach, (6) requesting to remain, and (7) dedicating merit.

Seven-point contemplation (*sems sbyong don bdun ma*) – A unique teaching from the SECRET HEART ESSENCE, which allows those unable to directly perceive the appearances of awareness to avoid the pitfall of mistrusting the HEART ESSENCE teachings, and to gradually perceive their own awareness. The seven points of this system are: 1) impermanence, 2) short-term and long-lasting happiness, 3) manifold circumstances, 4) the pointlessness of worldly activities, 5) the qualities of the BUDDHA, 6) the guru's key instructions, and 7) nonconceptuality. [TS 134-35] Not to be confused with the seven-point mind training of ATISHA (blo sbyong don bdun), a contemplative system that stems from the KADAM SCHOOL.

Shangpa Kagyü (*shangs pa bka' brgyud*) – A Buddhist lineage brought to Tibet by Khyungpo Naljor, closely related in substance to the TAKPO KAGYÜ. [TD 2833]

Shravaka (*nyan thos*) – See LISTENER.

Siddha (*grub thob*) – See ACCOMPLISHED MASTER.

Simple Beggar (offering of) (*ku sa li'i tshogs gsog*) – A meditation practice in which one gives away one's own body. [TD 14]

Six lineages (*brgyud pa drug*) – The six lineages of the TRANSMITTED TEACHINGS OF THE NYINGMA SCHOOL and TREASURES. This includes the three lineages that are common to both the Transmitted Teachings and the treasure tradition: (1) the LINEAGE OF THE VICTORS' REALIZATION, (2) the SYMBOLIC LINEAGE OF THE MASTERS OF AWARENESS, and (3) the HEARING LINEAGE OF PEOPLE, as well as three additional lineages that relate specifically to the karmically linked treasures: (4) the LINEAGE OF TRANSMISSIONS AND PROPHECIES, (5) the LINEAGE OF ASPIRATIONS AND EMPOWERMENTS, and (6) the LINEAGE

ENTRUSTED TO DAKINIS. [NS 745] In Longchenpa's *A Cloud on the Ocean of Profound Reality*, the lineage of transmissions and prophecies is referred to as "the lineage of compassionate blessings." [ZD 308]

Six perfections (*pha rol tu phyin pa drug*) – (1) Generosity, (2) discipline, (3) patience, (4) diligence, (5) ABSORPTION, and (6) KNOWLEDGE. [TD 1698]

Six stains (*dri ma drug*) – Six faults that should be eliminated when receiving teachings on the Dharma: (1) pride, (2) lack of faith, (3) disinterest, (4) distraction, (5) inward withdrawal, and (6) discouragement. [TD 1327]

Skillful means (*thabs*) – An activity that enables one to accomplish a given outcome easily. [TD 1148] See also PATH OF SKILLFUL MEANS and VEHICLE OF SKILLFUL MEANS.

Solitary buddha (*rang sangs rgyas*) – These beings, in their final existence, do not rely upon a spiritual master. Instead, they analyze the REALITY of INTERDEPENDENT ORIGINATION and, on that basis, realize the selflessness of the individual as well as half of the selflessness of phenomena. In so doing, they become FOE-DESTROYERS who have achieved the actualization of solitary enlightenment. [TD 2659] See also FOUNDATIONAL VEHICLE.

Space Class (*klong sde*) – See THREE CLASSES OF THE GREAT PERFECTION.

Sphere of reality (*chos kyi dbyings*) – (1) EMPTINESS; (2) the empty nature of the five aggregates. [TD 840]

Spiritual attainment (*dngos grub*) – The positive result that one aims to attain by practicing a particular set of spiritual instructions. [TD 675] See also MUNDANE SPIRITUAL ATTAINMENT and SUPREME SPIRITUAL ATTAINMENT.

Spiritual partner (*yab yum*) – See MALE AND FEMALE SPIRITUAL PARTNERS.

Sugata (*bde bar gshegs pa*) – See BLISSFUL ONE.

Sukhavati (*bde ba can*) – See REALM OF BLISS. [TD 1368]

Supreme Realm (*'og min*) – (1) The eight planes of existence associated with the fourth level of absorption; the gods born in this plane have reached the highest level of the FORM REALM. This realm, which is one of the five pure realms, is referred to as such because there are no other realms of embodied beings higher than this; (2) the Richly Arrayed Realm of Akanishta (Akanishtaghandavyuha), a SAMBHOGAKAYA realm located above the seventeen form realms. [TD 2529, 1103] According to Longchenpa, the genuine, true Supreme Realm "cannot be measured in terms of dimensionality. Rather, it is free of all elaborations. This essence is the sacred point where the buddha's journey ends." [CCM 35]

Sutra (*mdo*) – See SUTRA VEHICLE.

Sutra Vehicle (*mdo'i theg pa*) – The Buddhist teachings are often classified into two divisions, which represent two approaches to enlightenment—the Sutra Vehicle and the VAJRA VEHICLE. The former is often referred to as the "Causal Vehicle" because, in this tradition, practice consists of assembling the causes that lead to the attainment of liberation. This vehicle is further divided into the VEHICLES OF THE LISTENERS and SOLITARY BUDDHAS (which constitute the FOUNDATIONAL VEHICLE) and the VEHICLE OF THE BODHISATTVAS (the GREAT VEHICLE).

Svabhavikakaya (*ngo bo nyid sku*) – See ESSENCE KAYA.

Symbolic lineage of the masters of awareness (*rig 'dzin brda'i brgyud*) – The succession of teachers who are introduced to the unique key instructions of the NYINGMA SCHOOL'S SECRET MANTRA via symbols and various skillful means. [TD 2685]

Takpo Kagyü (*dwags po bka' brgyud*) – A Buddhist tradition founded in Tibet by Marpa Lotsawa, Milarepa, and Gampopa, and which spread widely under Gampopa. [TD 1312]

Tantra (*rgyud*) – (1) A continuum that remains temporally unbroken; (2) a thread; (3) a region or district; (4) bloodline; (5) the SECRET MANTRA and its related texts. [TD 573]

Tantra of the Secret Essence (*rGyud gsang ba snying po*) – This text, often referred to as the *Guhyagarbha Tantra*, is the most widely studied tantra in the NYINGMA SCHOOL. It was translated by Vimalamitra, Nyak Jnanakumara, and Ma Rinchen Chok. The full title of this twenty-two-chapter text is *Tantra of the True Nature of Reality: The Glorious Secret Essence*. [TD 574] While this tantra is most often linked with the MAHAYOGA tradition, it is also listed as an ANUYOGA tantra in certain contexts and an ATIYOGA tantra in others, which is due to the fact that the view of this set of literature is said to correspond to that of Atiyoga, while in terms of conduct it is linked with Mahayoga. According to Ju Mipam, it is fine to classify this text as belonging to any one of the THREE INNER TANTRAS, from the perspective of emphasizing its teachings on DEVELOPMENT, COMPLETION, or GREAT PERFECTION, respectively. [KG 10]

Tara (*sGrol ma*) – A female YIDAM DEITY whose name (literally, "the Liberator") signifies her capacity to liberate beings from the eight forms of fear. [TD 625]

Tatagata (*de bzhin gshegs pa*) – An epithet of the buddhas, referring to one who, in dependence upon the path of REALITY, abides in neither existence nor peace and has passed into the state of great enlightenment. [TD 1287]

Tengyur (*bstan 'gyur*) – Indian Buddhist treatises on the traditional academic subjects, sutras, and tantras that were translated into Tibetan and collected in a 218-volume collection. [TD 1126]

Ten Perfections (*pha rol tu phyin pa bcu*) – (1) Generosity, (2) discipline, (3) patience, (4) diligence, (5) ABSORPTION, (6) KNOWLEDGE, (7) SKILLFUL MEANS, (8) strength, (9) aspiration, and (10) WISDOM. [TD 1698]

Ten powers (*stobs bcu*) – The ten powers of the TATAGATAS: (1) the power to know the correct and incorrect; (2) the power to know the ripening of KARMA; (3) the power to know the variety of individual interests; (4) the power to know the variety of individual characters; (5) the power to know both superior and inferior faculties; (6) the power to know all paths that can be traveled; (7) the power to know the meditative concentrations of total liberation, absorption, stability, and so on; (8) the power to know previous births; (9) the power to know of death, transmigration, and rebirth; and (10) the power to know of the exhaustion of defilements. [TD 1119]

Ten riches (*'byor pa bcu*) – The five personal riches: being human, born in a central land, having the senses intact, not having a negative livelihood, and having faith in the Buddha's teachings; and the five circumstantial riches: a buddha having come, taught the Dharma, for the teachings to remain, for the teachings to have followers, and for there to be spiritual teachers. [TD 1986]

Terma (*gter ma*) – See TREASURE.

Tertön (*gter ston*) – One who reveals a terma, or TREASURE. [TD 1048]

Thirty-seven factors of enlightenment (*byang phyogs so bdun*) – The thirty-seven factors of enlightenment are qualities that occur at various stages of the Buddhist path. According to Maitreya's *Distinguishing the Middle from Extremes*, these are (1) the four APPLICATIONS OF MINDFULNESS that occur on the lesser path of accumulation; (2) the four authentic eliminations that occur on the intermediate path of accumulation; (3) the four bases of miraculous power that occur on the greater path of accumulation; (4) the five faculties that occur on the first two stages of the path of connection—the stages of heat and summit; (5) the five powers that occur on the last two stages of the path of connection—the stage of acceptance and the supreme state; (6) the seven aspects of enlightenment that occur on the path of knowledge; and (7) the eightfold noble path that occurs on the path of cultivation. [MV 732]

Thirty-two marks of the buddhas (*mtshan bzang po so gnyis*) – See MARKS AND SIGNS.

Thodgal (*thod rgal*) – See DIRECT LEAP.

Three classes of the Great Perfection (*rdzogs chen sde gsum*) – According to Longchenpa, the first transmission of the GREAT PERFECTION teachings in the human realm took place between Garap Dorjé and Manjushrimitra. The former passed on his teachings in the form of 6,400,000 verses. The latter then codified his master's teachings and divided them into three categories: the MIND CLASS, SPACE CLASS, and KEY INSTRUCTION CLASS. [TC 16] Explaining these three categories, Jigmé Lingpa writes, "There are no phenomena that exist apart from one's very own mind. Therefore, one is freed from the idea that there are things that need to be rejected. This is the Mind Class. In addition, all forms of phenomenal existence have nowhere to go other than reality itself—the expanse of Samantabhadri. Because of this, one is freed from the extreme of needing antidotes. This is the activity-free Space Class. Finally, the profound KEY INSTRUCTION CLASS involves being liberated from both factors that need to be rejected and antidotes by arriving at a decisive certainty concerning the true nature of things." [YT 608]

Three collections (*sde snod gsum*) – The three collections are a vehicle used to express the entire range of teachings given by the Buddha. Respectively, the VINAYA

COLLECTION, the SUTRA Collection, and the Abhidharma Collection relate to the THREE TRAININGS, those of discipline, meditation, and KNOWLEDGE. These three contain all the words and meanings found within the twelvefold collection of sacred Buddhist writings and encompass all the various topics that can be known, from form all the way up to omniscience. [TD 1473]

Three forms of enlightenment (*byang chub gsum*) – The fruition of the paths of the LISTENERS, SOLITARY BUDDHAS, and BUDDHAS. [TD 1872]

Three gates (*sgo gsum*) – Body, speech, and mind. [TD 595]

Three gates to total liberation (*rnam par thar pa'i sgo gsum*) – The three meditative concentrations that enable one to attain total liberation: (1) EMPTINESS, (2) the absence of characteristics, and (3) the absence of desire. [TD 1569]

Three inner tantras (*nang rgyud gsum*) – In the textual tradition of the NYINGMA SCHOOL, the three inner tantras constitute the final three of this tradition's NINE VEHICLES. They are listed as the tantras of MAHAYOGA, the scriptures of ANUYOGA, and the key instructions of ATIYOGA. [TD 1505] These three divisions are also associated with the practices of DEVELOPMENT, COMPLETION, and GREAT PERFECTION. As Dilgo Khyentsé explains: "Development and Mahayoga are like the basis for all the teachings, completion and Anuyoga are like the path of all the teachings, and the GREAT PERFECTION of Atiyoga is like the result of all the teachings." [WC 773]

Three Jewels (*dkon mchog gsum*) – The Buddha, Dharma, and Sangha. [TD 61]

Three kayas (*sku gsum*) – The DHARMAKAYA, SAMBHOGAKAYA, and NIRMANA-KAYA. [TD 125]

Three outer tantras (*phyi rgyud gsum*) – In the textual tradition of the NYINGMA SCHOOL, the three outer tantras are listed as KRIYA TANTRA (Activity Tantra), CHARYA TANTRA (Performance Tantra), and YOGA TANTRA (Union Tantra). These traditions are also referred to as the "Vedic Vehicles of Ascetic Practice," due to the fact that they include various ascetic practices, such as ritual cleansing and purification, that are similar to those found in the Vedic tradition of the Hindu Brahmin caste. [TD 1740]

Three realms (*khams gsum*) – The desire, form, and formless realms. [TD 226]

Three roots (*rtsa gsum*) – The three roots are the three inner objects of refuge: the guru, YIDAM DEITY, and DAKINI. A guru is a qualified spiritual teacher who has liberated his or her own mind and is skilled in the methods that tame the minds of others. The yidam deities are the vast array of peaceful and wrathful deities and those associated with the EIGHT GREAT SADHANA TEACHINGS. The dakinis are those associated with the three abodes. The latter refers to VAJRAVARAHI in particular, the divine mother who gives birth to all BUDDHAS. [KN 23]

Three spheres (*'khor gsum*) – Agent, act, and object. [TD 320]

Three trainings (*bslab pa gsum*) – (1) Discipline, (2) concentration, and (3) KNOWLEDGE. [TD 3056]

Three transformations (khyer so gsum) – To realize that all appearances, sounds, and thoughts are deity, mantra, and wisdom, respectively. [DMW 147]

Three vajras (rdo rje gsum) – VAJRA BODY, VAJRA SPEECH, and VAJRA MIND.

Three vehicles (theg pa gsum) – The VEHICLE OF THE LISTENERS, the VEHICLE OF THE SOLITARY BUDDHAS, and the VEHICLE OF THE BODHISATTVAS. [TD 1183]

Torma (gtor ma) – Torma is one of the primary offerings found in the SECRET MANTRA tradition, where, along with medicine and BLOOD, it constitutes the inner offerings. Though there are various divisions of torma, the outer torma offering consists of "the choicest types of edibles heaped upon a vessel of precious substances," which, as Jamgön Kongtrül explains, embodies "the indivisibility of the SPHERE OF REALITY and WISDOM." [LW 129] Explaining the significance of torma in different contexts, Dilgo Khyentsé writes, "Generally speaking, torma should be viewed as the MANDALA in the context of APPROACH AND ACCOMPLISHMENT, as sense pleasures in the context of making offerings, as the DEITY in the context of EMPOWERMENT, and as the SPIRITUAL ACCOMPLISH-MENTS at the conclusion of a practice." [WC 743]

Tranquility (zhi gnas) – One of the common denominators and causes of all states of ABSORPTION. This form of meditation involves settling the mind one-point-edly in order to pacify the mind's tendency to be distracted outward to external objects. [TD 2384]

Transmitted Teachings of the Nyingma School (rnying ma bka' ma) – The teachings of the NYINGMA SCHOOL have been transmitted through two lineages, the distant lineage of the Transmitted Teachings and the close lineage of the TREA-SURES. In the former, the teachings of MAHAYOGA, ANUYOGA, and ATIYOGA are preserved, respectively, under the headings of the Tantra of the Magical Net, the Sutra of the Condensed Realization, and MIND CLASS. [NS 396]

Treasure (gter ma) – The teachings of the NYINGMA SCHOOL have been transmit-ted through two lineages, the distant lineage of the TRANSMITTED TEACHINGS OF THE NYINGMA SCHOOL and the close lineage of the treasures. In the latter, the teachings that are passed on consist of three primary categories, those that relate to Guru PADMASAMBHAVA, the GREAT PERFECTION, and the GREAT COMPASSIONATE ONE, AVALOKITESHVARA. [NS 396]

True goodness (nges legs) – A lasting state of happiness—liberation and omniscience. [TD 659]

Twelve ascetic virtues (sbyangs pa'i yon tan bcu gnyis) – (1) Wearing cast-off clothing, (2) wearing only three Dharma robes, (3) wearing woolen garments, (4) eating only one meal a day, (5) begging for alms, (6) not eating after noon, (7) staying in isolated places, (8) staying at the foot of trees, (9) living in exposed places, (10) staying in charnel grounds, (11) sleeping only while sitting up, and (12) staying wherever one finds oneself. [TD 2023]

Twelve links of interdependent origination (rten 'brel yan lag bcu gnyis) – The

internal process of interdependent origination, that is, the twelve links of interdependent origination that relate to the emergence of the sentient beings that
inhabit the universe. These twelve consist of the three links that propel, the four
links that are propelled, the three links that are to be established, and the two
links that are established. [TD 1075]

Twenty-five disciples (*rje 'bangs nyer lnga*) – The twenty-five accomplished mas-
ters to whom Padmasambhava transmitted many VAJRA VEHICLE teachings.
This occurred during the reign of King Trisong Deutsen, who invited Padma-
sambhava to Tibet. The twenty-five disciples are 1) King Trisong Deutsen, 2)
Namkhai Nyingpo, 3) Sangyé Yeshé, 4) Gyalwa Chokyang, 5) Yeshé Tsogyal,
6) Palgyi Yeshé, 7) Palgyi Sengé, 8) Berotsana, 9) Nyak Jnanakumara, 10) Yudra
Nyingpo, 11) Dorjé Dudjom, 12) Yeshé Yang, 13) Sokpo Lhapel, 14) Shang Yeshé
Dé, 15) Palgyi Wangchuk, 16) Denma Tsemang, 17) Kawa Peltsek, 18) Shupu
Palgyi Sengé, 19) Gyalwé Lodrö, 20) Kyeu Chung Lotsawa, 21) Otren Palgyi
Wangchuk, 22) Ma Rinchen Chok, 23) Lhalung Palgyi Dorjé, 24) Langdro
Konchok Jungné, and 25) Lasum Gyalwa Changchup. [TD 910]

Two accumulations (*tshogs gnyis*) – The accumulation of merit and the accumulation of wisdom. The first of these involves a conceptual reference point and consists of wholesome endeavors, such as acts of generosity. [TD 3051] The second
is the accumulation of nonreferential WISDOM, which refers to the accumulation of the undefiled VIRTUE that enacts the attainment of the dharmakaya, the
fruitional wisdom in which EMPTINESS is embraced by BODHICHITTA. [TD
2594]

Twofold benefit (*don gnyis*) – One's own benefit and that of others. [TD 1302]

Twofold selflessness (*bdag med gnyis*) – The selflessness of the individual and the
selflessness of phenomena. [TD 1358]

Two forms of wisdom (*ye shes gnyis*) – The wisdoms of meditative equipoise and
postmeditation. [TD 2595]

Two obscurations (*sgrib pa gnyis*) – The AFFLICTIVE OBSCURATIONS and COGNI-
TIVE OBSCURATIONS. [TD 612]

Unexcelled Yoga (*rnal 'byor bla na med pa*) – See ANUTTARAYOGA TANTRA.

Universal ground consciousness (*kun gzhi'i rnam shes*) – This primary mental process is unobscured, neutral, and functions as the foundation for the infusion of
habitual tendencies. It functions as the basis for the entire range of karmic maturation, as well as for the seeds that are implanted within it, and is the awareness
of the essence of objects. [TK 2, 194]

Vairochana (*rNam par snang mdzad*) – As one member of the FIVE BUDDHA FAMI-
LIES, Vairochana represents the buddha family of enlightened form, the foundation of all positive qualities. [BT 408]

Vajra (*rdo rje*) – (1) That which is unchanging and indestructible; (2) an ancient
Indian symbol that symbolizes skillful means in the pairing of SKILLFUL
MEANS and KNOWLEDGE; (3) one of the twenty-seven coincidences in Tibetan

astrology; (4) an abbreviation of the Tibetan word for diamond. [TD 1438] In
VAJRAYANA practice, this SYMBOLIC IMPLEMENT is associated with a number
of important principles. Generally speaking, it is linked with the male principle,
compassion, skillful means, and the great bliss of unchanging REALITY. [YT
671]

Vajra body (sku rdo rje) – As one of the THREE VAJRAS, the vajra body is the KAYA
of indivisible appearance and EMPTINESS—the purification of ordinary form.
[TD 122]

Vajradhara (rDo rje 'chang) – Vajradhara is considered to be the sovereign lord of all
buddha families and the teacher of the TANTRAS. It is also said that this is the
form Shakyamuni took when teaching the SECRET MANTRA. [TD 1439]

Vajra Hell (rdo rje dmyal ba) – A term used in the SECRET MANTRA tradition to
refer to the Hell of Incessant Torment. [TD 1442]

Vajra holder (rdo rje 'dzin pa) – (1) Great VAJRADHARA; (2) VAJRAPANI; (3) a master of the SECRET MANTRA; (4) Indra. [TD 1440]

Vajrakilaya (rDo rje phur pa) – A YIDAM DEITY associated with the principle of
enlightened activity from the EIGHT GREAT SADHANA TEACHINGS.

Vajrakumara (rDo rje gzhon nu) – A YIDAM DEITY of the ANUTTARAYOGA TAN-
TRA; another name for VAJRAKILAYA. [TD 1440]

Vajra master (rdo rje slob dpon) – A vajra master is a guru who either grants EMPOW-
ERMENT into a MANDALA of the SECRET MANTRA or who teaches its liberating instructions. [TD 1442]

Vajra mind (thugs rdo rje) – One of the THREE VAJRAS; according to Jamgön Kongtrül, vajra mind is linked with the DHARMAKAYA and the union of bliss and
EMPTINESS. [LW 37]

Vajrapani (Phyag na rdo rje) – Vajrapani is the condensation of the enlightened
mind of all the BUDDHAS and the embodiment of their strength, might, and
power. [TD 1734]

Vajrasattva (rDo rje sems dpa') – Vajrasattva is a YIDAM DEITY who is considered to
be the sovereign lord of the hundred buddha families. He is white in appearance
and sits in the vajra posture. With his right hand, he holds a VAJRA at his heart,
and with his left, a bell at his hip. [TD 1442]

Vajra speech (gsung rdo rje) – One of the THREE VAJRAS; according to Jamgön
Kongtrül, vajra speech is linked with the SAMBHOGAKAYA and the union of
LUMINOSITY and EMPTINESS. [LW 36]

Vajravarahi (rDo rje phag mo) – Literally, "Indestructible Sow." A semi-wrathful
female YIDAM DEITY; the female counterpart of Chakrasamvara ('Khor lo bde
mchog). [TD 1440] The divine mother who gives birth to all BUDDHAS. [KN
23]

Vajra Vehicle (rdo rje theg pa) – Following the FOUNDATIONAL VEHICLE and the
GREAT VEHICLE, the Vajra Vehicle is the third and highest vehicle in the Buddhist tradition. In particular, it contains the teachings on Buddhist TANTRA.

Ju Mipam explains the significance of this appellation: "In this system, one does not accept or reject illusory, relative phenomena. Instead, the relative and ulti-mate are engaged as an indivisible unity and one's own three gates are linked with the nature of the THREE VAJRAS. Therefore, this vehicle is "vajra-like" insofar as these elements are seen to be indivisible and the very embodiment of primordial enlightenment, in which there is nothing to accept or reject, hence the term 'Vajra Vehicle.'" [KG 39] See also VEHICLE OF SKILLFUL MEANS, FRUITIONAL VEHICLE, and SECRET MANTRA VEHICLE.

Vajra wisdom (*ye shes rdo rje*) – Vajra wisdom is linked with the SVABHAVIKAKAYA and the union of AWARENESS and EMPTINESS. [LW 36]

Vajrayana (*rdo rje theg pa*) – See VAJRA VEHICLE.

Vase empowerment (*bum dbang*) – The vase empowerment is a maturing EMPOW-ERMENT that is common to both the OUTER TANTRAS and INNER TANTRAS. In the latter, a MANDALA (either one made from colored powders or painted on canvas) is used to bestow the various subdivisions of this empowerment upon the student. This includes the water, crown, and other sections. This process purifies physical impurities and, in terms of the path, empowers one to practice the DEVELOPMENT STAGE. In terms of fruition, a causal link is formed that leads to the attainment of the VAJRA BODY—the NIRMANAKAYA. [TD 853, 2865]

Vehicle of Perfections (*phar phyin gyi theg pa*) – An alternate name for the SUTRA VEHICLE.

Vehicle of Skillful Means (*thabs kyi theg pa*) – An alternate term for the VAJRA VEHI-CLE; Ju Mipam explains the significance of this appellation, "This approach is referred to as such due to the four characteristics of its SKILLFUL MEANS, which are great, easy, many, and swift. With the key points of this path, afflictive and pure phenomena are not engaged from the perspective of needing to be accepted or rejected. As this is the case, they do not obscure. In addition, its methods are great, insofar as they lead to the perfection of the TWO ACCUMULATIONS. In other systems, such skillful means do not exist." [KG 38]

Vehicle of the Bodhisattvas (*byang chub sems dpa'i theg pa*) – This vehicle is first entered by taking the vows of ASPIRATION BODHICHITTA and APPLICATION BODHICHITTA. Its view involves realizing the TWOFOLD SELFLESSNESS, while its meditation consists of meditating on the THIRTY-SEVEN FACTORS OF ENLIGHTENMENT. Its conduct consists of training in the FOUR WAYS OF ATTRACTING STUDENTS and the SIX PERFECTIONS. The fruition of this vehi-cle is twofold: on a temporary level, there are ten levels that are attained, while its ultimate fruition is the attainment of the level of universal illumination [the state of buddhahood]. [TD 1874] SEE ALSO BODHISATTVA, GREAT VEHICLE, and SUTRA VEHICLE.

Vehicle of the Listeners (*nyan thos kyi theg pa*) – In this vehicle, one starts out by accepting to adhere to one of the seven types of discipline associated with the vows of INDIVIDUAL LIBERATION and to keep this discipline from degenerating. In terms of the view, one recognizes that all the phenomena included within the five aggregates are devoid of a personal self, yet one still holds to the idea that the two subtle, indivisible phenomenal selves truly exist. Their meditation consists of TRANQUILITY and INSIGHT, the former referring to the nine ways to settle the mind and the latter to meditating on the sixteen aspects of the four noble truths. In terms of conduct, they maintain the TWELVE ASCETIC VIRTUES. The fruition of this vehicle entails attaining the levels of the stream-enterer, the once-returner, the nonreturner, and the foe-destroyer. Each of these contains two further divisions, abiding and remaining, making eight in total. [TD 933] See also LISTENER and SUTRA VEHICLE.

Vehicle of the Solitary Buddhas (rang sangs rgyas kyi theg pa) – On this path, one realizes the character of INTERDEPENDENT ORIGINATION, both in its normal progression and also in reverse order, doing so without relying upon a spiritual teacher. This realization brings about a realization of the selflessness of the individual and the elimination of AFFLICTIVE OBSCURATIONS. [TD 2659] See also SOLITARY BUDDHA and SUTRA VEHICLE.

View, meditation, conduct, and fruition (lta spyod sgom 'bras) – These four factors subsume the various elements involved in Buddhist practice. Jamgön Kongtrül explains, "Though there are a great many divisions when it comes to view, meditation, and conduct, they can all be applied to the individual mind. The view is absolute conviction in its actual nature, while meditation means to apply this to one's own state of being. Conduct involves linking whatever arises with this view and meditation and, finally, the fruition is the actualization of the true nature of reality." [ND 6]

Vima Nyingtik (bi ma'i snying thig) – See HEART ESSENCE OF VIMALAMITRA.

Vinaya Collection ('dul ba'i sde snod) – One section of a threefold division that constitutes the Buddhist teachings; this scriptural division emphasizes the training of supreme discipline. [TD 1407]

Virtue (dge ba) – The opposite of negativity; positive endeavors or good conduct; a phenomenon that is classified as having a definite mode of maturation, insofar as its result is [always] pleasant. [TD 450]

Wisdom (ye shes) – Inborn knowing; the empty and clear awareness that is self-occurring within the mind streams of all sentient beings. [TD 2593]

Wisdom being (ye shes sems dpa') – The wisdom being is one of the three beings set forth in DEVELOPMENT STAGE practice, and that which is visualized in the heart center of the SAMAYA BEING. Dza Patrul explains, "At the heart center of each of the assembly of deities you are meditating on, visualize a wisdom being that resembles the deity it inhabits, though without ornamentation and implements." [SS 422] While this is the most common presentation, according to Kongtrül, meditating on the wisdom being can occur in other forms as well. It can involve visualizing a form that resembles the samaya being, yet it can also entail meditating on a DEITY with a form, color, face, and arms that are different than those of the samaya being, or meditating on a symbolic implement that arises from the seed syllable. [TK 3, 209] This topic is discussed extensively in DMW.

Wisdom of equality (*mnyam nyid ye shes*) – The aspect of WISDOM in which one internalizes the fact that all phenomena are equal, in the sense that they are all devoid of characteristics. [YT 431]

Wisdom of the sphere of reality (*chos dbyings ye shes*) – The aspect of wisdom that is empty in essence and unchanging. [ZD 78]

Yidam deity (*yi dam*) – Yidams are the deities, BUDDHAS, and BODHISATTVAS that form the unique support for tantric practice. [TD 2565] Concerning the ultimate nature of the yidam deity, Jigmé Lingpa writes, "You must realize that it is your own mind, with its EIGHTFOLD COLLECTION of consciousness, that arises as the KAYAS and WISDOM of the deity." [JL 235] This topic is discussed extensively in DMW.

Yoga Tantra (*rnal 'byor rgyud*) – Yoga Tantra is the last of the THREE OUTER TANTRAS. In this system, emphasis is placed on the internal process of ABSORPTION. In terms of the path, there are two forms of practice: the practice of SKILLFUL MEANS and the practice of KNOWLEDGE. In the first, one practices DEITY YOGA in conjunction with the FOUR MUDRAS. In the latter, one realizes the inner REALITY of the mind and actualizes DISCERNING WISDOM. To supplement this internal process, external forms of ritual purification are also practiced. [SG 335]

Yoga Vehicle (*yo ga'i theg pa*) – See YOGA TANTRA.

Yogi(ni) (*rnal 'byor pa/ma*) – A male/female practitioner of a spiritual path. [TD 1579]

Youthful vase body (*gzhon nu bum sku*) – "Youthful vase body" is a concept unique to the tradition of the Great Perfection. It refers to the realization of Samantabhadra, the identity of which encompasses the ocean of wisdoms and kayas and possesses six particular characteristics. These six refer to the external illumination of consciousness turning inward and the state of inner illumination that follows. The inner illumination of the great, primordial ground and space of being (1) manifests in its own natural state, (2) emerges from the ground, (3) is differentiated, (4) is liberated through differentiation, (5) does not come from somewhere else, and (6) remains in its own place. [TD 2432]

RECOMMENDED READING

⸙

CONTEMPORARY PRESENTATIONS

Chagdud Tulku. *Gates to Buddhist Practice: Essential Teachings of a Tibetan Master.* Junction City, Calif.: Padma Publishing, 2001.

Chogyam Trungpa. *Cutting Through Spiritual Materialism.* Boston: Shambhala, 2002.

Dzogchen Ponlop Rinpoche. *Mind Beyond Death.* Ithaca, N.Y.: Snow Lion Publications, 2007.

Dzongsar Jamyang Khyentse. *What Makes You Not a Buddhist.* Boston: Shambhala, 2008.

Ray, Reginald. *Indestructible Truth: The Living Spirituality of Tibetan Buddhism.* Boston: Shambhala, 2000.

———. *Secret of the Vajra World: The Tantric Buddhism of Tibet.* Boston: Shambhala, 2001.

Sogyal Rinpoche. *The Tibetan Book of Living and Dying.* New York: HarperCollins, 1994.

Thinley Norbu. *The Small Golden Key.* Boston: Shambhala, 1993.

Yongey Mingyur Rinpoche. *The Joy of Living: Unlocking the Secret and Science of Happiness.* New York: Three Rivers Press, 2008.

TRADITIONAL INSTRUCTIONS

Dilgo Khyentse Rinpoche. *The Heart of Compassion: The Thirty-seven Verses on the Practice of a Bodhisattva.* Boston: Shambhala, 2007.

———. *The Heart Treasure of the Enlightened Ones: The Practice of View, Meditation, and Action.* Boston: Shambhala, 1993.

Jamgön Mipham. *White Lotus: An Explanation of the Seven-Line Prayer to Guru Padmasambhava.* Boston: Shambhala, 2007.

Kangyur Rinpoche. *Treasury of Precious Qualities*. Boston: Shambhala, 2001.

Kunzang Pelden. *The Nectar of Manjushri's Speech: A Detailed Commentary on Shantideva's Way of the Bodhisattva*. Boston: Shambhala, 2007.

Padmasambhava. *Advice from the Lotus-Born: A Collection of Padmasambhava's Advice to the Dakini Yeshe Tsogyal and Other Close Disciples*. Berkeley: North Atlantic Books, 2004.

———. *Dakini Teachings*. Berkeley: North Atlantic Books, 2004.

Shabkar. *Food of Bodhisattvas: Buddhist Teachings on Abstaining from Meat*. Boston: Shambhala, 2004.

Shantideva. *The Way of the Bodhisattva*. Boston: Shambhala, 2008.

Thrangu Rinpoche. *The Practice of Tranquillity and Insight: A Guide to Tibetan Buddhist Meditation*. Boston: Shambhala, 1994.

HISTORY AND BIOGRAPHY

Allione, Tsultrim. *Women of Wisdom*. Ithaca, N.Y.: Snow Lion Publications, 2000.

Chagdud Tulku. *Lord of the Dance: Autobiography of a Tibetan Lama*. Junction City, Calif.: Padma Publishing, 1992.

Chatral Rinpoche. *Compassionate Action*. Ithaca, N.Y.: Snow Lion Publications, 2007.

Dilgo Khyentse. *Brilliant Moon: The Autobiography of Dilgo Khyentse*. Boston: Shambhala, 2008.

Dudjom Rinpoche. *The Nyingma School of Tibetan Buddhism: Its Fundamentals and History*. Boston: Wisdom Publications, 1991.

Gyalwa Changchub. *Lady of the Lotus-Born: The Life and Enlightenment of Yeshe Tsogyal.*. Boston: Shambhala, 2002.

Kunsang, Erik Pema. *Wellsprings of the Great Perfection: The Lives and Insights of the Early Masters*. Berkeley: North Atlantic Books, 2006.

Ngawang Zangpo. *Guru Rinpoche: His Life and Times*. Ithaca, N.Y.: Snow Lion Publications, 2002.

Nyoshul Khenpo Jamyang Dorjé. *A Marvelous Garland of Rare Gems: Biographies of Masters of Awareness in the Dzogchen Lineage*. Junction City, Calif.: Padma Publishing, 2005.

Sangye Khandro. *The Lives and Liberation of Princess Mandarava: The Indian Consort of Padmasambhava*. Boston: Wisdom Publications, 1998.

Shabkar Tsogdruk Rangdrol. *The Life of Shabkar: The Autobiography of a Tibetan Yogin*. Ithaca, N.Y.: Snow Lion Publications, 2001.

Thich Nhat Hanh. *Old Path White Clouds: Walking in the Footsteps of the Buddha*. Berkeley: Parallax Press, 1991.

Tulku Thondup. *Hidden Teachings of Tibet: An Explanation of the Terma Tradition of Tibetan Buddhism*. Boston: Wisdom Publications, 1997.

————. *Masters of Meditation and Miracles*. Boston: Shambhala, 1999.
Tulku Urgyen Rinpoche. *Blazing Splendor: The Memoirs of Tulku Urgyen Rinpoche*. Berkeley: North Atlantic Books, 2005.
Yeshé Tsogyal. *The Lotus-Born: The Life Story of Padmasambhava*. Berkeley: North Atlantic Books, 2004.
Yudra Nyingpo. *The Great Image: The Life Story of Vairochana the Translator*. Boston: Shambhala, 2004.

PRELIMINARY PRACTICES

Chagdud Tulku. *Ngöndro Commentary: Instructions for the Concise Preliminary Practices of the New Treasure of Dudjom*. Junction City, Calif.: Padma Publishing, 1995.
Dilgo Khyentse. *The Excellent Path to Enlightenment: Oral Teachings on the Root Text of Jamyang Khyentse Wangpo*. Ithaca, N.Y.: Snow Lion Publications, 1996.
————. *Guru Yoga: According to the Preliminary Practice of Longchen Nyingtik*. Ithaca, N.Y.: Snow Lion Publications, 1999.
————. *The Wish-Fulfilling Jewel: The Practice of Guru Yoga according to the Longchen Nyingthig Tradition*. Boston: Shambhala, 1999.
Khenpo Ngawang Pelzang. *A Guide to "The Words of My Perfect Teacher."* Boston: Shambhala, 2004.
Padmasambhava, and Jamgön Kongtrül. *The Light of Wisdom, Vol. I*. Kathmandu, Nepal: Rangjung Yeshe Publications, 1986.
Patrul Rinpoche. *The Words of My Perfect Teacher*. Boston: Shambhala, 1998.
Thinley Norbu. *A Cascading Waterfall of Nectar*. Boston: Shambhala, 2006.
The Third Dzogchen Rinpoche. *Great Perfection, Volume I: Outer and Inner Preliminaries*. Ithaca, N.Y.: Snow Lion Publications, 2007.

DEVELOPMENT STAGE MEDITATION

Gyatrul Rinpoche. *The Generation Stage in Buddhist Tantra*. Ithaca, N.Y.: Snow Lion Publications, 2005.
Jamgön Kongtrül. *Creation and Completion: Essential Points of Tantric Meditation*. Boston: Wisdom Publications, 2002.
Jigme Lingpa, Patrul Rinpoche, and Getse Mahāpaṇḍita. *Deity, Mantra, and Wisdom: Development Stage Meditation in Tibetan Buddhist Tantra*. Ithaca, N.Y.: Snow Lion Publications, 2007.
Khenpo Namdrol Rinpoche. *The Practice of Vajrakilaya*. Ithaca, N.Y.: Snow Lion Publications, 1999.
Padmasambhava, and Jamgön Kongtrül. *The Light of Wisdom, Vol. II*. Kathmandu, Nepal: Rangjung Yeshe Publications, 1986.

Great Perfection

Chogyal Namkhai Norbu. *The Crystal and the Way of Light: Sutra, Tantra, and Dzogchen.* Ithaca, N.Y.: Snow Lion Publications, 1999.

Chokyi Nyima Rinpoche. *Present Fresh Wakefulness: A Meditation Manual on Non-conceptual Wisdom.* Berkeley: North Atlantic Books, 2004.

Drubwang Tsoknyi Rinpoche. *Carefree Dignity: Discourses on Training in the Nature of Mind.* Berkeley: North Atlantic Books, 2004.

———. *Fearless Simplicity: The Dzogchen Way of Living Freely in a Complex World.* Berkeley: North Atlantic Books, 2003.

Dudjom Lingpa. *Buddhahood without Meditation: A Visionary Account Known as Refining Apparent Phenomena.* Junction City, Calif.: Padma Publishing, 2002.

———. *The Vajra Essence.* Austin, Texas: Palri Parkhang, 2004.

Dzogchen Ponlop Rinpoche. *Wild Awakening: The Heart of Mahamudra and Dzogchen.* Boston: Shambhala, 2003.

The Fourteenth Dalai Lama. *Mind in Comfort and Ease: The Vision of Enlightenment in the Great Perfection.* Boston: Wisdom Publications, 2007.

Karma Chagme. *Naked Awareness: Practical Instructions on the Union of Mahamudra and Dzogchen.* Ithaca, N.Y.: Snow Lion Publications, 2000.

———. *A Spacious Path to Freedom: Practical Instructions on the Union of Mahamudra and Atiyoga.* Ithaca, N.Y.: Snow Lion Publications, 1997.

Khamtrul Rinpoche. *Dzogchen Meditation.* Dharamsala, India: Library of Tibetan Works and Archives, 2004.

Longchen Rabjam. *The Practice of Dzogchen.* Ithaca, N.Y.: Snow Lion Publications, 2002.

———. *The Precious Treasury of the Basic Space of Phenomena.* Junction City, Calif.: Padma Publishing, 2001.

———. *The Precious Treasury of the Way of Abiding.* Junction City, Calif.: Padma Publishing, 1998.

———. *A Treasure Trove of Scriptural Transmission.* Junction City, Calif.: Padma Publishing, 2001.

Namkhai Norbu. *The Cycle of Day and Night: Where One Proceeds along the Path of the Primordial Yoga: An Essential Tibetan Text on the Practice of Dzogchen.* Barrytown, N.Y.: Station Hill Press, 2000.

Padmasambhava, and Jamgön Kongtrül. *The Light of Wisdom, Vol. IV.* Kathmandu, Nepal: Rangjung Yeshe Publications, 1986.

Padmasambhava, et al. *Crystal Cave.* Kathmandu, Nepal: Rangjung Yeshe Publications, 1990.

Van Schaik, Sam. *Approaching the Great Perfection: Simultaneous and Gradual Methods of Dzogchen Practice in the Longchen Nyingtig.* Boston: Wisdom Publications, 2003.

Shabkar Tsokdruk Rangdrol et al. *The Flight of the Garuda*. Kathmandu, Nepal: Rangjung Yeshe Publications, 1993.

The Third Dzogchen Rinpoche. *Great Perfection, Volume II: Separation and Breakthrough*. Ithaca, N.Y.: Snow Lion Publications, 2008.

Tsele Natsok Rangdrol. *Circle of the Sun*. Kathmandu, Nepal: Rangjung Yeshe Publications, 1990.

Tulku Urgyen Rinpoche. *Quintessential Dzogchen: Confusion Dawns as Wisdom*. Berkeley: North Atlantic Books, 2006.

———. *Rainbow Painting: A Collection of Miscellaneous Aspects of Development and Completion*. Berkeley: North Atlantic Books, 2004.

Vidyadhara Jigmed Lingpa. *Yeshe Lama*. Ithaca, N.Y.: Snow Lion Publications, 2009.

Philosophy

Arya Maitreya. *Buddha Nature: The Mahayana Uttaratantra Shastra with Commentary*. Ithaca, N.Y.: Snow Lion Publications, 2000.

Jamgön Mipham. *The Adornment of the Middle Way: Shantarakshita's "Madhyamakalankara" with Commentary by Jamgön Mipham*. Boston: Shambhala, 2005.

———. *Introduction to the Middle Way: Chandrakirti's "Madhyamakavatara" with Commentary by Jamgön Mipham*. Boston: Shambhala, 2005.

———. *Luminous Essence: A Guide to the Guhyagarbha Tantra*. Ithaca, N.Y.: Snow Lion, 2009.

Ju Mipham. *Maitreya's "Distinguishing Phenomena and Pure Being": Commentary by Mipham*. Ithaca, N.Y.: Snow Lion Publications, 2004.

Ju Mipham. *Speech of Delight: Mipham's Commentary on Shantarakshita's "Ornament of the Middle Way."* Ithaca, N.Y.: Snow Lion Publications, 2004.

Khenpo Shenga and Ju Mipham. *Middle Beyond Extremes: Maitreya's "Madhyantavibhanga" with Commentaries*. Ithaca, N.Y.: Snow Lion Publications, 2007.

Köppl, Heidi. *Establishing Appearances as Divine: Rongzom Chokyi Zangpo on Reasoning, Madhyamaka, and Purity*. Ithaca, N.Y.: Snow Lion Publications, 2008.

Pettit, John. *Mipham's Beacon of Certainty: Illuminating the View of Dzogchen*. Boston: Wisdom Publications, 1999.

NOTES

⊰◉⊱

1 Rongzom is one of the earliest of the great scholar-adepts of the Nyingma school. His seminal work on the *Tantra of the Secret Essence* topic, *Jeweled Commentary on the Guhyagarbha Tantra*, was the first major Tibetan commentary on this tantra. To date, Rongzom has received relatively little attention from the academic world. One notable exception is Heidi Köppl's recent translation of *Establishing Appearances as Divine* (*sNang ba lhar sgrub*) (Ithaca, N.Y.: Snow Lion Publications, 2008). In addition to her lucid translation, Köppl also discusses the life, works, and philosophical views of Rongzom. Other important works by Rongzom include *An Introduction to the Principles of the Great Vehicle* (*Theg chen tshul la 'jug pa*) and his influential commentary on Padmasambhava's *Key Instructions on the Rosary of Views* (*Man ngag lta phreng*). I have translated this text and am preparing it for publication. It will be accompanied by commentaries on the same text by Jamgön Kongtrül (translated by Gerry Wiener) and Mipam.

2 Longchenpa's commentary on the *Guhyagarbha Tantra* is entitled *Dispelling the Darkness of the Ten Directions* (*Phyogs bcu mun sel*). His life and works will be discussed in detail later in the introduction.

3 Mipam's main commentary on the *Guhyagarbha Tantra* is actually an overview of Longchenpa's commentary (see previous note). Entitled *Luminous Essence*, this text is one of the most widely studied commentaries on the topic. The Dharmachakra Translation Committee has published a translation of this text entitled, *Luminous Essence: A Guide to the Guhyagarbha Tantra* (Ithaca, N.Y.: Snow Lion Publications, 2009).

   Mipam's influence on the trajectory of Nyingma thought can hardly be overestimated. In the present day, his texts are far and away the most commonly studied commentaries in Nyingma monastic colleges. Two excellent sources on Mipam are Douglas Duckworth's *Mipam on Buddha Nature* (Albany: SUNY Press, 2008) and John Pettit's *Mipham's Beacon of Certainty* (Boston: Wisdom Publications, 1999). Both contain extensive information on Mipam's life, works, and philosophical views.

4 Atisha initially refused the former king's request, stating that he was needed in India to help ensure that the Buddha's teachings would endure, as Buddhism was in the midst of a state of decline due to the Muslim invasions that were plaguing the Indian subcontinent. When Yeshé Ö learned of Atisha's refusal, he believed that his offering of gold to Atisha had been insufficient. To obtain more gold, he then traveled to another kingdom, but was thrown into prison by the ruler of the area. When Yeshé Ö's grandnephew, also a monk,

attempted to free him with more gold, the former ruler refused the offer and asked that the gold be used to convince Atisha to visit Tibet. Upon hearing this story, Atisha finally relented and agreed to travel to Tibet. Though there is some dispute, some believe that Yeshé Ö died in prison.

5 Perhaps the most well-known example of the influence of Atisha's *lojong* teachings is found in the work of Tsong Khapa, the founder of the Geluk school. Tsong Khapa's *Lam-rim Chenmo*, which has recently been translated as *The Great Treatise on the Stages of the Path to Enlightenment*, 3 vols. (Ithaca, N.Y.: Snow Lion Publications, 2000–2004), is considered a classic of Tibetan Buddhist literature.

6 Two of the earliest female masters of the Great Perfection are Princess Mandarava and Yeshé Tsogyal. These figures are often mentioned as the spiritual partners of Padmasambhava, yet they were also great masters in their own right. Yeshé Tsogyal in particular played a critical role in transmitting the Great Perfection teachings to Tibet and helping to ensure their preservation for future generations. Later female masters continued to practice, transmit, and teach the Great Perfection, and many were instrumental in maintaining and shaping their respective lineages. One such example is Mingyur Paldrön (1699–1769) of the Mindroling lineage, whose profound writings on the Great Perfection were included by Jamgön Kongtrül in his *Treasury of Precious Treasures*. Remarkable female masters of recent times include Shuksep Lochen Chönyi Sangmo (1865–1953) and Sera Khandro (1892–1940), two women who trained some of the foremost Great Perfection masters of the twentieth century, including Zhadeu Trulshik Rinpoche (b. 1924) and Chatral Rinpoche Sangyé Dorjé (b. 1913).

7 The nine vehicles are discussed at length in appendix 5.

8 Keep in mind that Tibetan books, called *pecha*, are much larger than Western-style texts. One Tibetan pecha, when translated, may fill two, three, or even four large English-language volumes.

9 Precedents for the treasure lineage can be found in the annals of the Indian Buddhist tradition. Many of the Mahayana Sutras, for example, were said to have been "hidden" in other realms, such as the Perfection of Knowledge Sutras that were retrieved from the realm of the nagas by Nagarjuna.

10 Mingyur Dorje revealed Space Dharma in the seventeenth century and codified this cycle with the help of the great Karma Chakmé. These teachings have been maintained at Palyul Monastery, one of the six "mother" monasteries of the Nyingma school. Likewise, the teachings revealed by Longsel Nyingpo, as well as those of his teacher, Dudul Dorje (1615–1672), have become mainstays of Katok Dorje Den, another one of the six "mother" monasteries.

11 The Rimé movement was not a specific school or lineage, but rather an approach to spiritual study and practice shared by a loosely affiliated confederation of lamas and monasteries. This approach held that there are many valid paths to awakening, and that while it is important to remain rooted in one particular approach, studying other systems and teachings can enrich one's understanding and practice. For more information on this topic, see Ringu Tulku's *The Ri-me Philosophy of Jamgön Kongtrül the Great: A Study of the Buddhist Lineages of Tibet* (Boston: Shambhala, 2007).

12 Both Jamyang Khyentsé Wangpo and Chokgyur Dechen Lingpa revealed numerous cycles, many of which are widely practiced to this day. Of those revealed by the former, the aforementioned Heart Essence of Chetsün deserves special mention, as this particular cycle has given rise to an extensive collection of commentarial literature, including

instruction manuals composed by Jamgön Kongtrül, Lerab Lingpa (1856–1926), and Adzom Drukpa (1842–1924). A compilation of these texts was recently published by Shechen Monastery under the title *lCe btshun snying thig gi chos skor* (New Delhi: Shechen Publications, 2004).

Chokgyur Dechen Lingpa was one of the most prolific tertöns, with revelations that fill thirty-nine volumes. Among his most well-known Dzogchen cycles are the Three Classes of Dzogchen and the Heart Essence of Samantabhadra. Dudjom Rinpoche Jigdral Yeshé Dorje and Dilgo Khyentsé were also active treasure revealers. Some of their better known cycles are, respectively, the Dakini's Heart Essence (not to be confused with the similarly entitled collection included in the Fourfold Heart Essence) and the Heart Essence of Self-Occurring Padma.

13 See appendix 4 for more information on this cycle.

14 Treasure revealers may rediscover cycles that were propagated by previous revealers, but which are no longer extant. This category of treasures is termed *yang ter*, or "rerevealed treasures."

15 The Third Dzogchen Rinpoche, *Great Perfection, Volume 2: Separation and Breakthrough* (Ithaca, N.Y.: Snow Lion Publications, 2008), p. 293.

16 Ibid., p. 295.

17 According to Tulku Thondup, most scholars agree that Sahor is the place currently referred to as Mandi, which is located in Himachel Pradesh, a province of northern India. Tulku Thondup, *Masters of Meditation and Miracles: Lives of the Great Buddhist Masters of India and Tibet* (Boston: Shambhala, 1999), p. 94.

18 A lake is said to have formed where this event took place. Known to Tibetans as Pema Tso and to Indians as Lake Rewalsar, it is an important pilgrimage spot to this day. Another important pilgrimage spot associated with Padmasambhava and Mandarava is Maratika Cave in Nepal.

19 See Sangye Khandro, *The Lives and Liberation of Princess Mandarava: The Indian Consort of Padmasambhava* (Boston: Wisdom Publications, 1998) for more information on Mandarava.

20 The Heart Essence of the Dakinis will be discussed in more detail in appendix 4.

21 Many of Rongzom's writings were lost over the centuries, but some important works remain. Of particular importance is his commentary on the *Tantra of the Secret Essence*, the first major commentary on this topic composed in the Tibetan language. To this day, Rongzom's commentary is regarded as an authoritative work on this seminal Nyingma tantra. Another important work, entitled *An Introduction to the Principles of the Great Vehicle*, provides a unique Great Perfection perspective on the various facets of the Buddha's teachings. He also penned a commentary on Padmasambhava's *Key Instructions on the Rosary of Views* and another text entitled *Establishing Appearances as Divine*, a short work that employs logical arguments to prove the purity of relative appearances, one of the central tenets of the Vajra Vehicle. See n. 1 for more information on this master.

22 The Seven Treasuries are considered the most authoritative Tibetan writings on the unique approach of the Great Perfection. Though all seven deal with the Great Perfection to some degree, they vary greatly in terms of form and content. The *Precious Treasury of the Supreme Vehicle*, for example, spans two thousand pages and deals primarily with the Great Perfection. Meanwhile, the *Precious Wish-Fulfilling Treasury* is less than two hundred pages and presents the entire Buddhist path in a series of elegant verses,

with more emphasis on the Sutra Vehicle teachings. All in all, these seven works address virtually every aspect of Buddhist thought and practice and offer a remarkably complete picture of the view of the Great Perfection. This collection is being translated by Lama Chökyi Nyima and published by Padma Publishing. See the recommended reading list for more details.

23 This collection contains three texts: *Resting in the Nature of Mind, Resting in Illusion,* and *Resting in Deep Meditation.*

24 Boudhanath Stupa, located on the outskirts of Kathmandu, remains one of the most important pilgrimage sites in the Buddhist world. It is currently home to one of the largest communities of refugee Tibetans on the Indian subcontinent. More information on this power spot can be found in Keith Dowman, *The Legend of the Great Stupa: The Life Story of the Lotus Born Guru* (Emeryville, Calif.: Dharma Books, 1973).

25 This text will be included in a forthcoming book in the Heart Essence Series, along with Longchenpa's root text from the Heart Essence of Vimalamitra.

26 It is not uncommon for enlightened teachers to have multiple reincarnations. There are often said to be three reincarnations related to enlightened body, speech, and mind embodiments, or even five related to enlightened body, speech, mind, qualities, and activity.

27 Khenpo Ngagwang Pelzang is the author of an important commentary on *The Words of My Perfect Teacher,* entitled *A Guide to "The Words of My Perfect Teacher"* (Boston: Shambhala, 2004).

28 Nyoshul Khenpo wrote a wonderful work on the Heart Essence lineage, entitled *A Marvelous Garland of Rare Gems: Biographies of Masters of Awareness in the Dzogchen Lineage* (Junction City, Calif.: Padma Publications, 2005). Another book, *Natural Great Perfection* (Ithaca, N.Y.: Snow Lion Publications, 2008), contains some of his teachings and autobiographical accounts.

29 All three of these teachers have published numerous works. See recommended reading for more details.

30 See n. 11.

31 Depending on the edition and the number of page numbers in each volume, there may also be either two or four volumes in the collection.

32 In Khenpo Ngakchung's lineage, for example, the bodhichitta prayer is recited only thirty thousand times. Instead, more emphasis is placed on bodhichitta-related contemplations, such as sending and taking and the four immeasurables.

33 In the Longchen Nyingtik, the sadhana for the one hundred peaceful and wrathful deities is *Purifying the Lower Realms: A Ritual of the Peaceful and Wrathful* (Tib. *Zhi khro ngan song sbyong ba'i cho ga*). For Vajrasattva, the practice is entitled *Cultivating the Realm of Utter Delight: A Guru Yoga Related to Vajrasattva* (Tib. *rDo rje sems dpa' la brten pa'i bla ma'i rnal 'byor mngon dga'i zhing sbyong*). The practice associated with Padmasambhava is *The Inner Sadhana of the Gathering of the Masters of Awareness* (Tib. *Nang sgrub rig 'dzin 'dus pa*). Each of these sadhanas has its own empowerments.

34 The specifics of this approach are discussed in Khenpo Ngawang Pelzang, *A Guide to "The Words of My Perfect Teacher,"* p. 287. See appendix 3 for more details.

35 There are many sadhana practices in the Heart Essence of the Vast Expanse. The three peaceful guru sadhanas are as follows: an outer guru yoga associated with Padmasambhava (Tib. *Lamey Naljor; Bla ma'i rnal 'byor*); an inner guru yoga, entitled *Gathering of the Masters of Awareness,* associated with Padmasambhava and the eight masters

of awareness (Tib. *Rigdzin Düpa*; *Rig 'dzin 'dus pa*); a secret guru yoga, entitled *Great Compassion: The Self-Liberation of Suffering*, associated with Avalokiteshvara (Tib. *Tukjé Chenpo Dukngel Rangdrol*; *Thugs rje chen pos sdug bsngal rang grol*); and an extremely secret guru yoga associated with Vimalamitra and Longchenpa (Tib. *Tiklé Gyachen*; *Thig le rgya can*). There are also two wrathful guru sadhanas: *Gathering of Great Glorious Ones*, which is associated with the deities of the Eight Great Sadhanas (Tib. *Palchen Düpa*; *dPal chen 'dus pa*) and *Takyung Barwa*, which is associated with Hayagriva (Tib. *Takyung Barwa*; *rTa khyung 'bar ba*). The two feminine sadhanas are *Yumkha Dechen Gyalmo*, which is associated with Yeshé Tsogyal (Tib. *Yum mkha' bde chen rgyal mo*) and *Lion-Faced Dakini* (Tib. *Sengé Dongchen*; *Seng nge'i gdong chen*). Finally, there is also a sadhana of the one hundred peaceful and wrathful deities, entitled *Cleansing the Lower Realms: The Peaceful and Wrathful Deities* (Tib. *Shi-tro Ngensong Jongwa*; *Zhi khro ngan song sbyong ba*); a chöd practice, entitled *The Bellowing Laugh of the Dakinis* (Tib. *Khandro Gey Gyang*; *mKha' 'gro gad rgyangs*); and a Vajrasattva sadhana, entitled *Purifying the Realm of Complete Joy: A Guru Yoga on Vajrasattva* (Tib. *Ngönga Shing Jong*; *rDo rje sems dpa' la brten pa'i bla ma'i rnal 'byor mngon dga'i zhing sbyong*). The protector practices relate to Magön Chamdrel (Tib. *bKa' srung ma mgon lcam dral*) and the Five Medicine Sisters (Tib. *bKa' srung sman btsun mched lnga*).

36   The gradual approach to visualization is advocated in the Mahayoga teachings. In the Anuyoga and Atiyoga teachings, visualization takes place instantly. See Jigmé Lingpa, *Ladder to Akanishta*, in Jigmé Lingpa, Patrül Rinpoche, and Getse Mahāpaṇḍita, *Deity, Mantra, and Wisdom: Development Stage Meditation in Tibetan Buddhist Tantra* (Ithaca, N.Y.: Snow Lion Publications, 2006), pp. 24–31 for more details on the different approaches to visualization.

37   These texts have been translated into English and are included in Jigme Lingpa, Patrul Rinpoche, and Getse Mahāpaṇḍita, *Deity, Mantra, and Wisdom*.

38   See Patrul Rinpoche, *The Words of My Perfect Teacher* (Boston: Shambhala, 1998), pp. 351–365 for more information on this practice.

39   This refers to the three sacred principles: The sacred preparation is to form the correct motivation for practice, here referring to the altruistic mind-set of bodhichitta. The sacred main practice is to remain free from any reference point, without any agenda or expectation concerning the results of practice. The sacred conclusion is to dedicate the merit and virtue of the practice to the enlightenment of all sentient beings.

40   See Patrul Rinpoche, *The Words of My Perfect Teacher*, pp. 101–112, for an extensive explanation of these four aspects of a karmic act.

41   The seven-point mind training, not to be confused with the similarly named system of the Kadampa school, is an alternate version of the outer preliminaries included in the Heart Essence of the Vast Expanse. Jigmé Lingpa's commentary on this practice will be published in the fourth volume of the Heart Essence series.

42   These three forms of generosity involve giving away increasingly precious objects, until one is able to even give away parts of one's own body to others in need.

43   The completely pure sphere of activity mentioned here involves imbuing ordinary activities with positive aspirations. When a bodhisattva enters a house, for instance, he or she links this activity with the cultivation of bodhichitta, with the thought, "May all sentient beings attain the city of liberation!" When they lie down, they think, "May they attain the form of a buddha, and when they dream, may they dream that all phenomena are like a dream!" When they wake up, they think, "May they awake from ignorance!" When

they get up, "May they attain the form of a buddha!" Similarly, the eight thoughts of great beings are positive aspirations meant to benefit others.

44   The ten Dharma activities are 1) transcribing the words that form the basis of the sacred Dharma; 2–3) making offerings to and giving generously to the Dharma and those who teach it; 4) listening to Dharma teachings; 5) reading Dharma books; 6) memorizing the Dharma; 7) explaining the Dharma; 8) chanting the Dharma from memory; 9) taking its meaning to heart; and 10) meditating on its meaning.

45   The seven-point posture of Vairochana consists of keeping the legs in the vajra (lotus) posture, placing the hands beneath the navel in the meditation mudra, spreading the shoulders out like the wings of a vulture (i.e., opening the chest), straightening the spine like an arrow, lowering the gaze to the tip of the nose, placing the tongue on the roof of the mouth, and tucking the chin slightly inward.

46   See n. 39.

47   The terms "support" and "supported" refer to the pure buddha realms and the buddhas who reside there, respectively.

48   In his commentary on the Heart Essence of the Dakinis, the Third Dzogchen Rinpoche explains the traditional Buddhist cosmology and the meaning of the terms mentioned here: "A single solar system is made up of four continents, eight subcontinents, a central mountain, seven golden mountains, seven lakes of play, a sun, moon, and a surrounding ring of iron mountains. The perimeter of one thousand such solar systems is encircled by iron mountains whose height is the same as the Heavenly Realm of Thirty-three. Together, these constitute a first-order thousandfold universe. The perimeter of one thousand of these systems is encircled by another ring of iron mountains, this time equaling the height of the Heaven of Mastery over Others' Creations. This is an intermediate, second-order thousandfold universe. The perimeter of one thousand of these systems is encircled by iron mountains that are as high as the first state of absorption. This is the great, third-order thousandfold universe. If you count each set of four continents and iron mountains, a third-order thousandfold universe is composed of one billion solar systems." The Third Dzogchen Rinpoche, *Great Perfection: Outer and Inner Preliminaries* (Ithaca, N.Y.: Snow Lion Publications, 2008), pp. 48–49.

49   The bodhisattva Samantabhadra radiated billions of light rays from his heart, with a replica of himself on the tip of each ray. Each of these replicas then emanated light from their own heart centers. This process then continued until he had projected an infinite number of light rays and replicas of himself, each of which made an inconceivable number of offerings to the buddhas and bodhisattvas. These offerings came to be known as the offering clouds of Samantabhadra.

50   This prayer is found in full in Lotsawa House's translation of this text, www.lotsawa house.org.

51   *Calling the Guru from Afar* is found on p. 194.

52   The Vajra Master of Oddiyana is a form of Padmasambhava.

53   Pema Tötreng Tsel is an alternate name of Padmasambhava.

54   See Mipham's *Luminous Essence*, an important commentary on this tantra.

55   A short version of the Longchen Nyingtik ngöndro written by Jamyang Khyentsé Wangpo, entitled *The Sublime Path to Enlightenment*, is included in appendix 1. For more information on the various texts related to the Longchen Nyingtik preliminaries and English-language translations, see appendix 6.

56 In the long ngöndro liturgy, the refuge prayer and bodhichitta prayer are separate. In the short version composed by Jamyang Khyentsé Wangpo, refuge and bodhichitta are combined.

57 A multivolume translation of the *Lamrim Yeshé Nyingpo*, entitled *Light of Wisdom*, has been translated by Erik Pema Kunsang and published by Rangjung Yeshe Publications (Kathmandu, Nepal, 1986–2001). For an important commentary on the *Guhyagarbha Tantra*, the *Tantra of the Secret Essence*, see Mipham, *Luminous Essence*. There are numerous translations related to the practice of Vajrakumara, or Vajrakilaya. See recommended reading for more details on these texts.

58 Dzongsar Khyentse Rinpoche's father is Thinley Norbu Rinpoche, a respected Nyingma lama and son of Dudjom Rinpoche, the late head of the Nyingma lineage.

59 This presentation is based on two texts, both by Chatral Rinpoche: *Ri chos mtshams kyi khog dbub* and *Ri chos mtshams kyi lhan thabs* (Delhi, India: Chos spyod par skrun khang, 1996).

60 Tib. *Kusali Tsok Chö; Ku sa li tshogs mchod.*

61 Tib. *Rigdzin Düpa; Rig 'dzin 'dus pa.*

62 Tib. *Tukjé Chenpo Dukngel Rangdrol; Thugs rje chen pos dug bsngal rang grol.*

63 Tib. *Tiklé Gyachen; Thig le rgya can.*

64 Tib. *Palchen Düpa; dPal chen 'dus pa.*

65 Tib. *Yumkha Dechen Gyalmo; Yum mkha' bDe chen rgyal mo.*

66 Though this is the most commonly accepted version, there are alternate explanations concerning the exact contents of this collection. A discussion of these varying presentations can be found in Jamgön Kongtrül's *Dri med zhal lung*, pp. 127–128, in gDams ngag mdzod, vol. wa (New Delhi: Lungtok and Gyaltsan, 1971), pp. 115–281.

67 Nges don bstan 'dzin bzang po, *rDzogs pa chen po mkha' 'gro snying thig gi khrid yig thar lam bgrod byed shing rta bzang po* (Chengdu, China: Si khron mi rigs dpe skrun khang, 1997), p. 257.

68 One important exception is Longchenpa's commentary on the Heart Essence of the Dakinis, *An Ocean of Clouds of the Profound Nature*. Spanning nearly five hundred pages, this massive text offers one of the most comprehensive and systematic presentations of Great Perfection practice ever written. This is also the single largest text contained in the Fourfold Heart Essence.

69 The root tantra of the Heart Essence of Vimalamitra is entitled *Tantra of the Sole Offspring*. In the Heart Essence of the Dakinis, the root tantra is entitled *Tantra That Liberates Upon Wearing*.

70 One might think that such a dearth of sadhana-based materials would be common in Nyingtik cycles, but this is rarely the case. In the vast majority of Heart Essence cycles, sadhanas far outnumber texts devoted solely to the practices of breakthrough and direct leap. In the famed Longchen Nyingtik, for example, only the aforementioned *Wisdom Guru* deals explicitly with these two Heart Essence practices, while there are countless sadhanas, instruction manuals, and subsidiary practices that relate to the development stage practices of visualization and mantra recitation. For this reason, the Fourfold Heart Essence is quite unique, even within the Heart Essence tradition.

71 Chos grags bzang po, *Kun mkhyen dri med 'od zer gyi rnam thar mthong ba don ldan,* in sNying thig ya bzhi, vol. 6 (Darjeeling, India: Talung Tsetrul Pema Wangyal, 1976), p. 556.

72   Klong chen rab 'byams, *Theg pa mtha' dag gi don gsal bar byed pa grub pa'i mtha' rin po che'i mdzod* (Gangtok, Sikkim: Sherab Gyaltsen and Khyentse Labrang, 1983), pp. 393, 396.

73   Rang byung rdo rje, *Nyams len lag khrigs ma'i khrid ngo mtshar can,* in sNying thig ya bzhi, vol. 6 (Darjeeling, India: Talung Tsetrul Pema Wangyal, 1976), p. 274.

74   Klong chen rab 'byams, *gTer 'byung rin po che'i lo rgyus,* in sNying thig ya bzhi, vol. 7 (Darjeeling, India: Talung Tsetrul Pema Wangyal, 1976), p. 48.

75   Tsultrim Dorje and Trimé Özer are alternate names for Pema Ledrel Tsel and Longchenpa, respectively.

76   Padma las 'brel rtsal, *dBang gi rim pa khrid du bskur lugs,* in sNying thig ya bzhi, vol. 10 (Darjeeling, India: Talung Tsetrul Pema Wangyal, 1976), p. 276.

77   gTer bdag gling pa, *mKha' 'gro snying thig gi khrid yig zab lam gsal byed* (Chengdu, China: Si khron mi rigs dpe skrun khang, 1997) p. 518.

78   Dudjom Rinpoche, *The Nyingma School of Tibetan Buddhism* (Boston: Wisdom Publications, 1991), p. 586.

79   *Mind treasures* are one class of terma, or revealed treasure. In contrast to physical treasures, which are hidden in a physical location, mind treasures are hidden in the mind stream of an individual. They are revealed when the right circumstances trigger a memory of the teachings, at which point they are set down in writing. For more information on the varieties and history of the treasure tradition, see Tulku Thondup's *Hidden Teachings of Tibet: An Explanation of the Terma Tradition of the Nyingma School of Buddhism* (London: Wisdom Publications, 1986).

80   Nges don bstan 'dzin bzang po, *rDzogs pa chen po mkha' 'gro snying thig gi khrid yig thar lam bgrod byed shing rta bzang po,* p. 292 (Chengdu, China: si khron mi rigs dpe skrun khang, 1997).

81   Klong chen rab 'byams, *rGya mtsho ar gtad kyi mun khrid 'od gsal 'khor lo,* vol. 12 (Darjeeling, India: Talung Tsetrul Pema Wangyal, 1976), pp. 259–267.

82   This appendix is adapted from the introduction to The Third Dzogchen Rinpoche, *Great Perfection, Volume II,* pp. 9–20.

83   Tib. *tum mo.*

84   Tib. *ka dak.*

85   Tib. *lhun drup; lhun grub.*

86   Tib. *trekchö; khregs chod.*

87   Tib. *tögal; thod rgal.*

INDEX

⟨⟨⟩⟩

THE HEART ESSENCE SERIES

—— ❦ ——

The Heart Essence Series contains translations of seminal writings on the Great Perfection. Beginning with the works of the Heart Essence of the Dakinis and the Heart Essence of Vimalamitra, two cycles that lie at the core of the Great Perfection lineage, we hope to provide scholars, teachers, and practitioners of these profound teachings with accurate and readable translations of the most important Great Perfection texts. Our projects are carried out with the blessings and guidance of leading masters of the Great Perfection lineage.

Current Volumes:
► *Great Perfection: Outer and Inner Preliminaries* – The first half of the Third Dzogchen Rinpoche's *Excellent Chariot*, which includes extensive explanations of the outer and inner Great Perfection preliminary practices, as well as a foreword by Dzogchen Ponlop Rinpoche
► *Great Perfection: Separation and Breakthrough* – The second half of the Third Dzogchen Rinpoche's *Excellent Chariot*, which includes extensive explanations of the unique Great Perfection preliminary practices and instructions on the breakthrough stage of Heart Essence practice

Future volumes include:
► *Dzogchen Mind Training* – Writings by Longchenpa and Jigmé Lingpa on a unique form of mind training, or *sem-jong*, from the Heart Essence of Vimalamitra
► *Heart Essence of the Dakinis: Core Teachings on the Great Perfection* – The most important texts from the Heart Essence of the Dakinis, including the *Three Last Testaments* and the *Six Essence Tantras That Liberate Upon Wearing*
► *Heart Essence of the Dakinis: Origins of the Great Perfection* – A collection of texts on the history and contents of the Heart Essence of the Dakinis cycle

If you would like to learn more about these projects or support our work, please visit us online at www.rimefoundation.org or e-mail info@rimefoundation.org for more details.

THE RIMÉ FOUNDATION

⊰⊱||⊰⊱

The Tibetan word Rimé (pronounced ree-may) literally means "without bias." This term has most recently been linked with a spiritual movement that began in Eastern Tibet roughly one hundred and fifty years ago. Like all religions and cultures, Tibetan Buddhism has seen its fair share of sectarian strife and turmoil. The Rimé movement aimed to counter this tendency by promoting an atmosphere of harmony and goodwill between the various Buddhist schools and lineages of Tibet. Rimé is not a school or sect of Buddhism, but a unique approach to spiritual practice. Adherents of this outlook are often rooted in one spiritual tradition. At the same time, however, they maintain a respect for, and willingness to learn from, other approaches. The Rimé ideal, then, is not to create one "universal approach" to spirituality, but rather to honor the differences between lineages, sects, and religions, and to foster an environment of mutual support and harmony.

The vision of the Rimé Foundation is a world in which wisdom and compassion are the guiding forces in our individual and collective lives, and in which the traditions that enable us to cultivate virtue are honored, practiced, and preserved for future generations. Our mission is to facilitate this process by preserving the spiritual heritage of Tibet, providing access to its texts, teachers, and practices, and fostering the growth of a diverse and tolerant spiritual community.

Our programs include:
- Translating classic Tibetan literature into the English language
- Offering grants and support to dedicated spiritual practitioners in our communities to enable them to engage in spiritual study and retreat
- Creating resources and programs to facilitate interfaith and intercultural dialogue and promoting the practice of meditation in both secular and spiritual contexts

For more information about our organization and programs, please visit us online at www.rimefoundation.org or e-mail info@rimefoundation.org.

SAVING THE LIVES OF ANIMALS

⊰∦⊱

All royalties from the sale of this book will be used to save the lives of animals that would otherwise be killed. Whenever possible, proceeds will be donated to Chatral Rinpoche's annual animal release in Nepal and India. If you would like to learn more about the traditional Buddhist practice of ransoming life, or to make a tax-deductible donation to this program, please visit us online at www.rimefoundation. org or e-mail info@rimefoundation.org.

Printed in the United States
by Baker & Taylor Publisher Services